D1433996

THE PERFECT COURTIER

Baldésar Castilione

From the portrait by Raphael in the Louvre

THE PERFECT COURTIER

BALDASSARE CASTIGLIONE

HIS LIFE AND LETTERS, 1478–1529

BY JULIA CARTWRIGHT
(MRS. ADY)

'C' è chi, qual lui
Vedriamo, ha tali i cortegian formati.'
ARIOSTO.

'Lacrime, voce e vite a' bianchi marmi
Castiglion, dar potesti, e vivo esempio
A Duci nostri, anche in te sol contempio
Com' uomo vinca la morte, e la disarmi.'
TORQUATO TASSO

IN TWO VOLUMES
VOL. I

LONDON
JOHN MURRAY, ALBEMARLE STREET, W.

First Edition . . . . . *October,* 1908
Cheaper Edition 1927

PRINTED IN GREAT BRITAIN BY
BILLING AND SONS, LTD., GUILDFORD AND ESHER

PREFACE

Count Baldassare Castiglione is known to the
world as the author of 'Il Cortegiano.' He was a
distinguished soldier, diplomat, and poet, but his title
to immortality rests on this one book. 'The best
book that was ever written upon good breeding,' said
Dr. Johnson, when he was travelling with Boswell in
Skye—'the best book, I tell you, "Il Cortegiano,"
by Castiglione, grew up at the little court of Urbino,
and you should read it.' This frank and decisive
utterance, eminently characteristic of the speaker, and
yet hardly what we should have expected from him,
did but confirm the unanimous verdict of the last
two hundred years. Castiglione's book first issued
from the Aldine Press at Venice in April, 1528, and
before the close of the century more than a hundred
editions of the work had already seen the light.
Spanish, French, English, and German versions
followed each other in rapid succession, and the
'Cortegiano' was universally acclaimed as the most
popular prose work of the Italian Renaissance.
'Have you read Castiglione's "Cortegiano"?' asks
the courtier Malpiglio, in Tasso's dialogue. 'The
beauty of the book is such that it deserves to be read
in all ages ; and as long as courts endure, as long as
princes reign and knights and ladies meet as long

as valour and courtesy hold a place in our hearts, the name of Castiglione will be held in honour.'[1]

Nowhere has the popularity of Castiglione's treatise been greater than in our own country. From the time when, only thirty-four years after its first appearance in Venice, Sir Thomas Hoby's translation, 'The Book of the Courtier,' took the Elizabethan world by storm, no less than seventeen English versions of the 'Cortegiano' have been published. In those days, when to know Italian was held to be 'a grace of all graces,' and translations of Boccaccio and Bandello's novels 'were solde in every shop,' Castiglione's book was in the hands of all cultured Englishmen. Poets and dramatists alike quoted his sayings and borrowed his stories.[2] Florio, in his 'Second Fruites,' tells us that Castilion's 'Courtier' is one of the books most read by young men who would pick up a little Italian. Ben Jonson and Webster mention the 'Courtier'; Marston, in his 'Satires,' speaks of the author, not without a touch of scorn, as 'the absolute Castilio.'

There seems little doubt that Shakespeare was familiar with the book, if not in the original Italian, at least in Hoby's translation. As Mr. Wyndham[3] first pointed out, the platonic philosophy of the Sonnets was clearly borrowed from Bembo's oration; and a clever American writer, Miss Scott, has almost succeeded in convincing us that the characters of Benedick and Beatrice were derived from the Lord Gaspare Pallavicino and the Lady Emilia of the 'Cortegiano.[4]

[1] 'Il Malpiglio,' 251.
[2] See the Introduction to Hoby's 'Book of the Courtier,' by Professor Raleigh.
[3] Introduction to 'The Poems of Shakspeare.'
[4] 'The Book of the Courtyer,' by M. A. Scott, Ph.D.

Even Roger Ascham, that stern Puritan who looked on these 'fonde bookes' by foreign authors as 'enchantments of Circe, brought out of Italy to mar men's manners in England,' has a good word for the 'Cortegiano.' 'To join learning with comely exercises, Count Baldesar Castiglione doth truely teach; which book, advisedly read and diligently followed but one year at home in England, would do a young gentleman more good, I wiss, than three years' travel spent abroad.'[1]

The modern revival of interest in the Italian Renaissance has naturally led students to turn once more to Castiglione's 'Courtier,' in whom they justly recognise the ideal representative of that great age. No less than three new versions of the 'Cortegiano' have appeared in English during the last few years. In 1900 Hoby's translation was reprinted in Nutt's 'Tudor Classics,' with an excellent Introduction by Professor Raleigh, and another handsome edition, with woodcuts by Mr. Ashbee, was issued by the Essex House Press, to be followed in 1903, by a new translation, richly illustrated and carefully annotated from the pen of Mr. Opdyke.

But while the 'Cortegiano' has been widely read and highly esteemed in England, it is curious how little is known of its author. A few notices of Castiglione in the works of Hallam, Roscoe, Dennistoun, and John Addington Symonds, a memoir in a translation of the 'Cortegiano' published in 1727, two short biographical studies from the pen of Professor Raleigh and Mr. Opdyke, and a spirited sketch by Miss Scott, are all that have been written about him in English. Yet Count Baldassare is an exceedingly interesting and attractive figure. He himself, as his contem-

[1] 'The Scholemaster,' iii. 141.

poraries with one accord exclaimed, was a living
example of his ideal courtier, the perfect knight of
his own dreams. 'I am not surprised,' wrote Vittoria
Colonna, when the Count sent her his manuscript,
'that you have described a perfect courtier, since you
had only to hold up a mirror before yourself and
consider your external and internal qualities.' And
although Castiglione himself modestly disclaimed any
pretence at self-portraiture, there certainly was in
his case, as in that of most persons, an evident correspondence between what the man admired and
what he was. 'I will not deny,' he writes naïvely,
that I have striven to attain those qualities which I
desired to see in my courtier.' Just as Aristotle
defined the virtuous act as that which the good and
great man does, so Castiglione maintained that the
perfect gentleman must frame his own canons of
moral taste, and that his instinct must in the final
resort determine what right conduct is.

In his own person Count Baldassare affords the
most brilliant example of the union of chivalry and
scholarship, a type which always flourished on Italian
soil. Many other instances might be named—Luigi
da Porto, the brave Vicentine who wrote the story
of Romeo and Juliet; Niccolò da Correggio, the
condottiere and playwright; the Milanese cavalier,
Gaspare Visconti. But of all that gallant company
Castiglione was the brightest and the best. In his
threefold capacity of soldier, statesman, and scholar,
he holds a foremost place among the most distinguished figures of the sixteenth century. He was
employed by Popes and monarchs on important
missions, and enjoyed the favour of Leo X. and
Clement VII., of Francis I. and Charles V. Both
at the courts of Mantua and Urbino and in the larger

world of Rome he was a shining light, dear alike to
Elisabetta Gonzaga and Isabella d' Este, to Bembo
and to Raphael.   In an age when, as it has been
well said,[1] cleverness was abundant but character was
lacking, he not only believed in virtue, but practised
it.   In circles where crime and treachery were con-
doned, and to deceive others was held to be the
first duty of a diplomat, he spoke the truth boldly,
and remained absolutely loyal to his masters.   So
he moved through these dark scenes of intrigue and
bloodshed, wearing the white flower of a blameless
life, and gaining the confidence and respect of those
who were most unlike him.   His career was a
chequered one, overshadowed by heavy losses and
sorrows in private life, and by failures and disappointments in his public capacity.   But he was widely
honoured and greatly beloved, and left a stainless
name to his children.

The first biography of Castiglione was written in
1573, at his son Camillo's request, by the Mantuan
Bernardino Marliani, and published eleven years later
in Venice The author derived his information chiefly
from members of the Count's family, and especially
from Lodovico Strozzi, who had been his uncle's companion during the last years of his life in Spain, and
his record is on the whole accurate and trustworthy.
A few more details are supplied in Beffa-Negrini's
'Elogi della Famiglia Castiglione,' a work which
appeared in 1606, but is rather in the nature of a
panegyric than a biography.   Paolo Giovio introduced a notice of Castiglione among his Elogi of
illustrious men, and an eighteenth-century historian,
Mazzuchelli, wrote another Life of the Count in his
'Scrittori d' Italia, without, however, adding much

[1] A. J. Butler, 'Cambridge Mod. Hist.,' ii. 457.

to our knowledge. But the best and fullest biography of Castiglione was that written in 1760 by Abate Pietro Serassi, who had access to the family papers brought to Rome by Cardinal Valenti Gonzaga, secretary to Pope Benedict XIV., and who afterwards published an interesting selection of letters from the Count's public and private correspondence. In our own days the most important work on the subject has been the biographical essay by Dr. Martinati, whose excellent summary of Castiglione's life contains forty-five hitherto unpublished letters.

Like most of his contemporaries, Count Baldassare was an active correspondent, and his letters, both private and official, are, as Ginguené remarked, not only precious historic documents, but models of lucid and graceful style, grave and animated, witty and pathetic, by turns. Fortunately, a considerable portion of his correspondence has been preserved. The Valenti papers in the Vatican Library, from which Serassi drew most of his material, contain several hundreds of letters, many of which are given for the first time in my text, while a few of the originals are printed in the Appendix. Another large collection is to be found in the Gonzaga archives at Mantua, where Castiglione's correspondence fills eight volumes in the Biblioteca. Others are preserved in the Oliveriana at Pesaro and in the Archives of Turin and Florence. Many of these documents have been published at different times by historical writers, such as Dr. Pastor, Signor Luzio, Signor Contin, Signor Feliciangeli, Signor Zannoni, and Signor Vernazza di Freney. A considerable number are to be found in a very rare work, ' Delle Esenzioni della Famiglia di Castiglione,' published at Mantua in 1780, as well as in pamphlets, now out of print, by Professor Renier and Professor Vittore Cian. This

last-named writer has further earned our gratitude
by the valuable series of historical and biographical
notes with which he has enriched his admirable
edition of the ' Cortegiano.' Finally, among the count-
less notices of Castiglione which have appeared in
works on Italian literature, especial mention should be
made of the fine appreciations from the pen of Dr.
Adolf Tobler, Professor Bottari, and Dr. Gaspary.[1]

To all of these I desire to acknowledge my obligations, as well as to the keepers of archives and
libraries in many cities of Italy. Above all, my
heartfelt thanks are due to Padre Ehrle, the learned
Keeper of the Vatican Library, and to Signor Francesco Cagiati, for the unfailing courtesy and kindness
with which they have assisted my researches.

The painting by Justus of Ghent at Windsor is
reproduced by permission of the Lord Chamberlain,
the portraits of Federico Gonzaga and of Eleanor of
Austria by the kindness of their owners, Mr. Leatham
and Lord Roden, while I have to thank Lieutenant
Simondi for the valuable series of photographs which
he has placed at my disposal.

*   *   *   *   *

On September 6, 1904, exactly four hundred years
from the day when Castiglione first entered Urbino,
I stood in the ducal palace which was the scene of
his immortal dialogues. Here, surrounded by remains
of past splendour, it seemed worth while attempting
to revive these forgotten glories and to tell the story
of the perfect courtier's life. If the tale affords my
readers one half of the pleasure which it has given me,
my labours will not have been in vain.

JULIA CARTWRIGHT.

OCKHAM, *August 30,* 1908.

---

[1] For the full titles of works by these authors, see Bibliography.

BIBLIOGRAPHY

MANUSCRIPT SOURCES.

Archivio Segreto della Santa Sede : Lettere dei Principi, iii., iv.
v., vi.
Biblioteca Vaticana, Roma :
Codice Latino Vaticano, già Valenti, 8210, 8211, 8212, 8213 :
Lettere della famiglia di Castiglione.
Codice Vaticano, Urbino, 904. Commentaria del Duca Guido-
baldo I.—924 : Philippi Beroaldi Defensio Francisci Mariæ I.—
9063. Miscellanea.—1198. Federici Urbini Ducis Epistolæ.—
1248. Miscellanea.
Archivio Gonzaga, Mantova : Corrispondenza di Roma, 1519-1524.
Carteggio della Marchesana Isabella.
Biblioteca di Mantova : Carteggio di Baldassare Castiglione. 8 vols.
Archivio di Stato di Firenze : Carte di Urbino. Cl. i., Div. G.,
f. 125, 241, 265.—Carte Strozziane. Serie i., cl.-clx., ccclxiii.
Biblioteca Marciana, Venezia : Miscellanea. Cl. vii., Cod. mliii.,
Cl. x.-xxii.
British Museum : Harleian MSS. 3462, 4612, Lettere di F. Chieri-
cati, B. Scalona, V. Calmeta, Stazio Gadio, al Marchese
Francesco e alla Marchesana Isabella. Cronaca Mantovana,
1400-1524.
British Museum : Additional MS. 22,890. Valenti MSS.
British Museum : Egerton Papers, 18,521.

PRINTED SOURCES.

ADEMOLLO, A. : Alessandro VI., Giulio II. e Leone X. nel Carne-
vale di Roma.—Documenti inediti, 1499-1520. Firenze, 1891.
AFFÒ, I. : La Vita del Cavaliere Bernardino Marliani. Parma, 1780.
ALBERI, E. : Le relazioni degli ambasciatori Veneti al Senato
durante il secolo decimosesto. Serie ii., 5 vols. Firenze, 1839-
1863.
ALBERTINI, F. : Opusculum de Mirabilibus Novæ Romæ. Roma,
1510.
D'ANCONA, A. : Origini del Teatro Italiano. 2 vols. Torino, 1891.

ANSTIS, J. : The Register of the Order of the Garter, usually called
    the Black Book, with notes, etc.   2 vols.   London, 1724.
ANTOGNONI, O. : Appunti e Memorie.   Imola, 1889.
D'ARCO, C. : Delle Arti di Mantova.   Mantova, 1857.—Notizie di
    Isabella Estense Gonzaga.   (Archivio storico italiano.   Serie i.,
    Appendice ii.)   Florence, 1845.
ARIOSTO, L. : Lettere con prefazione storio-critico, documenti e note
    per cura di A. Cappelli.   Milano, 1887.—Opere minori in verso
    e in prosa, ed. Polidori.   2 vols.   Firenze, 1894.—Orlando
    Furioso, ed. Casella.   Firenze, 1877.
ARMSTRONG, E. : The Emperor Charles V.   2 vols.   London, 1902.
ASCHAM, R., The whole Works of.   London, 1864.
ASHMOLE, E. : The Institution, Laws, and Ceremonies of the Order
    of the Garter.   London, 1672.
ATANAGI, D. : Lettere di XIII Uomini illustri.   Venezia, 1554.
ATTI E MEMORIE delle R. R. Deputazioni di Storia patria delle
    Provincie Modenesi e Parmensi.   Vols. ii. and iii.   Modena,
    1863-1865.
AUTON, J. : Chronique de Louis XII., ed. Maulde de Clavière.
    Paris, 1890.
BALDI, B. : Della Vita e dei Fatti di Guidobaldo, Duca d' Urbino.
    Milano, 1821.—Della Vita e Fatti di Federigo di Montefeltro,
    Duca di Urbino.   3 vols.   Roma, 1824.—Descrizione del
    Palazzo di Urbino.   Roma, 1841.
BANDELLO, M. : Novelle, ed. Busdrago.   Lucca, 1534.
BANDINI, A. : Il Bibbiena e il ministro di stato delineato nella vita
    del Cardinale B. Dovizi.   Livorno, 1758.
BAROTTI, G. A. : Memorie istoriche di Letterati Ferraresi.   Ferrara,
    1777.
BARUFFALDI, G. : La Vita di Lodovico Ariosto.   Ferrara, 1807.
BASCHET, A. : Alde Manuce, Lettres et Documents.   Venise, 1867.
BASCHET-REUMONT : La Jeunesse de Catherine de Medici.   Paris,
    1866.
BAUDI DE VESME, C. : Il Cortegiano del Conte B. Castiglione,
    Firenze, 1856.
BAUMGARTEN, H. : Geschichte Karl V.   3 vols.   Stuttgart, 1888.
BEFFA-NEGRINI, A. : Elogi historici di alcuni personaggi della
    famiglia di Castiglione.   Mantova, 1606.
BEMBO, P. : Vita di Guido Ubaldo, Duca di Urbino.   Venezia, 1553.
    —Epistolarum familiarum.   4 vols.   Venezia, 1582.—Episto-
    larum familiarum Leonis X.   2 vols.   Venezia, 1552.—Lettere.
    5 vols.   Verona, 1743.—Poesie, ed. Serassi.   Padova, 1745.—
    Prose.   Verona, 1743.
BERGAMASKI, D. : Storia di Gazzolo.   Casalmaggiore, 1883.
BERTOLOTTI, A. : Artisti in relazione coi Gonzaga.   Modena, 1885.
BERGENROTH, G. : Calendar of Letters and State Papers relating to
    the Negotiations between England and Spain, preserved in the
    Archives of Simancas.   Vol. ii.   Henry VIII., 1509-1515.
    London, 1866.

BETTINELLI, S. : Discorso intorno le belle lettere e le arte Mantovani. Venezia, 1800.

BIAGI, DR. G. : A proposito di due sconosciute legature ' Grolier.'
Prato, 1904.

BIANCHINI, F. : La Spiegazione delle Sculture del Palazzo di Urbino.
Urbino, 1724.

BIBBIENA, B. : La Calandria (Teatro antico italiano, i.) Roma,
1808.)

BISTICCI, V. DE : Le Vite di Uomini illustri, ed. A. Mai. Firenze,
1859.

BOSWELL's Life of Johnson, ed. J. W. Croker. London, 1866.

BOTTARI, E. : Baldassare da Castiglione e il suo libro del Cortigiano.
Pisa, 1877.

BREWER, J. S. : Letters and Papers, Foreign and Domestic, of the
Reign of Henry VIII. 4 vols. London, 1862-1875.

BROSCH, M. : Julius II. u. d. Gründung d. Kirchenstaates. Gotha,
1878.

BROWN, RAWDON : Calendar of State Papers and MSS. relating to
English Affairs in the Archives of Venice. Vols. ii., iii., iv.,
1509-1533. London, 1867-1873.

BUFARDECI, G. : Su la vita letteriara del Conte B. Castiglione.
Ragusa, 1900.

BURCKHARDT, J. : Die Kultur der Renaissance in Italien. 2 vols.
Leipzig, 1899.

CAMBRIDGE Modern History, The. Vol. i., The Renaissance;
vol. iii., The Wars of Religion. Ed. by A. W. Ward and
G. W. Prothero. Cambridge University Press, 1902 and 1904.

CAMPORI, G. : Notizie sopra Raffaelle. Modena, 1870.

CASANOVA, E. : Lettere di Carlo V. a Clemente VII., 1527-1532.
Firenze, 1892.

CASTIGLIONE, A. P. : The Courtyer translated and annotated.
London, 1727.

CASTIGLIONE, BALDASSARE : Il Cortegiano, Venezia, 1528.—Opere volgari e Latine del Conte B. Castiglione, raccolte da Gio. Antonio
e Gaetano Volpi. Padova, 1733. (For annotated editions and
critical studies of letters, poems, and biographies, see Bottari,
Bufardeci, Cian, Contin, Feliciangeli, Gabotto, Giovio, Martinati, Mortara, Opdyke, Raleigh, Renier, Ronchini, Serassi,
Scott, Tobler, Toldo, Valdrighi, Vernazza di Freney, Zannoni.)

CASTIGLIONE : Dell' Esenzioni della famiglia di Castiglione e della
loro origine e fondamento. Mantova, 1780.

CASTIGLIONE, M. : De origine, rebus, gestis ac privilegiis gentis
Castelionæ. Venetiis, 1616.

CESAREO, G. : Papa Leone e Pasquino (Nuova Antologia, serie iv.,
vol. lxxv.). Roma, 1898.

CIAN, V. : Uno decennio nella vita di Pietro Bembo. Torino, 1885,
—Motti inediti e sconosciuti di M. Pietro Bembo. Venezia,
1888.—Candidature nuziali di Bald. Castiglione. Venezia.
1892.—Il Cortegiano del Conte Baldesar Castiglione annotato

ed illustrato. Firenze, 1894.—Una Ambasceria di P. Bembo.
(Archivio Veneto, xxx., xxxi.). Venezia, 1886.—Fra Serafino
Buffone. (Archivio storico lombardo, xiv.) Milano, 1887.—
Un Episodio nella censura in Italia nel secolo xvi. (Archivio
storico lombardo, xviii.) Milano, 1891, and other articles
in Arch. st. lombardo, xix., Milano, 1892; and Giornale
storico d. lett. italiana, iv., ix., xvii., Torino, 1885, etc.

Colonna, V., Carteggio di, ed. Ferrero. Torino, 1889.

Contin : Lettere diplomatiche di Castiglione. Padova, 1875.

Creighton, M. : A History of the Papacy from the Great Schism
to the Sack of Rome. 6 vols. 1904.—Historical Essays and
Reviews. London, 1903.

Crowe, J., and Cavalcaselle, G. : The Life and Works of Raphael.
London, 1882.

Cust, L. : The Royal Paintings. Vol. ii., Windsor. London, 1906.

Delaborde, H. : Études sur les Beaux Arts, i. Paris, 1864.

De Leva, G. : Storia documentata di Carlo V. in correlazione all'
Italia. 5 vols. Venezia, 1863, etc.

Delisle, L. : Recherches sur Grolier. Paris, 1866.

Dennistoun, J. : Memoirs of the Dukes of Urbino, 1440-1630.
3 vols. London, 1851.

Diario Ferrarese, 1409-1502, Muratori, Rerum Italicarum
Scriptores, xxiv.

Didot, A. Firmin : Alde Manuce et l'Hellenisme à Venice. Paris,
1875.

Donesmondi, R. P. F. I. : Della Storia Ecclesiastica di Mantova.
2 vols. Mantova, 1613-1616.

Dumesnil, A. : Histoire des Amateurs Italiens. 2 vols. Paris, 1860.

Einstein, L. : The Italian Renaissance in England. London and
New York, 1902.

Erasmi, D. : Opera Omnia. 10 vols. Lugd. Bat., 1703-1706.

Erasmus, The Epistles of, translated by F. M. Nichols. London,
1901.

Fabrickzy, C. von : Medaillen der Italienischen Renaissance.
Leipzig, 1903.—Adriano Fiorentino (Jahrbuch der k. pr. Kunst
Sammlungen, xxiv.) Berlin, 1903.

Fabronius, A. : Leonis X., P. M., vita. Pisa, 1797.

Feliciangeli, B. : Alcune lettere inedite di B. Castiglione in
Propugnatore, N.S., v. 346-369. Bologna, 1892.

Fiera, B. : Mantuanus Hymni Divini ; Sylvæ ; Melanysius Cœna.
1515.

Fischel, O. : Porträts des Giuliano de' Medici : Jahrbuch der k.
pr. Kunst Sammlungen, xxviii. Berlin, 1907.

Fitzmaurice-Kelly, J. : History of Spanish Literature. London,
1898.

Flamini, F. : Il Cinquecento—Storia dell. Lett. italiana. Milano,
1903.

Florio, J. : Second Fruites. London, 1591.

Francesconi, Abate D. : Congettura che una lettera creduta di
B. Castiglione sia di Raffaello. Firenze, 1799.

FRIZZI, A.: Memorie per la Storia di Ferrara. Vols. iv. and v. 1791.

GABOTTO, F. : Tre lettere di Uomini illustri nell' Archivio di Milano. Pinerolo, 1890.

GARDNER, E.: The King of Court Poets: a Study of the Works, Life, and Times of Lodovico Ariosto. London, 1906.

GASPARY, A.: Geschichte der italienischen Literatur   Vol. ii. Berlin, 1888.—Trad. da V. Rossi. Torino, 1900.

GAYANGOS, P. DE: Calendar of Letters, Despatches, and State Papers relating to the Negotiations between England and Spain, preserved in the Archives of Simancas. Vols. iii. and iv. London, 1873-1886.

GAYE, G.: Carteggio inedita di artisti dei secoli xv., xvi., e xvii. 3 vols. Firenze, 1840.

GIOVIO, P.: Elogia veris clarorum Virorum, Imaginibus apposita quæ in musæo Joviano Comi spectantur. Venetia, 1546.— Delle Imprese. Firenze, 1554.—Vite di 19 Uomini illustri di guerra. Firenze, 1554.— Historia sui temporis. 2 vols. Lutetiæ, 1554.—Vitæ Leoni X. et Adriani VI. Florentiæ, 1548.—Elogia illustrium virorum vitæ. Florentiæ, 1551.

GIRALDI, L.: De poetis nostrorum temporum, ed. C. Wotke. Berlin, 1894.

GIUSTINIANI, A.: Dispacci di Antonio Giustiniani, Ambasciatore Veneto in Roma, 1502-1505, ed. P. Villari. 3 vols. Firenze, 1876.

GNOLI, D.: Leone X. (Nuova Antologia). Roma, 1898.—Storia di Pasquino (Nuova Antologia). Roma, 1890.—Un Giudizio di Lesa Romanità sotto Leone X. Roma, 1891.—Le Cacce di Leone X. Roma, 1893.

GREGOROVIUS, F.: Geschichte der Stadt Rom im Mittelalter. Vols. vii. and viii. Stuttgart, 1880.

GRETHEN, R.: Die politischen Beziehungen Clemens VII. zu Carl V. in den Jahren 1523-1527. Hannover, 1887.

GRUYER, F.: Raphael, peintre de portraits. 2 vols. Paris, 1881.

GUALTERIO, F.: Corrispondenza segreta di G. M. Giberti col Cardinale Agostino Trivulzio in 1527. Torino, 1845.

GUASTI, C.: Le Carte Strozziane nell' Archivio di Firenze. 2 vols. Firenze, 1884.—MSS. Torrigiani. Arch. stor. ital., serie iii., xix.-xxi., xxiii.-xxvi. Firenze, 1865-1877.

GUICCIARDINI, F.: Storia d' Italia. 5 vols. Torino, 1874.—Translated by Fenton. London, 1618.—Opere inedite. 10 vols. Firenze, 1857-1867.

GUILPIN, E.: Skialethia; or, A Shadowe of Truth, in certaine Epigrams and Satyres. London, 1598.

HALLAM, H.: Introduction to the Literature of Europe, Fifteenth to Seventeenth Centuries. London, 1855.

HOLTZINGER, H.: Federigo di Montefeltro, Duca di Urbino. Cronaca di Giovanni Santi nach den Cod. Vat. Ott. 1305. Zum ersten male herausgegeben. Stuttgart, 1893.

VOL. I.   *b*

JANITSCHEK, H. : Die Gesellschaft der Renaissance in Italien und die Kunst. Stuttgart, 1879.

JONSON, B. : The Works of, ed. by Gilford, with Introduction by Cunningham. London, 1875.

KLACZKO, J. : Jules II. Paris, 1898.

LANCIANI, R. : The Golden Days of the Renaissance in Rome. London, 1906.

LANZ, K. : Korrespondenz des Kaisers Karl V. aus dem könig. Archiv und der Bibliothèque de Bourgogne zu Brüssel. 3 vols. Leipzig, 1844-1846.

LEONI, G. : Vita di Francesco Maria della Rovere, Duca d' Urbino. Venezia, 1605.

LEROUX DE LINCY, A. : Recherches sur Jean Grolier. Paris, 1866.

LIPPARINI, G. : Urbino (Italia Artistica, ed. C. Ricci.). Bergamo, 1903.

LITTA, P. : Le Famiglie Celebri Italiane. Milano, 1819-1858.

LUZIO, A., and RENIER, R. : Mantova e Urbino. Torino, 1893.—La Coltura e le Relazioni letterarie di Isabella d' Este Gonzaga. (Giornale storico dell. Lett. ital., vols. xxxiii. to xl. Torino, 1899-1902.)

LUZIO, A. : Federico Gonzaga, Ostaggio alla corte di Giulio II. Rome, 1887.—Isabella d' Este e Leone X. (Arch. stor. lomb. xxxii., Milano, 1906 ; and Arch. stor. ital., xl. Firenze, 1907.)

MARLIANI, B. : Vita del Conte B. Castiglione. (Opere, ed. Volpi.) Padova, 1733.

MARSTON, J., The Works of, ed. by Halliwell. London, 1856.

MARTINATI, C. : Notizie storico-biografiche intorno al Conte Baldassare Castiglione con documenti inediti. Firenze, 1890.

MAZZUCHELLI, G. : Gli Scrittori d' Italia. 2 vols. Brescia, 1753.

MIGNET, F. : La Rivalité de Charles Quint et de Francis Ier. 2 vols. Paris, 1875.

MILANESI, G. : Il Sacco di Roma del 1527. Firenze, 1867.

MOLINI, G. : Documenti di Storia Italiana. 2 vols. Firenze, 1836.

MORSOLIN, B. : Francesco Chiericati. Vicenza, 1873.—Giangiorgio, Trissino. Vicenza, 1894.

MORTARA, A. : Una lettera di B. Castiglione a Federico Gonzaga. Casalmaggiore, 1854.

MÜNTZ, E. : Raphael, sa Vie son Œuvre, et son Temps. Paris, 1855.—Leonardo da Vinci. Paris, 1899.

MUZIO, G. : Historia dei Fatti di Federico di Montefeltro, Duca di Urbino. Venetia, 1605.

NARDUCCI, E. : Vita inedita del Baldassare Castiglione scritta del Conte Gian Maria Mazzuchelli nel Cod. Vat. Lat. 9266. (Buonarroti, xii.) Roma, 1877.

NITTI, F. : Leone X. e la sua politica secondo, documenti e carteggi inediti. Firenze, 1892.

OPDYKE, L., The Book of the Courtier, by Count Baldesar Castiglione, translated and annotated by. London, 1902.

ORTI-MANARA G. : Intorno alla vita ed alle gesta del Conte Lodovico da Canossa. Verona, 1845.

BIBLIOGRAPHY xix

PARIS DE GRASSIS: Il Diario di Leone X., ed Delicati-Armellini. Roma, 1886.

PASSAVANT, J.: Raphael im Urbino, u. s. Vater G. Santi. 3 vols. Leipzig, 1839.

PASTOR, L.: Geschichte der Päpste seit dem Ausgang des Mittelatters. 3 vols. Freiburg-im-Breisgau, 1891-1895.—Geschichte der Päpste im Zeitaltar der Renaissance u. der Glaubenspaltung. Vol. iv., von der Wahl Leos X. bis zum Tode Klemens VII., 1513-1534. Freiburg-im-Breisgau, 1906-1907. —Die Reise des Kardinals Luigi d'Aragona durch Deutschland, die Niederlande, Frankreich u. Oberitalien, 1517-1518, beschrieben v. Antonio de Beatis. Freiburg-im-Breisgau, 1905.

PISTOFILO, B.: Vita di Alfonso d' Este, ed Cappelli. Modena, 1868.

PORTO, L. DA: Lettere storiche, 1509-1518, ed. Bressan. Firenze, 1857.

PUNGILEONI, L.: Elogio di Raffaello di Urbino. Urbino, 1829.

RALEIGH, W., The Book of the Courtier, by B. Castiglione, translated by Hoby, 1561; with introduction by. Tudor Translations. London, 1900.

RAYNALDUS, O.: Annales ecclesiastici. Vol. xiii. Lucca, 1755.

RENIER, R.: Notizia di lettere inedite di B. Castiglione. Torino, 1889.

REUMONT, A. VON: Della diplomazia italiana. Firenze, 1855.— Vittoria Colonna, Marchesa di Pescara, Vita, Fede e Poesia nel secolo decimosesto, ed. Müller-Ferrero. Torino, 1892.

RICHTER, J. The Literary Works of Leonardo da Vinci. 2 vols. London, 1883.

RONCHINI, A.: Due lettere di B. Castiglione nell' Archivio di Parma. (Atti e Memorie delle R. R. Deputazioni di Storia Patria per le Provincio Modenesi e Parmensi. Serie i., vol. ii.) Modena, 1864.

ROSCOE, W.: The Life and Pontificate of Leo X. 4 vols. London, 1827.

ROSSI, V.: Appunti per la storia della Musica alla Corte di Guidobaldo e Francesco Maria, Duci di Urbino. Modena, 1888.

RUSCELLI, G.: Imprese illustri. Venezia, 1570.—Lettere di Principi. 3 vols. Venetia, 1573-1577.

SADOLETO, J.: Epistolæ. Romæ, 1760-1764.

SANDRART, J. VON: L' Accademia Tedesca. 2 vols. Nürnberg, 1673.

SANUTO, M.: I Diarii, 1496-1533. 56 vols., ed. Stefano e Berghet. Venezia, 1879-1903.

SANTORO, D.: Della Vita e delle Opere di Mario Equicola. Chiet 1906.

SCHMARZOW, A.: Melozzo da Forli. Berlin, 1886.

SCHULZ, H.: Der Sacco di Roma. Karls V. Truppen in Rom, 1527-1528. Halle, 1894.

SCOTT, M., Ph.D.: The Book of the Courtyer, by Count Baldassare Castiglione. Baltimore, 1901.

SEARSSI, P. A.: Delle Lettere del Conte Baldassar Castiglione, con annotazioni storiche illustrate. 2 vols. Padova, 1769-1771.

—Poesie volgari e latine e vita del Conte Bald. Castiglione. Roma, 1760.

SOLMI, E. : Leonardo. Firenze, 1900.

SYMONDS, J. A. : The Renaissance in Italy. 7 vols. London, 1897 1899.—Sketches and Studies in Italy and Greece. 2 vols., ed. H. Brown. London, 1898.

TASSO, T. : Dialoghi. Vols. vii. to ix., Opere, ed. Rosmini. Pisa, 1821-1832.

TIGHE, R., and DAVIS, J. : Annals of Windsor. London, 1858.

TIRABOSCHI, G. : Storia della letteratura italiana. Vols. iv. to vii. Milano, 1805-1813.

TOBLER, A. : Castiglione und sein 'Hofmann.' (Neues Schweizerisches Museum, vol. iv.) Berne, 1864.

TOLDO, P. : Le Courtisan dans la littérature française et ses rapports avec l'œuvre du Castiglione. (Archiv für das Studium der neueren Sprachen und Litteraturen. Vols. civ. and cv Braunschweig, 1900.

UGHELLI, F. : Italia sacra, sive de episcopis Italie et insularum adjacentium. 9 vols. Romæ, 1644-1662.

UGOLINI, F. : Storia dei Conti e dei Duchi d' Urbino. 2 vols. Firenze, 1859.

VALDÈS, J. DE : Due Dialoghi, l' uno di Mercurio et Caronte, l' altro di Lattanzio et di Uno Archidiacono, nel quale puntalmente si trattano le cose avenute in Roma nell' anno 1527. Vinegia, 1545.

VALDRIGHI, A. : Due lettere inedite del Conte B. Castiglione (Indicatore Modenese, i., 18, 19.) Modena, 1851.

VARCHI, B. : Storia Fiorentina. 2 vols. Milano, 1805-1813.

VASARI, G. : Le vite de' più eccellenti pittori, scultori ed architettori, ed. Milanesi. 9 vols. Firenze, 1878-1885.

VENTURI, A. : Gian Cristoforo Romano, Scultore. (Arte, vol. i.) Roma, 1888.

VERDI, A. : Gli ultimi anni di Lorenzo de' Medici, Duca d' Urbino, 1515-1518. Este, 1889.

VERNARECCI, A. : Di alcune Rappresentazioni drammatiche alla Corte di Urbino nel 1513. (Archivio storico per le Marche e per l' Umbria.) Foligno, 1886.

VERNAZZA DI FRENEY, A. : Lettere inedite di B. Castiglione. (Accademia di Torino. Vol. xxi.) Torino, 1811.

VETTORI, F. : Sommario della storia d' Italia, 1511-1527. (Arch. stor. ital., appendice vi.) Firenze, 1848.

VILLARI, P. : Niccolò Machiavelli e i suoi tempi. 3 vols. Firenze, 1877.

VOLTA, L. : Mantovani illustri. Mantova, 1845.

WEALE, W. H. J. : Josse van Wassenhove. (Petite Revue de Gand.) Gand, 1901.

WYNDHAM, G. : The Poems of Shakespeare. London, 1898.

XENOPHON : Hellenica. Venezia, 1503.

ZANNONI, G. : Nuovi contributi per la Storia del Cinquecento in Italia. (La Cultura, serie i., vol. xi.) Roma, 1890.

CONTENTS TO VOL. I.

CONTENTS

CONTENTS

CONTENTS

CHAPTER XVIII

1509–1510

CHAPTER XIX

1510–1511

CHAPTER XX

1511–1512

CHAPTER XXI

1512–1513

CHAPTER XXII

1513

CONTENTS

LIST OF ILLUSTRATIONS TO VOL. I

CHAPTER I

1478–1490

On the heights above the gorge of the Olona, about ten miles from the Lake of Varese and twenty or more from the city of Como, stands the ruined castle of the ancient Castiglione family. It is a wild and romantic spot, with the rushing waters of the mountain torrent in the ravine below, and the steep streets and stone walls of the old town straggling among the chestnut and acacia woods along its banks. The road winds through gardens of vine and maize, of fig and olive, and between the overhanging boughs of the trees we look back at the distant range of Alps and the snows of Monte Rosa.

According to one historian — Bonaventura Castiglione, who was himself a member of the house— the name of the place in Roman times was Castrum Stiliconis, and owed its origin to the Vandal general Stilicho, who fixed his camp here in the days of Theodoric. Afterwards it became a flourishing town, but was destroyed by Attila and restored by Archbishop Ansferto of Milan, as recorded on a tablet placed in the church of S. Ambrogio, at the time of his death in 886.

In the tenth century this fair and fruitful land was granted to a certain Corrado, son of Count Berengaria, who had rendered important services to the Archbishops of Milan, and now settled on the banks of the Olona. Here he raised the famous Castello, with its four square towers, from which his descendants took their name. This citadel, with crenellated turrets borne in the lion's paws, figures in the armorial bearings of his house, and the old town down in the hollow at the foot of the Rocca still retains the name of Castiglione d' Olona.

The Captains of Castiglione, as they were termed in medieval days, rose to high honour under Otho the Great and the successive German Emperors who visited Italy ; and two members of the family, Gottifrede and Tealdo, were advanced to the dignity of Archbishops of Milan by Henry IV. But in the thirteenth century, when Guido Castiglione was podesta of Como, his castle was razed to the ground by a rival lord, Ottone Visconti, and the fortifications were not rebuilt for 150 years. Then an illustrious ecclesiastic, Branda Castiglione, who enjoyed the favour of the Visconti dukes and was created a Cardinal by Pope John XXIII., obtained leave to rebuild his ancestral fortress on the old site.

Close by, on the summit of the same hill, this splendid prelate reared the noble collegiate church with the lofty campanile and red sandstone walls, that are still standing. Within, its stately choir and baptistery were adorned with frescoes by Masolino, the Florentine painter, whom Cardinal Branda had met in Hungary, when he was sent by the Pope as

Legate to this distant land. Here we may recognize
the keen face and white hair of the aged Cardinal,
as Masolino painted him when he was past eighty,
kneeling with the shepherds at the manger of Beth-
lehem, or seated at King Herod's banquet in his robes
of purple and ermine. The Castello which he raised
again from the dust is a heap of ruins to-day, but
down in the town, in a street bearing the name of
the Via del Cardinale, we may still see the fair
palace, with Lombard Gothic portals and windows,
which Branda built for himself, and which Masolino
decorated with friezes of portraits and views of the
distant Alps.

Like many other members of his house, Branda
was an able lawyer and statesman as well as a distinguished ecclesiastic. During his mission to Hungary
he rendered important services to the Emperor Sigismond, who in return created him and all the members
of his house Counts Palatine, and granted them perpetual exemption from imperial tolls, tribute, and
customs. By the same deed, drawn up at Buda-
Pesth in 1412, the members of this 'ancient, numerous,
privileged, and most illustrious race,' were empowered
yearly to elect one of their house to hold jurisdiction
over their family and dependents in the county of
Castiglione.[1]

On his return to Lombardy the Cardinal was
appointed President of the ducal council by Filippo
Maria Visconti, and founded a college for poor
students at Pavia that was only suppressed in the
last century. But Corio tells us that he incurred the
displeasure of the Milanese by endeavouring to sub-
stitute the Roman liturgy for the Ambrosian rites in
the Duomo on Christmas Day, 1440, a proceeding

[1] Beffa-Negrini, 'Elogi,' 404.

which enraged the mob to such a pitch that they stormed and sacked the Cardinal's palace in Milan. After this Branda retired to Castiglione d' Olona, where he spent his last years in peaceful retreat, and celebrated the rites of the Church after his own taste in his collegiate foundation. Here he died three years later, at the age of ninety-three, and was laid to rest in an imposing sarcophagus, adorned with his recumbent effigy, watched over by guardian angels and his chosen saints, Francis and Anthony.

Another illustrious member of the Cardinal's family, Franchino Castiglione, filled the chair of jurisprudence in the University of Pavia for many years, and was sent on embassies both to Florence and Ferrara by Filippo Maria Visconti. In 1441 he was employed to draw up the marriage contract of the Duke's daughter, Bianca Maria, with Francesco Sforza, and delivered a nuptial oration when the wedding was celebrated at Cremona. After Filippo Maria's death, Franchino took an active part in the establishment of a popular form of government, and became one of the chief magistrates of the short-lived Ambrosian Republic. None the less, he remained on friendly terms with Francesco Sforza, who made him a member of his council when he became Duke of Milan. From that time the Castiglioni were loyal subjects of the Sforza princes, and served Francesco and his sons faithfully and well. A second Branda, a grand-nephew of the Cardinal, became Bishop of Como, and celebrated high mass at the church of S. Stefano on the Feast of St. Stephen, when Galeazzo Maria was murdered as he entered the doors. In the following year, 1477, he was sent by the widowed Duchess Bona as ambassador to her brother-in-law, Louis XI. of France, and afterwards commanded the Papal fleet in the war against Venice. In 1483 Sixtus IV. appointed the Bishop Governor of Rome, but the enmity of the Pope's nephew, Girolamo Riario, soon led him to abandon this office and retire to his diocese. Three years later he was sent by the Regent, Lodovico Sforza, to congratulate Innocent VIII. on his accession to the Papacy, and died during his absence in Rome. He was succeeded in the bishopric of Como by his nephew, a third Branda, who became ducal councillor, and was employed by the Moro on confidential business, and sent to the help of his niece, Caterina Sforza, when her subjects rebelled and murdered her first husband, the hated Girolamo Riario.

Several other members of the family enjoyed Lodovico's favour and held high office during his reign. Gian Stefano Castiglione was sent on missions to Pope Alexander VI. and the Signory of Florence, and married Lucia, daughter of the Moro's confidential secretary, Bartolommeo Calco. After Lodovico's fall, however, Gian Stefano was among the first councillors who took the oath of fealty to Louis XII., and received the lands of Saronno, which the Duke had given to his mistress, Cecilia Gallerani, in reward for this desertion. His younger brother Branda was also a ducal councillor and prime favourite of the Moro. On his death in 1495, he was buried by the Duke's command in the choir of S. Maria della Grazie, where Duchess Beatrice was laid to rest two years later, and where a beautiful monument records his rare virtues and the grief of his kinsfolk. One of Branda's sons, Gian Giacomo, was made Archbishop of Bari in early youth, by Lodovico Sforza, but never visited his distant diocese until after his patron's fall, as he was constantly

employed on diplomatic missions.   While Gian Giacomo remained loyal to the exiled Sforzas, his brother
Girolamo embraced the French cause, and was
rewarded with lands and honours by Louis XII.
Another distinguished member of the family, and
descendant of Franchino the jurist, was Sabbà da
Castiglione, the gallant and accomplished Knight of
St. John of Jerusalem, who, after defending Rhodes
against the Turks, returned to spend a peaceful old
age at Faenza and write his famous ' Ricordi.'

All of these Milanese knights and courtiers claimed
the author of the 'Cortegiano' as their kinsman, although
he was only remotely connected with their branch of
the house. His great-grandfather, Cristoforo, a cousin
and contemporary of Cardinal Branda, was one of the
foremost lawyers of the age, and filled the chair of
jurisprudence at the University of Pavia.   Unlike his
illustrious kinsman, he never enjoyed the favour of the
Visconti princes, and after the murder of Duke Gian
Maria in 1412, by his wife's brother, he found it
prudent to leave Pavia and settle at Parma.   There
he was treated with the honour due to his learning,
and received the title of Count Palatine from the
Emperor Sigismond, and the confirmation of all the
privileges which had been granted to his kinsman,
Cardinal Branda, for himself and his descendants in
perpetuity. In his old age Cristoforo returned to Pavia
and still pursued his legal studies, although he had
the misfortune to lose his large and valuable library
by fire three times.   *Legum monarcha et subtilita-
tum princeps* was the title bestowed upon him by
his fellow-jurists, and more than a century after his
death his ' Discourses ' were published at Venice, in
the year 1560.

Cristoforo's youngest son, Baldassare, embraced the

BOOKS OF HISTORY AND REMINISCENCES

Etc.

LONDON: JOHN MURRAY
ALBEMARLE STREET : W. 1

¶ The Original Six-Volume Edition of the Standard Life Complete in Two Volumes. With 16 Photogravures. 3312 pages. 21s. net the set.

THE LIFE OF BENJAMIN DISRAELI
EARL OF BEACONSFIELD.

By WILLIAM FLAVELLE MONYPENNY and GEORGE EARLE BUCKLE. Revised by GEORGE EARLE BUCKLE.

LORD ERNLE, in *The Times* : 'The value of the biography can never be superseded. It must always remain the final authority on the full career of Disraeli.'

THE KINGS OF ENGLAND, 1066-1901

By the HON. CLIVE BIGHAM, C.M.G., C.B.E., Author of 'The Prime Ministers of Britain, 1721-1924,' etc. With 37 Illustrations. 21s. net.

This is a short account of the lives and characters of the thirty-six sovereigns of England from William the Conqueror to Victoria. The personal histories of the Kings and Queens are illustrated by by the occupations, amusements and other incidents of their private lives as well as by the public policy that they pursued. A complete study of this nature has never been attempted hitherto.

THE AMAZING CAREER
OF BERNADOTTE (1763-1844)

By the RT. HON. SIR DUNBAR PLUNKET BARTON, Bt., Author of 'Bernadotte and Napoleon, etc.' Illustrated. 21s. net.

The career of Jean Baptiste Bernadotte presents features of almost unique interest. Starting as a runaway recruit, he became a Marshal of France, a Prince of the French Empire, King of Sweden and Norway and a founder of the Royal throne of Sweden. Some scattered writings on the subject have appeared from the pen of Sir Dunbar Plunket Barton who now presents in a single volume a true portrait and a vivid biography of the man.

THE NARRATIVE
OF A NAVAL NOBODY, 1907-1924

By DOUGLAS FAIRBAIRN, Lt.-Commr. (retired) R.N.
With a Preface by 'Bartimeus.' 10s. 6d. net.

This is a personal account of the experiences of a naval officer throughout his service in the Royal Navy, a most interesting period of 16 years before, during and after the Great War. He is seen in the work and play of life afloat in the Fleet, in peace and war, in many parts of the world where his ships were stationed.

A DOORKEEPER OF MUSIC

By J. A. FULLER-MAITLAND, Author of 'The Spell of Music,' 'The Musician's Pilgrimage.' Illustrated. 10s. 6d. net.

The author, who was for 20 years musical critic of *The Times*, tells of an unconventional childhood and youth, in the course of which he came across many notable and some notorious people; many eminent figures in the literary and artistic world pass across the pages, from Disraeli and Gladstone to Browning and Samuel Butler, from Ruskin and Leighton to Du Maurier and Whistler.

ODDS AND ENDS OF MY LIFE

By the COUNTESS CAVE, Author of 'Memories of Old Richmond.' With Illustrations. 7s. 6d. net.

This little book can best be likened to an evening talk round the fireside with one who has touched life at many points and is willing to ramble over the fields of reminiscence, grave and gay, with kindly and humorous comment and criticism.

THE STORY OF SAN MICHELE

By AXEL MUNTHE, Author of 'Letters from a Mourning City,' 'Memories and Vagaries,' etc. 16s. net.

'Romantic, realistic, pitiful and enchanting, this is the record of a citadel of the soul . . . a treasure house of incidents and dreams. A miracle? Well, every work of art is a miracle, and every beautiful thing the shrine of a realised dream.'—*Daily Telegraph.*

GILBERT AND SULLIVAN
OR, THE 'COMPLEAT' SAVOYARD.
By ISAAC GOLDBERG. Illustrated. 21s. net.

'He draws together almost all the established facts—the great mass of tradition and anecdote and critical and uncritical appreciation—which goes to make up the romantic story of the Savoy operas. The book has a real value. He has produced by far the best book of reference, up to date, in the Gilbert and Sullivan library . . . Fresh and stimulating.'—*Saturday Review*.

LORD CHIEF BARON POLLOCK
By the LORD HANWORTH, P.C. Illus. 10s. 6d. net.

The Rt. Hon. LORD HEWART, Lord Chief Justice, in the *Morning Post* says:—'The Master of the Rolls is warmly to be congratulated upon this most admirable biography of his distinguished grandfather. The reader is reluctant to say farewell to the learned, unwearied and essentially kind and affectionate man who lives again in these pages.'

DAISY, PRINCESS OF PLESS
By HERSELF. Illustrated. 6th Impression. 25s. net.

'A private commentary of the frankest character; vivid, intimate, human.'—*The Observer*.

'Extraordinarily vivid and interesting. They are the best things of the kind that have appeared for a long while.'—*Truth*.

THREE PERSONS :
FIELD-MARSHAL SIR HENRY WILSON, COLONEL HOUSE AND COLONEL LAWRENCE.
By SIR ANDREW MACPHAIL, O.B.E., LL.D. With Portraits. Second Impression. 10s. 6d. net.

'This cruelly clever book is a contribution to the interpretation of history, and a remarkable analysis of historical matter.'—*Daily Telegraph*.

HIGH PRESSURE.
By COLONEL LIONEL JAMES, C.B.E., D.S.O., sometime War Correspondent of *The Times*. Maps. 12s. net.

'Colonel James is one of the last of the old breed, and this book will be enjoyed by everyone who likes good yarns of adventure. Apart from the record it gives of a clever journalist, his book ought to have other interests for present-day readers.'—*The Times*.

profession of arms from his boyhood, and became renowned as a wise and valiant soldier. Francesco Sforza appointed him Commissioner-General of his armies and sent him to the court of the Emperor Frederic III. to obtain the investiture of the duchy of Milan. On his return from this embassy, Baldassare was induced to enter the service of Lodovico Gonzaga, who had at one time been Captain of the Milanese forces, and eventually left Milan to settle at Mantua. While he was still in the service of the Sforza Duke, he married Polissena, the daughter and heiress of Alessandro Lisca of Verona. This wise and beautiful maiden brought him, as her dower, the castle and lands of Casatico, on the river Oglio, near Marcaria, in the Mantuan territory, where forty years later his illustrious grandson, the author of the ' Cortegiano,' was born. After his marriage, Baldassare sold his Milanese estates, and spent the proceeds in enlarging and improving his property at Casatico. When he finally left Milan, the Marquis Lodovico granted his favourite a palace at Mantua, in the street leading to the Castello di Corte, then known as the Via Pradella, close to the ancient church of S. Jacopo. This house was pulled down during the Austrian occupation in 1822, to make room for the present Teatro Sociale, and Palazzo Bonacolsi, on the Piazza Sordello, close to the Castello, is now the family residence of the Castiglioni. Here the Milanese knight spent his declining years enjoying the favour of the good Marquis and his German wife, Barbara of Brandenburg. His sons Cristoforo and Baldassare grew up in close companionship with the Gonzaga princes, whose forms and faces are familiar to us in Mantegna's frescoes on the walls of the Sala degli Sposi. According to one Mantuan chronicler, who wrote the history of the Castiglione family,[1] Cristoforo's own portrait was introduced into one of these groups, and the fine-looking courtier standing behind the Marquis Lodovico's chair in the act of receiving his lord's commands is our hero's grandfather. The intimacy which the young Castiglione brothers enjoyed with the Gonzagas was strengthened by the marriage of the elder brother with Luigia, or, as she is often called, Aloysia Gonzaga. This remarkable woman, whose force and elevation of character were destined to exert so great an influence on her son's future, was the daughter of Antonio Gonzaga, a descendant of Corrado, Podesta of Mantua, and great-uncle to the Marquis Gian Francesco I. Although only distantly related to the reigning house, the members of this younger branch of the family were recognized as kinsmen by the reigning Marquis, and bore the title of *Signori nobili*, which gave them precedence at court next to the princes of the blood. Antonio Gonzaga himself was a brave soldier who received the honour of knighthood from the Emperor Frederick III., and his wife, Francesca degli Uberti, a descendant of Dante's Farinata, was connected with many illustrious Lombard houses. Their daughter's marriage to the son and heir of Baldassare Castiglione was celebrated with great rejoicing in the summer of 1477. Soon after this, Baldassare himself was sent to Tuscany to arbitrate between the Florentines and Lucchese, and decide a quarrel which had been referred to the Marquis Lodovico. He returned home towards the end of the year, and died a few weeks later, on January 14, 1478. His lord and master, Lodovico Gonzaga, soon followed him to the grave, dying on June 12, at his villa of Goïto, deeply lamented by the subjects over

[1] Beffa Negrini.

Photo, Anderson.

LODOVICO GONZAGA AND HIS FAMILY.

BY MANTEGNA (SALA DEGLI SPOSI, MANTUA)

To face p. 8, Vol. I.

whom he had reigned so long. Six months afterwards, on December 6, 1478, Cristoforo Castiglione's young wife gave birth to a son at Casatico, that ancient castle which, in the words of the family chronicler, 'we now regard with a reverence as great as the house of Virgil at Pietola, the Tower of Boethius at Pavia, or the home of Petrarch.'[1]

The boy whose birth was to endow this old country house with immortal fame received the name of Baldassare, after his grandfather, who had been the first of his race to settle at Mantua. In 1481, Chiara Gonzaga, the eldest child of the Marquis Federico, Lodovico's son and successor, and of his wife, Margaret of Bavaria, was married to Gilbert, Count of Montpensier, the French king's cousin. Duke Ercole of Ferrara, who came to Mantua for the wedding, and agreed to the betrothal of his daughter Isabella with the son of his good friend the Marquis, knighted Luigia's brother Gianpietro on this occasion, and Luigia herself and her husband, Cristoforo Castiglione were chosen to escort the young Princess to her new home. Together they crossed the Alps, in the train of the wedded pair, and travelled to France, taking with them among the wedding gifts Mantegna's painting of S. Sebastian to adorn the chapel of the Montpensier château in Auvergne.

From the first the young Marquis Francesco, who succeeded his father in 1484, and his wife Isabella d' Este, honoured both of Baldassare's parents with marks of signal favour. Cristoforo accompanied Francesco through all his campaigns, and fought gallantly at his side in the fiercely-contested battle of the Taro. On that disastrous day, when the Marquis's uncle, Rodolfo Gonzaga, fell in the thick

---

[1] Beffa-Negrini, 404.

of the mêlée, and Francesco himself narrowly escaped with his life, Cristoforo was severely wounded. He lived four years longer, but never recovered from the effect of his injuries.

Meanwhile young Baldassare grew up in his home at Casatico, under the eye of his watchful mother, who instilled her own high sense of honour and lofty principles into the boy's soul, while at the same time she herself inspired him with that deep affection and unbounded confidence which lasted until his dying day. His brother Jeronimo was many years younger, but for companions Baldassare had his uncle Gianpietro Gonzaga's sons, Luigi and Cesare, who were about his own age, and who both of them shared his cultured tastes and love of music and poetry. In the year 1492 all three lads were sent to complete their studies at the University of Milan, where the enlightened liberality of the Sforza dukes attracted the foremost scholars of the day. Nothing was more natural than that Cristoforo should send his son to a court where his kinsmen held high office, while the maternal uncle of Luigi and Cesare Gonzaga, the Marchesino Stanga of Cremona, was the confidential secretary and chamberlain of the all-powerful Moro.

CHAPTER II

1492-1499

Milan under the rule of Lodovico Sforza—Castiglione's teachers and studies—His love of learning and the fine arts—His friends at the court of Milan—He enters the Duke's service—Death of Duchess Beatrice—Castiglione recalled to Mantua by his father's death—Fall of Lodovico Sforza—Castiglione enters Milan with Louis XII.—His description of the triumphal entry and dislike of the French victors—Recollections of the court of Milan in the 'Cortegiano.'

THE seven years which young Castiglione spent at Milan, between the age of thirteen and twenty, were a memorable period in his life. Nowhere else could he have acquired so full and complete a training in all the arts and graces necessary for the equipment of a perfect courtier. 'This court,' wrote Isabella d' Este, from the Moro's palace, 'is the school of the Master of those who know.'

The young scholar who came to Milan from Virgil's birthplace with his heart full of enthusiasm for classical learning, for art and poetry, soon found himself at home in this 'new Athens,' and drank deeply of the celestial spring that flowed from Lodovico's Parnassus. He sat at the feet of Giorgio Merula, the sun of Alexandria, as the great humanist was called by his contemporaries, and learnt Greek from the venerable Athenian Demetrius Chalcondylas. The importance of acquiring some knowledge of this language in early

11

youth was a point upon which Castiglione always insisted in after-years, and which he took care to impress upon his own son. 'It is the opinion of the best judges,' he wrote to his mother from Rome in 1521, 'that a boy should begin by learning Greek, because Latin is, so to speak, our own language, and therefore easily acquired and spoken by men of our race, but this is certainly not the case with Greek.'[1]

At the same time Baldassare attended the lectures of Filippo Beroaldo, and, under the guidance of this eminent Bolognese humanist, devoted much of his time to the study of rhetoric and Latin authors. Among prose-writers, Cicero, who was afterwards to become his chief model; among poets, Virgil and Tibullus, Abbot Serassi tells us,[2] were his favourites. But while classical literature formed the chief object of his serious studies, Italian poets from the first attracted his fancy. The writers in that *lingua volgare*, whose claims he was to defend so vigorously in future days, appealed to him in an especial manner. He loved the energy and sublime power of Dante's line, the grace and elegance of Petrarch's verse, while among living poets none had greater fascination for him than the Tuscan singers, Lorenzo de' Medici and Poliziano. Both of these Florentine poets were already popular at the court of Milan. Duke Lodovico had been on friendly terms with the Magnifico, and honoured Poliziano with his patronage, and one of the first books which we find mentioned in Castiglione's letters is Poliziano's 'Stanze Volgari.' Nor was the young squire's training in knightly exercises neglected. He learnt jousting and fencing, wrestling and vaulting, from Messer Pietro Monte,[3] that past-

---

[1] 'Lettere fam.,' ed. Serassi, i., p. 181.
[2] 'Vita,' p. 94.   [3] 'Cortegiano,' i. 25.

master in these arts, who was the instructor of the
Duke's son-in-law, Galeazzo di San Severino, and whose
trick of flinging darts excited Leonardo's admiration
as much as his interest in engineering and philosophy.[1]
Soon young Castiglione became an adept at handling
the lance, riding at the ring, and all those other
feats of horsemanship and military exercises which
were held to form an important part of a courtier's
education. He looked on with kindling eyes when
Messer Galeazzo, that mirror of chivalry, vanquished
all his rivals in the tournament, and bore off the prize
in the presence of the whole court. Perhaps he rode
out in the train of that brilliant knight when he
escorted the young Duchess on her gay hunting-
parties, and Beatrice and her courtiers went singing
on their way, or disputed merrily over the rival
claims of Roland and Rinaldo.

Castiglione was on intimate terms with Beatrice's
secretary, Vincenzo Calmeta, who became known at
Urbino as *l' elegantissimo Calmeta,* and wrote a touching record of his dear mistress seven years after her
death. Her favourite violin-player, Jacopo di San
Secondo, and Cristoforo Romano, the accomplished
master who carved her bust in marble and charmed
her with his exquisite singing, were both well known
to him, and his natural love of music and painting
brought him into connexion with many of the artists
at the Moro's court. Often as he waited on Messer
Galeazzo's pleasure, or watched Pietro Monte jousting,
in the courts of the Castello, he met Leonardo, the
Florentine, whom the court-poet described as 'the
new Apelles,' leaving the equestrian statue of the
great Duke Francesco, on which he was at work, to
put the last touches to his fresco in the Dominican

---

[1] Leonardo, ed. Solmi, p. 81, and Manoscritti I.

convent without the gates. He was among the spectators on the memorable day when the plaster model of the great horse was set up on the arch in front of the Castello in honour of Bianca Maria's marriage to the Emperor Maximilian, and the voice of poets and applauding multitudes together hailed the completion of the work. He saw the comedies that were given in honour of the Marchesa Isabella's visit, and heard the wonderful performances of the famous improvisatore, Serafino of Aquila, whose gnome-like appearance caused him to be compared to a carpet-bag, and whose premature death was lamented by all the ladies at Mantua and Urbino. He may have been in the Duchess's rooms on those evenings when cantos of the 'Divina Commedia' were read aloud, and the architect Bramante and Gaspare Visconti, the poet, discussed the rival merits of Dante and Petrarch. And the gay and witty conversations which he heard in that brilliant society may well have suggested the idea of recording those animated scenes in a more enduring form. The sight of all these wonders, and the intercourse with these rare artists and gifted scholars, whom he describes as the flower of the whole world, made a deep impression on the young courtier, whose sensitive soul was keenly alive to beauty in every shape and form. It was natural that, as Serassi and Marliani tell us, he was soon fired by an ardent desire to attach himself to a Prince who was so enlightened a patron of art and letters, and who was endowed with so fine and discriminating a taste in these matters. At the age of eighteen, his education being held to be completed, Castiglione entered the Duke's service, and soon became a general favourite at court.

This was in 1496, when the unfortunate Gian

Galeazzo was dead and Lodovico had gained the object of his ambition, and been proclaimed Duke in his nephew's stead. But Fortune, which had granted the Moro his heart's desire, and raised him to these giddy heights, now suddenly withdrew her smile, and Castiglione, who had seen the court of the Sforzas in its greatest splendour, lived to be the witness of its downfall. He was in Milan on that winter evening when the young Duchess died in the bloom of her youth and beauty. 'Then,' in her secretary's words, 'everything fell into ruin. The court, which had been a joyous paradise, was turned into a dark and gloomy hell, and poets and painters were forced to seek another home.' After this terrible catastrophe, the rift between the Moro and his brother-in-law, Francesco Gonzaga, gradually widened, and mutual suspicion and distrust parted the rulers of Milan and Mantua. Castiglione, however, remained in the Duke's service, and endeared himself to Lodovico daily more and more. One of his Milanese kinsmen, the able jurist Stefano Castiglione, speaks of the young courtier's popularity in a letter which he addressed to Baldassare's father in February, 1499. After appealing to Cristoforo's generosity on behalf of a poor relation who owed him money, the writer adds : 'I must tell Your Magnificence that your son, Messer Baldassare, is very well and highly esteemed, not only by our illustrious lord the Duke, but by every one here, and that with good reason, for, indeed, there could not be a more charming or talented youth. You should really come to Milan yourself soon and contract some honourable marriage for him, which would prove a source of consolation to you and all your family.'[1]

Two months after this letter was written, in April,

[1] Cod. Vat. Lat., 8213. Appendix I.

1499, Cristoforo Castiglione died, as we learn from a
letter addressed by Gianpietro Gonzaga to Jacopo
d' Atri, Count of Adria and Pianella. The Count,
who is mentioned in the second book of the 'Cortegiano,' was at this time Mantuan ambassador at
the court of Naples, and will be remembered as the
secretary whose advice Isabella d' Este sought when
she wished to raise a statue to Virgil. Now, Gianpietro, the widowed Luigia's brother, wrote to inform
Jacopo d' Atri of his kinsman's death, and assure him
at the same time of Baldassare readiness to serve
his father's old friend. ' I am certain,' he writes on
April 24, 'that Your Magnificence will have grieved
sincerely for the great loss we have sustained here in
the death of our Magnifico Cristoforo, in whom I
have lost a good friend and brother. When Baldassare,
his son, who is now in Milan, returns to this city, I
will desire him to do what you ask, and you may
certainly depend upon him as you did on his father.
Both he himself and all that he has will be at the
disposal of Your Magnificence.'[1]

Cristoforo Castiglione was buried at his father's side
in the family chapel in S. Agnese, the church built
early in the century by the Augustinian friars on
the shore of the Lago di Mezzo, and eight years later
his son and widow raised a noble monument above
his grave. Both church and tomb perished in the
evil days that overtook Mantua, and the street which
bore the name of Via S. Agnese is now known
as Via Cavour. After his father's death Baldassare
returned to comfort his widowed mother and take
his father's place in the management of his estates.
He had three sisters, two of whom were already

---

[1] Archivio Gonzaga, Carteggio di B. Castiglione.   Martinati
Notizie intorno al Conte B. Castiglione, 75.

Photo, Anderson.

LODOVICO SFORZA.

BY BOLTRAFFIO (TRIVULZIO COLLECTION).

To face p. 16, Vol. I.

married. The eldest, Polissena, was the wife of
Jacopo Boschetto, a gentleman of Modena, who lived
at Gonzaga, in the neighbourhood of Mantua, and
seems to have been a martyr to gout. The second,
Francesca, had married Tommaso Strozzi, a courtier
of the Mantuan princes, who often accompanied the
Marchesa and her son on their travels. Baldassare
entertained a sincere regard for both his brothers-in-
law, although Messer Jacopo's bad temper and grasp-
ing nature were often a source of trial, and only to be
excused on the ground of ill-health. But the one of
all his family to whom he was most deeply attached
was his youngest sister, Anna, who took the veil in
1504, in the convent of Santa Paola, a community
of Poor Clares, to which many of the Gonzaga
princesses belonged. His early letters abound in
affectionate references to this maiden, whether he
calls her by her baptismal name of Anna or by that
of Suor Laura, which she adopted on her profession;
and in after-years he named his first daughter Anna
after this favourite sister.

Besides these sisters, the young Count had a
brother, Jeronimo, who was many years younger than
himself, and whom his mother insisted on keeping
at home. For his benefit Castiglione engaged a
young tutor named Falcone, whom he had known at
Milan, and of whose learning and character he had
the highest opinion. Falcone came to live at Casatico,
and took charge of Jeronimo, who was destined for
an ecclesiastical career, and for whom Baldassare and
his mother early obtained a grant of several rich benefices, which he did not live to enjoy. Castiglione
himself now became attached to Francesco Gonzaga's
person, and soon won the favour both of the Marquis
and of his accomplished wife. Strangely enough, the

first public occasion on which he was required to attend his lord was in October, 1499, when the French King, Louis XII., made his triumphal entry into Milan.   During the same month of April in which Baldassare was recalled to Mantua by his father's death, the treaty between France and Venice, which sealed the fate of Lodovico Sforza, was signed at Blois. After this a series of disasters brought about the Moro's ruin, and by the end of August the French armies were at the gates of Milan.   Lodovico and his children fled to Innsbrück, and the Castello—that impregnable citadel of the Sforzas—was treacherously surrendered to the enemy.   Louis XII. now hastened to take possession of his new dominions, and the exiled Duke's nearest relatives, trembling for their own safety, lost no time in making peace with the victorious monarch.   On October 2 Duke Ercole of Ferrara and his son-in-law, the Marquis of Mantua, met King Louis at Pavia, and four days later entered Milan with him in state.   Castiglione, who had by this time almost completed his twenty-first year, rode through the streets in his master's suite, and wrote a letter to his brother-in-law, Jacopo Boschetto, in which he describes this triumphal progress, not without a pang of natural regret for the lost glories of Lodovico's court :

' *To the Magnificent Cavalier, Messer Jacopo Boschetto da Gonzaga, my Kinsman and Honoured Brother.*

'MAGNIFICENT AND HONOURED BROTHER,
     ' If I were not sure that your kindness and indulgence were not far greater than my culpable neglect, I should fear that my conduct might have excited your displeasure.   But the certainty that I

could never wilfully offend you leads me to commit
this fault ; and this same confidence which leads me to
err prevents me from attempting to make any longer
valid excuses for not having written before. I think
you have already been informed of His Majesty the
King's entry into Pavia. Our most illustrious lord
remained at Pavia with His Majesty until Saturday
evening, when he came to Milan. On Sunday after
dinner, we rode out to meet His Majesty, who came
to S. Eustorgio, a church outside the Porta Ticinese,
and remained there for some time. Signor Messer
Giovangiacomo [Trivulzio, the French Commander-in-
Chief] here presented him with the bâton of state and
a sword. The King gave the sword to Monsignore de
Ligny, who is Grand Chamberlain and Marshal of
France, and returned the bâton to M. Giovangiacomo.
This took place in a chamber at S. Eustorgio. I did
not see the ceremony, but heard of it from others who
were present. Meanwhile many companies of archers
and other French troops arrived in great confusion,
together with chariots and prelates and cavaliers, and
a good many Milanese gentlemen rode out in some
degree of order. About twelve chariots belonging to
the Pope's son [Cesare Borgia, Duke of Valentinois]
drove up, covered with black velvet and gold brocade,
followed by many pages on splendid horses, clad in
the French fashion, who were a fine sight. Then
there rode out to meet the King, Cardinal Borgia the
Legate, Cardinal S. Pietro in Vincula [Giuliano della
Rovere, afterwards Pope Julius II.], and the Cardinal
of Rouen [Georges d'Amboise], all of these riding
together. Meanwhile French gentlemen, lords, and
knights went riding continually up and down the
street, looking at ladies and making their horses prance
and gambol ; they had good horses, but handled them
badly and struck out at every one who ventured to
come in their way. There was one archer who drew
his knife and gave our Master of the Horse, M. Evangelista, a great blow on the back of his neck, and yet

he had not said or done anything in the world to pro-
voke such treatment !   At length, God be thanked !
the King appeared.   First the trumpets sounded ;
then we saw the German infantry, with their Captain
on horseback at their head, and they themselves on
foot, bearing their lances in rest as usual, and all wearing green and red uniforms and hose.   There were a
hundred of them, as splendid-looking men as you can
wish to see, and these formed the vanguard.   Then
came the King's own body-guard, all of whom are said
to be gentlemen.   There were 500 archers on foot,
with halberds instead of bows in their hands, and
helmets on their heads, wearing red and green doublets,
embroidered with the King's badge of the porcupine
with its quills spread out, on the back and breast.
Then came the King's trumpeters and those of the
other Princes, with our own among them, wearing
satin vests like the cross-bowmen.   Immediately after
these came His Majesty the King, and just in front
of him Signor Giovangiacomo da Trivulzio with the
bâton of command in his hand, and some of his
barons at his side, Monsignori di Begnino [Stuart
d'Aubigny], di Lignino [Ligny], the Grand Connétable,
and others whom I do not know.   Behind him were
the three Cardinals, each in his proper rank, and the
Duke of Ferrara and our Signor, who rode between
Montpensier and another lord whose name I cannot
remember, and the Pope's son, who has a very
gallant bearing, all according to their rank.   After
that came a multitude of other lords and gentlemen
innumerable, and prelates and Milanese and foreigners.
Then 200 French gentlemen-at-arms, all well armed
and mounted, making altogether a very gallant show.

  ' These all accompanied His Majesty along the road,
which was covered with cloth up to the Castello, and
lined on each side with ladies and adorned with
tapestries and other decorations.   Some one who
wished to show his affection for the French had placed
the King's arms above his doors as the best ornament

that he could have. The street was crowded with
people, and the King rode on, looking up at the ladies,
who are said to please him greatly. Over his head a
baldacchino of gold brocade was carried by doctors
wearing purple robes, and capes and birettas lined with
fur. Several of the first gentlemen in Milan walked on
foot at his horse's side, in good order; the horse itself
is a roan, not very large, but a nice horse, only a little
poor about the mouth. His Majesty wore the ducal
mantle of white damask and the ducal cap, lined with
fur, also of white damask. So he rode up to the
Castello. The piazza was thronged with people, and
the road was kept for His Majesty by Gascon archers
on foot, armed with helmets and the same liveries, but
without embroideries. These Gascons are little men,
and the archers are very stout. With all this pomp
His Majesty the King of France entered the Castello
of Milan—once the place where the flower of the men
of this world were assembled, but now full of drinking booths and dung-heaps. It is said that, on entering the gates, His Majesty laid his hand on his sword,
and his action caused the bearers of the baldacchino
some alarm. However, he did not draw blood, but
only flourished his sword in the air a moment. On
Monday morning we went to court in attendance on
our most illustrious lord, and the King went to mass
at S. Ambrogio, escorted by the halberdiers and
accompanied by all the Princes whom I have already
mentioned. Mass was sung by the Bishop of Piacenza.
After mass we escorted the King to the Castello,
and went home to dinner, and then back to court.
On Tuesday morning our lord went to court at break
of day with two or three horses, and a falcon on his
wrist, because this was the King's pleasure, and they
rode out into the country. This morning I have not
yet been out of the house. I do not write about our
illustrious lords affairs, because you will soon see
persons who are better informed on these matters than
I can pretend to be. But from the great demonstra-

tions of affection and familiarity which I have seen, it seems to me that there is a strong similarity of tastes between His Majesty and our most illustrious lord, so that I hope all may go well and our affairs prosper. I will say no more now, but commend myself to Your Magnificence and beg you to try and get well soon.

'Your brother,

'BALDASSARE CASTIGLIONE.

'From MILAN, *October* 8, 1499.'[1]

This first letter that we have from Castiglione's pen is eminently characteristic of the writer. His frank and childlike nature, the quickness of his observation, and the simple loyalty of his soul, are all revealed in this account of the first martial pageant in which he had taken part. The accuracy of his description is confirmed by the records of the Benedictine chronicler, Jean d'Auton, who accompanied the French king to Italy, and looked with admiring eyes on this new and glorious city of Milan. He, too, describes the splendour of the street decorations, the houses hung with white draperies and shields wreathed with leafy garlands, with fleurs-de-lis and ermines. Two things above all struck his fancy : the tall white lilies that blossomed all along the route from the city gates to the great church of 'Notre Dame du Dôme,' and the beautiful ladies with flowing locks and eyes more radiant than the morning sun, who, clad in robes of cloth of gold and rainbow-coloured silks, looked down from every window and balcony. Like Castiglione, the good monk singles out the good order and proud bearing of the German halberdiers for special praise, and dwells on the superb air and sumptuous attire of the Pope's son, Cesare Borgia, Duke Valentino.

[1] Cod. Vat. Lat., 8210.

At the age of twenty it was only natural to be moved by the sight of all these splendours, and yet Baldassare could not repress a sigh at the sight of Gascon archers and foreign soldiery camping in these halls decorated by Leonardo and Bramante, where the foremost scholars and artists of the age had met at the Moro's court. 'The French are a dirty people,' wrote another eyewitness of the scene, a Venetian, who, with all his hatred of the Moro, could not but feel saddened at the sight of the present condition of Milan. 'Everywhere in the Castello there is dirt and foulness, such as Signor Lodovico would not have allowed for all the world ! The French captains spit upon the floor of these splendid halls, and their soldiers outrage women openly in the streets.'[1] A touch of contempt for these foreigners from beyond the Alps, with their rude speech and manners, is apparent throughout Castiglione's narrative, and certain passages in the 'Cortegiano' show that these first impressions were not dispelled by closer acquaintance with the French invaders. 'The French,' he writes, 'only believe in the nobility of arms, and count all the rest as nothing. They not only despise learning, but they abhor it, and hold scholars to be the vilest of men, and think that the worst reproach they can address to anyone is to call him a clerk !'[2] It was necessary, however, to put aside these prejudices for the moment. King Louis and the Marquis Francesco had become fast friends, and the best that Mantua had to give—the paintings of Mantegna, and falcons and horses of rarest breed, were laid at the victor's feet. Henceforth the Gonzagas and the Bourbons were to be close allies, and it was under

[1] Marino Sanuto, 'Diarii,' iii. 31.   [2] Book i. 42.

the banner of France that Castiglione's first laurels were to be won.

But the memory of the brilliant court where he had grown up to manhood never faded from his mind. Long years afterwards, when the splendour of the Moro's rule had vanished like a dream, when Beatrice was in her grave, and death had at length ended Lodovico's weary captivity in the dungeons of Loches, Castiglione, who by this time was himself a sober, middle-aged man, recalled the different actors on that brilliant stage, and took up his pen to celebrate their fame. Where, he asks in the chapters of his 'Cortegiano,' are the equals of these men and women to be seen? Where, for instance, can you find a woman to compare with Duchess Beatrice or with her sister and mother, my lady Isabella of Mantua, and the saintly Leonora of Aragon? The passionate fires and enthusiasms of youth were dead, but Galeazzo di San Severino was still for him the model of a peerless knight, *sans peur et sans reproche*, and Leonardo the foremost painter in the world. Cristoforo Romano and Vincenzo Calmeta were honoured with a place among the august company which met in Duchess Elisabetta's rooms. Jacopo di San Secondo was held up to fame as the prince of musicians, and Pistoja the poet, who sang the glories of Lodovico's court and declared that God reigned in heaven and the Moro upon earth, was mentioned in the same breath as the incomparable singer, Serafino. The names of these men and women who were familiar figures when the Moro reigned over Milan, are enshrined in the pages of the 'Cortegiano,' and live for all time in Castiglione's immortal prose.

CHAPTER III

1500–1503

DURING five years after the French conquest of Milan, Baldassare Castiglione remained in the service of his natural lord, the Marquis of Mantua. Both Francesco and his wife treated him with marked favour, and realized from the first that his presence was a great addition to court circles at Mantua. Everything, indeed, combined to make Castiglione an ornament to society. He was young and singularly handsome. There are, unfortunately, no early portraits of him in existence, but those of a later period, with the help of contemporary descriptions, enable us to form some idea of his appearance. He was above middle height, well proportioned, and erect in bearing, with regular features and deep grey eyes full of thought and seriousness, a broad open forehead, and brown hair, which he wore short, with a pointed beard and moustache, after the fashion set by the Marquis Francesco at the court of Mantua. There was an air of refinement and high breeding about him, an expression of mingled dignity and gentleness which made him the very pattern of a courtier such as he has himself described, fearless in battle and skilled in courtly exercises, a finished scholar and elegant poet, a pleasant companion and a trusted friend.

As might be expected, this brilliant cavalier won the smiles of all the court ladies, and before he had been many months at Mantua two marriages were proposed to him. First of all the Marchesana, always eager to arrange a suitable match, made it her business to find him a well-dowered bride, and suggested a daughter of Messer Girolamo Stanga, of Cremona, one of Lodovico Sforza's most trusted servants. Messer Girolamo, however, does not seem to have considered Baldassare's fortune sufficient, and in 1502 Agnesina Stanga married his kinsman and her first cousin, Luigi Gonzaga of Borgoforte. The next proposal came from the Marquis's uncle, Bishop Lodovico Gonzaga, whose home at Gazzolo was only a few miles from Casatico, and who was on very friendly terms with Madonna Luigia and her children. In a letter addressed to Count Maffeo da Gambara, he suggests an excellent match for one of his daughters in the person of 'M. Baldassare da Castiglione, my kinsman through his mother, sister of M. Gian Pietro Gonzaga.' The Bishop goes on to draw a glowing picture of the young man, whom he describes as exceedingly handsome, learned, eloquent, discreet, and singularly virtuous ; in fact, so generously endowed by Nature and Fortune that it would be hard to find his equal. 'He receives from his estates,' adds the writer, 'a yearly income of 1,500 ducats, which he shares with his brother, who is a priest, and whom we are trying to endow with benefices in order that M. Baldassare may enjoy the whole of his patrimony undivided.'[1] The Bishop's proposals, however, met with no better success than those of the Marchesana. Baldassare himself had evidently no wish to plight his troth and remained for many years to come far more eager to gain military glory and diplomatic renown than domestic happiness.

Before long Francesco Gonzaga discovered that Messer Baldassare possessed qualities of head and heart even more valuable than his attractive exterior and manifold accomplishments, and began to realize that his quick intelligence, exquisite tact, and perfect self-control, his inviolable honesty and fidelity, fitted him in an especial manner for the conduct of delicate negotiations in affairs of state.

But loyally as Castiglione served his master, Francesco Gonzaga's personality, it is evident, never attracted him. This rough, fiery soldier was of too coarse a mould to appreciate the finer shades of Baldassare's nature, and was as insensible to the purity and nobility of Castiglione's character as he was to his elegant scholarship. A born intriguer himself, who had little consideration for others, and cared solely for his own interest, Francesco's brutal temper and recklessness in the means which he used to attain his selfish ends, must often have jarred on Baldassare's nobler and more elevated nature. It is, accordingly, not to be wondered if the Marquis failed to inspire his faithful servant with any strong feeling of personal attachment, and if Castiglione soon found a master whose service was more congenial. With the Marchioness Isabella it was altogether different. This gifted lady, with her heaven-born instinct for discerning excellence in any shape or form, quickly recognized the rare charm and beauty of the young

[1] S. Bettinelli, 'Delle lettere e delle arti Mantovane,' 147.

courtier's nature, and lost no time in attaching him
to herself.   The trust which she reposed in him was
repaid with interest.   Wherever Castiglione found
himself during the next thirty years, whatever private
or public business he had in hand, his best powers of
body and mind, his wide knowledge of men and
infinite resource, were always placed at Isabella's
disposal.   And she on her part never failed him.   It
was to her that he turned in the darkest and most
difficult moments of his career, when his lord frowned
upon him and slanderous tongues reviled him, and he
had no other friend whom he could trust at court.
In his letters to his mother he speaks of her as our
pillar—*la nostra colonna*—the one unshaken rock
upon whom his hopes were fixed, and on whose help
and friendship he could rely with absolute certainty.

As yet, however, no clouds had risen to darken the
young courtier's horizon, and strong of arm and blithe
of heart he rode out to do his lord's bidding.   The
Marquis, we know, declined to take up arms on Lodovico Sforza's behalf when, early in February, 1500,
that unfortunate Prince crossed the Alps in the
forlorn hope of recovering the Milanese.   Just at
that time we find Baldassare in command of the
garrison of Castiglione, a fortification on Mantuan
territory.   The post was a solitary one, and the
young soldier grew restive in this enforced inaction.
On January 27 he sent his mother the following note,
begging for supplies for himself and his servants:

'MAGNIFICENT LADY AND HONOURED MOTHER,
      'I send Andrea with the mule for the bread
and other things you wrote about, if they are ready,
and by him some fish which was given me yesterday.   This morning I sent Spagnolo to Brescia for

Photo. Premi.

GIOVANNI FRANCESCO GONZAGA II.

(MUSEUM OF MANTUA.)

To face p. 28, Vol. I.

that blessed cuirass, but do not know if he will secure it. Carlo asks me to let Francesco go on Sunday to carve at Messer Lodovico's[1] table. I promised to let him go, and begged Messer Lodovico at the same time to ask our lord's leave for me to come to Mantua for these three days. This, I think, he will easily grant, as it cannot matter if I am away for this short time, and I am very anxious to come. I beg you to send me some salt and sausages. Sebastian would be glad if you could send him enough horsehair to stuff a saddle, and I should be grateful if you would also let me have a piece of salt meat.'

The leave for which he asked was evidently granted, and a month later, when he had returned to his post after a visit to Mantua, he wrote again to announce his safe arrival :

'Until this moment I have had no time to write to Your Magnificence. We arrived all safe, and the horses too. These peasants are certainly rather poor creatures, and have to be driven like donkeys. I had much rather stay at Mantua, not so much for my own convenience or to escape work, but because this place is very lonely. I beg you to let me have two pounds of candles and a pair of boots for Marcello. I am trying to find a trusted messenger to send to Brescia, and beg Marco Secco to see if he can possibly obtain this tiresome cuirass, and find out if it costs more than the six gold ducats which I paid Maestro Michelotto. . . .'[2]

From another letter, written a year later, we find that Baldassare was sent by his lord to Carpi to arrange some business matters with Alberto Pio and his brothers. On April 2, 1501, he informed his

[1] Lodovico or Luigi Gonzaga, his cousin.
[2] Cod. Vat. Lat., 8210.

mother of the success which had attended his efforts, and of the courtesy with which he had been received by these cultured princes.

'To-morrow,' he adds, 'we intend, by God's will, to go and dine at San Benedetto ; and, if Your Magnificence has no objection, I intend to remain there during Holy Week, and communicate in this quiet retreat, which seems to me well fitted for these devotions.' He proceeds to consult his mother about some private affairs which had to be arranged with Messer Amato Boschetto, Jacopo's brother, who was with him at Carpi, and ends by sending greetings to his brother Jeronimo, his sister Anna, and all the others at home.[1]

That year witnessed Cesare Borgia's invasion of Romagna and the marriage of his sister Lucrezia to Alfonso d' Este. These events were followed a few months later by the treacherous conquest of Urbino. Guidobaldo and his wife Elisabetta took refuge at the court of Mantua, and Baldassare, whose mother was a kinswoman of the Duchess, was for the first time brought into close relations with these illustrious exiles. In all probability he accompanied the Marquis Francesco when he and his father-in-law, the Duke of Ferrara, went to meet the French king at Asti, and entered Milan in his train on July 28. Here Guidobaldo and Giovanni Sforza, both of whom had been deprived of their dominions by Cesare, came to plead their cause with King Louis ; and Francesco Gonzaga was already boasting that he would soon avenge their wrongs, when, to the dismay of the assembled Princes, the hated Borgia suddenly appeared in person on the scene.

One August evening, about nine o'clock, when the

[1] Cod. Vat. Lat., 8210.

King was returning from a banquet given by his
general Trivulzio, Jean d' Auton, the chronicler, who
lodged in a street near the Castello, heard a clatter
of horses' hoofs under his window, and, putting his
head out quickly, saw Duke Valentino, mounted on
a *cheval de poste*, in the act of saluting His Most
Christian Majesty. By the light of the French
guards' flaming torches, the monk was able to distinguish Cesare's travelling suit of black velvet and
his German hat still covered with white dust, as
he rode by the King's side, in friendly and animated
conversation, to the gates of the Castello. 'There,'
he adds significantly, ' were the Marquis of Mantua,
the Duke of Urbino, and many others, who hated
Borgia with a deadly hatred. But, in spite of the
presence of these open enemies, the King gave the
Duke a cordial welcome, embracing him affectionately,
ordering his supper, and placing his own wardrobe
and carriages at his guest's disposal. His Majesty,'
adds honest Jean, ' goes nowhere without the Duke ;
and if he should wish to get off his horse or into the
saddle again, it is the Duke who plays the part of
a good squire and holds stirrup and bridle.'[1]

After that it was plain that Guidobaldo and his
companions in misfortune had little hope of obtaining
any redress for their wrongs from the French monarch;
and Borgia's insolence grew to such a pitch that he
would not allow the exiled Duke and Duchess to
remain at Mantua, and compelled them to seek
shelter at Venice. Louis XII., however, still treated
Francesco Gonzaga with marked favour, and at his
pressing invitation the Marquis spent Christmas at
the French court at Loches, and did not return to
Italy until the end of January.

[1] Jean d' Auton, 'Chroniques,' ii. 192, 194.

The following year was memorable in Castiglione's life as the date of his first visit to Rome. He was evidently sent there by the Marquis or his wife Isabella, who frequently exchanged letters and presents with Duke Valentino, in her anxiety to keep on good terms with the powerful usurper, and had actually agreed to the betrothal of her three-year-old son Frederico with Cesare's infant daughter.[1] Unfortunately, we have no details of his journey or of the impressions which the first sight of the Eternal City made on the enthusiastic young scholar. A single sentence in a letter to his mother is the only record that is left us of his feelings on this occasion. 'We are all well, thank God,' he wrote from Rome on March 16, 1903, 'and hope you will tell me all that is happening at home, how you are, and what people are doing over there, and how our friends are. Here there is no news that concerns us, but Rome is a wonderful place ! (*gran cosa è Roma*).'[2] Two months later he was at home again, and we find an interesting mention of him in a letter from the Mantuan secretary Tolomeo Spagnoli, who had been sent to pay his master's respects to the French Viceroy of Milan, Charles d'Amboise.

'The illustrious Signor Zoan Giacomo Trivulzio,' writes the envoy on May 24, 1505, 'tells me that in the last rebellion of Milan, when the Moro recovered the city in 1500, he lost many of his private possessions, and among these nothing which he regretted as much as a volume of Quintus Curtius, with marginal notes in his own hand. This book, he hears, is now in the hands of Baldassare da Castiglione, and since he is anxious to recover it, and hears that Baldassare is now at Mantua, he begs Your Excellency to ask Baldassare for the book and send it to him at

---

[1] 'Isabella d' Este,' i. 247-250.
[2] Cod. Vat. Lat., 8210.   Appendix II.

Milan, and the said Signor Zoan Giacomo will gladly pay Baldassare whatever he has spent upon it, and will remain eternally obliged to Your Excellency.'[1]

Castiglione, it appears, was already a collector of rare books, and his interest in classical literature was shared by the veteran who had driven out the Moro.

The Marquis now received a commission from Louis XII. to raise a force and join the expedition which La Trémouille was about to lead southwards, to recover Naples from the Spanish captain, Gonsalvo de Cordova.

Baldassare accompanied his lord on this occasion, and left Mantua early in July to join the French army at Parma. On the eve of his departure he wrote to his mother at Casatico : ' Our expedition to Parma is arranged, but I know not how it will succeed. Time will show.' He goes on to tell her that he has executed her commissions in town, and had sent off the linen which she required, and that the tapestries will soon follow. What is more impor- tant, he informs her of a confidential communication which he has just received regarding a valuable benefice which Monsignor di San Marco is ready to resign in favour of Jeronimo, at a word from the Marquis. 'In my present circumstances,' he adds, ' I hardly know what to do, but I have so many friends that I hope this may be effected. I have not, however, spoken of it to a single living person ; neither Messer Gian Pietro nor anyone else, and I beg you not to mention it to a creature.' Mantua, July 6, 1503.[2]

After prolonged delays the French army at length started for Naples on August 20. But just before

---

[1] ' Archivio storico italiano,' Appendice, ii. 268.
[2] Cod. Vat. Lat., 8210.

the Marquis left Parma, a courier from Rome arrived, bringing him word of the Pope's sudden death, an event which changed the whole aspect of affairs. Castiglione appears to have been sent back to Mantua with the news, which was the signal for the exiled Duke's immediate return to Urbino.   La Trémouille continued his march southwards, as far as Viterbo, where he found the conclave was sitting, and halted at the urgent request of Cardinal Georges d'Amboise, who hoped that the presence of the army would ensure his own election.   But the confident expectations of the French prelate, who, in Jean d'Auton's words, ' already saw the keys of St. Peter dangling from his girdle,'[1] were doomed to disappointment, and on September 22, 1503, the venerable Cardinal Piccolomini of Siena was proclaimed Pope, with the title of Pius III.   A week later the French army marched through the suburbs of S. Maria del Popolo, ' in fine order and great numbers,' and since La Trémouille was dangerously ill of fever and unable to proceed further, the Marquis of Mantua assumed the command.   Meanwhile Francesco's loyal servant, Baldassare Castiglione, was hurrying from Mantua to join his lord, cursing the Fates who had hindered his journey by a series of untoward accidents.   When at length he reached Rome early in October, he found to his bitter disappointment that the French army had already left the neighbourhood.   In his disgust he addressed the following letter to the Marquis, explaining the causes of his delay and his impatience to rejoin him:

' MY DEAR LORD,
        'Since I have been unable to join Your Excellency as quickly as I hoped, and as it was my

---

[1] 'Chroniques,' iii. 13.

duty to do, I must tell you that I have arrived here in Rome with Matteo Grigna, Marsilio Tombetta, Rigellino, Carlo da Bardellone, and Carlo del Gallo, and that we are all of us in the greatest despair to find that it is impossible to join Your Excellency. I have no other desire in the world than to serve you, especially at this moment, but the roads are so unsafe that if we travel without an escort we are certain to be robbed. So we hope to come as soon as a company of the Orsini or any other sufficient escort shall be going the same way. The reason of my delay has been the impossibility of procuring a good horse. I had to seek through the whole State of Milan as far as Piedmont before I could find one, and as soon as I had succeeded in this a series of misfortunes delayed my departure. However, I hope soon to continue my journey, and desire nothing else but to be where Your Excellency is, and whether on foot or on horseback devote this poor life to your service. God grant me this prayer, for I can ask no greater favour in this world !

' Your Excellency's most faithful servant,
       ' BALDASSARE CASTIGLIONE.

' ROME, *October* 4, 1503.'[1]

The young soldier's prayer was granted, and in the short but arduous campaign which followed he faced peril and hardship valiantly at his lord's side. After a fruitless attempt to take the fortified town of Rocca Secca, Francesco Gonzaga took up his position on the banks of the Garigliano, between San Germano and Gaeta. The Spanish captain, Gonsalvo de Cordova, whose forces were considerably inferior in numbers, prudently entrenched himself on the opposite bank, and prepared to offer a vigorous resistance to the enemy. After repeated efforts, the French

[1] Archivio Gonzaga, and Martinati, p. 76.

succeeded in crossing the river, but were repulsed and driven back with heavy loss. 'If the Frenchmen,' writes Guicciardini, 'had boldly advanced forward, they had that day remained superiors; but while they proceeded slowly, and with demonstration of timorousnesse, they did not only lose the occasion of the victory that day, but they diminished greatly all hope in time to come. From that daye, all things tooke with them very ill successe, and there was already among the captaines rather confusion than concord; and according to the custome of the French souldiers with the Italian captaines, very little obedience to the Marquis of Mantua, the King's lieutenant.'[1]

Francesco's difficulties were increased by scarcity of provisions as well as by the unusual severity of the season. 'Winter was very colde and sharpe,' continues the historian, 'raining and snowing almost continually, much more than had been accustomed in that country, whereby it seemed that Fortune and the heavens had conspired against the French, who staying there, did not onely spend the time unprofitably, but received by that aboade, almost the like harmes which mens bodies receive by a poison that worketh slowly.'[2] The Marquis himself fell ill, or else, according to most authorities, feigned sickness because he was unable to endure the pride, quarrels, and disobedience of the French any longer,[3] and resigned his command to the Marquis of Saluzzo. The Venetian Envoy in Rome reported that Francesco had fallen ill with fever and pains in his limbs, and been carried in a litter to Traietto, but another informant added

---

[1] 'The Historie of Guicciardini reduced into English by Geffray Fenton,' 1618, p. 237.
[2] Guicciardini, pp. 231, 237.   [3] Muratori, 'Annali d' Italia.'

significantly : 'He is not ill, but has left the camp and is gone to Rome, seeing the probable result of the campaign. He is a wise man, and I need say no more.'[1]

Throughout the earlier stages of the campaign Castiglione remained in close attendance upon his master, and endeared himself greatly to the Marquis by the cheerful courage with which he bore the hardships to which captain and soldiers were alike exposed. Now he left the camp with his lord, and returned to Rome, where his cousin, Cesare Gonzaga, was eagerly expecting him, as we learn from the letters which he wrote early in December to Baldassare's anxious mother.

After their departure the quarrels of the French captains became daily more bitter, while the soldiers died by hundreds of cold and hunger. At length, on December 20, a decisive battle took place in which the French were completely routed, and Piero de' Medici, who was fighting in their ranks, together with a large number of fugitives, were drowned in the river Garigliano. The destruction of the French army on that fatal day sealed the fate of Naples, and established the Spanish dominion firmly throughout the kingdom. But neither the Marquis of Mantua nor his servant Castiglione, as most of his biographers have stated, were present in the rout of Garigliano.[2]

[1] Sanuto, v. 387, 483.   [2] Marliani, Serassi, etc.

CHAPTER IV

1503–1504

GREAT events had happened during the few weeks
which had elapsed since Castiglione left Rome on
the morrow of Pope Pius III.'s election. On October 17, after a brief reign of twenty-six days, the
new Pontiff died, and on the vigil of All Saints the
conclave met once more to elect his successor. This
time there could be little doubt as to the result. Although Cardinal d'Amboise, in Jean d'Auton's quaint
phrase, 'came very near to the gates of Paradise,'
being only short of two votes, on that same evening
Giuliano della Rovere, Cardinal of S. Pietro in Vincula,
was elected Pope. On the morning of All Saints'
Day, November 1, this able and ambitious prelate—
'mightie in friends, reputation, and riches'—was proclaimed supreme Pontiff and assumed the title of
Julius II.

The elevation of this Cardinal to the chair of
St. Peter produced a complete revolution in the
Papal policy. Already, only ten days after Alexan-
der VI.'s death, Duke Guidobaldo had returned to
Urbino, where his old subjects welcomed him with

an enthusiasm which Castiglione himself has described in eloquent language. 'Guidobaldo,' he writes in his Latin Epistle to our Henry VII., 'came back to his own and recovered the State of which he had been so unjustly deprived, amid the rejoicing of all Italy. Troops of children flocked to meet him with olive branches in their hands, singing for gladness at the sight of their beloved Prince. Old men, tottering under the weight of years, hurried out to meet him with tears of joy streaming down their cheeks, mothers with babes in their arms, and persons of every age and sex joined the crowds that thronged the streets. The very stones seemed to dance and exult in his coming.'[1]

The accession of his kinsman, Giuliano della Rovere, to the Papal throne, two months later, secured the permanence of Guidobaldo's restoration. The new Pope's brother, Giovanni della Rovere, who in his lifetime held the office of Prefect of Rome, had married the Duke of Urbino's sister, Giovanna, the Lady Prefetessa who was the patron of Perugino and Raphael, and her young son, Francesco Maria, was tacitly recognized as Guidobaldo's heir. One of Julius II.'s first acts was to summon Guidobaldo to Rome and promise to appoint him Gonfaloniere of the Church in the place of Cesare Borgia. Castiglione's cousin, Cesare Gonzaga, had accompanied the Duke on his return to Urbino, and, after taking part in his campaign against Borgia's forces in Romagna, now followed him to Rome. Thus, when Baldassare reached Rome with the Marquis of Mantua on his return from the French camp, he found his kinsman already settled in the Vatican. On December 7 Cesare wrote the following letter to his aunt

[1] Serassi, ii. 351.

Luigia, who was anxiously expecting news of her absent son :

'I did not answer Your Magnificence's two letters before, because I have been daily expecting our Messer Baldassare's return. Now he is here, I must thank you for your dear letters, which are a fresh proof of the love which I know you bear me, although no letters are needed to assure me of this. And I pray you to continue your prayers for me, for I firmly believe they are the cause that God has not allowed me to perish in the great dangers to which I have been exposed. For when I look back upon them, I feel more terror than I did at the actual moment, God be praised ! As for Dorotea da Crema, about whom you write, I regret that I can give you no satisfaction. I have made many inquiries of persons who had good reason to know the truth, but all I could learn from a friend of mine, who was one of her guards, is that some days ago he gave her 400 ducats, in order that she might take a long journey. I entreated him to tell me more, but he refused, and I can find out nothing further. I am sorry not to be able to give you more information, but I think she is alive, and will do my utmost to find out more, as our most illustrious Lord Marquis also desires. I pass on to Your Magnificence all the Papal blessings which I have received, excepting one which is intended for Madonna Orsina. Please do me the favour to present this to her in my name, with infinite respects. I will say no more, as you will doubtless hear more fully from our Messer Baldassare, and only commend myself to you and all the members of our family. And when yon see the Lady Marchesana, I pray you commend me to her good graces.'

We have no clue as to the mysterious disappearance of Dorotea da Crema, but she was probably one of Cesare Borgia's victims, and had been carried off by

one of his captains. Valentino himself, as he was
generally called in Italy, was himself in Rome at this
moment, endeavouring to obtain the Duke of Urbino's
pardon and the new Pope's favour.

On the very day when Cesare Gonzaga wrote to
inform his aunt of her son's safe arrival, a strange
meeting took place in the Vatican between Guidobaldo and the man who had wronged him. The
Duke, as one of his gentlemen wrote to a friend at
Castel Durante, was resting on a couch in the Pope's
antechamber, when suddenly Valentino appeared in
the room, cap in hand, and fell on his knees before
him. Guidobaldo, startled at the sight of his old
enemy, rose and drew back a few paces. Then he
courteously raised Valentino to his feet and listened
patiently while Cesare begged his pardon for the
wrongs which he had done him, excusing himself on
account of his youth, and ascribing his evil deeds to
the rapacity of his father, Pope Alexander, whose
memory he loaded with curses. At the same time he
promised to restore the library and most of the other
treasures of the ducal palace, which were safely housed
in the citadel of Forli. ' To all of which,' continues
our correspondent, 'the Duke replied in a noble and
fitting manner : " Truly a strange example of the
changes of Fortune, which fulfils the words of the
Psalmist, ' He hath put down the mighty from their
seat, and exalted the humble and meek.' " ' [1]

According to Castiglione, on this occasion Guidobaldo behaved with his wonted magnanimity, and
interceded on his old enemy's behalf with the Pope,
who detained him for the present in the Vatican, and
afterwards allowed him to go to Ostia, where he was
arrested and sent to Spain by Gonsalvo de Cordova.

[1] Ugolini, 'Storia di Urbino,' ii. 514.

Castiglione, we learn from his cousin's letter, arrived in Rome on December 7, and obtained his master's leave to remain there when Francesco himself went on to Mantua for Christmas. The Marquis might not have agreed so readily had he foreseen the consequences of his action. Baldassare remained in Rome, and saw so much of Guidobaldo during the next few months that he was inspired with an ardent wish to enter the Duke's service. This feeling was no doubt strengthened by the fact that both Cesare Gonzaga and his other kinsman and intimate friend, Lodovico, Count of Canossa, were already attached to the Duke's person. On the other hand, Castiglione's personal charm, his talents and accomplishments, made him peculiarly acceptable to the Duke, who asked nothing better than to secure the services of so finished a cavalier. A mutual regard sprang up between Prince and courtier, and when, at the end of May, Baldassare at length returned to Mantua, he pledged his word to join the Duke in Romagna as soon as he could obtain the necessary permission from the Marquis.

Guidobaldo himself was impatient to return to his own home at Urbino, where the Duchess was governing the State in his absence. But all through the winter months, Julius II., who was genuinely fond of the Duke, insisted on keeping him at the Vatican on one pretence or another, and it was only on May 10 that the long-delayed consistory was held in which the succession of the Pope's nephew, Francesco della Rovere to the duchy of Urbino was publicly confirmed. Two days afterwards, three English Ambassadors, Sir Gilbert Talbot, Richard Bere, Abbot of Glastonbury, and Dr. Robert Sherborne, Dean of St. Paul's, arrived in Rome, bearing King Henry

VII.'s congratulations to the new Pope, and bringing with them the habit and collar of the Garter for the Duke of Urbino—thus, in the old chronicler's quaint phraseology, 'stopping two gappes with one bushe.' In a Latin epistle addressed to his most dear friend, the Lord Guido Ubaldo, the English monarch informed his Sublimity that in a Chapter of the Most Noble Order of the Garter recently held in the palace of Westminster, he had been created a Knight of that august company, as his father, of happy memory, had been before him, in recognition of his singular merit and virtue. The envoys were received by Silvestro Gigli, the Italian Bishop of Worcester and English resident at the Vatican, and lodged in the house of Cardinal Adriano Castellesi, Bishop of Hereford. This prelate, as Lodovico Sforza's envoy to the English court reported,[1] kept King Henry well informed in Italian affairs, and was especially useful in obtaining favours from the Vatican. In the present instance, the Cardinal's ambassador was well paid for his hospitality by the announcement which the envoys brought of his preferment to the See of Bath, with a yearly income of 12,000 ducats. In recognition of this signal favour, Castellesi, we learn from the Venetian ambassador in Rome, presented his splendid new palace in the Borgo to King Henry VII.[2]

In a consistory held on May 20, the English envoys were received by the Pope, and a Bull was promulgated granting special indulgences to Henry VII.'s newly-built chapel in the Abbey of Westminster, and sanctioning the removal of

---

[1] Calendar of State Papers in Archives of Venice, i. 281.
[2] Giustiniani, 'Dispacci,' ii. 97 ; Dennistoun, 'Dukes of Urbino,' ii. 447.

Henry VI.'s ashes to this shrine.   On the 22nd the
Duke of Urbino's appointment as Captain of the
Church, with a yearly salary of 5,000 ducats, was
publicly proclaimed, and he was solemnly invested
with the robes and insignia of the Garter in the
Vatican.   There, in the presence of the Pope and
Cardinals, the Abbot of Glastonbury recited the
ancient formula, in Norman French, to the new-made
Knight who knelt before him : ' *La Soveraiyne et
l'amyable compagnie des Chivaliers de l'Ordre de la
Jarretière vous ont reçu et choisi pour leur Amy,
Frère et Compaignon';* and proceeded to invest the
Duke with the crimson robe, velvet mantle of celestial
blue, and collar and garter of the Order, in the
name of God Almighty, His spotless and undefiled
Mother, and the blessed martyr St. George.   ' *Si que
estant armé de beaux vertus, vous pouvez passer parmi
les ennemis et les confondre, et après avoir vaillamment
guerroyé en ce monde vous pouvez parvenire a les
éternelles et triomphanz joyes célestes.*'[1]   After this
ceremony the Duke and ambassadors were entertained at a banquet in the Vatican, and Guidobaldo
rode in state through the town in his Garter robes, to
the great admiration of the people.   On the following
evening he left Rome, and returned to Urbino, to
lead an expedition against the citadels of Forli and
Cesena, which Cesare Borgia's captains still refused to
surrender.

On May 27 he reached Foligno, and that same
evening addressed a note to his brother-in-law,
Francesco Gonzaga, asking his permission to invite
the Marchese's subject and servant, Baldassare da
Castiglione, to enter his service.   ' This would be

---

[1] Elias Ashmole, ' The Institution, Laws, and Order of the
Garter,' 1672, Appendix.

especially acceptable to me,' writes the Duke, 'since I desire to raise a company of men-at-arms which will do me honour and serve me well ; and I promise to treat him in such a manner as to show Your Excellency how highly I esteem your servants, and if ever you should require his services, you will be able to avail yourself of them as easily as if he were still in his own home.'

The request was one which the Marquis could hardly refuse, but from the curtness of his reply it is plain that he was by no means pleased at the prospect of being deprived of his most brilliant servant.

'My Lord Duke,' he wrote from his villa at Gonzaga on June 9, 'if Baldassare da Castiglione chooses to enter your service, we are well content, and shall be ever ready to oblige you in anything that you may desire.

'FRANCESCO GONZAGA.'

Meanwhile Castiglione himself had reached Mantua, and on the following day he sent a gracefully worded petition to the Marquis, asking for leave to enter the Duke of Urbino's service :

'MY DEAR LORD,
        'Yesterday I received a letter from the Lord Duke of Urbino, asking me if I am willing to enter his service, with Your Highness's leave, and promising to treat me liberally and well. He also tells me that he has written to Your Excellency on the subject. Since I must ever remain your servant, and can never think of anything but serving and obeying Your Highness, my only desire is to do what you command. So I await the knowledge of your wishes before I send any answer, and will only obey the will of Your

Excellency, to whom I commend myself with the utmost devotion.'

On the next morning the following brief answer came from Rovere, where the Marquis was now staying:

'BALDASSARE,
      'As we have replied to the Lord Duke, who asked our leave to take you into his service, so we repeat to you that, as regards ourselves, we are content, and give you free leave to serve him.

'*June* 11, 1504.'[1]

The bitter resentment secretly cherished by the writer of these lines was to make itself felt in many ways during the next few years, but at the moment Baldassare cared little as long as he could have his way. His choice was made, and, with the desired permission in his hands, he humbly thanked His Excellency for his gracious answer, and hastened to join his new master in the camp at Cesena. There his cousin Cesare Gonzaga gave him a cordial welcome and the Duke appointed him to the command of a company of fifty men-at-arms and promised him a salary of 400 ducats. 'Here I lack nothing,' he wrote to his mother in high spirits from Cesena; 'the Duke and all the others treat me with infinite kindness, and soon we hope to go to Urbino, where we shall be very happy and glad of heart. So I hope you will try and be of good courage, and all the rest of the family too, for I can have no greater joy than to know that you are satisfied.'   And in a postscript he begs his brother Jeronimo to send him a song beginning 'Essi Diva

---

[1] Archivio Gonzaga, and Martinati, 76,

AUTOGRAPH OF BALDASSARE CASTIGLIONE.

(VATICAN LIBRARY.)

To face p. 46, Vol. I.

Diana,' and let him have both the music and the words.[1]

Unluckily, on the day after his arrival, his horse fell under him and crushed his foot so badly that for several weeks he was unable to walk. In a letter to his mother from the camp before Forli, the last fortress which still resisted the Papal forces, Baldassare complains that since he joined the army he has had nothing to do but to nurse himself.

'This foot,' he writes, 'has made me see the stars at midday. Would to God it were cured now! This is certainly not yet the case, although it does not hurt if I walk slowly; but this is all that I can do, and it is still very much swollen.' In the same letter he thanks his mother for giving him the news of the birth of a nephew—probably Lodovico Strozzi, the son of his sister Francesca, who was one day to accompany his uncle to Spain.

'God be thanked for this good piece of news!' writes the young soldier. 'Pray congratulate both the parents for me. You ask about my new post. This illustrious Lord Duke gives me 400 ducats for myself, and the command of fifty men-at-arms, which I share with a comrade, who will be, I think, Messer Cesare. We have no fixed quarters yet, as we have been engaged in the cursed task of besieging this Rocca, which has now surrendered owing to the extreme dearth of provisions. This is the same throughout the whole of Romagna, which is indeed in a pitiful state. I have as yet received no pay, because when I arrived every penny was spent. But to-day I hope to receive 100 ducats, as the Duke has just sent me word that 1,000 ducats reached him yesterday. . . . I will not say more now, as I

[1] Cod. Vat. Lat., 8210

have already written by an armour-bearer, and also by Sigismondo, from Ferrara, only beg Your Magnificence to be as cheerful and of good courage as I am.   And if it is true that I am far from home and from many persons whom I love dearly, at least I am happy and can suffer misfortunes willingly now my mind is at rest.

'Forli, *August* 12, 1504.'

Madonna Luigia, who had all along felt some misgivings at the course which her son had chosen, was further relieved by a letter from her nephew Cesare, who wrote in high spirits to assure his aunt of Baldassare's well-being and of the marked favour which the Duke showed him :

'If until now, my dear and honoured Aunt, I have shown myself all too negligent a son, I will no longer persist in these bad courses.   Therefore, putting excuses for my past negligence aside, I will pay my addresses to you, feeling sure that you have already forgiven me, on many grounds ; and if you have not forgiven me of your own free will, I am quite certain that no words of mine will be of any avail.   Here I am alive and well, and always ready to execute Your Magnificence's commands.   Messer Baldassare is also well, and his foot is beginning to mend.   And he is treated with such kindness by this illustrious lord that every day he feels better satisfied to be here. We are both of us gay and happy, and hope that you and all our kin are the same.

'Forli, *August* 11, 1504.'

'P.S.—Your Magnificence will kindly commend me to Messer Jeronimo and to Falcone, as well as to Messer Jacopo and Madonna Polissena, with whom I rejoice cordially in whatever good fortune falls to their share.'

[1] Serassi, ii. 235.

On the very day that this letter was written, the citadel of Forli surrendered to the Duke's arms, and a messenger was promptly dispatched to Rome with the news. On the evening of Sunday, August 11, Pope Julius, having been very restless and irritable all day, was induced by his servants to take a ride with one of the Cardinals in the meadows along the banks of the Tiber. They went as far as Ponte Molle, and as they were returning through the fields, they met a courier from the Duke of Urbino riding at full speed. On hearing the good tidings the Pope burst into joyful exclamations, and hurried home to send his congratulations to the victorious leader.

The Papal army now occupied Forli, and on August 24, Baldassare wrote again to his mother, expressing a lively interest in his newly-born nephew, and assuring his anxious mother that he was taking the utmost care of his injured foot, and had no greater wish in the world than to be able to use it again. As for the minute particulars which Madonna Luigia desires regarding sundry small expenses, he declares it to be beyond his power to satisfy her.

' I certainly bought three yards and a half of velvet from the Jew Agnolo, and made out the bill myself. I cannot at this moment recollect the exact price of the material, but know that it was cheap. Excepting my foot, J am exceedingly well. Here it is very hot, and we stay at Forli reluctantly on account of the great scarcity here, but do not yet know when we shall leave, as the Duke has had an attack of fever, which has grieved us all. God send him better health ! I have no other news, but should like to hear some from Mantua.

' Your obedient son,
' B. C.'[1]

[1] Cod. Vat. Lat., 8210.

A day or two later Guidobaldo disbanded his troops and returned to Urbino, taking with him four waggons laden with his own recovered treasures, including the famous library of the ducal palace, which Cesare Borgia had carried off and stored in the citadel of Forli.

It was then that the Duke took Castiglione with him to the city which was to be his home during the next ten years. In the midst of the confusion of these first days he found time to write a few hurried lines, informing his mother of his safe arrival :

'Since Maestro Antonio is going to you, I must inform Your Magnificence that last Friday, on the 6th of the present month, we at length reached Urbino safe and sound, and with great rejoicing, since we had all of us been longing to be here. We have done what little was possible, in these three days, to put our house in order, and now we shall get on capitally. Maestro Antonio can tell you all that you care to know about us. The Lady Duchess and Madonna Emilia commend themselves very warmly to you. My foot is improving, but only very slowly. I beg you to send me, by the first opportunity, a piece of fine white cloth to make a new pair of hose for myself, as I cannot procure any here, and also some dark green cloth to make a pair for Smeraldo [his groom]. Please ask Jeronimo also to send me my copy of Poliziano's " Stanze Volgari." And I commend myself to Your Magnificence. [1]

'URBINO, *September* 9, 1504.'

---

[1] Serassi, i. 8.

CHAPTER V

1504

Urbino — The court of the Montefeltro princes — Castiglione's description — Reign of Duke Federico — His character and paternal government — Patronage of art and letters—The palace of Urbino — Its present condition — Contemporary accounts—Giovanni Santi and Antonio di Mercatello—The ducal library — Artists employed at Urbino — Piero della Francesca, Melozzo da Forli, and Justus of Ghent.

' On the slopes of the Apennines, almost in the centre of Italy, towards the Adriatic Sea, there lies, as every one knows, the little city of Urbino. Although situated in a mountainous region, less pleasant it may be than some that we may have seen, it is favoured by Heaven in that the country is exceedingly fertile and rich in fruits of the earth. And besides the pure and health-giving air of the region, all things necessary for human life are to be found here in great abundance. But among the greatest blessings which it enjoys, this I count to be the chief, that from remote times it has always been governed by the best of Princes, although, in the universal calamities of Italy during the recent wars, it was deprived of them for a time.'[1]

In these words Castiglione describes the city which he entered in Guidobaldo's train, in September, 1504, and which his eloquent prose has rendered immortal.

[1] 'Cortegiano,' i. 2.

This narrow strip of hill-country, only sixty miles long, lying between Umbria, the March of Ancona, and the Adriatic Sea, had during the last half-century become famous as the seat of a model court, upon which the eyes of all Italy were fixed. Here during forty years the good Federico had reigned over a loyal and contented people, who still kept his memory alive in their hearts. A wise and able ruler as well as a brave captain, this great Montefeltro prince was foremost among his peers both in the arts of war and peace. The best record of his career is given in the Latin inscription which his son Guidobaldo placed above the arcades in the court of the ducal palace :

‘ Federico, Duke of Urbino, Count of Montefeltro and of Castel Durante, Gonfaloniere of the Holy Roman Church and Captain of the Italian Confederation, built this house from its foundations for his own glory and the good of posterity. He fought many battles, went out six times to war, defeated his enemy eight times, and, having been victorious in all his campaigns, extended the borders of his dominions. His justice, clemency, liberality and religion in time of peace equalled and adorned his conquests.’

‘ In his days,’ says Castiglione, ‘ Duke Federico of glorious memory was the light of Italy, nor is there any lack of truthful witnesses still living, who can bear testimony to his prudence, humanity, justice, liberality, unconquered courage, and military skill. His great qualities were further proved by his many victories and swift and sudden campaigns, by the capture of impregnable fortresses, and the repeated occasions on which he put numerous and powerful foes to flight, without ever losing a single battle.   So

Photo, Lieut. Simondi.

URBINO.

that he may, not without cause, be compared to the most renowned heroes of olden time.'[1]

Angelo Poliziano praises Duke Federico as the equal of Lorenzo de' Medici in learning and patronage of letters; Marsilio Ficino calls him the pattern of a wise ruler and perfect man; and his own subject. Giovanni Santi, extols him as the ideal of a great and good Prince. In his boyhood Federico was a pupil of the illustrious Mantuan teacher Vittorino da Feltre, whose portrait he kept before his eyes as a constant reminder of his teaching. The court of Urbino was framed on the precepts which he had learnt in Casa Giocosa, and became in its turn a school where Italian princes sent their sons to be trained in knightly exercises and elegant manners. Although much of his time was spent in active warfare, he never ceased to cultivate his mind. Every week he visited the Franciscan convent, and discussed philosophical and theological subjects with the friars. In his last years he studied Aristotle with a learned Dominican, Messer Lazzaro, and mathematics with a German professor, known as Messer Paolo. Pope Pius II. records how, when riding by his side at Tivoli, under the burning sun and amid the dust raised by the cavalry, the Duke discussed the Trojan war with him, and could not come to any decisive conclusion as to the precise boundaries of Asia Minor.[2] His household, we learn from Vespasiano, was regulated on the pattern of a religious community. No gambling or bad language was allowed, and every member of the family had a definite office with a time-table, and definite instructions as to the discharge of his duties. Federico's own fare and habits were of the simplest kind. Livy or Tacitus were usually read aloud at

[1] 'Cortegiano,' i. 2.   [2] Pio II., 'Comm.,' p. 131.

his meals, excepting in Lent, when he liked to hear passages from the Fathers or his favourite author, Aquinas. He rose early and rode out into the country, attended by a few young squires, and on his return attended mass and walked in the palace gardens, conversing freely with any of his subjects who craved access to their lord. On summer evenings he often watched the youths, who were being educated at court, wrestling and playing ball in a meadow of the Franciscan convent behind the palace, and encouraged the lads with his applause, or reproved them if they were awkward and lazy.[1] The Urbino poet, Antonio di Mercatello, describes how he walked daily in the market-place, jesting with the peasants who rode in from the country, and greeting brides on their way to church. He often entered the shops and houses, and taking one man by the hand, or leaning on the arm of another, asked them in a friendly way about their family or their affairs. ' How is your old father ?' he would say to one ; ' Are your daughters married yet ?' to another ; or, ' How does your business prosper ?' And when he spoke he always lifted his hat with chivalrous courtesy, so that it became a common jest in Urbino to tell anyone who was very busy that he had more to do than Federico's cap.[2]

Architecture was one of the subjects in which he took especial interest, and Mercatello tells us that ' the good lord ' was himself an admirable architect, and often designed his own buildings. He certainly was a great builder, erecting churches, bridges, and palaces in all parts of his dominions, and improving the ducal residences at Gubbio and Fossombrone, Castel

[1] ' Uomini illustri,' pp. 92-94.
[2] Muzio, ' Historia dei Fatti di Federigo Duca d' Urbino,' Dennistoun, i. 258-268.

Photo, Lieut. Simondi.

DOORWAY, PALACE OF URBINO.

To face p. 54, Vol. I.

Durante and Cagli.   But his most splendid achieve-
ment in this direction was the palace at Urbino.

'On the rugged heights of Urbino,' writes Castiglione, in the opening sentences of his 'Cortegiano,'
'Federico reared a palace which, in the opinion of
many, is the finest in Italy, and furnished it so richly
with all things needful that it seems to be rather a
city than a palace.   For he adorned it not only with
all things required for ordinary use, such as silver
plate and sumptuous hangings of gold and brocade,
but with an infinite number of antique marble and
bronze statues, of precious paintings, and musical
instruments of every variety ; neither would he allow
anything within its walls which was not most rare
and excellent.'[1]

The architect who transformed the medieval fortress
of Urbino into this fair Renaissance palace was
Luciano da Laurana, a native of Lovrana in Istria,
who had already built a wonderful pleasure-house at
Poggio Reale for King Ferrante of Naples, and had
more lately been employed by Alessandro Sforza to
adorn his palace at Pesaro.   In June, 1468, Federico
appointed him to be *Capo-maestro* of works in the
palace of Urbino, and set forth his pleasure in the
following terms :

'Having resolved to build in this our city of
Urbino a fine house worthy of the birth and renown
of our fathers and ourselves, and having vainly
searched everywhere, but more especially in Tuscany,
that home of good architects, for a man skilled in this
profession, and having first heard by report, and then
satisfied ourselves by our own eyes, of the learning
and genius of Messer Luciano, we do now appoint

---

[1] 'Cortegiano,' i. 2.

this distinguished architect chief of all those employed upon this our fabric.'

During the next fourteen years the Istrian architect's genius and Federico's vast wealth were devoted to this task, and in their hands the palace of Urbino became one of the wonders of the world. Even to-day, when the halls have been stripped of their priceless treasures, and only the shell of the building remains, its beauty and grandeur still fill us with admiration.

The site is unrivalled, from whichever side it is approached. Whether the traveller enters Urbino by the Roman road that leads across the Apennines, and through the Furlo ravine, or comes from Tuscany by the upper valley of the Tiber, a steep ascent leads to the city gates, and long before the journey's end he sees the ducal palace on the heights above. The twin towers, with their delicate pinnacles soaring into the sky, and fronting the western sun, lend the whole an atmosphere of romance—a faery glamour that might well make the poets declare this was no work of mortal hands, but a house reared by the gods. This first impression is deepened by the height of the stately portals, the admirable proportions of the pillared court, and what Vasari calls the *extravaganza* of the grand staircase, with its steps, easier and wider than any other in the world. A whole wealth of exquisite sculpture is lavished upon pilasters and doors, cornices and mantelpieces, all wrought in fine white limestone, brought, according to the oldest writers, not from Istria, but from the neighbouring valleys of the Metauro and the Foglia.[1] On the vault of the throne-room is the eagle of Monte-

---

[1] Baldi, ' Descrizione del palazzo ducale di Urbino,' p. 580.

Photo, Lieut. Simondi.

COURTYARD, PALACE OF URBINO.

To face p. 56, Vol. I.

Photo, Lieut. Simondi.

SALA DEGLI ANGELI.

To face p. 56, Vol. I.

Photo, Lieut. Simondi.

PALACE OF URBINO.

To face p. 56, Vol. I.

feltro ; on the mantelpieces opposite the six imposing
windows, are the ducal arms and initials, with the
badge of the Garter, and its time-honoured motto. A
frieze of warlike guns and engines, of military trophies
and banners, runs round the central courtyard ; a
troop of dancing children and *putti* bearing flaming
torches and pots of roses and carnations adorns the
mantelpiece of the Sala degli Angeli, where the dukes
held private audiences. Medallions of Federico and
Guidobaldo, devices and monograms of dukes and
duchesses, the viper of the Sforza, the oak-tree of
the della Rovere, the palm-tree bending under the
storm, with the motto *Resurgam*, the Garter of
England and the Ermine of Naples, are introduced
above the doorways and corridors. Garlands of flowers
and fruit, of roses and lilies, of acanthus and ivy ;
candelabra and cherubs, sphinxes' and rams' heads.,
birds and shells, are carved on the pilasters ; figures
of Apollo and Pallas are wrought in the inlaid wood-
work of the doors.

One little room on the first-floor, close to the
Sala degli Angeli, still retains its original decoration
of rich *intarsiatura*. This was Federico's private
study, the peaceful retreat where he loved to
meditate over his favourite books or listen to his
chosen melodies. The portraits of great writers
once painted on the walls are gone, but the shelves
which held his library, and the seats ranged round,
retain their exquisite coloured and inlaid wood-
work. All that the *buon Signor* loved best is represented in the decorations of this little sanctuary,
which for elegance and invention may well compare
with Isabella d' Este's Paradiso in the Castello of
Mantua. The sword that he could wield so well ;
the helmet and spear, the cuirass and spurs worn

in many battles ; the Bible, and his favourite Greek and Latin authors—Homer, Virgil, Cicero, Seneca, and Tacitus—are all figured here.   Here, too, are symbols of the recreations with which he beguiled his spare moments: geometrical and musical instruments, lute and viols, a shelf filled with musical scores, his favourite organ, with the maker's name — *Johani Castelano*—on the case, and the motto *Virtutibus itur ad astra*.   On the tessellated pavement of the floor, his pet squirrel is represented, feeding on a cluster of ripe fruit.   Classical porticoes and temples, framing views of familiar hills and valleys in the neighbourhood of Urbino, are seen on one wall ; on the other a cage of parrots, a clock, a bell, a lighted candle, and flagons of embossed silver, have been introduced by the artist, either as appropriate emblems of home life, or merely to show his realistic skill.   The larger panels at the end of the room are filled with allegorical figures of Faith, Hope and Charity, and a portrait of Federico himself, wearing the ducal cap and mantle, and holding the Gonfaloniere's bâton in his right hand.

One door of this study leads into a small oratory, decorated with coloured marbles and stucco reliefs ; the other opens on to the loggia between the central towers, looking down on the crowded roofs and narrow streets of the medieval city below, and far away across smiling valleys and fruitful plains to the long ridge of Monte Nerone and the lofty peak of Catria.

These beautiful fragments help us to realize what the home of the Montefeltro princes must once have been.   Many are the descriptions of the famous palace that contemporary writers have left us.   Some of these, like Raphael's father and Mercatello, themselves watched Laurana's towers rise to the music of

Apollo's song ; others, like Baldi and Vasari, knew
Urbino in the days of the later dukes, before the
palace was shorn of its ancient splendour, and the contents were carried off to Florence and Rome. Giovanni
Santi sings of the marvellous house, which has no
equal on the face of the earth ; Antonio calls it an
earthly paradise, that attracts strangers from all parts
of the world. They describe the lofty halls and
spacious courts, the grand stairway and fair chapels,
the 250 rooms and 660 windows, the beds hung with
silken tapestries and cloth of gold, the marble baths
and paved yards where the game of palla was played,
the vast kitchens and stabling for 300 horses, the
storehouses for corn and wine which held supplies
for this large household. Perfect order, we are told,
reigned throughout this vast establishment. Each
fretted cornice and delicate ornament was daily kept
bright and polished by the hands of servants and
pages, who stood ready to do their lord's will and
carry out his orders with scrupulous exactitude. Our
poets devote their most eloquent periods to the grand
banquet-hall, hung with the famous tapestries of the
siege of Troy, wrought by skilful weavers whom
Federico brought from Flanders, and which in Vespasiano's opinion were unequalled for beauty and delicacy
of workmanship.[1] Here, too, were the services of
gold and silver, the costly bowls and dishes, cunningly
chased and enamelled with precious gems, which,
ranged in tiers on a sideboard at state banquets, made
as fine a show as any that adorned the table of kings
and emperors. Without were the Duchess's hanging
gardens, raised on pillars cut in the rock, and commanding a view of the wide plains and far Apennines.
Here the terraces and stone seats were shaded with

[1] 'Uomini illustri,' p. 94.

pergolas of trailing ivy, rose and jessamine, and the
fountains and basins were fed by a conduit which
brought water from a tank in the roof, and also supplied the stables.[1]

But the chief pride of the palace of Urbino was the
ducal library, which occupied two halls on the ground-
floor, to the left of the central doorway. The first of
these was a vaulted corridor, 40 by 18 feet, with
shelves ranged along the walls, and above them small
windows looking north, which Baldi tells us diffused
a soft light, and kept the room warm in winter and
deliciously cool (*freschissima*) in summer. The inner
and larger hall went by the name of La Cancelleria,
because it contained the ducal archives and state
papers. Here the space between the shelves was
decorated with a series of allegorical frescoes, representing the Arts and Sciences, painted, according to
Dr. Schmarsow, by Melozzo da Forli, but ascribed
by most recent critics to the Flemish master, Justus
of Ghent. Portraits of Federico's three elder
daughters, Elisabetta, Giovanna and Costanza, with
their betrothed husbands—Roberto Malatesta of
Rimini, Giovanni della Rovere, and Antonio, Prince
of Salerno—were introduced in these paintings ; while
his brother-in-law, Costanzo Sforza of Pesaro, is said
to be the youth represented in the panel of Music,
which, together with that of Rhetoric, is now
in the National Gallery. His nephew and minister,
Ottaviano Ubaldini, appears as Ptolemy in the subject
of Astronomy, and Federico himself, in the red ducal
cap, is seen kneeling at the feet of the teacher who
discourses on Dialectics. Both of these *pitture
singularissime*,[2] as they are called by the poet

---

[1] Baldi, p. 588.
[2] Mercatello in Schmarsow, ' Melozzo da Forli,' Appendice.

Mercatello, are now in the Berlin Museum. Round the frieze of this hall ran the following inscription in rude Latin hexameters, curiously characteristic of the aspirations of Renaissance humanists :

' In this house you have wealth, golden bowls, abundance of money, crowds of servants, sparkling gems, rich jewels, precious chains and girdles. But here is a treasure that far outshines all these splendours. In these halls you have pillars of snowy marble and gold, painted figures set in deep recesses ; within the walls are hung with the tale of Troy, without are gardens fragrant with bright flowers and green foliage. Both within and without the house is glorious. But all these things are dumb ; only the library is eloquent. Whether they speak or hold silence, books have power to profit and charm the reader. They teach the story of the past and unfold the meaning of the future. They explain the labours of earth and impart the knowledge of heaven.'

These words introduced the stranger to the library, which Federico called the finest jewel of his crown. 'With great expense,' writes Castiglione, 'the Duke collected a large number of very rare and precious Greek, Latin, and Hebrew books, all of which he adorned with gold and silver, counting them the supreme excellence of his great palace.' Both Mercatello, who wrote in 1473, and Santi, whose poem was dedicated to Federico's son Guidobaldo, ten years later, dilate on the size and excellence of the collection and praise the beauty and value of the manuscripts which it contained. But the best account of the ducal library that we possess is from the pen of Vespasiano de' Bisticci, who after being employed by Cosimo de' Medici and Pope Nicholas V. to collect manuscripts and arrange their libraries, came to Urbino

in 1472, and devoted the remaining years of his life
to Federico's service.   He it was who classified the
ducal library and divided it into the four groups of
theology, philosophy, history, and poetry, an arrange-
ment first adopted at the Vatican and afterwards
illustrated in Raphael's frescoes.   The Florentine
bookseller cannot restrain his wonder and admiration
at the sight of this famous and excellent library,
which he pronounces far superior to any that has
been formed during the last thousand years.

'What goodly books!' he exclaims, 'what rare
manuscripts! what fine works! All collected regard-
less of expense, all superlatively beautiful, all written
with the pen and all elegantly illuminated!   Whenever the Duke hears of any rare manuscript, he sends
for it at once, and during the last fourteen years
he has kept thirty-four copyists constantly employed
at Urbino, Florence, and in other parts of Italy.   Thus
he has succeeded in obtaining something that is unique
in the world.'

On a brass eagle in the centre of the hall was the
famous Urbino Bible, bound in gold and silver brocade
and richly adorned with miniatures, which is still the
pride of the Vatican.   Then there was the Hebrew
Bible, which the Duke was said to have brought back
from the siege of Volterra, and the illuminated Dante
with the eagle of Montefeltro and Garter embroidered
in pearls on the cover.   A Polyglot Psalter in Hebrew,
Greek, and Latin, *cosa mirabile ed eccellentissima*,
especially excited the admiration of Vespasiano, while
Mercatello dwells with enthusiasm on a copy of
Ptolemy's 'Cosmografia,' with illustrations of the
mountains, rivers, and bridges described by the Greek
geographer.   All the Latin poets, with their best
commentaries, all the known Greek and Roman

historians, the complete works of Cicero, the writings of the Fathers and of the chief medieval and modern doctors, from Aquinas to Pope Pius II., were included in the collection. Besides these historical and theological works, the most important treatises on geometry, astrology, mathematics, law, medicine, and physics, were to be found on the shelves, together with numerous works on military tactics, architecture, painting, and music. Each book was bound in crimson and fastened with gold or silver clasps, and each was a complete copy—'a perfection,' remarks the Florentine writer, 'not to be found in any other library.' Vespasiano could speak with authority on the subject, since in 1482, shortly before the Duke left home for his last campaign, the librarian compared the catalogue which he had drawn up with those of the Vatican, of S. Marco of Florence, of Pavia, and of the University of Oxford, and found that it was the only one which contained no duplicates and no imperfect copies. No wonder that the most renowned scholars were attracted from all parts of the world to the palace which contained such priceless treasures. 'I myself,' writes Giovanni Santi, 'have seen men of the finest taste buried in the study of these precious volumes.'

A whole army of artists and skilled workmen were employed in the decorations of the palace, under Laurana's direction. Francesco di Giorgio of Siena, an able engineer, whom Vasari incorrectly calls the chief architect of the palace, built the stables in 1475, and, with Ambrogio da Milano as his assistant, executed the seventy-two reliefs of military weapons and trophies which originally adorned the central court. The Florentine Baccio Pontelli, who lived at Urbino from 1479 until his death in 1482, and is buried in the church of S. Domenico, had a large share in the decorative sculpture which was the chief beauty of the interior. When Lorenzo de' Medici asked this artist for a plan of the famous palace, he replied that he only wished the Magnifico could see for himself what a thing of beauty it was, while the Duke courteously sent word that he regretted it was impossible to send Lorenzo the house itself. The *intarsia* decoration of Federico's study is said to have been the work of a Bergamo friar, Maestro Giacomo by name. A Lombard sculptor, Domenico Rosselli, carved the mantelpieces of the throne-room and Sala degli Angeli; while Brandano, Diotalevi, and several other local artists, were employed upon the stucco ornaments and reliefs of halls and corridors.

Many other artists of renown came to Urbino in Federico's reign. Desiderio da Settignano, the young Tuscan sculptor whom Giovanni Santi calls '*si dolce e si bello,*' was employed by the Duke to carve a bust of his fair daughter Gentile. Another Florentine master, Maso di Bartolommeo, designed the portals of the Dominican church opposite the old wing of the ducal palace, and Luca della Robbia, with whom he had worked on the bronze gates of the sacristy in the Duomo of Florence, executed the beautiful terra-cotta Madonna over the doorway. In those days, too, Pisanello and Sperandio designed their admirable medals of Federico, and the Umbrian master, Piero della Francesca, painted his masterly portraits of the Duke and Duchess when he came to Urbino in 1469, and lodged in the house of Giovanni Santi. Paolo Uccello was there in the previous year, and executed an altar-piece for the brotherhood of Corpus Domini, to which the curious predella of the Miracle of the Host, now in the ducal palace, originally belonged. Yet another great master, Melozzo da Forli, was at Urbino from 1473 to 1476, and superintended the decoration of the library. Giovanni Santi, who assisted him in his task, and talks with so much affection of his master—'Melozzo a me si caro'—was attached to the Duke's person, both as painter and poet, and wrote verses and arranged pageants for the court festivities. His sweet-faced Madonnas still adorn the churches of Cagli and Urbino, and his metrical chronicle, in *terza-rima*, is the best record that we have of the life and deeds of the great Duke.

Flemish artists also enjoyed the favour of this enlightened prince. A picture of 'Women Bathing' by John of Bruges (Jan Van Eyck) is mentioned by Vasari as one of the gems of his collection.[1] Another master whose presence excited some jealousy among his Italian rivals was Justus of Ghent, or, more accurately, Josse van Wassenhove, the friend of Hugo van der Goes, who came to Urbino at the Duke's invitation, and painted twenty-eight portraits of celebrated authors in his study. These paintings, which the humanist Vespasiano singles out for special praise, were removed to Rome by Cardinal Barberini in the seventeenth century, and, although badly damaged, still retain traces of their rich colouring. Fourteen of the series, including half-lengths of Homer, Boethius, Moses, Solomon, Cicero, Petrarch, and Pius II., are still in the Barberini palace, as well as a fine portrait of Federico in armour, with his little son, clad in gold brocade, at his knee, hearing mass in the ducal chapel. The other fourteen panels, including portraits of Solon, Plato, Aristotle, Virgil, Dante, Sixtus IV., and Vittorino da Feltre, are now in the Louvre; while the most interesting of the series—the group which

[1] 'Vite di Pittori,' i. 321.

Dennistoun saw at Florence in 1845—was bought by Queen Victoria seven years later, and is now in the royal collection at Windsor.[1] Here, under the vaulted roof of a spacious hall, Federico, wearing the ducal mantle of crimson velvet and the order of the Garter, is throned in a chair of state, with three councillors behind him, and Guidobaldo, a fair-haired boy of six or seven, in court dress, standing at his side, listening to a black-bearded professor—probably the German Messer Paolo—lecturing on mathematics. In this noble head of the Duke we recognize the portrait which Vespasiano describes as the best likeness ever taken of his lord, and only wanting breath to be alive. But the finest and best preserved of the Flemish master's works still in existence is the 'Last Supper,' painted in 1474, for the Confraternity of Corpus Domini, and now in the ducal palace. In this noble altar-piece we have a portrait of Federico, with his minister, Ottaviano Ubaldini, standing immediately behind him, which is a masterpiece of realism. The Venetian envoy, Caterino Zeno, who visited Urbino in 1474 on his way to Hungary, is introduced in the background, sitting at table clad in Oriental dress and turban, and a nurse is seen standing in the open doorway with Federico's only son and successor, the infant Prince Guidobaldo, in her arms.

[1] L. Cust, 'The Royal Collections of Paintings,' vol. ii. ; W. H. J. Weale in ' Petite Revue de Gand,' 1901.

CHAPTER VI

1504

FEDERICO'S first marriage was childless; but after
the death of his wife, Gentile Brancaleone, in 1460,
he married Battista Sforza, the young daughter of
Alessandro of Pesaro, and niece of his intimate friend
and close ally Francesco Sforza, Duke of Milan.
The new Duchess had been educated at her uncle's
court with her accomplished cousin Ippolita, the
wife of Alfonso of Naples, and is described by contemporary writers as a being endowed with every
grace and virtue. Giovanni Santi speaks of her
modest and majestic eye, her grave and gentle
character; and Pope Pius II. praised the discretion
and wisdom with which she ruled her husband's State
in his absence. Their union was a singularly happy
one, and, after bearing her lord seven daughters during
twelve years of married life, Battista gave birth to a
son at Gubbio in January, 1472. The boy was named
Guido Ubaldo, after the hermit who was the patron
saint of the ancient city, and whose shrine may still

be seen on the cliffs above the ducal palace. His birth was hailed with general rejoicing, and the Duke hastened home from his victorious campaign at Volterra to the cradle of his new-born son.

'Alas for the vanity of human bliss!' sang Giovanni Santi, 'more slender than the spider's web of gossamer!' Federico reached Gubbio on a July day, to find his wife dying, and was only just in time to receive her last farewell. 'With the most bitter and heartfelt grief,' wrote the bereaved husband to his kinsfolk, 'I inform you that my wife Battista sickened on Tuesday last with headache and fever, and that Our Lord God took her soul to himself at eleven o'clock on this 6th instant, leaving me as miserable, distressed, and inconsolable as anyone can be in this world.' 'She was my wife,' he told Pope Pius II., who had known and highly esteemed the young Duchess, 'precious above all others, the beloved partner of my toil and cares, the joy of my public and private life! No greater misfortune could have befallen me!'[1]

The Duchess, who was only twenty-six at the time of her death, was buried with great pomp in the church of S. Bernardino, outside the city gates, on the hill opposite the ducal palace. This beautiful Renaissance building had been erected by Federico on the site of another shrine where his ancestors were buried, and is supposed to be an early work of the great architect Bramante, who left home for Milan about 1472. The Duke was on friendly terms with the Zoccolanti friars, who occupied the neighbouring convent; and his biographer Muzio relates how one winter night, when the friars were snowed up and rang their bells to call for help, Federico himself went

[1] Cod. Vat. Urb., 1198; Dennistoun, i. 204.

out armed with a pickaxe at the head of his servants, and cut a road to the convent through the snow-drifts. After his wife's death he employed Piero della Francesca to paint the fine altar-piece now in the Brera at Milan, for this little sanctuary. The artist reproduced the fair features of the young Duchess in the Madonna, who is here enthroned, with the Duke in black armour kneeling at her feet. During the remaining years of his life Federico's time was spent partly in active warfare beyond the limits of his own duchy, and partly in building and decorating the new palace, which became his chief interest. In April, 1482, he was appointed Captain of the armies of the League that had been formed between Milan, Florence, and Naples for the defence of Ferrara against Venice, and left home on St. George's Day with a foreboding that he would never return. Five months afterwards he died of malarial fever in the ducal palace of Ferrara, to the bitter grief of his subjects, who loved him as a father. His body, clad in robes and mantle of crimson velvet, with his sword at his side and the Garter on his breast, was brought back to Urbino and buried by his wife's side in the vaults of S. Bernardino.

Guidobaldo, the ten-year-old child whom Federico had confided to the care of his nephew Ottaviano Ubaldini, when he left home for his last campaign, now succeeded to the ducal honours, and reigned over a loyal and contented people, who counted themselves fortunate to be the subjects of a Monte-feltro prince. A charming portrait of the young Duke, by Melozzo da Forli, is preserved in the Colonna Palace in Rome. The boy wears a red cap on his long locks, and a massive gold chain round his neck. His refined features and gentle expression recall the young mother who died in giving him birth, and the white forehead, blue eyes, and fair hair agree with Castiglione's description. Guidobaldo, we are told, grew up tall and handsome, with long delicate features and well-shaped limbs, until, as his biographer sadly remarks, prolonged illness marred the beauty of his face and form. From early years he was noted for his literary tastes and love of learning. Odasio, to whom Federico entrusted his education, and whose misfortune it was to survive his pupil, describes him as a child of exceptional intelligence. Both Castiglione and Bembo were struck by his remarkable powers of memory and wide knowledge of classical literature. He could repeat whole books of Homer and Virgil by heart, and spoke Greek as if it were his own language. Like Federico, he was particularly fond of history and theology. Xenophon and Chrysostom were his favourite authors. The rites and ceremonies of the Church also interested him deeply, and laymen and ecclesiastics alike were surprised to hear the clearness and accuracy with which he could explain the differences that are to be found in the Greek and Roman liturgies.

It was the hard fate of this thoughtful youth to live in the most troubled times, and to be engaged in almost perpetual warfare. At the age of ten he was elected Captain of the armies of the League in his father's place, and although this appointment was naturally purely nominal, he took the field as soon as he was old enough to bear arms. His father's friend, King Ferrante of Naples, enlisted him in his service, and Pope Innocent VIII. employed him to repress the turbulent barons of the Marches. But he was as unfortunate in battle as his father had been for-

Photo, Alinari.

GUIDOBALDO, DUKE OF URBINO.

BY CAROTO (PITTI).

To face p 70, Vol. I.

tunate. Success rarely attended his arms, and from
the age of twenty, he suffered repeatedly from severe
attacks of gout. When he fought under the banner
of the Church in 1498, he was taken prisoner by the
Orsini, and only released on payment of a heavy
ransom; and when he led the Venetian forces into
Val d' Arno, his health broke down under the hardships of a winter campaign, and he was compelled
to retire from Bibbiena. When he visited Venice
in the following year, and was splendidly entertained
by the Doge and Senate, Marino Sanuto remarks
that he was unable to dance at a ball given in
his honour. Three years later came the crowning
disaster of his life, when the treachery of Cesare
Borgia deprived him of his State and fortune in a
single day, and he was forced to wander homeless
from city to city.

But if Guidobaldo was unfortunate in all else, he
was, as Bembo justly says, 'supremely fortunate
in his marriage.' At the age of fourteen he was
betrothed to Elisabetta Gonzaga, sister of the young
Marquis of Mantua, a princess about a year older
than himself, and already remarkable for the charms
and virtues which made her, in the eyes of her most
distinguished contemporaries, unrivalled among the
women of her day. Two years later—in 1488—the
wedding was celebrated with great festivity at Urbino,
and in a pageant arranged by Giovanni Santi for the
occasion, all the gods of Olympus came down from
heaven to welcome the bride and chant the praise of
Hymen.

The portrait which the young Raphael painted of
Elisabetta has perished. There remain, however, a
small but very interesting miniature in an Umbrian
manuscript, that has been preserved in Paris, and

the well-known picture in the Uffizi. This last was formerly ascribed to Mantegna, but is now generally recognized as the work of the Veronese artist, Caroto, who painted Guidobaldo's likeness in the Pitti.[1]

In both these portraits we see the same noble and regular features, the same tired and serious expression, but neither give us any idea of the charm which fascinated men and women alike. If, however, painters failed to do justice to Duchess Elisabetta's beauty, writers and poets have made ample amends for their short-comings. There is a universal agreement in the homage paid to her by men of every rank and age that is very remarkable. When she died, Pope Clement VII. paid a splendid tribute to her great and noble character, and the Mantuan ambassador lamented her as 'the rarest lady of her times.' Both Castiglione and Bembo have celebrated her name in immortal prose. 'I have seen many excellent and noble women,' wrote Bembo, 'and have known some who were conspicuous for certain virtues in their time, but in her alone all virtues were summed up.'[2]

'There is no need for me to dwell on her perfections,' writes the author of the 'Cortegiano,' 'since they are already well known to the world, and yet more, because it is beyond the power of my tongue or pen to express them. They might, indeed, have remained hidden, if Fortune, who admires rare virtues, had not revealed them to us by many adversities and stings of calamities, in order to show the world that in the tender breast of a beautiful woman you may find wisdom and fortitude of soul, and all those sterner virtues which are most rare in man.'[3]

[1] Bibliothèque Nat., MS. Ital. 1,507 ; Arte, 148.
[2] 'Lettere,' ii. 65.   [3] 'Cortegiano,' 18.

These expressions were no mere common-places of flattery in the lips of either courtier or Cardinal. The tears which Bembo shed over Elisabetta's grave, the cry that broke from Castiglione's heart when he remembered that the Lady Duchess was dead, are more eloquent than any courtly phrase. But it was the same with all who approached this gentle and charming lady. The keynote of her character was a sweet reasonableness, a serenity of soul which made her face peril and calamity with uncomplaining fortitude, and an unselfishness which led her to place herself unreservedly at the disposal of others.

Her quick sympathy with joy and sorrow, her readiness to help the needy and relieve the oppressed, made her beloved by all. No prayer for succour or comfort was ever addressed to her in vain; no suppliant for pardon or favour ever left her doors unsatisfied. Her fine womanly tact was ever ready to smooth away difficulties, to lend a helping hand, and counsel patience or submission, delay or prompt action, as the case might require. We see her watching anxiously by the death-bed of the court-painter Giovanni Santi, grieving over his untimely end and protecting the youth of his orphan son, the boy Raphael, for his father's sake. We find her mourning over her old friend Mantegna's death, and interceding with her brother on behalf of the master's scapegrace son, 'because of Andrea, whom I loved so well.' In later years we see her curbing the violent temper of her adopted son, Duke Francesco della Rovere, teaching him to be tender to his young wife, and kind and thoughtful for others. We see her taking infinite trouble to obtain a place or pension for persons whom she did not even know, but who were the friends of her friends; or else excusing the faults and follies of old servants, craving pardon for Tebaldeo's delinquencies, and soothing her brother the Marquis's just anger with wise and gentle words.

'The Lady Duchess,' writes Bembo to the friends in Venice who urged him to leave Urbino and return home, 'has worked, and is working, for me in a way that has surpassed my fondest expectations. She never ceases to do things that may help and benefit me, and takes more thought for my affairs than I do myself. Even if Fortune should deprive her of the power to help me as she desires, I can never forget that she, for whom I have never done anything in my life, has done more for me than all the other people put together for whom I have often done a great deal.'[1]

Such a princess could not fail to inspire deep and ardent affection. In her old home at Mantua, Elisabetta had been a favourite with brothers and servants alike. The rude and passionate Marquis Francesco and the gay and thoughtless Giovanni, who cared for nothing but horses and gambling, were both devoted to this gentle sister, and ready to take any trouble or run any risks for her sake. Her delicate health only increased their affection for her when she left home for Urbino. Francesco was ready to fly to her side at a moment's notice if the doctors gave a bad report of her, and was always trying to induce her to come to Mantua for the good of her health and that he might enjoy the pleasure of her society. And one of the few occasions on which she aroused his displeasure was when, in spite of his warnings and suspicions of the Borgias, she persisted in her determination of going to Rome rather than disappoint her sister-in-law, Agnesina Colonna.

---

[1] 'Lettere,' ii. 61

' Never was there such a Madonna !' exclaimed the
reckless Giovanni, when he came to Urbino at the
time of Guidobaldo's death, and found how wisely and
well the Duchess had ordered all things in her lord's
State. Women as well as men owned the power of
her spell. Young and old, they all loved Elisabetta.
Her brilliant sister-in-law, Isabella d' Este, a highly
critical lady, easily jealous, and quick to resent any
claim to superiority in a rival, cherished her with
a deep and enduring affection that remained unchanged through every vicissitude of fortune. And
she quickly inspired both her young sister-in-law,
Agnesina,[1] and Emilia Pia, the accomplished wife of
her husband's illegitimate brother, Antonio di Montefeltro, with the same devotion. From the moment
that the Duchess Elisabetta came to Urbino she was
adored by her husband and subjects. Guidobaldo
found in his young wife the intelligent sympathy that
he needed, and although the blessing of children was
denied them, during twenty years their union was one
of unclouded happiness. Under their rule the court
of Urbino maintained the high position which it had
acquired in the days of the good Duke Federico, and
became even more famous as a school of art and
letters.

' It is a noteworthy thing, and impossible of con-
tradiction by the most malicious tongues,' wrote
Ruscelli,[2] ' that the court of Urbino in our times has
been a fountain, which, in no poetic phrase, but in
sober earnest, may be termed a true Pegasean spring,
a fortunate garden or field in which were reared an

---

[1] Agnesina, Guidobaldo's youngest sister, was still unmarried
when Elisabetta came to Urbino. In the following year she
became the wife of Fabrizio Colonna, and was afterwards the
mother of Ascanio and Vittoria Colonna.

[2] ' Imprese illustri.'

infinite number of great men whose names will be celebrated for all time.'

The death of Duke Federico and that of his architect Laurana in the following year, naturally interrupted the progress of the ducal palace, and Guidobaldo's enforced absence from home and lack of money seriously interfered with its completion. But he made several important additions to the fabric, and took especial interest in the decoration of the interior, which, Baldi tells us,[1] became much richer and more sumptuous during his reign, 'being adorned with gilding and colour and inlaid panelling.' He built a new and larger studio for his own use on the ground-floor, and employed Timoteo Viti to decorate its walls with paintings of Apollo and the Muses, which are still preserved in the Corsini Palace at Florence. A chapel enriched with stucco and coloured marbles was also Guidobaldo's work, as well as a new and spacious hall for the game of palla, which he liked to watch, although unable to take part in it himself.

Francia's pupil, the Urbino master, Timoteo Viti, mentioned above, returned from Bologna in 1495 to succeed Giovanni Santi as court-painter and become the teacher of his son Raphael. Several works by Timoteo's hand are preserved at Urbino; amongst others an altar-piece, in which Guidobaldo and Bishop Arrivabene are seen kneeling before St. Martin and St. Thomas. This picture, now in the Cathedral sacristy, was painted after the death of Bishop Arrivabene in 1504, for the chapel of St. Thomas à Becket in the Duomo which this prelate had endowed.

Both Guidobaldo and his wife shared the passion for antiques that was prevalent in their age, and

[1] Baldi, p. 574.

The Fine Art Publishing Co. Ltd. photo.

Emery Walker Ph. Sc.

Federico of Urbino and his son
listening to a lecture

From a picture by Justin of Ghent at Windsor Castle

brought many precious marbles and bronzes to adorn the ducal halls. Chief among these, we know, were the famous Venus and the Cupid of Michelangelo. This last passed as an antique statue in Rome, and in Isabella d' Este's opinion, was unequalled among modern works of art. Both of these were originally presented to Guidobaldo by Cesare Borgia when the Pope's son was on friendly terms with him, and after the conquest of Urbino were given by the victor to the Marchioness of Mantua, who refused to restore them to her kinsman.

Among the artists employed at Urbino during Guidobaldo's reign we find the names of Luca Signorelli, who painted his fine altar-pieces of the Descent of the Holy Ghost and the Crucifixion in the church of San Spirito; Girolamo Genga, who decorated the cathedral with frescoes; and Francesco Francia, who is said by Vasari to have painted a panel of the Roman Lucretia and a pair of horses' bards for the Duke.

Cristoforo Romano, the accomplished sculptor and musician, was, as we shall see, a frequent and welcome guest at the ducal court, a favourite here, as elsewhere, with all fair ladies. The portrait medals of Elisabetta and of Emilia Pia, however, that have hitherto been ascribed to him are now pronounced by some experts to be the work of Adriano Fiorentino, another distinguished sculptor and gifted musician, who spent three months at Urbino in 1495.[1] Elisabetta was herself an accomplished musician, and sang to her own accompaniment on the lute, while Guidobaldo inherited his father's love of music, and took lessons from one of his subjects, Ottaviano de' Petrucci of Fossombrone, the inventor of the art of type music-

[1] E. v. Fabriczy in ' Jahrbuch,' xxiv., p. 82.

printing. Several other distinguished musicians visited Urbino during this Duke's reign, and lingered there many weeks. The Veronese singer Marchetto Caro, who was in the Marquis of Mantua's service, and had been sent by him to cheer Elisabetta's exile at Venice, found a warm welcome at Urbino, and would gladly have remained there if his own lord had not sent him an imperious summons to return home. Jacopo di Sansecondo, the famous viol-player, who, like Cristoforo Romano, had been a great favourite with Duchess Beatrice of Milan, settled at Urbino after the Moro's fall. Here, too, often came the Roman lute-player Terpandro to make his home with his friends Bembo and Bibbiena, Castiglione and Tebaldeo, at this court, which was the favourite resort of 'every pleasant and amusing person, and of all those who were most excellent in every branch of knowledge throughout Italy.'

But the library which Federico had founded was, as might be expected, his son's especial care. He added a great number of valuable works to the collection, spending large sums in obtaining ancient manuscripts, and employing the best humanists to assist him in the task. Several noted scholars, Agabito, Lorenzo Abstemio, and the chronicler Federico Veterani, held the post of librarian at his court in succession, and a set of curious and minute regulations were drawn up for their guidance and the benefit of students who visited Urbino.

'The librarian should be learned and of good presence, equable in temper and gracious in manner, accurate and fluent of speech. He must keep a complete inventory of the books in the library, and see that they are well arranged and easily accessible, whether Latin, Greek, Hebrew, or Italian; and he must also keep the halls in good condition. The books must be preserved from the ravages of damp and vermin, as well as from the hands of ignorant, dirty, and careless persons. When personages of learning and importance visit the palace, he ought himself to show them the treasures of the library, courteously pointing out their beauty and chief characteristics, their miniatures and characters, but being watchful to see that no pages are removed. When strangers ask to see the books out of mere curiosity, a single glance will be sufficient, unless the visitor should be one of distinction and influence. When new clasps or locks are required, he must take care that they are provided without delay. No book may be taken out of the library excepting by order of the Duke, and the librarian must take care that a written receipt be given for each volume, and see that it is carefully returned. And when many visitors come together, he must be especially watchful that no books are stolen.'[1]

The fame of Guidobaldo's own learning attracted many scholars to his court, and works of the most varied description were dedicated to him by distinguished writers. A reprint of an ancient astronomical work by Maternus, and a 'Treatise on the Dignity and Office of a Cardinal,' by Paolo Cortesio, were both inscribed to him. To him the venerable painter, Piero della Francesca, dedicated his work on the Five Bodies, a practical application of Euclid's propositions to art, begging the Duke to place his *libellus* 'in some corner, as a humble handmaid to the innumerable books of his vast library.' Again, Piero's fellow-citizen and Leonardo's friend, Fra Luca Pacioli, of Borgo San Sepolcro, inscribed his great mathematical work, the 'Somma di Arit-

[1] Cod. Vat. Urb. 1248, f. 58, and Dennistoun, i. 158.

metica,' in 1494, to the same generous patron.
Another celebrated book mentioned in the 'Cortegiano,' the famous 'Hypernotomachia Polyphili,' or
'The Combat of Love in the Dream of Polyphilus,'
one of the first volumes that issued from the
Aldine press, was also dedicated to Guidobaldo.
A Dominican friar of Venice, Francesco Colonna,
was the author of this strange and powerful romance,
which reflects in so vivid a manner the different
currents of Italian thought in the fifteenth century,
its yearnings for the old Greek and Roman world,
its love of rich colour and sumptuous pageantry,
its dreams of beauty and aspirations after a more
perfect order. It was printed by Aldo in 1499, at
the expense of Leonardo Crasso of Verona, whose
brother had served in the campaign of Bibbiena, under
Guidobaldo, and dedicated by him in terms of high
eulogy to this Prince ' learned above others in Greek
and Latin, in the knowledge of ancient history, and
equally renowned for his wisdom and goodness.' The
Veronese scholar's choice was singularly appropriate,
and it seems in the fitness of things that a work
steeped in classical mythology and illustrated with a
profusion of admirable woodcuts, should be connected
with the court of Urbino.

Four years later Aldo himself dedicated his edition of
Xenophon to Guidobaldo. During the weary months
of exile which the Duke and Duchess had spent at
Venice, they had made many friends among the circle
of cultured patricians to which the printer belonged,
and had endeared themselves to all who knew them
intimately. When, in November, 1503, they were
recalled by a grateful people, Aldo availed himself of
this auspicious occasion to address an elegant Greek
epistle to the Duke, in which he congratulates him on

his restoration to home and throne, and begs him to accept the book as a mark of devotion to his person and of admiration for his character.

'O good son of an excellent father,' he exclaims, quoting from the 'Iliad,' 'could I, O Zeus! father of the gods Athene and Apollo, see ten such kings and princes! In these unhappy times, what would not be our good fortune if our States were governed by Kings who, according to the divine Plato's precepts, were also philosophers! You at least as a sovereign answer to this description, since you have no wish but to make your subjects happy, and your people, aware of this, have twice recalled you to your realm after you had been vanquished by the enemy's forces, to be restored amid universal joy and acclamation. See, then, how good, how useful it is even for a monarch to be a philosopher! But philosophy secures us many greater benefits, such, among others, as unshaken courage in all the changes and chances of life. "Let Fate and Fortune destroy all things mortal to please their caprices, Hippoclides will take no heed." Yes, in joy as well as in sorrow, the true philosopher remains the same. Of this history has given us many examples. As for you, we all know how admirable you have been in the different phases of fortune. In prosperity you have ever been just and kind, filled with a gracious and unceasing benevolence, and when Fortune has not smiled on you, as your virtues deserved, your conduct has been such as to make men think that you suffer nothing from adversity. I need only point to your courage and wisdom, in all the troubles that you endured, in that hour when you fled before your foes to escape capture, and God Himself came to your help. And we are not the only witnesses of your courage in evil fortune. All Venice has seen and admired you. This, then, is one of the advantages of philosophy.

'It is as a token of the high idea that I have of your

worth, that I offer you the " Hellenica " of Xenophon, a work full of interest, which I have just printed.   The author was so eloquent and so deeply imbued with the Attic spirit that the Greeks called him the Attic bee. In this also he resembles you.   Like yourself he was the captain of an army, like you he was learned, well educated, and distinguished by his virtues.   These are indeed great and noble qualities.   But I have said enough.   Accept this present, which I hope will please you, and which you will keep as a remembrance of my regard, and of my devotion to you and your realm.   Greetings.'[1]

   ' VENICE, *November* 14, 1503.'

This dedication deserves to be remembered as a proof of the love and admiration with which Guidobaldo was regarded beyond the walls of Urbino. But there were two events which, more than the grateful praises bestowed upon him by scholars and artists, more even than the eloquent words of Aldo, have made the name of this Duke memorable in the eyes of posterity.   During his reign Raphael was born, in the old stone house that is still standing in the narrow street leading up the steep mountain-side, and twenty years later, while the century was still young, Baldassare Castiglione first came to Urbino.

   [1] Xenophon ' Hellenica.'   In Aldi Neacademia, 1503.

LODOVICO SFORZA.
(BRITISH MUSEUM.)

ELISABETTA GONZAGA.
(BRITISH MUSEUM.)

ISABELLA D' ESTE.
(BRITISH MUSEUM.)

To face p. 82, Vol. I.

CHAPTER VII

1504

It was a memorable moment in Castiglione's life when he rode up the long ascent from Pesaro, and for the first time beheld the golden spires of the ducal palace flashing in the evening sun. Wonderful tales of its splendour had reached Mantua from the servants who escorted the young Duchess Elisabetta on her wedding journey, and the ladies who accompanied the Marquis and Marchioness on their frequent visits to Urbino. Isabella d' Este herself could not contain her admiration at the sight of the superb tapestries and treasures of art that were displayed before her eyes, and confessed that in the natural loveliness of the situation, in the stateliness of its architecture and the wealth of its decorations, the palace far surpassed her expectations. Now Castiglione saw all these wonders for himself. His love of beauty was satisfied as his eye rested on the masterpieces of Melozzo and Piero della Francesca, or surveyed the incomparable prospect from the windows and balconies of the ducal apartments. Here he found, in fuller measure than

83

ever before, all that he most needed—rare books
and manuscripts with leisure to study their contents,
congenial society and friends that were dear to him as
his own soul; the *alta quiete, la vita dolce e lieta*,
which Giovanni Santi calls the greatest boon that can
be granted to mortals in this troubled world.

During the next twelve years he made Urbino his
home, and shared a house with his cousin Cesare
Gonzaga in a street near the ducal palace. When
he was not engaged in close attendance on the
Duke, his mornings were generally spent in the
library. There he might be seen in the cool recesses
of the frescoed halls, studying his favourite classical
authors—Cicero and Virgil, Plato and Aristotle,
Plutarch and Tacitus—or those poets in the *lingua
volgare* for whom he had so great an affection. In
the Duke he found a sympathetic friend who
shared his love of the Mantuan bard, and who
was as keenly interested in classical texts and
metaphysical problems as he was himself. Guidobaldo, we know, took great pleasure in the society
of studious and cultivated persons. ‘It was the
Duke’s habit,’ Castiglione tells us, ‘to surround
himself with gentlemen of birth and breeding, with
whom he lived on easy and familiar terms, enjoying
their conversation, and giving them as much pleasure
as he received, because he was himself learned in
both Greek and Latin, and combined the utmost
affability and pleasantness with infinite knowledge on
all manner of subjects.’

The Venetian envoy Mocenigo describes how,
being disabled by broken health from taking part in
active pursuits, the Duke resolved to fill his household
with men who were distinguished in every profession.
‘Thus with the help of the Duchess, who was as

eager as her lord in welcoming and entertaining accomplished guests, he collected a greater number of fine spirits than any Prince of his age, and held up to the world the model of an admirably regulated court.'[1]

Some of these noble youths and talented guests became Castiglione's most intimate friends. In the autumn of 1504, Giuliano de' Medici had not yet come to seek a refuge in his exile at Guidobaldo's court, and Pietro Bembo was still struggling in vain to escape from the political or commercial career for which his father had destined him. But Cesare Gonzaga, and several of the other personages with whom the pages of the 'Cortegiano' have made us familiar, were already at Urbino. Here Baldassare found another kinsman—our Count, as he calls him in his letters home—Lodovico Canossa, a member of a noble Veronese family, who, after spending his youth at Mantua, came to Urbino in 1496, at the age of twenty, with an introduction from Isabella d' Este, and entered the Duke's service. Here, too, were the sons of Guidobaldo's half-sister, the beautiful Gentile di Montefeltro, Ottaviano and Federico Fregoso, who had lived at their uncle's court since they had been driven out of their native city of Genoa by rival factions in 1497. Ottaviano was a gallant soldier who distinguished himself in defending Urbino against Cesare Borgia, and afterwards served under his uncle in the wars of the Church. His younger brother, although he took orders and was made Archbishop of Salerno in 1507, also played an active part in the wars of Genoa, and fought in the galleys of Andrea Doria. Both brothers were followers of the Muses and composed sonnets, and joined Castiglione and

[1] Alberi, ' Relazioni degli ambasciatori Veneti,' Serie ii., i. 98.

Cesare Gonzaga in the different games and pastimes that were the order of the day at Urbino.   And both were men of noble and affectionate character, especially Federico, who remained Bembo's attached friend until his death in 1541.   'Certainly,' wrote the Cardinal on that occasion to Leonora Gonzaga, the widowed Duchess of Urbino, 'Your Highness, as you truly say, has not only lost a rare friend and relative and a most wise and holy prelate, but the whole Church has suffered a great and incomparable loss.   Of my own sorrow I will not speak, for Your Excellency knows the close and ardent affection that linked us together from the days of tender and early youth, and was never injured by a single word on his part or mine.'[1]   Here, too, were the young Lombard Count Gaspare Pallavicino, who plays the part of Benedick in the 'Cortegiano,' but who, in spite of his declared aversion to women, was exceedingly popular both with men and ladies; the Milanese Captain, Alessandro Trivulzio ; the aged Neapolitan, Baron Sigismondo Morello, of Ortona, who owned vast lands in the Abruzzi, but had long been attached to the Duke's person ;[2] and those two youthful courtiers, Roberto da Bari, the boy-shepherd of Castiglione's pastoral play, to whom he was so tenderly attached, and Luigi da Porto, of Vicenza, the author of the well-known 'Lettere storiche' and of the original tale of 'Romeo and Juliet.'   This last-named knight, who, like Baldassare himself, was destined to acquire as much renown in letters as in arms, was related to the Gambara and Pio families, and seems to have returned to Urbino with Guidobaldo in 1503.   He was one of Pietro Bembo's intimate friends, but left Urbino towards the end of 1505, to the grief of the whole

[1] 'Lettere,' iv. 71.   [2] Ugolini, ii. 159.

court, and is therefore not mentioned in the 'Cortegiano.'

The ladies in attendance on Duchess Elisabetta
were most of them already well known to Castiglione
when he came to Urbino.   There was, first of all,
Emilia Pia, her beloved sister-in-law and inseparable
companion, whose name is familiar to every reader of
the 'Cortegiano.'   This brilliant and accomplished
lady was the youngest daughter of Marco Pio, Lord
of Carpi, and renowned, like all the members of
this illustrious house, for her natural wit and love
of literature.   She was connected by birth and
marriage with most of the great families of Northern
Italy.   Her brother Giberto—who in 1494 succeeded to half of the principality of Carpi, and
promptly seized on the other half, which belonged
to his cousin, Alberto Pio—was married to Elena
Bentivoglio ; her eldest sister, Alda, was the wife
of Count Gambara of Brescia, and mother of the
famous Veronica.   Another sister, Agnese, married
Count Francesco Rangone, of Modena ; while a third,
Margherita, was the gentle lady who wedded Antonio
San Severino, and after his death refused to be
comforted, and turned a deaf ear to her poet Trissino's
addresses.   One of her brothers, Galeotto, entered
the service of Lodovico Sforza, and served him loyally
to the end ; another, the condottiere Lodovico, fought
under the banner of the Church, married Bembo's fair
Milanese friend, Graziosa Maggi, and spent much of
his time at Urbino.   Her cousin Alberto Pio, the
nephew of Aldo Manuzio's patron Giovanni Pico
della Mirandola, was also a frequent visitor at the
ducal court, and claimed kinship with the Duchess
through his first wife Camilla and his mother, the
widow of Rodolfo Gonzaga.   In 1487, when she was

still very young, Emilia Pia came to Urbino as the bride of Antonio da Montefeltro, Guidobaldo's elder half-brother. This natural son of Duke Federico had been legitimized in 1454, by Pope Nicholas V., before his father's marriage to Battista Sforza, and is described by Vespasiano as a youth of great promise and military prowess. He was knighted by King Ferrante of Naples at the age of twenty, and fought gallantly at his father's side in his last campaign of Ferrara, after which he entered the Venetian service, and was present at the battle of the Taro.

In spite of the wide difference of years between them, Emilia was devotedly attached to her husband, and when he died, after a long illness, in 1500, her grief was such as to cause her relatives the greatest anxiety for her own life. ' Madonna Emilia's sorrow,' wrote the gentle Elisabetta, who had, from her first arrival at Urbino, found a true sister in Antonio's young wife, ' is so great that it would move the hardest heart to compassion.[1] My lord and I cannot on any account leave her.' And the Marchioness Isabella wrote affectionately to the poor young widow, begging her to take comfort and to endure life for the sake of the friends who loved her so well. After the first shock was over, Emilia recovered health and spirits, and showed the same tender solicitude for others, and the same keen interest in passing events, which had made her a general favourite before. But although her charms still attracted suitors of all ages, and she was courted and loved by many, she rejected all advances and remained faithful to her dead lord's memory.

During the Duchess's exile, Emilia Pia was her constant companion, and became intimately acquainted

---

[1] Luzio e Renier, ' Mantova e Urbino,' 106.

with several leading Venetians. One of her chief
friends and admirers was Pietro Bembo, who often
corresponded with this 'valiant lady,' as he calls her
in one of his letters. He describes her as a ' woman
of great soul and wise counsel, as remarkable for
prudence as for virtue ';[1] while in a set of carnival
verses he salutes her as *Alma gentil,* at once cruel and
pious [*pia*], and pronounces her charms worthy to
be sung by Homer, the greatest of all poets. In
a charming letter of March, 1504,[2] he declares that
Madonna Emilia's letters, however long delayed,
are as welcome as flowers in May, and sends her
and the Duchess ' as many greetings as there are
leaves this springtide on the forests between Venice
and Urbino.' Such fragments of Emilia's correspondence as have been preserved, especially her
letters to the Marchioness Isabella, justify these expressions, and show that her pen could be as lively and
amusing as her tongue. Her quick wit, sparkling
gaiety, and womanly tact are displayed in the many
passages of the ' Cortegiano,' which make us realize
the important position that she held at the ducal
court.

' " These Princes indeed," writes Abate Serassi,
" loved and honoured her more than if she had been
their own sister. And she was undoubtedly worthy
of this high consideration, since few women ever lived,
at any period of the world, who could in any way
compare with her. Not only was she endowed with
singular grace and the most lively wit, but her wisdom
and ripe judgment have rarely been equalled, so that
at this Court, which, as every one knows, contained
the noblest men in the world, the Lady Emilia
appeared to be the mistress of all, and was a pattern

[1] ' De Urbini Ducibus,' p. 45.   [2] ' Lettere,' iv. 31.

of wisdom and prudence. To these virtues she joined
a certain modesty and sweetness that were apparent
in all her words and movements, and made her
the unconscious arbiter of the deeds and wishes of
others. Thus Castiglione, in his pastoral play of
'Tirsi,' sings :

> Una fra tutte lor v' è dolce e pia
> Ch' accanto della Dea sempre si vede
> Questa non porta mai seco arme in caccia,
> Sol col dolce parlar le fiere allaccia.

But what above all made her worthy of the greatest
honour and reverence was her great and singular
chastity. For, although she was young and beautiful
and lived at the gayest of Courts, among constant
dancing and festivity, and was admired and courted
by many gallant knights, not only did she remain
chaste and modest in word and deed, but knew how
to instil the same pure sentiments and modesty into
other ladies. For these virtues, as well as others,
Madonna Emilia was especially worthy to be the
sister, counsellor, and inseparable companion of
Duchess Elisabetta.'[1]

This invincible virtue, as Serassi goes on to say, was
not altogether approved of by the gay cavaliers at
court, some of whom complained of the fair lady's
tyranny, and wrote sonnets and epigrams 'Alla Signora
Emilia impia.' Even the Goddess of Love, Bembo
tells us, and her son Cupid, had cause to lament the
cruelty of the Lady Emilia, and sent messengers to the
court of Urbino to ask why the winged darts of Love
were shot in vain along the banks of the Metauro, and
fair maidens there laughed at the fiery rays of the
Evening Star. The medal struck at Urbino in
honour of Emilia, bears witness to the inviolable

---

[1] Serassi, ii. 270.

chastity which she maintained during her long widow-
hood. On one side we see her portrait, with the
regular features and long tress of hair coiled in the
Lombard style, and her name *Emilia Pia Feltria ;* on
the other we have a pyramid bearing an urn, with
the inscription *Castis cineribus.* But if Emilia Pia
refused to accept any one of the courtiers as her lover,
she was always ready to welcome them as her friends.
And Castiglione, whose mother had known her from
girlhood, and with whom she had recently renewed
her old friendship at Mantua, was cordially welcomed
by her on his arrival, and treated with unchanging
kindness in after-years.

Among the other ladies at the ducal court, our
cavalier also found Elisabetta's niece Margherita, an
illegitimate daughter of the Marquis of Mantua, who
accompanied the Duchess on her return to Urbino,
and whose youthful charms attracted many suitors.
Alberto Pio, who was now a widower, courted her for
several years, and was at one time recognized as her
betrothed husband, but political troubles delayed
their union, and eventually he consoled himself with
another bride. The wealthy Roman banker Agostino
Chigi next paid addresses to Margherita, but although
his suit was encouraged by the Gonzaga family, she
herself showed so much reluctance to the union that
the marriage was eventually abandoned. Castiglione
alludes to a third suitor in a well-known letter to
Canossa,[1] 'a Count of Correggio, young, handsome,
and rich,' as being about to wed 'our Madonna
Margherita'; but this project also seems to have fallen
through, and when the Marquis died, in 1519, his
daughter was still unmarried. The Duke's half-sister,
Madonna Gentile Fregoso, the mother of Castiglione's

[1] Serassi, ii. 159.

friends Ottaviano and Federico, was also living at Urbino at this time, and is often mentioned in letters of the period. Her daughter Costanza, afterwards the wife of Count Landi of Piacenza, took an active part in the pastimes of the court, danced French and Spanish dances with Margherita, to the delight of the spectators, and corresponded with Pietro Bembo, who stood sponsor to her first-born son. Another fair maiden, Raffaella by name, was among the Duchess's ladies, and not only honoured Castiglione with her friendship, but wrote letters to him when he was absent in the camp. We have, however, no particulars of her history and family, nor yet of her companion, Ippolita, whom Alessandro Trivulzio courted, and whose charms Bembo praised in his verses.

But more to Castiglione than any of these lovely maidens, more to him than the wise and witty Madonna Emilia, or Bembo, or his own kinsmen, was the Duchess Elisabetta herself. He had known this gentle Princess in his boyhood at Mantua, and seen her go forth as a young bride to her new home beyond the Apennines. He had met her again on the frequent visits which she paid to her brother's court, when she and her lord were driven into exile. For him, in those early days, she had been the bright, particular star whom he worshipped from afar. Now he learnt to know her intimately, and enjoyed that easy and familiar converse with the Duke and Duchess which, Bembo tells us, was a leading feature of life at Urbino. Guidobaldo's favour and his own connexion with the Gonzagas brought the young courtier into close relations with Elisabetta, who quickly recognized his noble character and honoured him with her friendship; while he on his part regarded her with deeper reverence and affection than any other woman. For him

Elisabetta was not only the fair Galatea for whom all
the shepherds on the banks of Metaurus sighed in
vain, the divine Dido whose lament would have melted
the hardest heart, or the Siren whose voice charmed
mortal cares away, but the object of his silent worship,
the mistress to whom his allegiance was pledged, and
whom he served with true and lifelong devotion.

Chroniclers and biographers agree in ascribing these
sentiments to Castiglione, and give us many instances
of the secret passion that he cherished for his mistress.   Beffa-Negrini,[1] the family historian, tells us
of the two sonnets, evidently inspired by hopeless
love for some exalted object, that were placed by him
in 1517, together with the portrait of a most beautiful
and illustrious lady, by the hand of Raphael of
Urbino, at the back of a splendid mirror in his house
at Mantua.   Here they were found forty-three years
later by his daughter-in-law, Countess Caterina
Mandello, who touched a secret spring at the back of
the glass and discovered Raphael's painting and the
sonnets composed by Castiglione among the ruins of
ancient Rome, and written by his own hand.   The
portrait has unfortunately never come to light, but
the sonnets are printed in Serassi's collection,[2] and
are among the best which the Count ever wrote.

It is difficult to say whether Castiglione's devotion
to Elisabetta was more than a merely poetic senti-
ment, common to courtiers and poets in that age; but
there are passages in his ' Cortegiano ' which seem to
show that the feelings which he cherished for the
Duchess were of a deeper and more enduring nature.

' I must confess,' he writes in his dedication to

---

[1] 'Elogi di B. Castiglione,' 415 ; Marliani, 330 ; A. Dumesnil
' Histoire des Amateurs italiens.'
[2] Serassi, ii. 286.

Dom Miguel de Silva, 'that I have not expressed or even indicated the perfections of the Lady Duchess, because my words could never describe them nor could my intellect imagine them.' And when in a foreign land, long years after he had left Urbino, the news of her death reached him, it came as a great shock, and wrung from him a cry of pain. 'But what cannot be told without tears is that the Lady Duchess is herself dead ; and if my soul is troubled by the loss of so many of my friends and masters, who have left me in this life as in a desolate wilderness, it is natural that I should grieve more bitterly for the death of the Lady Duchess than for all the rest, because she was worth far more than all the others, and I was more deeply attached to her than to any of them all.'

CHAPTER VIII

1504

Castiglione's recollections of life at Urbino—Society at the ducal court — Intellectual and physical exercises — Poems and comedies—The study of language—Evenings in the Duchess's room—Music and games—Poets and jesters—The Nuncio delivers the banner of the Church to Guidobaldo—Francesco della Rovere proclaimed the Duke's heir — Raphael at Urbino.

THE best and happiest days of Castiglione's life were those which he spent at the court of Urbino in Guidobaldo's reign. We know how fondly he looked back on those joyous times in later years; how tenderly he recalled each little incident of the vanished days, and sighed for the faces of the friends whom he had lost. Nor was he alone in this respect. There were other survivors of that brilliant group who looked back on the years spent at Urbino as the best time of their life. Many and frequent are the allusions to those 'good old days' that we find in Bembo's correspondence. In letters written twenty and thirty years later, we find the Papal secretary and future Cardinal recalling the 'happy days when I lived at Urbino in such content and gladness of heart,' and speaking to the Duke's successor, or to Federico Fregoso, who had gone back to end his days as Archbishop of Gubbio in the beloved *contrade*, of

' that pleasant land where the most joyous years of my life were spent.'[1]

It is Castiglione himself who has enabled us to realize in some degree the manner of life that these men led at the court of Urbino.   In the pages of the ' Cortegiano ' he has, in his own words, given us 'a faithful portrait of Guidobaldo's court, not indeed by the hand of Raphael or Michelangelo, but by a humble painter who could only trace the chief outlines of the picture, and knew not how to adorn the truth with gay colours, or by the art of perspective make that which is not appear as if it were.'

In spite of these modest expressions, the picture is drawn by a master-hand.   The outlines of the sketch are clear and vigorous ; the colours are laid on, the lights and shadows filled in, with rare literary skill.   The form is taken from classical models, but the pulse of warm human life beats through the even flow of the narrative at every page.   The dialogues are interspersed, after the fashion of contemporary plays, with lively interludes, with merry jests and witty stories, with games and dances, and the whole reflects, as in a mirror, the calm and joyous life which the author and his friends led at the court of Urbino in the golden days of the Renaissance.

The time, Castiglione begins by telling us, was divided between intellectual and physical exercises, honourable and enjoyable both to body and mind. The high ideal held up in his book had penetrated deeply into the heart of Italian society, and there was no one at the ducal court who doubted the truth of his assertion that mental culture formed part of a perfect knight's equipment.   Guidobaldo's

---

[1] ' Lettere,' iii. 69, iv. 39.

own love of literature and the refined tastes of
Elisabetta and her ladies lent a strong stimulus to
literary production. Sonnets and *canzoni*, *stanze*
and *rime*, were composed and recited, now by one
member of the group, now by another. Most of
Castiglione's finest poems and many of Bembo's most
elegant verses belong to this period. Other courtiers
less accomplished, but no less anxious to please,
caught the prevailing fashion, and tried their hand at
rhyming. Cesare Gonzaga, Ottaviano Fregoso, even
Giuliano de' Medici, were among the poets in those
days. Bembo's correspondence abounds in allusions to
these poetic effusions which reached him from all
parts of Italy, and were read and recited to the whole
court, whether they were composed in Rome or
Venice, at Mantua or Ferrara. At carnival time
flights of a higher order were attempted ; pastoral
plays and comedies were composed and acted before
the Duchess and her ladies. Vincenzo Calmeta,
Beatrice d' Este's old secretary, who since the death of
his lamented mistress had been a wanderer from one
court to another, came to Urbino in the early spring
of 1504, and delighted the ladies by a comedy of his
invention, not without exciting the jealousy of Bembo,
who wrote from Venice to Madonna Emilia, that he
would like to pull his rival's ears were he not afraid of
Calmeta's superior stature ! Next year it was the
turn of Castiglione and Cesare Gonzaga, then of
Bembo and Ottaviano Fregoso, who were all called
upon to contribute to the amusements and pleasures
of the court.

Graver and more solid works were also produced
by leading scholars and humanists. Here during
many years Bembo pursued those studies of the
lingua volgare that were ultimately to find shape

in his famous 'Prose.' A portentous work in nine books, dedicated to Duchess Elisabetta, was Vincenzo Calmeta's contribution to the subject, and had the effect of again rousing the animosity of his friend Bembo. No theme was more frequently and hotly discussed at Urbino than this vexed question of the rival claims of Latin and Italian poetry. Bembo tells us how, one winter evening in 1502 four distinguished personages—Messer Ercole Strozzi, the Magnifico Giuliano de' Medici, Federico Fregoso, and his own brother, Carlo Bembo—met by the fireside in his father's house in Venice, and began a discussion on the subject, which was prolonged during three successive meetings. Messer Ercole, the talented Ferrarese poet, strongly advocated the superior claims of Latin verse, while Giuliano and Carlo Bembo, who represented his brother's views, defended the *lingua volgare*, and Fregoso brought his knowledge of Provençal and Sicilian dialects to bear upon the controversy, and suggested that Tuscan poets owed much to both those sources. At Urbino, however, the partisans of the *lingua volgare* were in the ascendant. Both Castiglione and Bembo, who wrote the most elegant Latin verse and prose of the day, were strong supporters of the vulgar tongue, and did much by their own works to form a national literature.

But there were plenty of minor points which afforded debateable ground for scholars who were interested in this new study. Bembo and Fregoso, in their anxiety to preserve the purity of the Tuscan tongue, defended the use of obsolete phrases ; while Castiglione and Canossa were all in favour of greater freedom, and could see no objection to the introduction of colloquial expressions in writing as well as in speaking. How far, again, the use of foreign words, of French and Spanish terms, could be permitted was another question which gave rise to much animated discussion, as we learn from the pages of the ' Cortegiano.'[1]

While these and similar intellectual themes supplied the courtiers of Urbino with material for endless arguments, Castiglione is careful to inform us that manly sports and knightly exercises were by no means neglected. In the early days of Guidobaldo's reign the young Duke excelled in these chivalrous amusements, and took great delight in riding, jousting, and all forms of sport. When Elisabetta came as a bride to Urbino in 1489, riding and hunting parties were constantly planned for her diversion. Every day the Duke and Duchess, accompanied by Madonna Emilia and Guidobaldo's unmarried sister Agnesina —the future mother of Vittoria Colonna—rode out to visit the churches and towns in the neighbourhood. Sometimes, especially when the Marquis Francesco or his brother Giovanni came to visit their sister, hunting-parties on a large scale took place, and the chase was extended to the parks of Fossombrone and Castel Durante. But now gout and general ill-health had so much weakened the Duke's limbs that he was often unable to walk or stand, and all the active sports in which he had formerly taken pleasure were reluctantly abandoned. Such, however, Castiglione tells us, was his greatness of soul, that he retained keen interest in watching others jousting and riding at the ring, and often looked on when the knights and pages were engaged in sports and feats of horsemanship, encouraging them by his presence, and showing his excellent judgment in these matters. Messer Baldassare

[1] Book i., 29, 30.

himself and his cousin Cesare Gonzaga, Gaspare
Pallavicino, and young Roberto da Bari, were all
experts at these exercises; while among the distinguished visitors at Urbino that year was Pietro
Monte, the Milanese condottiere who had been
Castiglione's own teacher at the court of Lodovico
Sforza, and who is praised by our author as 'the true
and only master in every branch of this art.'[1]   'And
thus both in jousts and tournaments, in riding and
handling arms of all kinds, as well as in games and
music—in fact, in all the exercises meet for noble
cavaliers, every one strove to prove himself worthy of
such noble fellowship.'

But since the Duke was compelled by his increasing
infirmities to retire to rest soon after supper, the
company generally met to spend the evenings in the
rooms of the Duchess, 'with whom,' Castiglione tells
us, 'was always to be found Madonna Emilia Pia,
who, being endowed with such quick intelligence and
judgment, seemed to be the mistress of all, and
inspired all present with her own wit and wisdom.'
Here cavaliers and ladies grouped themselves in a
circle, and sat down as far as possible in pairs, only
that the number of men was nearly always larger
than that of the women present on these occasions.
Each chose the place that seemed good to him,
or was his by chance, and the Duchess—or more
often, at her desire, Madonna Emilia — decided
how the evening was to be spent. Often it was
devoted to music and singing, 'pastimes most
fitting,' in the courtier's opinion, 'when ladies are
present.' String quartets and motets for different
instruments were performed, especially those of
Josquin de Près, the renowned Flemish composer,

---

[1] 'Cortegiano,' i. 25.

who, after spending some years in the service of Pope Sixtus IV. and Lorenzo de' Medici, was now the Duke of Ferrara's choir-master. Sometimes the Duchess herself or one of her ladies would sing Petrarch's verses to the lute, or else Josquin de Près' own setting of Virgil's lament of Dido, which was one of Elisabetta's favourite songs. Jacopo di Sansecondo would charm his listeners with the melodious strains of his viol ; or Morello, the aged lord of Ortona, would play the lute with his wonted skill. Then all of a sudden Barletta would strike up a merry tune on his instruments, and Madonna Margarita and Costanzo Fregoso would join hands and dance a stately Spanish *bassa* or sprightly French *roe garze*, to the delight of the assembled company. On winter nights the whole party often joined in these dances, and in January, 1505, Fra Serafino wrote that every evening cavaliers and ladies danced in the Sala Grande of the palace, to the music of four pipers from Ferrara. Dancing, we know, in Castiglione's opinion, was an accomplishment in which every courtier was bound to be proficient, even if he could not attain to the perfection of Messer Roberto da Bari, who had no rival in this art, and danced with such grace and enjoyment that he often allowed the cloak to fall from his shoulders and slippers drop off his feet, without ever pausing to pick them up.[1] At other times round games of different sorts, such as the Sienese *proposito*, when questions were passed round the circle, and forfeits paid for inappropriate answers ; or that of *invidia*, when a battledore was brought into use, and repartees were swiftly exchanged as the shuttlecock flew from one to the

---

[1] 'Cortegiano,' i. 27.

other.[1] Or else riddles were propounded and enigmas guessed, jests and merry anecdotes were told or witticisms passed round, and sharp retorts freely exchanged, between such lively speakers as Count Gaspare and Lady Emilia, who loved nothing better than a passage at arms with some quick - witted opponent. One favourite amusement, we learn from Castiglione, was that of choosing devices or mottoes for each member of the company. Another consisted in reciting impromptu verses and sonnets. Often, as Ariosto tells us, thoughts and feelings that could not be openly declared, found expression in these veiled forms, and by this means lovers revealed the secrets of their hearts to the unconscious objects of their adoration.[2] 'And in all these different modes of conversation,' Castiglione tells us, 'marvellous pleasure was taken, because, as I have already said, the house contained so many fine intellects.'

'Here, then,' in our courtier's words, 'sweet discourses and innocent jests were heard, and the faces of all present shone with mirth and gaiety, so that this house could indeed be called the very home of joy; nor do I believe that in any other place all the sweetness which flows from dear and cherished companionship was ever tasted as fully as it was here at that time. For, letting alone the honour it was, for each of us, to serve such a master as him of whom I have already spoken, there sprang up in the hearts of all a sense of supreme content each time we entered the presence of the Lady Duchess ; and it seemed as if this were a chain that held us all bound together in love, so that there was never greater union of will, or more cordial love between brothers, than that which reigned between us all. It was the same among the ladies, with whom there was the freest and most

---

[1] V. Cian, 'Motti inediti di M. Pietro Bembo,' 91.
[2] 'Orlando Furioso,' vii. 21.

innocent intercourse. Every one was free to speak, sit, joke, and laugh with whom he chose. But so great was the reverence paid to the wishes of the Duchess, that this same liberty became a check; nor was there anyone who did not count it the greatest pleasure he could have in the world to be able to please her, and the greatest pain to displease her. For this reason the most refined manners went hand in hand with the greatest liberty, and in her presence games and laughter were tempered, not only with the keenest wit, but with a grave and gracious majesty; because that greatness and modesty which marked all the acts, words, and movements of the Lady Duchess, whether she jested or laughed, were such, that even those who had never seen her before would have recognized her as an august lady. And thus she impressed herself upon those of us who were round about her, in such a way that we all seemed to conform to her quality and conduct, and every one tried to copy her example, and take, as it were, a lesson of beautiful manners from the presence of so rare and virtuous a lady.'[1]

Not only Castiglione, but Pietro Bembo, Filippo Beroaldo, and many of their correspondents, dwell on this atmosphere of freedom and easy familiarity which added so much to the happiness of life at Urbino, and speak of it as a thing without precedent among the courts of Europe at that time. So, from all parts of Italy, distinguished visitors came, attracted by the fame of Guidobaldo's court, to pay their respects to the Duke and Duchess and enjoy their hospitality. Whatever the rank and estate of the guest might be—whether, as Bembo remarks, he were of princely birth, or lowly origin—a Cardinal's brother like the Magnifico, or a poor scholar like himself, he was sure of a gracious welcome and of

[1] 'Cortegiano,' i. 4.

honourable entertainment. 'I came to Urbino,' he
wrote long afterwards, when the Duke and Duchess
were dead and all the actors in that stately pageant
had passed away—'I came to Urbino with only forty
ducats in my pocket, and there I stayed for six years.'
Merit was the only passport required of the stranger
who presented himself at the palace gates—*virtù*, as
the phrase ran—that is to say, excellence in one form
or another. 'I beg you to receive our friend Bembo
kindly,' wrote Madonna Emilia to Isabella d' Este,
when the Venetian scholar left Urbino, a few months
after this, to visit Mantua on his homeward journey,
' as his talents deserve, for truly he is a man worthy
to be held in high account.'[1]   At this particular
moment, when Castiglione came to Urbino, he found
many accomplished visitors assembled in the ducal
palace. 'This court,' wrote a Mantuan secretary
that September to his mistress, 'is full of talent just
now,' and among the poets who were present he
proceeds to name Vincenzo Calmeta and l' Unico
Aretino, whose brilliant improvisations delighted the
assembled company night after night.[2]

Another guest who is honoured with a place in the
'Cortegiano,' and whose jests and sallies frequently
provoked the laughter of the ducal circle, the Mantuan
buffoon Fra Serafino, was also at Urbino on this
occasion. Like the Aretine, this friar was one of the
Marchesa Isabella's prime favourites, and addressed
frequent letters in prose and rhyme to his mistress in
his absence, signing himself habitually, 'Your slave
and that of my Lady Duchess.' These effusions
abound in proofs of the strange licence that was
allowed to these buffoons, whose mad freaks afforded

[1] V. Cian in 'Giornale d. Lett. It.,' ix. 99.
[2] A. Luzio in 'Giornale d. Lett. It.,' iv. 382.

so much amusement to our illustrious ladies. Fra
Serafino tells Isabella that the letter which she sent
to him by Count Lodovico Canossa, filled him with
such transports of delight that he rushed into the
Duchess's bedroom, to the amazement of her waiting-
women, and danced and capered about madly, until
Elisabetta herself caught him by the hair and asked
what had happened.[1] In spite, however, of his vaunted
devotion to the Marchesana, Fra Serafino evidently
found Urbino a very pleasant sojourn ; and although
he returned to Mantua in October, by Christmas he
was back again, enjoying the flesh-pots of the ducal
court, and playing the fool for the benefit of knights
and ladies

There were other and more exalted personages
among the guests who spent that autumn at the court
of Urbino. Foremost among those who hastened to
rejoice with the Duke and Duchess, on their happy
restoration, was Guidobaldo's eldest sister, Giovanna
della Rovere, the widow of Pope Julius II.'s brother,
the late Prefect of Rome. The Lady Prefetessa, as
she was still called, arrived from the Papal court,
bringing her son Francesco, the Duke's adopted heir,
and her youthful daughter, Costanza, a girl of fifteen,
whom Castiglione describes as being as good and
gentle as she was fair to look upon. With them
came two other Princesses, the Prefetessa's elder
daughter Maria, the widow of Venanzio Varano, Lord
of Camerino, and her niece Felice della Rovere,
the beautiful and accomplished daughter of Pope
Julius II. Both had suffered from the cruelties of
Cesare Borgia, and had narrowly escaped with
their own lives. The poor young wife of Varano
had seen her husband murdered with his father

[1] V. Cian in ' Archivio storico Lombardo,' viii. 406.

by Cesare Borgia, when he seized the Rocca of Pergola, and had fled for shelter with her infant son Sigismondo to her uncle's court. Felice, while still a child, had been rescued by faithful servants, after her sister and brother-in-law had been murdered, and carried by sea to join her father in his diocese of Savona. Castiglione himself tells the story of the high-spirited girl's courage on that occasion, and how, when the Pope's galleys were seen in pursuit, she told her attendants that she would throw herself into the sea rather than fall alive into the hated Borgia's hands.[1] But now times were changed, and the Pope's daughter was held in high honour in Rome, both for her father's sake and her own charms. This fascinating lady, 'our own Madonna Felice,' as the author of the 'Cortegiano' calls her in one passage of his book, soon made herself very popular, not only in Rome, but among all the court circle at Urbino, and became one of Castiglione's best friends.

On September 14, a week only after Guidobaldo's triumphal entry, the Papal nuncio, the Archbishop of Ragusa, arrived from Rome, to present the standards of the Church and the bâton of Gonfaloniere to the Duke. His coming had been long expected, as we learn from Madonna Emilia's letters, and was the signal for great rejoicings. On the following Sunday high mass was celebrated in the Duomo before the whole court and chief citizens of Urbino. These insignia of office were solemnly blessed by the nuncio, who, after censing and sprinkling them with holy water, finally delivered them to the Duke. Guidobaldo received them, kneeling on the altar steps, and handed the bâton to his lieutenant and brother-in-law, Giovanni Gonzaga, and the banners to

[1] 'Cortegiano,' iii. 49.

Ottaviano Fregoso and Morello of Ortona, after which, writes the chronicler of Urbino, the Duke and the whole assembly returned to the palace amid the joyful shouts of the people and martial music of drums and trumpets.[1]

Three days later, on September 18, a still more imposing function took place in the Duomo. The Papal nuncio, sitting between the Duke and his nephew the Prefettino, before the altar, pronounced a Latin oration, setting forth the reasons which led the Duke to adopt his nephew as his successor, with the consent of the Pope and the Emperor Maximilian. The Papal bull was then read aloud, and Francesco Maria, standing on the altar steps with an illuminated missal open before him, at a miniature of the Blessed Sacrament, swore by the body of Christ to be loyal to His Holiness. After this, he received the oaths of fealty from Messer Battista Ceci, Gonfaloniere of Urbino, and the representatives of the other cities in the duchy, each of whom knelt in turn to do the young Prince homage.

When these stately ceremonies were over, and after much feasting and music the nuncio had departed, a humbler visitor entered the palace gates and craved audience of the Duchess. It was a young artist, the son of Giovanni Santi of honoured memory, the court painter and poet who had served Guidobaldo and his father faithfully and well for many a year, and who in his last days had been the object of the kind Duchess's tender anxiety. She had watched the orphan boy's career with affectionate interest, had given him his earliest commissions, and rejoiced to hear the high praise which his genius had won from that worthy master, Messer Pietro of Perugia. Her

[1] Cod. Vat. Urb., 904 ; Baldi, 'Vita di Guidobaldo,' ii. 173.

protégé had just finished an important altar-piece for the Franciscans of Città di Castello, and had proudly signed the picture with his name—Raphael of Urbino. Now the young painter came to ask for leave to go to Florence, that he might continue his studies there and see the wonderful cartoons that Leonardo and Michelangelo had designed for the decoration of the Council-hall. The result of this interview was that, on October 1, the Lady Prefetessa gave him a letter of introduction to Piero Soderini, the Gonfaloniere of Florence, and with this in his pocket, Raphael descended the steep hillside and set out on his journey.

Castiglione, whose fine taste in art was well known, no doubt saw the works which this native artist had already executed for the Duke and Duchess, the poetic little panel of the Dream of a Knight, the St. Michael which he had painted on the back of a draught-board, and the Madonna with the pure brow and heavenly smile, which hung in Elisabetta's chamber. He probably conversed with the young painter, whose romantic air and charming manners made him a favourite wherever he went, and thus in these early days, the foundations of that friendship were laid, to which the world, it may be, owes more than it has yet realized.

CHAPTER IX

1504–1505

Castiglione's correspondence with his mother—His private affairs—
Need of money—Prospects of his brother Jeronimo—Marriage
proposals — Visit to Ferrara — The Este Princes and their
court—Warlike designs of Pope Julius—Castiglione accom-
panies the Duke to Rome—Marriage of Francesco Maria and
Leonora Gonzaga—Felice della Rovere's wedding.

AMID the manifold distractions of his new life, Baldassare did not forget his home at Mantua. His letters
to his mother show the same deep interest and affectionate solicitude for every member of the family
which he had left behind. He begs to be informed
of the smallest events at home, and repeatedly pro-
fesses his anxiety to gratify his young brother Jeronimo's wishes and to be guided by Madonna Luigia
in every particular of business. He sends kind messages to his married sisters and their families, does
not forget to inquire after the health of his brother-in-
law, Messer Jacopo Boschetto, and never fails to send
his love and greetings to each one of them, and 'most
of all to Suor Laura,' the sister Anna for whom he
cherished so deep and enduring an affection. Com-
munications between Mantua and Urbino were frequent, owing to the close relationship of the Gonzagas
and Montefeltros, and the intimate friendship between
the Marchesana and the Duchess. Castiglione availed
himself of the messengers, who were constantly

journeying from one court to the other, to send home letters and parcels at every possible opportunity. Thus, early in October, when he had as yet hardly been a month in his new home, he dispatched a letter to his mother by Fra Serafino, and a fortnight later received two letters from her by Giovanni Suardo, which he immediately applied himself to answer.

Madonna Luigia, however, was not always easy to satisfy. After the habit of anxious mothers, she plied her absent son with perpetual questions as to his welfare, his doings and domestic matters, and complained if she did not receive a prompt reply.

'In one of your letters,' wrote her son on October 26, 'you say you are anxious to learn what reception I had from the Lady Duchess, and if I have hired a house or live in one belonging to the court, and what provision we make for our household, and if the scarcity is great, etc.—things which I had omitted to mention as unnecessary, being myself more in need of supplies than of counsel. But to take your questions in order : The Duchess received me and continues to treat me with far more kindness than I deserve. The house is one that has been rented by Messer Cesare, and he and I live here together very comfortably. The scarcity is great, and we have never received any more pay from the Duke, so our pockets are very light. However, we expect some every day, and are very well, thank God. As you see, I have not been at the trouble to answer every particular of Your Magnificence's inquiries, but only those which are most important. It is certainly true that I like to hear everything that goes on at home and wish our affairs were more prosperous. However, as long as we can keep out of debt let Fortune do her worst ! You must not take these things too much to heart, but try and remedy what you can, and let the rest go, as I do, with a gay heart ! . . . As to our affair of importance,

I am glad to hear Messer Francesco Pusterla is of this opinion, but wish he had told me more fully what I am to ask the Cardinal, and what my petition to the Pope is to contain, and would give me in writing the reasons why this should be done. For I am sure that some one else will start up and tell me that this thing cannot be done. However, if you will tell me M. Francesco's opinion on the subject, I will go at once to Ferrara, and will send immediately from there to tell you when to send me this letter, because, for my part, I do not mean to come to Mantua at present.'[1]

The affair of importance was plainly a request to the Pope for some benefice or office which Madonna Luigia wished to secure for her younger son, and which Baldassare thought he might obtain through Cardinal Ippolito d' Este, whom he had known intimately in his boyhood at the court of Milan, and with whom he always remained on friendly terms. For this object he was quite ready to take a journey to Ferrara, where he suggested that his brother's tutor, Falcone, might meet him with instructions from Madonna Luigia. But nothing on earth, he repeats, will induce him to come to Mantua and brave the displeasure of the Marquis. Accordingly he writes on November 2:

'Since Francesco [his servant] wishes to go to Mantua on account of his illness, I have settled to send him there and let Your Magnificence know that we are, thank God, safe and sound, as you will hear from his lips more fully. We get on happily here, but our pockets are still light; for we have not yet received a farthing, and expect our pay every day with great devotion. The Lady Duchess and Madonna Emilia are very well, and commend them-

---

[1] Serassi, i. 9.

selves to Your Magnificence, and so does Madonna Ginevra,[1] who pays me a thousand attentions every day. My dear Lord Duke is suffering from a quartan ague, which distresses us all. I send the enclosed letter to Carlo,[2] open. If you approve of it you can give it to him, and for the rest do as you like in the matter. Since time presses, I have decided not to wait any longer to arrange our important affair, because if I were to await the instructions and advice of which I wrote, the thing might drag on too long. So I have settled to go to Ferrara and there await Your Magnificence's instructions, and it would be well if Falcone could tell me your wishes more fully by word of mouth. In any case, I hope to be at Ferrara in a fortnight's time, and I hope you will arrange for me to find Falcone there ; and if I have not arrived, he can await me in the house of Messer Timoteo [Bendidei] or that of the Strozzi. I would not come to Mantua now for anything in the world. For the present I must be content to visit Your Magnificence by means of these letters, for I never think of Mantua without one of my hairs turning grey, and if you were not there, I should never think of the place at all. Francesco will tell you of our life here, which is certainly happy and tranquil, and I commend myself to you and all our family.'

Three weeks later Baldassare wrote again to his mother from Ferrara, where he had met Falcone, at the house of his kinsmen, the Strozzi, and discussed many things with his old friend. Madonna Luigia apparently was anxious that her son should come to Mantua, not only on his brother's business, but because she had fresh marriage proposals on his own

[1] Ginevra Rangone, wife of Giangirolamo da Correggio, and afterwards of Luigi Gonzaga.

[2] A dependent who wished to rent one of the houses at Casatico.

account to discuss with him. We do not learn from what quarter these proposals came, or whether it was the Marchesa who, as before, was anxious to find a good match for her favourite cavalier, and thus, it may be, obtain his return to court. But whoever was responsible for these suggestions, Baldassare would have none of them. His mind was made up on this point, and nothing would induce him either to come to Mantua or entertain these marriage proposals. He was perfectly happy in his present surroundings, and he had no wish to undertake new and grave responsibilities. So he wrote to his mother from Ferrara, firmly declining to enter on any negotiation which would compel him to leave the Duke of Urbino's service.

' Speaking as my conscience directs, I must say that, having so lately entered the service of these Princes, I should be very reluctant to leave them to come home, which it seems to me would be necessary. I should no longer be able to arrange anything for Jeronimo, whereas, if he really wishes to find a career, and if God grants His Holiness life and health, I may be able to help him. Besides, there is plenty of time, and I feel, perhaps presumptuously, that I need have no fear of failing to obtain a wife. And although this may be a good offer, none the less it is not so good that I might not easily find a better. Your Magnificence will understand what I mean, and I pray God to be my guide, that I may act for the best.' [1]

Unfortunately, the post which Castiglione had hoped to obtain for his brother was apparently not yet vacant, and his errand in this respect was doomed to failure. On December 3 he wrote again to his mother :

[1] Cod. Vat. Lat., 8210.

'In reply to the letter which Francesco brings me, I must tell you that by the grace of God we are all in good health, and are in no danger of suffering from exposure to the bad weather, being uncommonly well lodged, so that I listen to the rain that is falling now with great satisfaction. I have not yet said anything to the Most Reverend Lord Cardinal, but will be sure to speak to him on the subject and let you know his reply. I am only sorry to have had so little sense as to come here for a thing that cannot be done now ; however, I will find some explanation to give my Lord Duke. I hear that the illustrious Lord Marquis will be here to-morrow, and shall be glad of this opportunity to kiss his hand. . . . What I have to tell you now is that at this hour, which is eleven o'clock at night, this illustrious Lord Duke's life is despaired of, and the doctors let him eat whatever he fancies. A little while ago he asked for some cabbage, and was, I believe, allowed to have some, which must, I should think, help to hasten the accession of a new Duke.'

Ercole d' Este was, as Castiglione said, at the point of death, and intrigue was busy round his bedside in these last moments of his life. This did not prevent Baldassare from finding a cordial welcome at Ferrara, and spending a very pleasant time among his friends at the court, as he tells his mother in another letter, written on the eve of his departure, and dated December 9 :

'I write to Your Magnificence to fulfil my duty, as I shall probably be unable to find messengers for some time to come. I leave Ferrara to-morrow and return to Urbino, and shall travel by water as far as Ravenna. I have been most kindly treated by these illustrious Lords, not only by my friend the Most Reverend, but by all the others, and most of all by the most illustrious Lady,[1] who has shown me greater

---

[1] Lucrezia Borgia, wife of Alfonso d' Este.

honour and kindness than I deserve, and so have all
the other ladies, whether they belong to the court or
not. Many have asked after you—namely, Madonna
Laura Calcagnina, M. Barbara Torella Bentivoglio,[1]
M. Polissena of Bologna with the big voice, and
several others. For the rest I will only beg you to
keep well and be of good courage, as I am also. As
to my horses, I would sell them gladly, in the hope
of buying better ones. These affairs of the Church
still seem likely to give trouble, and may end in war;
and we others may have a chance of doing some
honourable deeds, especially now my Lord Duke is
ill, so that it will not do to be found unprepared. I
will give your messages at Urbino. Francesco can
stay with you as long as he likes, and you can keep
the least ill-looking of the beasts. I do not remind
you of the clothes for which I asked, feeling sure that
you will bear this in mind, knowing how much I need
them.'[2]

Hardly had Castiglione reached Urbino than he
received orders to accompany his lord the Duke to
Rome, and the next letter which he addressed to his
mother was written from the Eternal City.

All through that autumn the Pope had been
urging Guidobaldo to come to Rome and prepare for
a fresh campaign to recover the cities of Romagna
from the Venetians. The Duke pleaded ill-health as
an excuse for remaining at home, and on September 23
sent the popular Count Lodovico Canossa as his envoy
to the Vatican, to thank His Holiness for the honour
done him by the nuncio's mission to Urbino. Pope
Julius received the Count graciously, but when the
ambassador ventured to explain Guidobaldo's aversion to warlike measures, he broke into a furious

---

[1] Barbara Torelli, the wife of Ercole Bentivoglio, and afterwards
married to the unfortunate Ercole Strozzi.

[2] Serassi, i. 11.

passion, and denounced the Duke as a coward and a traitor.[1] In spite, however, of this violent language, the Pope had a sincere regard for Guidobaldo, and would not take any decisive measures without consulting him. At length, early in December, he sent a litter drawn by four magnificent white horses to Urbino, and ordered the Duke to come to Rome without further delay. Accordingly, on December 15 Guidobaldo started on his journey, to the grief of the Duchess and all the citizens, who, in the chronicler's words, were sorely displeased—'*malissimi contenti*'—at the loss of their beloved Prince. But a severe attack of gout delayed his progress and detained him at Narni for nine days. Castiglione and Cesare Gonzaga, with the chief part of his suite, were sent on to Rome, and arrived there on Christmas Eve, while the Duke and his nephew, the Prefettino, did not reach the city until January 3.

'Your Magnificence,' wrote Baldassare from Rome on January 5, 1505, 'will have heard of my sudden departure from Urbino by this time, through my servant Sebastiano, although, from what I hear, he did not start on his journey as soon as I had ordered him to do, which thing displeases me greatly. I must beg Your Magnificence to tell him from me, and for this once only, that when I give him an order, and he does not execute it with greater promptitude and diligence than he showed on this occasion in leaving Urbino, or the other day in taking the horse from Casatico to Forli, we shall agree very badly, and I must, in fact, dismiss him from my service, for, whatever happens, I am determined to be obeyed.'

Having relieved his feelings by this unusual display of severity, the writer resumed the tale of his travels,

[1] Giustiniani, 'Dispacci,' ii. 239.

Photo, Alinari.

POPE JULIUS II.

BY RAPHAEL (PITTI).

To face p. 116, Vol. I.

and told his mother of the Duke's illness, which had hindered his lord from entering Rome until after the New Year.

'So we have been some days alone here. His Excellency only reached the gates on the 3rd, and hoped his arrival was a secret ; but of course it soon became known, chiefly through the Lord Prefect, who arrived some time before. That evening both Princes slept at S. Maria del Popolo, where several Cardinals went out to visit them, and the next day they entered Rome in state. All the households of the Cardinals now in Rome, the Captain of the Papal Guard, and many other gentlemen, rode out to meet them. My Lord Duke's own gentlemen certainly did him honour, and were all mounted on fine horses and clad in suits of gold brocade. I myself wore one, which I procured at the Duke's expense. When we reached the Pope's palace, His Holiness received the Duke with great honour, and we all kissed his holy foot. He looks remarkably well, and is very gay and lively.'

The Venetian ambassador, who watched the splendid cavalcade pass through the Campo Fiore to the Vatican, was much impressed by the fine appearance of the Duke's suite and the honour paid to him by the Pope, who received him at the entrance of the palace, attended by all the Cardinals.[1] But the Master of the Ceremonies was struck by Guidobaldo's look of suffering, and noted that he was unable to walk alone and had to be supported by two servants.

In this first letter from Rome, Baldassare alludes to two important matters which concerned the ducal family. The one was the proposed marriage between Guidobaldo's nephew, Francesco Maria, and Elisabetta's niece, Leonora Gonzaga, which the Duchess

---

[1] Giustiniani, iii. 357 ; Burcardo, 'Diarii,' iv. 163.

was especially anxious to see arranged. The other was the Cardinalate which had long been the object of her brother Sigismondo's ambitions and intrigues. The fulfilment of these hopes, as Castiglione could not but feel, must prove advantageous to himself, and especially to Jeronimo's prospects.

'I have nothing to tell Your Magnificence,' he continues, 'regarding the things that concern Mantua. Neither the marriage nor our red hat are yet definitely arranged. But if the Duchess were to come here in person, I think that it would be less difficult, and we expect that she may have to come at any moment. God grant that she may succeed! It can only bring us good, and would benefit Jeronimo most of all, and I should like to feel that, once for all, his feet were planted firmly in the ground. I should also be very glad if you would let me know of any vacant office that you may hear of through friends, as, being here on the spot, I could obtain it without difficulty. I have nothing more to write to Your Magnificence saving that we are all well by God's grace, and, as usual, without a farthing in the world! I should much like to know how our affairs at home are prospering, but when you write be careful not to say anything that may not be seen by every one, unless the messenger is a tried one, as many letters are intercepted. I commend myself to Your Magnificence, and beg you to commend me to all our family, and tell M. Jacopo that his brother M. Galeazzo is well. We —that is to say, M. Cesare and I—are lodged here in St. Peter's, in the house of Cardinal d' Este. Our M. Cesare commends himself to you.[1]

'ROME, *January 5, 1505.*'

For some time the Duchess herself had wished to come to Rome, and there had been quite a flutter among her ladies at the prospect. But the Pope pleaded

[1] Serassi, i. 12.

poverty as an excuse for his reluctance to entertain guests that winter, and the plan was abandoned,
greatly to the displeasure of Madonna Emilia and her
companions, who poured scorn on the Pontiff's nig-
gardly habits. 'The Pope has given up all his old
liberality,' wrote the Venetian ambassador, ' and only
cares to save money. He sells every office, and will
not even pay his bills, if he can discharge them in any
other way. And I hear that he has already accumu-
lated 100,000 ducats since he took possession of the
Papal throne.'[1] He goes on to remark that Guidobaldo and his suite are lodged in the Cardinal of
Ferrara's house and expected to pay their own expenses
without even receiving a subsidy. This explains the
straits to which Castiglione and his comrades were
reduced, when he wrote that they had not a farthing
between them.

In spite of these drawbacks, our young courtier
found life in Rome very pleasant that winter. His
letters to his mother reflect the gay and varied scenes
among which he moved, the stately functions which
he attended, the friends who came and went on
missions to the Vatican. The Prefect's marriage
negotiations were briskly carried on, if the bestowal of
the red hat, from which Castiglione hoped so much
for his brother, was still delayed. Count Lodovico
Canossa was sent to Mantua with formal proposals
for Leonora's hand, and returned to Rome early
in February accompanied by Giovanni Gonzaga, so
that Castiglione and his mother were in constant
communication.

' As I know that you like to have letters from
me,' he wrote on January 22, ' I begin one, although

[1] Giustiniani, iii. 346.

I have no news of any description. We are all well, excepting Smeraldo, who has been indisposed lately, but I hope it will prove nothing serious. You will have heard most of the events that have been happening here from our Count Lodovico, so I need not describe them at length. Here in Rome we have had a bitterly cold wind for the last days. Before that it was so warm that the roses were in bloom and it might have been May. Many masks are being made in Rome. Princes, Cardinals, and prelates all intend to wear them; I expect it is the same in Mantua, or better still. For my part, I cannot say that these things give me much pleasure. We expect Count Lodovico's return with great impatience, and hopes of many good things; but I fear that he, too, has allowed himself to be detained by these pleasant festivities or by their prospect, and will forget to come on here. If it were of any use to desire things ardently, and to wish for what one has not got, I should have abundance of happiness. Above all, I am very impatient to get letters from home, for since I left Ferrara I have had none, not even an answer to the last one which I wrote from there. So I implore you to write to me about our private affairs, and beg our M. Tommaso and M. Francesco and M. Luigi Gonzaga to write to me and forgive my infinite neglect! For if I owed them some letters, now that I have kissed the Pope's foot, I am absolved from all guilt and obligation for past sins. Your Magnificence will commend me to all our friends, especially to Suor Laura and Jacopo Boschetto, and M. Cesare and I commend ourselves to you.'[1]

When he next wrote, the long-expected letters had arrived, and he did his best to gratify Madonna Luigia's reiterated prayer for news and explain his silence regarding public affairs.

[1] Serassi, i. 13.

'I have received two letters from Your Magnificence by our illustrious Lord Giovanni, and together with these the velvet, for which I thank you very much. I should like to send a long reply to your first letter, so as to please you ; but, to say the truth, these Roman affairs do not belong to our corner of the world, and if I were to tell you what these prelates, Bishops, and Cardinals say and do, I think it would give you little pleasure, as you do not know them personally. It is true that here in Rome one hears news from France, Spain, and all parts of the world ; but these things, I feel, do not concern us, and as for those which concern my Lord Duke, I am reluctant to mention them, because letters often go wrong, and I would not for the world give him any reason great or small to be vexed with me. The favour which he enjoys with His Holiness is very great. The Pope is ready to grant him whatever he chooses to ask, without ceremony, and comes frequently to His Highness's rooms, has long talks with him, and is most friendly without any formality. I fear I cannot send you any fruit from the March this year, because we shall be in Rome till April. To our Suor Laura I hardly know what to send. If the messenger would or could carry it, I would send her the candle which the Pope gave me on the Feast of Our Lady at Candlemas, but I fear it would get broken on the way. I will have the Papal dispensation for your confessional made out and send it without delay. I have nothing more to say excepting that we are well and happy. From Count Lodovico's report, the plague does not appear to have done much harm. I should be glad if, when you write, you would tell me what you know, and how Carlo is, and what new dignity M. Amato of Ferrara has received from the new Duke. I do not write to M. Jacopo ; Your Magnificence will kindly commend me to him and Madonna Polissena and to all the rest.[1]

'*February 23, 1505.*'

[1] Serassi, i. 14.

Ten days later this good son took up his pen again, and sought to gratify his mother by telling her the latest news from Rome. This time, at least, he had more to tell. The funeral of Queen Isabella of Spain, the entry of the Polish ambassadors—above all, the marriage of the Prefect and Leonora Gonzaga—were naturally of deep interest to Madonna Luigia.

'Since you wish to hear what is happening in Rome, I must tell you that last Wednesday, February 26, the funeral of the great Queen of Spain, of blessed memory, was celebrated with much solemnity, after the Spanish rites, in the church of S. Jacopo of the Spaniards. All the Cardinals were present, clad in dark purple, which is their mourning garb ; all the Ambassadors and His Excellency my Lord Duke, wearing a black mantle down to the ground ; the most Illustrious Lord Prefect, in black velvet ; the Spanish Ambassador and all his household, clad in coarse black cloth. Nothing else worthy of note took place on this occasion. Yesterday being March 1, the Polish Ambassadors made their state entry, having come to pay homage to His Holiness. All the Cardinals' households and that of the Pope, as usual, rode out to meet them ; then the Captain of the Papal Guard, followed by the whole guard ; then the Illustrious Lord Prefect, whom we escorted.

'These Ambassadors were attended by fifty servants mounted on roan horses, and were nearly all clad in red like Germans, and all wore the same kind of hats with a jewelled plume and device in pearls. Some of them had the same device embroidered in pearls on one sleeve and stocking, and most of them wore silver chains. Before them rode two Turks on Arab horses, with Oriental turbans on their heads ; and behind four Tartars strangely attired, with bows and arrows and curious fur caps. All these six were slaves, who had been taken prisoners in battle. The Ambassadors are three in number, a Bishop, a

Captain, and a Chamberlain, and each is richly clad according to his office. Thus were they honourably escorted to the hostelry of Cappello. But His Holiness has not yet given them an audience.'

The Papal Master of Ceremonies, Burcardo, who dilates on the barbaric splendour of the Polish envoys, and the Venetian ambassador, Giustiniani, explain that this delay was caused by an attack of gout which gave the Pope acute pains in one knee and compelled him to remain in bed. There was some talk of putting off the Prefect's marriage until the following Sunday, but, as this would have been Passion Sunday, His Holiness refused to defer the ceremony, which took place in the Vatican on March 2, as Castiglione relates.

'To-day being Sunday, the happy marriage of our Illustrious Lord Prefect with the Lady Leonora was celebrated, to the great satisfaction of the friends of both parties. These nuptials took place in the palace, in the Hall of the Popes, in the presence of eighteen Cardinals—Recanati, Portugal, Naples, Sta. Prassede, S. Giorgio, Alessandria, Gurk, Grimani, Como, Volterra, Bologna, Fiesco, S. Pietro ad Vincula, Aragona, Medici, Sanseverino, Ascanio Sforza, Colonna—and many other prelates. The Marquis of Mantua's brief of procuration was recited, and the Illustrious Lord Giovanni made this contract on the part of the bride, and my Lord Duke and the Prefect on the other side. His Holiness could not be present, owing to a slight fit of gout.'[1]

Another marriage which closely concerned both the Pope and the Duke of Urbino, and had been publicly announced at the same time as the union of Francesco Maria and Leonora, was that of the Pontiff's

----

[1] Serassi, i. 15.

daughter, Felice della Rovere. This charming lady, who had already won all hearts at Urbino — 'our Madonna Felice,' as Castiglione calls her — was to wed Guidobaldo's nephew, Antonello di Sanseverino, the exiled Prince of Salerno. The Pope wrote to the King of Spain to demand the restitution of the Prince's estates in Calabria, and offered to endow his daughter with a large fortune, if the bridegroom would renounce his claims on the duchy of Urbino in favour of Francesco della Rovere. 'All these things,' remarked the Venetian envoy, 'indicate new dreams and ambitions on the Pope's part.' But in this case the fair lady herself resolutely opposed the marriage which had been arranged for her, and boldly declared that she would not become the wife of a landless and penniless Prince. In vain the Pope stormed and the Duke of Urbino entreated his lovely kinswoman to consent to a project eminently convenient to all parties ; Felice stood firm, and the marriage, as Madonna Emilia had prophesied, ended in smoke. 'We hear no more of the wedding which had been arranged for the Pope's daughter,' wrote Giustiniani[1] on the day of Francesco Maria's marriage. A year later this lady, who was to play an important part in the politics of the Holy See, became the bride of Giangiordano Orsini, the chief of this great Roman house.

[1] 'Dispacci,' iii. 438.

CHAPTER X

1505

MEANWHILE Castiglione was not forgetting to forward his brother Jeronimo's interests. With this end in view, he took care to pay assiduous court to the most powerful Cardinals at the Vatican. He was already intimate with several of these prelates, notably with three of the younger members of the Sacred College. There was Luigi of Aragon, a scion of the royal house of Naples, who bore a remarkable likeness to his grandfather, King Ferrante, and proudly styled himself ' illustrissimo,' as well as ' reverendissimo,' in token of his august lineage. After the death of his young wife, Battistina Cibo, within a year of her marriage, Luigi took orders and became a Cardinal before he was twenty. His close relationship with the Este princes, his scholarly tastes and love of music and travel, all endeared him to Castiglione, whom he had known from boyhood, and whom he frequently met at Mantua and Ferrara. There was also Giovanni de' Medici, the great Lorenzo's youngest

son, who had been made a Cardinal at twelve years
of age and inherited the cultured tastes of his
house. He, too, was on friendly terms with Guidobaldo and Elisabetta, while his brother Giuliano, who
spent this winter in Rome, was soon to become one
of Castiglione's dearest friends and companions at the
court of Urbino. And there was lastly the young
Cardinal Galeotto della Rovere, who had succeeded
to his uncle Pope Julius's titular church of S. Pietro
in Vincula, and was said to have more influence at
the Vatican than any other person. The son of
Lucchina della Rovere, the sister whom the fiery old
Pontiff really loved, and at whose funeral he was seen
to shed tears, Galeotto is described by Marco Dandolo
' as the apple of the Pope's eye,' the one man who
knew how to soothe his uncle's violent moods by his
tact and gentleness.[1] At twenty-four he became in
turn Bishop of Lucca, Governor of Avignon, and
Cardinal, and was daily loaded with new honours and
benefices. But, as all contemporary writers agree,
he made a noble use of his wealth, and was already
renowned as the most generous patron of art and
learning in Rome. Cardinal de' Medici was deeply
attached to him, and his connexion with the ducal
family made him a frequent guest at Urbino, as well
as an intimate friend of the Duchess and Madonna
Emilia.

In Castiglione's letters to Mantua, we find constant
references to these three Cardinals, and if once
Jeronimo could come to Rome, his brother had little
doubt that with the help of these powerful friends he
would be able to obtain some lucrative post. Before
long too the Marquis of Mantua's brother, Sigismondo
Gonzaga, would, no doubt, receive the red hat that

[1] Sanuto, v. 668.

had so long dangled before his eyes, and was said to be the bait which had induced the Duke of Urbino to recognise Francesco Maria as his heir and give him Leonora Gonzaga in marriage. The prospect of seeing his mother's kinsman exalted to the Cardinalate, roused fresh hopes in Castiglione's breast, and he wrote to share his new plans with Madonna Luigia, on the day after the Prefect's marriage:

' As for Jeronimo's affairs, this is my plan. Since our Monsignore will now undoubtedly become a Cardinal, it will be necessary, or at least convenient, for His Highness to come to Rome. It would please me if Jeronimo came here in his service, since as yet he has obtained no benefices. The many promises which His Highness has made me in former days, and the loyalty of our house towards him and his family, convinces me that, whenever he has the chance, he will not fail to remember us. And if he should fail us, we are not so friendless, nor is our good fortune so entirely dead, that we may not still look for some good thing to come our way, especially now that offices with large salaries attached to them are being sold every day in Rome. Although we are short of money, we have some interest ; and if we had no other means of help, it would be no small thing to know the chief personages in the court of Rome, and enjoy the friendship of so many Lord Cardinals, all of which I can promise him. I further intend to get my illustrious lord to write the warmest letter possible to our Cardinal [when the hat is his !], so that between the favour with which His Highness regards our house and my Lord Duke's recommendation, I am certain Jeronimo will soon obtain a good and honourable post. Besides this, I shall not cease to exert any small influence that I may have on his behalf, and indeed, I am already enduring fatigue and toil, more in order to gain some promotion for him than for myself. For if by God's grace I can give myself up to a quiet life, I shall not be worse off, nor will any regard me as otherwise than an honourable man, seeing the life that I have led till now. So I hope to be able to effect this much, that through my exertions Jeronimo may attain through his own deeds to some worthy place ; and this does not seem to me a bad beginning, as things are. He need not take any further orders, nor deprive himself of liberty, nor sacrifice the half of that property to which he has succeeded, but can lead a free life in Rome, with good hope of future greatness, if, as I trust, his acts deserve it and Fortune proves kind. This is my advice. I hope that it agrees with your wishes and his own.'[1]

Both Madonna Luigia and Jeronimo, as might be expected, responded gratefully to Baldassare's suggestions, and the boy asked nothing better than to join his elder brother in Rome. 'Indeed, I think,' wrote Castiglione in another letter, 'that this ought to satisfy him fully ; and if he had nothing else in view, the prospect of holding office in this great court would be no small attraction. Then he who risks nothing gains nothing ; and the fact of being in Rome need not hinder his studies, for this is the fount of all learned men. . . .' For the present, however, all that Jeronimo himself could do was to visit Monsignore Sigismondo occasionally and remain in his company, which would not only have the good effect of interesting the future Cardinal in him, but would at the same time help the boy to put aside his own shyness and timidity. Then, as soon as ever the Pope's pleasure was announced and Sigismondo was created Cardinal, Baldassare promised to write to him on his brother's behalf and procure a letter of recom-

[1] Serassi, i. 17.

mendation from Guidobaldo. 'And I am certain,' he adds, 'that since the Duke has obtained this Cardinal's hat for him, he will not refuse to gratify him by taking an honourable youth into his service. But if you and the Magnifico Giovan Pietro think that this plan of mine ought to be made known to our most Illustrious and Excellent Lady and Mistress [the Marchioness Isabella], I should be well pleased, for in all ways Her Excellency is our pillar and support. But do just as you like about this.'

A rumour concerning Baldassare himself now reached Madonna Luigia's ears, which excited her keenest curiosity.

'As to what you say, of my probable journey to England,' her son wrote on March 2, 'I know nothing. My lord has not mentioned it to me, either with his own lips or through anyone else. All I know is that some one will have to go. Who it may be, I have not the least idea.'

The next day he is more explicit in his remarks upon the subject :

'As for my mission to England, all I know is that my Lord Duke must send a representative, and has, it appears, told some one that he is determined to send me. And when I consider the gentlemen of his household and their different offices, it is easy to see that the task is likely to be mine. The reason which renders this mission needful is the confirmation of the privileges of the Order of the Garter, an order something like that of St. Michel in France, of which His Majesty the King of England is the head. For this task it is necessary to send a man of birth who will be acceptable to His Majesty the King, and will be treated with much honour. It would take too long to describe all the formalities of the proceedings, as the investiture of this order entails much ceremony. So that if it should please His Excellency to choose me for this office, I could not refuse so honourable a task, and one which may also prove of great use to me, for I know I should go with the best and highest recommendations. So that I beg Your Magnificence to be content if this takes place ; for such things do not happen every day, and although the journey is rather long, it will be very pleasant. I beg of you not to mention this to any of our family or to others, because I should look very foolish if this were given out, and after all there should be nothing in it. Messer Gio. Pietro knows it already through M. Cesare's letters, but I do not think he will speak of it. If any one excepting M. Gio. Pietro mentions this to you, you can say that you know nothing of it and do not believe it, because I know it is that beast Messer Gian Lucido [the Mantuan agent in Rome] who has sent the news to Mantua in an evil hour, having heard it from a certain Bishop to whom the Duke had spoken. If you like to read Jeronimo that part of this letter relating to himself, in order to find out his wishes on the subject, I shall be very glad, but I do not wish him to see what I have said about England.

A fortnight later Baldassare's uncertainties were happily ended, and he wrote joyfully to tell his mother the good news :

'Our Lord Duke has at length told me that I shall do him the greatest pleasure if I will consent to go to England in his service. So I feel that it is impossible to refuse, and I hope to find great satisfaction in this mission—first of all in serving His Excellency, and secondly in seeing so large a tract of country, especially as we are sure to have an excellent journey, now the fine season is before us. I hope to travel in the company of Monsignor Gigli, a Florentine who holds a rich bishopric in England and is His Majesty's ambassador to His Holiness here in Rome, and is also one of my greatest friends. So I shall go with great honour on all sides, and hope to satisfy His Excellency my Lord Duke, which I desire above all things. A few days after Easter I will come to Mantua and spend eight or ten days with you, after which, if it pleases God, I will set out on my journey, and trust it will prove of advantage to you and me and all our friends. If you could send me the small sum of money of which I spoke, before I start, it would be a great kindness, as then I can procure a few necessary things.

'ROME, *March* 15, 1505.'

But many disappointments were to damp the young courtier's high hopes, and many long months were to pass away before he started on his journey or saw his mother's face again. That spring was rendered memorable by the unusual severity of the season. Easter fell early, and the weather was bitterly cold. Snow fell heavily at Urbino, and was twelve inches deep on April 7. Wheat rose to four florins a bushel, and ague and feverish colds were everywhere prevalent. Guidobaldo was laid up for several weeks with an acute attack of gout, and the Venetian envoy paid him repeated visits while he was in bed, trusting to him more than anyone else, to appease the Pope's anger. At Mantua, Castiglione's uncle, Gian Pietro, and his cousin Luigi, were both seriously ill, and he and his comrades in Rome did not altogether escape.

'I have received two of your letters at once,' he wrote to his mother on March 24, 'and am very glad to hear your cough is better, and our kinsfolk are well, or at least recovering. Here I have little to tell, excepting that the usual Lent ceremonies have been held. His Holiness attended the Holy Week offices with much devotion, and sang mass in St. Peter's,

as usual, on Easter Day. To-day mass was celebrated in the Papal chapel, and the golden rose
was presented to the Polish Ambassadors, who are
soon leaving Rome. They brought fine gifts to
the Holy Father—*i.e.*, three large and beautifully
worked silver bowls, made in Germany, and very well
gilded ; also three long mantles, one of white satin
or damask, lined with the finest sables, another of
crimson satin lined with ermine, the third of some
other colour lined with squirrel ; and with them about
150 sable-skins, so beautiful that the like have never
been seen in Italy. We are impatiently expecting the
settlement of our Mantuan affairs. Both the marriage
business and that of the Cardinal's hat are progressing
most happily. As to my mission to England, I think
you will have heard enough by the letters which I sent
by the horseman Zoppo. Since the Duke spoke to
me, I have heard no more, but expect my journey to
be put off for at least two months. But whether it
takes place then or later, Your Magnificence may be
sure that I will not set out on the journey without
coming to spend some days with you, for I really am
not so undutiful as you appear to think ! I will say no
more, but pray you to commend me to all my friends
and especially to Madonna Alda Boiarda [Isabella's
favourite maid of honour] who, I am delighted to
hear, has become one of our family.'[1]

In this last sentence we have probably an allusion
to some report regarding Madonna Alda's marriage ;
but although this brilliant and popular lady always
remained fast friends with Madonna Luigia and her
son, we hear no more of her contemplated union with
any of their family. All Baldassare's letters, at this
time, contain urgent requests for money, of which he
stood in great need, having been reduced to borrow
thirty ducats of his cousin Cesare to pay for the black

[1] Serassi, i. 19.

velvet suit and mantle which he wore at the Queen of
Spain's funeral.   But money was scarce at Mantua,
and first Giovanni Gonzaga's stud-groom, Evangelista,
then the Marquis's agent, Brognolo, then another
messenger, Alessandro Cattaneo, arrived without the
ducats that were so impatiently awaited, until at
length Baldassare declared that he would ask no more.
But he gives minute instructions about a pair of
hounds and a falcon, which he has asked a friend to
send to Mantua, and begs Jeronimo to watch over
them, until some way is found of bringing them to
Rome.   These dogs and falcon, he explains, are to
be a present to Cardinal de' Medici, the future Pope
Leo X., whose love of hunting was well known, and to
whom Castiglione expresses himself as deeply indebted.   'We are well here,' he adds, 'thank God,
and I am very sorry not to hear the same of our kinsfolk at Mantua. God send them better health!' And
when he wrote again, it was to express his relief at
learning that his uncle and Luigi were out of danger.

Meanwhile his departure for England, he explained,
was put off in order that he might attend a review
of the Papal troops on the piazza, which the Duke
was to hold, by the Holy Father's desire, on St. Peter's
Day.   There had been some idea that Castiglione
should be knighted by the Pope at Easter, but this
ceremony had been deferred.   'Still I think,' he
writes on April 23, 'this will take place before I
start on the journey.'   Here he breaks off hurriedly,
because some fools have come to interrupt him, and
adds a postscript, begging his mother to tell him if a
good harvest may be expected this year, and all that
is happening at home.

Five days later the embassy sent by the Doge and
Senate of Venice, at Guidobaldo's suggestion, to con-

clude an agreement with the Pope, entered Rome.
Throughout the past winter, whether sick or well, the
Duke had not ceased to plead the cause of Venice
with the irascible Pontiff.   At his entreaty the Doge
and Signory had agreed to evacuate Ravenna and the
whole of Romagna, excepting Faenza and Rimini, and
now sent ambassadors to lay their submission before
the Pope.   Bembo's father and the future Doge,
Andrea Gritti, were among the eight ambassadors
chosen for this delicate task, and Pietro Bembo
himself was one of the 200 members of the suite
who set out for Rome, as soon as the snows were
melted and the Apennines could be crossed in safety.
At Urbino the ambassadors were royally entertained
by the Duchess, in her lord's absence, and Bembo
once more enjoyed the company of Elisabetta
and Emilia Pia.   'Would to God,' he wrote from
Venice that March, ' would to God I were living in a
little shepherd's hut on the mountain-slopes looking
down on Urbino!'   And he prayed that the Fates
might grant him to see the sweet spot once more
before he died.'[1]   Now he left the Duchess, promising
to pay her a longer visit on his return, and went on to
Rome, where Castiglione and many other friends were
eagerly awaiting him.

About six o'clock on the evening of April 28, the
ambassadors of the Republic entered the city by the
Porta S. Pietro. The highest honours, as the Venetians
were proud to record, were paid them by the Sacred
College on this occasion. The officers of the Pope's
household and the servants of all the Cardinals rode
out to meet them at the gates, followed by the French,
Polish, Florentine, Ferrarese, Bolognese, and Rhodian
ambassadors, who offered their congratulations in a

[1] 'Lettere,' iv. 30, 38.

Latin oration, to which Bernardo Bembo replied also
in Latin, 'with great decorum and gravity.' Then the
Lord Prefect met them on the bridge of Sant' Angelo,
attended by 100 horsemen and 300 foot-soldiers, and
received the ambassadors in the Pope's name with
every sign of reverence. He was followed by the
gentlemen of the Duke of Urbino's suite, led by
Cesare Gonzaga and Castiglione, 'noble personages
mounted on superb horses,' who saluted the ambassadors in the name of their illustrious lord, he himself
being ill in bed. But the most memorable incident of
the reception was the unexpected appearance of Pope
Julius himself at a window that was suddenly opened
in the Castello Sant' Angelo. In his curiosity to witness the ambassadors' entry, His Holiness had hurried
across from the Vatican, accompanied by most of the
Cardinals, and presently looked out of the window
and with a smiling face gave his blessing to the
assembled multitude. Then the guns of Sant' Angelo
were fired and the procession went on its way towards
Monte Giordano, where the envoys were hospitably
received by their Orsini allies.[1]

On May 5 the ambassadors were received by the
Pope in full consistory at the Vatican. Hieronimo
Donato explained the object of their mission in a
most elegant and ornate Latin oration, after which
His Holiness replied in convenient terms, and Bernardo
Bembo was allowed the privilege of bearing the Holy
Father's train into the Camera de' Pappagalli. But
although the Pope spoke very pleasantly to these
grave Signors and was graciously pleased to admire
the magnificence of their robes and ornaments, he
firmly refused to issue a brief confirming the Republic
in the possession of Faenza and Rimini, and sent them

[1] Sanuto, vi. 162.

home much dissatisfied with the result of their mission. The Pope was evidently bent on recovering the whole of Romagna, and only awaited a favourable moment to break his pledges and make open war on the Republic. 'The Venetians wish to treat us as if we were merely their chaplains,' he exclaimed to Giustiniani, ' but that they shall never do ! It is not in our power to surrender the possessions of the Church. It is enough that I should pledge my word.'[1]

There was, however, one member of the Venetian embassy who thoroughly enjoyed his visit to Rome. After his long exile in Venice, Pietro Bembo was enchanted to find himself once more in the city for which his soul hungered and thirsted 'like another Tantalus.' He found many old friends there, and made new ones wherever he went. Cardinal Galeotto invited him to stay in his house, and treated him so courteously and kindly that he became his slave for life. He was present at the splendid banquet which Cardinal Grimani gave in honour of his countrymen, and revelled in the rich decorations and sumptuous fare set forth on this occasion. The halls were hung with blue velvet and gold brocade, and adorned with priceless antique marbles. Gilded stags, and boars' heads, bearing the lion of St. Mark on their horns, peacocks and pheasants of glittering plumage, were carried in on golden plate by pages in scarlet liveries, to the music of harps and lutes, of drums and trumpets, of tambourines and singing.[2] No wonder that, after this brief taste of Roman festivities, the young Venetian longed for another draught of those fresh and invigorating waters of Tiber, and wished himself back 'under the shadow of Cardinal Galeotto— the young and stately oak that has stuck its roots

[1] Giustiniani, iii. 408.　　　[2] Sanuto, vi. 175.

deep into that happy soil, and spreads fruit-laden
boughs towards the fostering sunshine of heaven.'
He had not left Rome a fortnight, when the death
of Ascanio Sforza, Lodovico Moro's brother, placed
the important office of Vice-Chancellor at the Pope's
disposal. Julius promptly conferred this post, together
with the bishopric of Cremona and the rich abbey of
Chiaravalle, which the late Cardinal had held, on his
fortunate nephew. ' Never again will I say with the
poets that Fortune is blind !' wrote Bembo from the
palace of Gubbio, where he was once more the guest
of the kind Duchess, on his homeward way, ' since she
has showered new and abundant gifts upon you, without waiting to be asked, and has hastened to meet you
with both hands full of precious things, as letters from
Rome have informed us, to the joy of this whole
court.'[1] Castiglione also rejoiced in the young Cardinal's good fortune, while he lamented the death of
an old and tried friend in Ascanio Sforza, whom he
had known in his boyhood at Milan.

' To-day,' he writes to his mother on June 6, ' the
only news I have to give you is the lamentable death
of Cardinal Ascanio, which has been universally
deplored by all men, great and small, because
to all alike he was a father. And indeed this
death has happened in an evil hour for Italy. May
God grant him peace ! The King of Portugal's
Ambassadors have arrived to make obeisance to the
Pope, in fine and gallant array, and have brought
these Cardinals many presents, chiefly of animals no
longer seen in Italy—parrots, leopards, monkeys of all
sorts, and many other things from his land. Our
review is to be held on St. Peter's Day, and then we
shall leave Rome, and I hope to visit Mantua on

[1] 'Lettere,' i. 17-19.

my way North. As soon as possible I will send a
messenger to fetch those dogs and falcons which you
say are ready. But if before then you see any safe way
of sending them, I should be very glad, especially if it
could be by Brognolo, whose coming we all expect
impatiently, and I most of all, because of the money
which I hope he will bring, as I have not received
it yet.'

In this letter Baldassare complained of a sudden
attack of fever which had fortunately yielded to
prompt treatment. When he writes again, a month
later, he pleads a return of the ailment as an excuse
for his delay in answering his mother's letters and
acknowledging the money which the Mantuan gentleman, Valenti, had at length brought him :

'The truth is that, just after Valenti arrived, I had
several fits of fever, which, thank God, have now
passed away. But suddenly one night I was seized
with a terrible pain in the foot, which I crushed at
Cesena, together with a contraction of nerves and
cruel spasms—the result, I believe, of some medicine
which I had taken. Many remedies were applied,
and I am well now, thank God, but this leg is not
cured yet. This has kept me several days in the
house, so that at least I have escaped the intense
heat from which we are now suffering. Here our
only news is that Monsignor S. Pietro ad Vincula has
been given the Chancellorship, which was Monsignor
Ascanio's, of happy memory, and brings in 12,000
ducats a year, so that this youth of twenty-five, finds
himself with an income of 40,000 ducats ! God
prosper him as he deserves ! Our parade, which was
to have been on St. Peter's Day, has been put off for
another eight or ten days. As soon as possible after
that I mean to go to the Baths near Siena to cure my
foot, which is not yet right. My visit to Mantua will

not be just yet, I fear, as we go to Urbino first,
and then I shall see my way better. But you must
not expect me until I tell you for certain, and I will
take care to let you know eight or ten days before my
arrival. We are all well now, which is saying a good
deal in Rome at this season, and most of all our
illustrious lord, who, contrary to his usual habit, is
in remarkably good health. Here we have received a
small part of our salary—that is to say, twenty-five
ducats, and shall need more than that to prepare for the
review, since we must spend freely if we are not to
disgrace ourselves. Your dispensation is drawn up
and signed. I will bring it with the other objects of
devotion for which you asked.[1]

'Rome, *July 3, 1505*.'

Three weeks later the much-talked-of parade was
finally held, apparently to Castiglione's entire satisfaction. On the 30th he wrote to his mother :

'We have at last had our review, which was really
a beautiful sight, and greatly praised by all who were
present. I exerted myself more than all the rest to
do honour to my dear lord, and also to myself. Now
I think that we shall start for Urbino in four days'
time, and expect my departure for England will take
place very soon, but will tell you in good time. For
the present I have told Valenti all I know about it, so
that he will inform you by word of mouth.'

The Pope was highly pleased, and entertained the
Duke of Urbino before his departure at dinner and
supper in the Vatican, and presented his nephew, the
Prefect, with two magnificently engraved dishes for
his bride. But Castiglione's pleasure in these events
was dimmed by the sad news of his friend Falcone's
death, which he received from Casatico that week.

[1] Serassi, i. 23.

Madonna Luigia, knowing the depth of her son's feeling for the young Mantuan scholar, sent the first intimation of his premature death to her nephew Cesare, begging him to break the news gently to Baldassare.   On August 2 Cesare replied to his aunt's letter in the following words:

'I have received a letter from V. M. in which you tell me of our dear Falcone's death.   This has caused me the utmost grief, because of his excellent parts and goodness and our intimate friendship, but more than all because M. Baldassare has lost in him so true and faithful a friend.   This alone would grieve me as much as anything that could happen now.   But since sooner or later we all have to tread the same path, let us make a virtue of necessity, and seek to endure these sorrows with courage and patience.   Therefore, knowing M. Baldassare to be well and strong at present, and endowed with these qualities, I did not think it necessary to employ any artifice in telling him the news, which naturally distressed him no less than you expected, because of the love that he bore to our poor friend.   But since he realizes what we must all feel in regard to those things, he has no need of teaching to enable him to bear his misfortune, and, as I think he is writing to you on the subject, I will say no more.   Only I will beg you to remember that we are all of good courage, and leading a joyous life here, and are trying to keep ourselves in good health, as we all are, thank God, at present.   To Your Magnificence I commend myself, and to M. Jeronimo, who will, I hope, not abandon the good path on which he had started with our poor friend, even though he has lost his guide.'

How deep and real Baldassare's sorrow was we learn from the following letter which he addressed to his mother two days before Cesare wrote:

' I can think of nothing but the death of poor
Falcone, which is always present to my mind. I
know not when I shall get over the sadness that
oppresses me, and feel that Fate has become my
enemy When I think how few friends in the world
I have left, and how I could always depend on this
poor fellow, and reflect how from boyhood we had
been brought up together, so that there was no one in
the world who knew my whole mind so entirely as he
did ; when I recall his excellencies, intelligence, and
all his rare qualities, and remember how he had
always been my companion in those toilsome studies,
of which the poor fellow was just beginning to reap
the fruit ; when I think how unexpectedly he has
been taken from me in the flower of his age, without
a word of farewell, which will, I know, have grieved
him more than death itself—when I remember all
these things, I feel that I have good reason to complain, because I am sure and certain that this is a
loss from which I can never recover. God knows, I
thought of obtaining some good post for him, no less
than for my brother, feeling that his long and loving
service deserved this. But Fortune has not suffered
me to reward him with aught but my tears, which
I would at least have liked to shed over his
grave. God send him such peace and blessedness
as I should seek for my own spirit, whenever it
pleases Him to deliver me from this evil world. I
can say no more. But I beg you kindly to let me
have some particulars of his end : if he died in a good
frame of mind, and how he arranged the affairs of his
soul and the rest, and where he is buried, because I
am very anxious to know these things. Besides this,
I hope that Jeronimo, out of regard for the debt that
he owes to Falcone's memory, will take the trouble to
collect all his writings, and will not allow them to
pass into any other hands, but will keep them safely
until I come. For if his death is an irredeemable
loss, at least let us not allow those things which

remain to perish with him. I will say no more, but commend myself ever to you and M. Jacopo, Madonna Polissena, and all the others; most of all to Jeronimo, who must not cease to navigate his bark, although he has lost a safe and trusted pilot.'[1]

If ever a man had a genius for friendship, it was Castiglione. No one loved his friends more tenderly, or clung to their memories with greater faithfulness. He sorrowed over his brother's tutor as he sorrowed fifteen years later over Raphael, and treasured the fragments which Falcone left behind him as carefully as every sketch by the great master's hand. Many years afterwards, a drama written by Falcone was performed at Mantua in honour of Castiglione's wedding, and, thanks to this loyal friend, the young poet's name was honoured in his native city long after his death. Nor was this touching letter the only tribute which Castiglione paid to his friend. The most beautiful and spontaneous of all his Latin poems, the elegy of 'Alcon,' was written in memory of Falcone. Since in these verses he alludes to his brother Jeronimo's untimely end, an event which took place in the summer of 1506, it is clear that Castiglione's poem was not written for more than a year after his friend's death, probably during his journey to England. But whenever these fine hexameters were composed, they were inspired by genuine love and sorrow—a love and sorrow that everywhere breaks through the thin disguise of pastoral romance and mythological fable in which, after the fashion of the day, he chose to clothe his thoughts.

Alcon, dead Alcon, is the theme of his song—Alcon, the beloved youth, whose song charmed the

Fauns and Dryads of the woods, whose death the shepherds lament to-day:

' Alcon, darling of Apollo and the Muses; Alcon, half of my soul, more than half of my heart, what God, what cruel fate, has torn thee from my side? With thee the happiness of the fields, all our love and joy, have passed away. The foliage of the trees withers, the forest loses its pride and denies the shepherds its shade, the meadows lose their charm, the grass dies, the fountains cease to flow, and the rivers are dried up. The soil is no longer fertile, and the flock wanders without a shepherd. Alas! unhappy boy, torn from us by cruel Fate! Never again shall I see thee wrestle with thy comrades or bear off the victory with winged shaft and spear, while the shepherds stand around; never again shall I fly with thee from the sun's glare on the long summer days to rest in the shade; no more shall thy pipe soften the stony rocks and thy tuneful song resound through the shady vale. . . . For we lived together from our tenderest years, and shared the heat of the day and the cold of winter nights, and reared our flocks by our common labour. My fields were thine; we lived one and the same life. Why, then, art thou taken while I am left? Alas! in an evil hour the gods led me from my native land! My hands were not allowed to close thy dying eyes; my lips were not able to kiss thy cold brow.'

Here the poet turns to his brother, and envies him for having been present at Alcon's death-bed, for having heard his last words and received his dying breath; aye, more fortunate still, in that he has followed him so soon to that silent land, where they wander hand-in-hand through the Elysian shades, enjoying sweet converse together, while he is left alone to mourn his lost friend. Fondly he recalls the dreams he once cherished of bringing Alcon to the famous shore, dear to the gods of old, where the temples of Latium rise on the banks of Tiber, and in his sleep he seems to see once more the face and hear again the voice of his beloved. But then he wakes, and knows it is all a dream. For his comfort he will raise a tomb to Alcon's shade by the winding Anio, and call youths to scatter fragrant flowers on the grassy mound—narcissus and roses and fair purple hyacinths, ivy and laurel—not forgetting cassia, cinnamon, and balsam, to fill the gentle breeze with delicious scents. Here the woodland nymphs will bring violets woven with amaranths, and strew flowers over his grave, and inscribe the stone with this lamentable song :

'We loved Alcon greatly, and he was worthy of our love, and worthy, too, of the honour we pay him ; and now that unkind Fate has torn him from us, the stony rocks weep over him. For day is turned into night, light to darkness, and sweet to bitter.'

Two things strike us when we read Castiglione's poetic lament over his dead friend. Virgil has throughout been his model, the bard whom Mantua had never ceased to honour, whose bust still looked down on the market square of his native city, and to whom Isabella d' Este was even then seeking to raise a more worthy monument. The metre of Baldassare's elegy is Virgilian ; the metaphors are borrowed from the 'Georgics' and the 'Bucolics'; the lament over Alcon recalls the wail of Mopsus for Daphnis, the fairest shepherd of the woods. The very name of Alcon, which Castiglione adopted from its similarity to the name of his lamented friend, is borrowed from the fifth eclogue. As in his pastorals Virgil openly adopted the characters and metaphors employed by

Theocritus, so Castiglione honestly tried to copy the Latin poet's example, and fashion his thoughts in the same mould. And as the Renaissance poet caught the notes of the Roman singer, so he in his turn found an imitator in an English bard of the seventeenth century. The form of Milton's 'Lycidas' was, it is plain, suggested by Castiglione's elegy of 'Alcon'; his sorrow for his friend's death found expression in the same pastoral strains. He too weeps over a gifted youth, linked to him by the closest ties of friendship, and cut off by an untimely end; he, too, fondly remembers the vanished hours of happy years spent together:

> ' For we were nursed upon the self-same hill,
> Fed the same flock by fountain, shade, and rill.'

The Englishman employs the same imagery as the Italian, and invokes the same gods—Apollo and Pales, Pan and the Dryads. He tells how the woods and desert-caves with all their echoes mourn, and calls on the nymphs and shepherds to bring their flowers— musk-rose and glowing violet, woodbine, amaranth, ' pansy freak'd with jet,'

> ' To strew the laureat herse where Lycid lies.'

It is interesting to note the succession of literary methods in these matters, and to trace the way in which the same ideas and metaphors are handed on by Greek, Latin, Italian, and English poets through different ages and nationalities. In this distinguished company our courtier is able to hold his own. Virgil's song may have a sweeter and more melodious sound; Milton's verse strikes a higher note; but it is Castiglione's pride to stand between the two, and to have left us a poem which can compare not unworthily with the strains of either bard.

CHAPTER XI

1505–1506

In the middle of August the Duke of Urbino finally
left Rome and returned to his own realm. But the
severe winter had produced a terrible famine in
Urbino, and this in turn had been followed by an
outbreak of the plague. 'As many as 300 died in
the city, more from hunger than disease,' writes the
diarist; 'corn rose to five and six ducats a bushel,
and every one left Urbino, which was quite deserted
till Christmas.' In May the Duchess moved to
Gubbio, and remained there with the court throughout the summer and autumn. This ancient city, on
the southern slopes of the Apennines, looking down
on the valley of the Tiber, had been a favourite
residence of Elisabetta from the day of her marriage.
The warm climate of this sheltered spot suited her
delicate health better than the more exposed situation
of Urbino, and it was Guidobaldo's delight to beautify
the palace which had been his birthplace. The noble
central court still retains its lofty columns and
graceful arches, and was probably the first work

designed by the architect Laurana for Duke Federico, whose name and arms adorn the doorways. Giovanni Santi praises the beauty of the site, and describes the palace as turned towards the south and western skies, with its back resting against the mountain-side, sheltered from rude Boreas, and commanding a view over the Tiber Valley, so fair and wide that it even surpasses the loveliness of Urbino.

'Cum si dolce veduta che Urbino excede e le sue dolce calle.'[1]

Guidobaldo proceeded to adorn the interior with elegant carved bas-reliefs and rich ceilings of gilded and painted wood, and a local artist—Antonio Maffei—decorated his study with exquisitely wrought *intarsia* representing books, musical instruments, military weapons, birds and flowers. Sixty years ago the inscription *G. Ubaldo Dux* and the badge and motto of the Garter were to be seen in this little room which rivalled Federico's cabinet at Urbino. But Time has dealt still more hardly with the ducal *corte* at Gubbio. In the last century it was stripped of all its rich decorations; the carved mantelpieces and priceless *intarsias* were put up to auction, and sold to the highest bidder; while the palace itself was turned into a silk manufactory. Nothing of the Duke's once splendid home now remains but the shell of the building and the fountain in the garden that was Elisabetta's especial delight.

It was here, in this magnificently furnished palace, which charmed the eyes of Isabella d' Este when she visited Gubbio eleven years before, that Castiglione and his comrades joined the Duchess on their return from Rome.

[1] 'Rime di Giovanni Santi.'

'By the grace of God,' he wrote to his mother on August 23, 'we have arrived safely and well at Eugubbio, where we have found our Lady Duchess also in good health. I do not know how long we shall stay here, as we may have to go to Fano on account of some events which are happening there.'

He goes on to tell her of the heavy expenses which he has incurred during the last few months, owing to the high price of corn and provisions, and confesses that he has been obliged to borrow 140 ducats in Rome, 55 of which must be repaid to an agent at Bologna by the end of September.

'I know,' he adds, 'that this part of my letter will not please you; but I was compelled to borrow this money, and am anxious to keep my credit in Rome, so that if I should suddenly require a larger sum I should be able to raise it without difficulty. So I pray you kindly to supply me with the needful sum by the time I name. I hear that many persons are still dying of the plague at Mantua, which seems to me very strange. God help them!'[1]

But neither anxieties about money, nor the ravages of the plague in other cities, nor even his grief over Falcone's death, prevented Baldassare from enjoying the next few weeks at Gubbio. The Duchess, as usual, was surrounded by a brilliant company, and the Duke's return became the signal for new festivities and amusements. Bembo, indeed, had been once more obliged to tear himself away from the pleasant society which he enjoyed so much; but his rival Vincenza Calmeta, l' Unico Aretino, Fra Serafino, Ottaviano and Federico Fregoso, were all there, and

[1] Serassi, i. 25.

the Duchess's brother, Giovanni Gonzaga, Cesare,
and Lodovico Pio of Carpi, arrived from Rome with
the Duke. On the same day that Castiglione wrote
to his mother, Serafino addressed an epistle in Latin
verse to the Marchesana Isabella, telling her that
l' Unico Aretino has just been reciting a *capitolo*
and sonnet of his own composition—'with what
charm I cannot tell you!'—in the presence of the
Lady Duchess, Madonna Emilia Pia, Messer Baldassare Castiglione, M. Cesare Gonzaga, the Fregoso
brothers, Lodovico Pio, Calmeta, Hieronimo Gallo,
and Giovanni Andrea Ruberto.[1]

Serafino proceeds to tell Isabella of his own visit
to Rome, and laments that he has left that glorious
city, but says that the Duchess is even greater and
dearer in his eyes than Rome, and that neither the
Eternal City nor heaven itself can tear him from her
side! Another visitor who came to Gubbio that
summer, although he is not mentioned by name in
Serafino's doggerel verses, was Isabella's chosen artist
and faithful servant, Lorenzo da Pavia. On July 8
this gifted organ-maker, who had known Castiglione
both at Milan and Mantua, arrived at the court
with letters from the Marchesa, and was graciously
welcomed by Elisabetta and her music-loving lord.
But in September Guidobaldo fell seriously ill, and
for a few days his life was in danger. Happily,
this time he recovered, and as soon as he was
fit to travel the court moved to Fossombrone,
the Forum Sempronii of the Romans, where Duke
Federico had built a fair villa in a sheltered valley,
watered by running streams and open to the sea-

---

[1] V. Cian, in 'Archivio st. Lombardo,' viii. 412.

breezes of the Adriatic. Castiglione himself now went to the Baths of S. Casciano, in Tuscany, and wrote the following letter to his mother on September 20 :

'As I have been absent from home so many days and months, and see no prospect of coming to see you at present, I have decided to send Francesco, who will tell you about my affairs better than I can do by letter. I know you are longing to hear from me, and he can bring me your letters For ever since I received one from you, together with another directed to M. Cesare, telling him of the death of poor Falcone, I have heard nothing. But this, I expect, has been owing to want of messengers. In this letter I need not say much, as Francesco will tell you all you want to know. Now I am at the Baths of S. Casciano for my foot, which was never properly cured. It is already very much better, and would have been quite cured if I had come here a little sooner ; but the cause of my delay was the grave and dangerous illness of the Lord Duke, who, how-ever, thank God, is now convalescent. But he gave us all a great fright, especially the poor Lady Duchess. God in His mercy would not allow so terrible a disaster ! I wrote to you the other day by M. Gio. Pietro's servant about the debt which, owing to the famine and other inevitable expenses, I incurred in Rome. Now I send my servant on the same errand, because the fifty-five ducats will be due at the end of this month, and I would not lose my credit in Rome for a thousand reasons, especially as I have managed to keep it till now. For if I required half a thousand ducats, I need only open my lips to have them ; and this is important if I am to effect anything for my brother as well as for myself. So I beg Your Magnificence to manage by some means to let me have this money as quickly as possible. I shall await Francesco at Fossombrone, and when he is back, if, as I trust God may grant, the Duke is out of danger

and there is no business of importance, I hope to
come to Mantua, if possible, for a fortnight; for I
wish above all else to see you and the other members
of our family.   Meanwhile you must try and keep
well, and I will do the same.   My journey to England,
as far as I can make out, is not to take place this
winter.'[1]

Fortunately, Castiglione found the Duke restored
to health on his return to Fossombrone.   The court
resumed its former gaiety, and new visitors arrived
to add lustre to the daily gatherings in Elisabetta's
rooms. In November Bembo arrived from Venice, on
a flying visit to the March, with another popular personage, whose musical talents and witty conversation
made him as great a favourite at Mantua and Urbino
as he had been at Milan—the sculptor Cristoforo
Romano.   Castiglione greeted him as an old friend,
and heard many interesting particulars regarding both
Milan and Mantua from his lips.   Now the sculptor
was on his way to Rome, and brought with him as a
present to the Duchess his beautiful portrait-medal
of the Marchesana Isabella, which excited as much
admiration at the court as it does in our own time.
Not a little mirth was caused on this occasion by a
trick which the Duchess played upon her adorer,
l' Unico Aretino.   At her suggestion Cristoforo
showed Accolti the medal which he had been desired
to give the poet, and told him that he could not
spare one for him, upon which the jealous Aretine
broke into bitter reproaches.   So violent was his
anger that some months later Isabella felt obliged to
write a letter to the sculptor, feigning the greatest
displeasure at his forgetfulness in obeying her orders,
and begged Cristoforo to show Accolti this note, 'in

order to keep the secret and save the Duchess's reputation.'[1]

By December most of the guests were gone; Bembo was back in Venice, and Cristoforo in Rome, where he gave Isabella's messages to the Holy Father, and told her how eagerly her presence was desired by Madonna Felice and the Cardinals. Guidobaldo, who remained at Fossombrone for the good of his health throughout the winter, now decided to send Castiglione to Mantua, on a secret mission to his brother-in-law, Francesco Gonzaga. He wished the Marquis to be informed of the Pope's designs against Venice, and of the more immediate attack upon Perugia and Bologna which His Holiness was meditating. No one seemed to him better fitted to discharge this delicate and important task than Francesco's own subject and loyal servant. Hitherto Castiglione had only acted as one of the gentlemen in attendance on his lord, whether in private or public, in the camp at Cesena and Forli, or at solemn functions of state in Rome and at Urbino. We have seen him successively in the part of student, soldier, and courtier. Now for the first time he entered on the diplomatic career in which many of the best years of his life were spent. The Duke had by this time known him long enough to realize how admirably fitted he was by nature and education for such a task. Not only was his presence handsome and dignified, his manners courtly and persuasive, but he possessed a rare tact and quick observation that made him invaluable in business transactions of a difficult and delicate nature. His fine scholarship and ready command of language were further qualifications of great im-

[1] A. Venturi, in 'Arte,' i. 151.

portance in these days, when Latin was the recognized means of diplomatic communication, and ambassadors were constantly required to deliver long and eloquent orations. But, above all, Castiglione, as the Duke knew well, was absolutely loyal and trustworthy, and he could place the most implicit confidence in him. Since his journey to England had been put off till the spring, and Castiglione was eager to see his mother, he accepted the task gladly, and set off before Christmas on this errand. But when he reached Ferrara his high hopes were suddenly dashed to the ground by a secret intimation which he received from one of his friends, not to proceed to Mantua, as the Marquis had given orders for his arrest. He at once sent a messenger to his mother, explaining his delay, and received a reply, telling him on no account to set foot in Mantua. The letter which he wrote to Luigia in answer shows how bitterly he felt this disappointment and how keenly he resented his old master's injustice:

'When I sent Alessandro to Mantua, I purposely endeavoured to conceal the fact that I was here on my Lord Duke's service, fearing that it might produce a bad impression to see his servant treated with such little regard. So this morning I rode out of Ferrara as if I were going to Mantua, and took shelter in a house two miles off, where I am in hiding, and only my own friends know that I am still here. Now that I have seen your short letter, merely saying that I must not come for all the world, I feel that I was well advised, since you are aware that I was sent here by the Duke, who is always very careful in the choice of his envoys, especially in these times, and when they are sent on such important missions. I am sorely perturbed at the thought of the grave and serious danger of the obstacle that blocks my way, although you do not clearly state what it is. All the same, I would not turn back, but have sent an urgent dispatch to the Lord Duke, begging him to let me know his pleasure, and have made up my mind to await his answer, and come to Mantua without fear of danger or respect of persons, if this seems best to him. The messenger cannot return for five or six days, so I am waiting here. My presence is hidden from most people, and only known to a few, chief among whom is my Lord Cardinal.[1]

'Just now I met some one who told me he had travelled from Mantua with a messenger who was sent by the Lord Marquis to arrest me in his name ; but Messer Cesare Gonzaga, the brother of M. Giulio, told him that I had already left Ferrara for Mantua, and repeated this so decidedly that the rider turned back on his authority. So I settled to ask you to consult M. Gio. Pietro on this subject ; for if the danger is not very clear and manifest, I will gladly come, and should like the Marquis to know that I am here. If I do not come, I know my Lord Duke will feel great indignation, and I should be very sorry if he should be annoyed, most of all on my account. For my own part, I would not hesitate to come, even without receiving the Duke's answer, because I know his mind, although I have had as yet no letters or orders from him. So that I trust you will take prompt action, for the thing is very serious, and may be attended with evil results—all the more that I really could not say why I am turning back, and every one here knows that I was coming as an ambassador. I beg you to send a messenger as soon as possible, and commend myself to you.

'FERRARA, 5 p.m., *December 24, 1505.*'[2]

---

[1] Ippolito d' Este.   [2] Serassi, i. 27.

Fortunately, Castiglione's doubts and difficulties were quickly settled by a message from the Duke, recalling him at once, and early in the New Year he set out on his journey southward. On January 5, 1506, he wrote as follows to his mother :

'To-day—Monday—I have received your letter by Carlo da Villanova, and the day after to-morrow at latest I return across the mountains. His Excellency my Lord Duke and my Lady Duchess have recalled me, although my lord writes that he should not dream of doing this because of the Marquis's objections, and would have been glad to see what might have happened ; but after hearing the warnings which I have received, he would not allow me to run any risks, as I am too dear in his eyes. So I will return to yonder place, where, if other things are lacking, at least I am sure of a welcome. I beg you to send me those things which I need so much by Brognolino or some other way. Jeronimo must certainly have a mule. I will endeavour to procure him one in our part of the world. I send you the Confessional by Francesco, who has begged me to let him go home on account of his mother's death, and hope you will listen to certain things which I have desired him to tell you, chiefly as to one M. Niccolò Frisio, who, I hear, is at Mantua. I very much hope you will be good to him, because he was exceedingly kind to me during my illness in Rome. I do not expect you to receive him with great ceremony, but only to treat him as well as you can, for I know that he loves me much. Madonna Barbara Torella, or Bentivoglia [wife of Ercole Bentivoglio, and afterwards of Ercole Strozzi], and her sister, Madonna Orsina, commend themselves to you, and also Madonna Simona Strozzi.[1] I have borrowed ten ducats from

---

[1] Simona degli Uberti, wife of Tito Strozzi's son Guido, and cousin of Luigia.

Messer Timoteo [Bendedei], and have told him that you will repay them.'

Once back at Fossombrone, Castiglione was received with marked favour by the Duke and Duchess, and consoled himself in the society of his friends for the annoyances which he had received elsewhere. Unfortunately, Francesco Gonzaga's displeasure had a baneful influence on his brother's prospects, and caused Madonna Luigia great distress. Baldassare did his best, like the good son that he was, to comfort and reassure his mother; but the task was not always easy. Then his sister Polissena's husband, Jacopo Boschetto, a gouty, querulous invalid, was always taking offence at some supposed affront or wrangling over his wife's portion with his mother-in-law.

'I have not yet answered your letters, because I have been always on the move, and Francesco found me at Sinigaglia. I was glad to see your statement of expenses, and one thing alone vexed me, which was that Your Magnificence should be worried. But we are all born into this world for trouble, and as I know, the thought that you are working for me lightens the burden greatly, so of this I will say no more. Some day I hope to rest, and you shall do the same. As for M. Jacopo, you must decide as you think best; and, indeed, there is nothing in the world I would not do to satisfy him. If he is not content with the interest we pay him, I will gladly sell any part of my estate that he wishes to buy, all the more because I am convinced that he thinks he is doing us a great favour in only asking eight per cent. from us; and I, on the contrary, feel sure this sum would not produce as much if it were put out at interest. For one thing, whoever takes over the mortgage will not complain all day as he does! I have written to him four or five times without getting

an answer, which is contrary to my habit. I know
not why I do this, but will write once more, and
after that never again. I am not writing to Jeronimo now, but will write to him by the muleteer.
The Cardinal has sent me word by Signor Giovanni
[Gonzaga] that he has finally decided not to take
Jeronimo into his service, for fear of annoying the
Marquis by favouring persons of whom he is not over-
fond, especially since I have incurred his displeasure
so lately. If I thought well to ask my Lord Duke,
or, better still, the Duchess, to speak to the Marquis
on the subject, he would be very glad; but I do not
deceive myself as to the true state of things, and
know that one lady alone has already done her best
for me. If I importunate the Duke and Duchess
again, it shall be for something more useful and
honourable for Jeronimo than this post, so do not
say a word of this to anyone, for good patrons will
not be lacking. I think my journey to England
will certainly take place in April, but do not speak
of it to many people, for fear some obstacle should
intervene and I should be held up to ridicule.

'FOSSOMBRONE, *February* 26, 1506.'[1]

The 'one lady' to whom Baldassare alludes in
this letter as having already exerted herself warmly
on his behalf was, of course, Elisabetta. The
Duchess had taken advantage of her brother Sigis-
mondo's recent elevation to the Cardinalate, through
Guidobaldo's influence, to ask Francesco's leave for
M. Baldassare to pay his respects to the Most
Reverend Monsignore. Early in February the new
Cardinal set out for Rome, laden with costly presents
from his fellow-citizens, and the Duchess sent a
letter to the Marquis by Isabella's secretary, Battista
Scalona, begging leave for Castiglione to meet Sigis-

[1] Cod. Vat. Lat., 8210.

mondo on his journey. The Marquis, however, vouchsafed no answer, and on February 6 Elisabetta renewed her request, saying that her lord had gone to Sinigaglia for a few days, and had desired her to write in his stead and beg him to grant M. Baldassare this favour. 'I pray Your Excellency to allow this,' she added, 'that so he and Monsignore may enjoy a few days together, to their mutual consolation and pleasure.' But the Marquis preserved a stony silence, and Baldassare wisely judged it best to take no further steps to conciliate him.[1]

At the end of February the court returned to Urbino. Guidobaldo, who had not been there since he left for Rome, more than a year before, received an enthusiastic welcome from his subjects, and carnival was celebrated with a gaiety unknown since the days before Cesare Borgia's invasion. The chief feature of the festivities was the performance of a pastoral play composed by Castiglione and Cesare Gonzaga, and recited by them in costume before the Lady Duchess and a brilliant company. In the following dedicatory epistle, addressed to Elisabetta by Cesare Gonzaga when this play of 'Tirsi' was printed during Castiglione's absence in Rome, the two friends are named as the joint authors of the piece :

'Since, last carnival, some pastoral verses were composed by the most noble cavalier Messer Baldassare Castiglione and myself, which, as Your Highness will remember, were pastorally recited in your presence; and as we seek no other reward for our small labours than to see them graciously acknowledged by Your Highness, it has seemed good to me to put

---

[1] Archivio Gonzaga, Carteggio di B. Castiglione.

them together and send them to you. We dedicate
them to you with the greatest pleasure, both because we know that no one will receive them more
kindly, and because they contain some mention of
yourself under the veil of allegory, although not, indeed, in those terms of infinite praise which you
deserve . . . But you will deign to look graciously
on our good intention, and remember that even the
gods are pleased with the honours paid them by
mortals.'[1]

But although Cesare certainly took part in the
representation, and probably helped his cousin with
his advice and suggestions, the composition was
chiefly, if not entirely, Castiglione's work, and we find
the poem described by Bembo in a letter to the
Duchess as ' Messer Baldassare's Eclogue.'[2]

These ' Stanze Pastorali ' were the first ambitious
effort of Castiglione's Muse in the *lingua volgare*,
whose claims Bembo and his companions defended
so resolutely. The *ottava rima* adopted by him on
this occasion, and the general style of the eclogue,
are plainly borrowed from Poliziano's ' Orfeo,' that
pastoral drama which had been first acted at the
court of Mantua, and remained a favourite model of
Renaissance poets. But the imagery and metaphors
introduced show once more how deeply he had
drunk from classical sources, and how familiar he was
with the works of Virgil and Horace, of Ovid and
Catullus. Petrarch's influence is also strongly felt,
while not a few passages bear a strong likeness to
Bembo's ' Asolani,' a book that was already popular at
the court of Urbino. To us the chief interest of the
poem consists in the allusions which it contains to
the different personages of the ducal court. The

---

[1] Serassi, ii. 237.   [2] ' Lettere,' iv. 36.

allegory, as usual in these palace representations, is
thinly veiled. The Duchess is the central figure of
the group—the milk-white Galatea, for whom the
shepherd Iola (Castiglione) pours forth his love and
pain in strains that melt the hard rocks and draw
the wild beasts from their lair—the goddess who has
her home on the winding banks of ' bel Metauro,'
and moves along these happy shores, attended by
lovely maidens, robed in white and garlanded with
flowers, singing and making music as they go. To
her all the shepherds of the country bring their
flocks and herds, singing of their love and lost freedom, and strewing flowers in her way. With them
come a troop of strangers from other lands, attracted
by the fame of her beauty and goodness. One there
is, famous above all others—a shepherd from the
shores of Adria, who for her sake would fain leave
his own land and come to dwell in this country, and
is heard singing softly ' Alma cortese.'[1] Next comes
another from the banks of Mincio, whose name is
honoured and beloved by every shepherd in yonder
land, and who has been crowned victor in every contest.[2] Here, too, we have the aged seer,[3] the Nestor of
the troop, with the laurel on his brow and Apollo's
lyre in his hands, whose counsel is precious to all his
comrades, attended by another youthful swain[4] who
has suffered cruelly at Love's hands and fills the air
with the sound of his complaints. Yet one more there
is, a wise and learned shepherd, skilled in all the arts,
whose praises are heard on every shore and by every

[1] Bembo, who had lately added a dedication to the Duchess to
his poem on his brother Carlo's death, beginning with these words.
[2] Count Lodovico Canossa, Castiglione's cousin.
[3] Morello da Ortona.
[4] Roberto da Bari.

fountain. He has come across the mountains from Etruria, and as he goes he sings a love-lorn lay:

'Se fusse il passo mio cosi veloce.'

From this description we recognize Giuliano de' Medici, the youngest and best of the great Lorenzo's sons. Born in 1479, and exiled from Florence with his brothers in 1494, he had found a refuge in Rome, and was always a welcome guest at the court of Urbino, where he probably spent this carnival. The Magnifico, as he was commonly called there, inherited his illustrious father's love of splendour and keen interest in letters, together with much of the charm which had made his uncle Giuliano so popular in Florence. Beneath his taste for fine clothes and luxurious surroundings, there was a kindliness and gentleness that endeared him to his companions, and more especially to Castiglione, who became one of his most intimate friends. His naturally dreamy and melancholy turn of mind made him take delight in poetry, and the line which is quoted here belongs to a sonnet preserved in the Biblioteca Nazionale at Florence.

Other well-known personages are also introduced —the rare viol-player, Jacopo di Sansecondo, called the 'Secondo,' but first in skill among all the musicians who pay homage to the goddess and her nymphs; the peerless lady, Emilia Pia, who never leaves her mistress's side, and charms the savage beasts with her gentle voice:

'Una fra tutte lor v' è dolce e pia
Ch' accanto della Dea sempre si vede.'

Last of all we have Guidobaldo himself, the *buon Pastore*, who reigns over these blessed regions, where under his paternal rule shepherds and sheep enjoy eternal peace and rest secure from the snares of cunning wolves. He is the good Duke, the Prince whose fame has gone out into all lands, glorious as the sun in its splendour, clement and just, wise, learned, and good. This, then, was the dramatic eclogue that was 'pastorally recited' in the halls of Urbino on the last day of carnival, 1506, in the presence of Elisabetta and her court. Castiglione himself and his cousin Cesare took the two chief parts of Iola and Dameta, and at the end a chorus of shepherds joined in singing the praises of the divine lady who had stooped from heaven to bless this land with her presence. A *moresca*, or morris-dance, 'the most beautiful,' we are told, 'that had ever been performed at Urbino,' concluded the entertainment, and nymphs, shepherds, cavaliers, and ladies, passed hand-in-hand into the banquet-hall, singing as they went. We can imagine the delight with which Castiglione's graceful verses were received, and the compliments and praises that were showered upon the author. The Duchess was graciously pleased to ask for a copy of the play, which she sent a few weeks later to Bembo at Venice. This copy, there can be little doubt, was the book of verses 'written in beautiful characters on parchment, with a dedicatory letter from Cesare Gonzaga, and bound in black velvet with wrought silver clasps,' which the Duchess preserved among her most precious treasures, and which her great-nephew, Guidobaldo II., presented long afterwards to Castiglione's grandson Cristoforo.[1]

[1] Beffa-Negrini, 415 ; Marliani, 330.

Photo, Alinari.

GIULIANO DE' MEDICI.

BY ALLORI, AFTER RAPHAEL (UFFIZI).

To face p. 162, Vol. I.

CHAPTER XII

1506–1507

WHEN the fêtes of this gay carnival were over, Baldassare found time to write to his mother again, and sent her a present of four bunches of figs by his muleteer. These figs, he explained, were to be divided between herself and his sisters, Polissena, Francesca, and Suor Laura.

'And since it is Lent I will confess my sin, which is that I lend these figs out at interest, and expect that you in return will send me some salt meats or cheese. Madonna Polissena will do the same, and Madonna Francesca might add some of her quince jelly or other preserved fruits. From Suor Laura I ask for nothing but prayers, especially now my expedition to England is to take place soon, if nothing, as I trust in God, should come to interfere with it this time. I should be very glad if you could send me the shears from Milan, and the chest which I ordered a thousand years ago from those carpenters in town. I should also like to have any canvas that

163

was left after making that old tent, as I want clothing for my horses. When I was at Ferrara I asked you for some black cloth for making a pair of hose, but you did not reply. I wish to have it now, but prefer white to black, and should like it to be very fine and sufficient to make me a pair, and would rather have too much stuff than too little. I do not like to write about my own affairs, as I see you are so fearful that you hardly dare speak of them. But I am anxious to know what is happening; if things have settled down, and if kinder words, or at least less unkind ones, are spoken of me. Directly after Easter I think the Lord Prefect will come to Mantua. Most of the Duke's servants will accompany him; but I shall not come, either then or later, until I can be quite sure of a better reception than I should have at present. Here, by the grace of God, we are all well and happy. The Lady Duchess is going to Rome, at any rate before Lent is over. I have no other news, but my servant, Il Rosso, will be able to tell you more by word of mouth. I hope that you will send me some of your good salt meats, for here they are much appreciated, especially by His Excellency our Lord, and I should be very glad for him to taste some of our own. In order to escape paying toll, you might get a pass for them in the name of the Marquis or Madonna, so that they should appear to be sent to the Duke—if, indeed, I am held worthy of so great a favour! Do not forget the money that I owe M. Timoteo. When our Monsignor of Mantua is here with us, I mean to thank him for his kind intention to take my brother into his household if it had been possible, and beg to be allowed to find him another patron, with a thousand fine words! Then when I go to Rome, as I must do before my journey to England, I am sure to be able to find a new patron. I will also contrive to see you, only you must on no account mention my expedition.

'URBINO, *March* 5, 1506.

'The Lady Duchess my mistress begs to be commended to you and to Mad. Polissena, and sends the enclosed for her *comatre* Mad. Francesca.'[1]

The precarious state of Guidobaldo's health led Elisabetta to abandon her intended visit to Rome, but towards the middle of April the young Prefect was sent to wait on the Pope in his uncle's stead. Castiglione accompanied him, together with several of his friends—Lodovico Canossa, Giuliano de' Medici, and Lodovico Pio. They were a joyous party and lodged in Canossa's house, and enjoyed the beauty of the spring-time, the sights of Rome, and the splendours of the Vatican to the full. Baldassare was treated with marked favour by the Pope and the ladies of the Rovere family. But the Marquis Francesco's suspicions followed him even in Rome, where a certain Augustinian friar, Girolamo Redini,[2] who was fond of meddling in politics, acted as a spy upon his actions and reported them to Mantua. On April 20 the Prefect and the gentlemen of his suite were present at an audience given by the Pope to the envoys of the Duke of Savoy. On this occasion Girolamo Eremita made good use of his eyes and ears, and the next day sent the Marquis the following letter containing the result of his observations :

'The coming of Baldassare Castiglione has, I find, nothing to do with his mission to England, which he tells me is not to take place for another month. I have not seen him again since the day after my arrival. Count Lodovico Canossa tells me that the Magnifico Giuliano de' Medici has taken him away from his house, and that he has not seen him since. But that is their usual way of talking ! I will spy

1 Cod. Vat. Lat., 8210. Appendix III.
2 'Isabella d' Este,' i. 125.

out their actions and let you know what his movements are.' And then, as if a qualm of conscience had suddenly seized him, he adds : ' It is true that I am sorry to be mixed up in this sort of business, in which one cannot speak well of every one, and in which one is obliged not to mention the names and actions of certain persons.'[1]

Castiglione and his friends could afford to laugh at the prying friar, but the sore rankled in the young man's breast, and he felt more convinced than ever that his lord's ears had been poisoned by malicious slanders. Unluckily, Madonna Luigia chose this moment to administer a rebuke to her son for his extravagant habits. In spite of her regard for the Duchess, she had never cordially approved of Baldassare's exchange of masters, and now she began to realize that the path he had chosen was not likely to lead to fortune. Money was scarce at Urbino, his salary was small and irregulary paid, and expenses were heavy. So the cautious mother took this opportunity of exhorting her son to greater prudence and more rigid economy. Baldassare not unnaturally resented this good advice, as we see from the following letter :

' I received the letter which you sent me by Il Rosso here in Rome, where I came on business ten days ago, and where I shall remain another four or five days, after which I hope to return to Urbino, and soon come to Lombardy on my way to England. I will not reply to all that you say, because I wrote fully the other day by Signor Giovanni's messenger. But in answer to your remark that it is sometimes necessary to use self-restraint, and not spend more than one has, I must say that I do not think I deserve this reproach. If you consider how many

---

[1] ' Archivio storico Italiano,' appendice, ii. 278.

servants and horses I have had to keep during the last two years, and where I reside, you will own that I have not been as extravagant as you suppose. If you consider what you spend a year in Mantua, where you do not have to buy bread, wine, or wood, nor yet corn for horses, and live in your own house, while I am deprived of all these advantages, you will see that I could hardly have spent less. Sometimes, indeed often, I have not known in the morning what I should have for supper at night, but am ready to bear anything gladly rather than lose the small reputation which I have acquired; not that I intend to play the part of a noble lord or fine gentleman, which I neither can nor wish to be. I do not deny that I might have practised a more strict economy in some things; none the less, there is no serious disorder in my affairs, and of this I will say no more now. . . . I think my coming will be very soon, but after the fine reception that I met with last time I do not intend to show so little regard for the Most Illustrious Lord Marquis of Mantua's wishes as to set foot in his territories. I think my best plan will be to come to Gazzolo,[1] where I would gladly meet you if you would consent to come there. Give me your advice on the subject and I will act upon it. I have no time to write to Madonna Francesca or M. Tommaso. Please kindly commend me to them, and thank them for their present, which was most welcome.

'Your obedient son,
'B. C.

'ROME, *April* 28, 1506.'[2]

A fortnight later Baldassare returned to Urbino with the young Prefect and his companions. They would have gladly remained another week to be present at the wedding of Francesco Maria's fair

---

[1] Bishop Lodovico's residence, near Casatico.
[2] Cod. Vat. Lat., 8210. Appendix IV.

cousin Felice, who, after refusing to wed the landless Prince of Salerno, now became the bride of Giangiordano, the strong-willed and eccentric chief of the Orsini house. But the Pope, fearing to recall the splendours of Lucrezia Borgia's wedding, would not allow any festivities to be held at his niece's marriage, which was celebrated, not in the Vatican, but in her brother Cardinal Galeotto della Rovere's palace of the Cancellaria. Full details of Giangiordano's strange proceedings on this occasion were duly reported to the court of Urbino, where Madonna Felice's marriage was a topic of absorbing interest.

Both the Pope's Master of Ceremonies, Paride de' Grassi, and Emilia Pia describe how the bridegroom kissed the blushing bride at the conclusion of the ceremony, much to her confusion and to the surprise of her kinsfolk, after which he insisted on walking through the streets to his house on Monte Giordano, amid a shower of confetti from the spectators at the windows. Here no preparations had been made for the bride's reception. The rooms were in disorder, and the supper was of the scantiest kind. Two shoulders of mutton, half a lamb, half a kid, one capon, and three bowls of blancmange, fragments of the dinner held at the Vice-Chancellor's palace, had been brought round, and lay heaped together in the same dish, without even a knife or fork, so that the guests had to help themselves with their fingers. Worse than all were the antics of the bridegroom. He put his hat on Felice's head as they walked through the streets, and kept one of his pages' hats on his own head during the meal, talking Spanish and French at random all the while.[1] How-

[1] Giustiniani, 'Dispacci,' iii. 439 ; Luzio e Renier, 'Mantova e Urbino,' 179.

ever, this marriage, which began in so inauspicious a manner, turned out very happily. Felice's good sense and cleverness prevailed, and, as the Pope had foreseen, the influence which she obtained over her strange husband proved no inconsiderable factor in Italian politics. Throughout the changes of the next twenty years she was loyal to her own family, and remained one of Castiglione's best friends to the end of her life.

On Baldassare's return to Urbino, preparations for his journey to England were pressed forward. The Duke was anxious to show his appreciation of the high honour paid him by King Henry VII., and took great pains in choosing suitable presents for his acceptance. Beside the customary gifts of valuable horses and dogs and falcons which his father, Duke Federico, and other Italian princes had sent to Edward IV. and Henry VII. on similar occasions, Guidobaldo determined to give the English monarch a present which should gratify his well-known interest in the art of Italy. This was a picture painted by one of the Duke's own subjects, that would give King Henry some idea of the perfection to which art had attained at Urbino. The subject of the picture was St. George, the patron saint of the order of the Garter, and the painter selected for this honourable task was Raphael of Urbino. Although for the last two years the young master's time had been chiefly spent in Florence, he still paid occasional visits to his home, and was at Urbino for some weeks during this spring. So in obedience to the Duke's orders—it may be at Castiglione's own suggestion—he painted the beautiful little panel of St. George riding full tilt at the dragon which now adorns the Hermitage at St. Petersburg. His father

had devoted several stanzas of his poem to the praise
of 'il gran Re Eduardo' and this illustrious order
worn first of all, according to him, by King Pepin
of France. The poet had in eloquent language
described the insignia of the Garter, and the device
inscribed in gold letters upon the blue ribbon : '*Possa
perir chi pensa altri che benè*'—'*Honi soit qui mal y
pense.*' Now his son placed the word *Honi* on the
Garter worn by the warrior saint, and his own name,
Raphello V., and delivered the panel to Castiglione's
keeping, to be presented by him to His Majesty of
England.

As Castiglione had told his mother, it was necessary
that he should be knighted before he set out on his
journey, since, in the quaint wording of the ancient
statutes of the Order of the Garter, the proctor or
deputy who was installed in place of the new member
'must be in degree at least a knight, ennobled with
arms and of unblamable conversation, incorruptible
fame, without any manner of reproach.' Accordingly,
the Duke invested Castiglione with the honour of
knighthood at Urbino, probably at the Easter festival
since in Cesare Gonzaga's dedicatory letter of the
eclogue the author is described as 'the Most Noble
Knight Baldassare Castiglione.' And the letters
addressed to him on his journey are inscribed with
the title *Eques.*

Baldassare's departure, however, was delayed for
some months, chiefly owing to the difficulties made by
Francesco Gonzaga, whom Guidobaldo had asked for a
horse of his famous Mantuan breed, as a present for
His Majesty of England. There can be no doubt
that Francesco's unwonted reluctance to oblige his
brother-in-law on this occasion arose from the spite
which he still cherished against Castiglione. Yet

Baldassare did his utmost to remove this antipathy. On May 19 he himself addressed a humble petition to the Marquis, asking for leave to pay his respects to His Excellency on the way to England, and assuring him that he was still his devoted servant, and that he hoped to live and die his subject. The concluding words of this letter show how deeply Castiglione felt the imputation of disloyalty under which he rested : ' God grant that one day Your Excellency may at least allow me to know the cause of my disgrace, and bring me face to face with those who have persuaded you that I am not your true servant, for then I should count myself to be most fortunate.'[1]

This letter Baldassare sent to his uncle, Gian Pietro, begging him to deliver it to the Marquis, while by the same messenger he wrote a note to his mother, informing her of the step that he had taken :

' Whatever answer I receive, good or bad, I hope to see you at Casatico, or, failing this, at Gazzolo. But as for making an excuse of the plague for not going to Mantua, that I think would be superfluous, all the more since the whole of Urbino knows that the Lord Marquis would not allow me to come to Mantua last time, and I expect this is also well known at Mantua. . . . I am preparing to start very soon, and will let you know my movements shortly. Meanwhile, if you can beg, borrow, or buy a good horse for my journey I shall be very grateful.

' URBINO, *May* 30, 1506.'[2]

At length the Marquis so far relented as to agree to let the Duke have the horse and falcons for which he had asked, and on July 4, we learn from the

---

[1] Contin, ' Lettere Diplomatiche,' p. 11.
[2] Cod. Vat. Lat., 8210.   Appendix V.

Urbino diarist,[1] 'Messer Francesco Ceci, a son of the Gonfaloniere of this city, and M. Giulio da Cagli, were sent by the Duke to England with M. Baldassare di Castiglione, to take presents of three horses to the King of England, who gave him the Garter last winter.' But since the Marquis vouchsafed no reply to Baldassare's request, the kind Duchess made a last attempt to soften his heart, and wrote to beg permission for Baldassare to visit Casatico and embrace his mother and brothers and sisters before he started on his long and perilous journey. This letter, couched in the most persuasive terms, was sent to Mantua on July 8 with another from the Duke, informing his brother-in-law of Messer Baldassare's departure, and begging that he might take the horse and falcons which Francesco had at length agreed to send to England.

' We thank you infinitely for your promised gifts, and feel sure they will redound to your honour and credit with His Majesty of England. Messer Baldassare will start on his journey from here to-morrow. Be so good as to send these things to him on his passage through your dominions, a road which he will gratefully take by your leave. You can then tell M. Baldassare if you have any business in those lands, and I have charged him to execute any orders that you may give him with the same faithfulness and diligence as our own.'[2]

But the Marquis still remained obdurate, and Castiglione was not allowed to visit Casatico. In his fit of bad temper he made difficulties about the horse, and told his brother-in-law that the charger in

---

[1] Cod. Vat. Urb., 904.
[2] Archivio Gonzaga, Carteggio di B. Castiglione.

question would be thrown away, since in England no one cared for big horses. Guidobaldo, in reply, expressed great surprise at this objection, and recalled the examples of his father, Duke Federico, of Ercole d' Este, and of King Ferdinand, who had all sent horses of this size to the King of England, on being invested with the Order of the Garter, because they understood them to be more acceptable than any other present. 'So that, having considered the subject long and seriously, and having heard from England that, among other gifts, a big horse would be especially acceptable to His Majesty, we have decided to send this one.'

This letter was written on August 4, before Castiglione left Gazzolo. But his troubles with the Mantuan charger were not yet at an end. When he reached Milan, ten days later, he found that the horse which the Marquis had finally sent in reply to Guidobaldo's renewed request was nearly blind. In his perplexity at this vexatious discovery, he confided his difficulties to the Marquis's old Master of the Horse, Niccolò Christo, whom he met in Milan, and who immediately pronounced the horse in question quite unfit for a present to a royal sovereign, and promised to take it back to Mantua. Soon after his return on September 8, the honest servant addressed the following letter to his master, in which he gives a full explanation of this unfortunate accident, which was probably the work of some of Baldassare's enemies at court :

'When I was at Milan with Signor Alberto di Carpi, Messer Baldassare di Castiglione arrived with two horses on his way to England. One of these belonged to Your Excellency's breed, but had a serious infirmity, being blind of one eye and seeing little with the other. This being the case, he naturally felt it would not do Your Excellency honour to take anything to England but what was exquisite and perfect of its kind. And as I had to return to Mantua, he begged me to take it back, which I am about to do. I left Milan last Thursday, and reached Casatico on Sunday evening. There I left the horse in good hands. I spoke to the Most Reverend Lord Cardinal, who replied that he would not meddle in this affair, so I write to ask for Your Excellency's orders, and will do what you will. The horse is in the stable of Madonna Luigia di Castiglione, who will do as Your Excellency commands.'

The Marquis was at Perugia with the Pope's forces when his old servant's letter reached him, and sent a brief note to his brother, Cardinal Sigismondo, whom he had left in charge at Mantua, begging him to attend to the matter. ' I beg your Highness,' he wrote on September 18, 'to send to Casatico for the horse which Baldassare di Castiglione has sent back, and see that it is placed in a stable and properly tended.'[1]

In a letter to his mother from Milan, Baldassare thus alludes to this vexatious incident:

' I do not know if this will reach you before our good friend M. Niccolò's arrival. He is bringing back the horse which has been, and is still, the cause of infinite trouble. However, I have endured so many worse things that I must bear this, too. I entreat you not to vex yourself, as perhaps even this mischance will be for the best in the end—at least, so I try to persuade myself. I beg you to see that the greatest care is taken of the horse, saddle, and all his trappings, headpiece and clothing, and especially that the iron-

---

[1] Archivio Gonzaga, Carteggio di B. Castiglione.

work of the saddle is not allowed to get rusty, so that the horse be restored exactly as we received it, excepting, it may be, in better condition ! . . . M. Niccolò,' he adds, 'will tell you more about this blessed horse—would to God I had never seen it !— and you can put implicit faith in him. I should like the groom to return as soon as possible, and for this reason you might lend him a horse, which I will have sent back by Crema. Please do not fail to tell me if you hear what the Marquis says on the subject.'[1]

But Baldassare had heavier cares than this on his mind when he started on the mission to which he had looked forward with such high hopes. Early in August, probably while he was still at Gazzolo, his brother Jeronimo died. The death of this poor lad, following so quickly on that of his beloved Falcone, was a great shock. Baldassare, as we have seen from his letters, was full of hopes for Jeronimo's future, and had through his powerful friends in Rome already secured him one lucrative benefice, the Priorate of Marcaria, close to Casatico. A letter addressed to Castiglione by Cardinal Gonzaga shows how general was the sympathy felt for him and his widowed mother in this fresh bereavement :

'*Magnifice Vir, Amice noster charissime*,—We are deeply grieved to hear from your letter of the sudden and melancholy death of your brother Jeronimo, whom we loved for many reasons. The great loss which both you and your mother have sustained must cause you profound sorrow. But knowing as we do that both of you are full of wisdom, and seeing that for death there is no remedy, we exhort you to be patient, remembering that we must all of us journey by the same road. It is needless for you to commend your

[1] Cod. Vat. Lat., 8210.

mother to me, because we have that honour and
reverence for her which a matron, endowed as she is
with every virtue, deserves.   Go happily on your
journey, which, we pray God, may prosper according
to your wishes.   Your mother will be ever in our
thoughts, and so will everything else that belongs to
you.   We beg you to condole with her in our name,
and tell her that we will do all that is in our power
to help both her and you.   *Et bene valete.*

'Ex Marengo, *August,* 1506.'[1]

The Cardinal, we see from this letter, entertained
the kindliest feelings for Baldassare and his mother,
although he prudently shrank from meddling in his
brother's quarrels.

After waiting at Milan some days longer in hopes
of receiving important dispatches from Urbino,
Castiglione decided to continue his journey on September 4.   The evening before his departure he
wrote two letters to his mother, and sent them by
Scaramella.   In the first, after repeating his orders
regarding the Marquis's horse, he added :

'I hope to start to-morrow, and trust I may have
a good journey.   I leave Francesco here to await the
return of the groom who is taking the horse back,
and the two will join me together, and will, I hope,
bring me letters from you and those from Urbino
which I have been anxiously expecting.   For the
future, please send all letters to the house of the
Vismari or of Monsignor della Torre, and they will be
forwarded to me.   I send Madonna Francesca a fan,
which I did not let her have before because I was so
muddle-headed as to fancy it was meant as a remembrance for you, but which I find M. Margherita
meant for her.   By the by, when M. Francesca

[1] Cod. Vat. Lat., 8211.

writes to her again, I hope she will address her letter
"*Alla Signora mia onoranda*," not "*majora mia
onoranda.*" This, you may say, is a trifling error;
but I should prefer to see it corrected. The fan
seems to me very beautiful, although I do not think
there will be much use for it this season, as the
mosquitoes are not very troublesome. I should like
the enclosed letters for Urbino to be sent by some
trusted messenger—not by post, but by some safe
channel, for the love of God! One of the Cardinal's
servants would do well, if he has not yet started.
Post-scripta: I have taken the liberty of opening the
letter which M. Francesca wrote to Sig. Margherita,
and see that she did not understand what I said,
which was that M. Margherita sent her this fan as a
present, and also these veils, for which I paid nothing,
and am now sending.'

In a second letter, written a few hours later, he
acknowledged the receipt of one of August 27 from
Madonna Luigia, informing him of the death of his
sister Polissena's poor little boy, who had, it appears,
been ill for some time :

'It seems indeed as if God had visited us very
often of late. I am deeply grieved for M. Jacopo
and M. Polissena, who are, I am sure, sorely distracted. I send by Niccolò the mourning veils for
which you asked, and the fan which the Illustrious
Lady Margherita Sanseverina sends you to give
M. Francesca, having heard that I was going to
send her one. It would be well for her to write and
thank her. I am sorry M. Tommaso is ill. I will
say no more for the present, but only beg you
to try and keep well and of good courage, for
there is nothing I desire more earnestly than this.
Messer Niccolò will supply all my omissions by word
of mouth.

'MILAN, *September 3*, 1506.'[1]

---

[1] Cod. Vat. Lat., 8210.   Appendix VI., VII.

Castiglione's concern for his sorrowing mother, whose tears he was not allowed to dry, is evident from the letter which he addressed to her on September 20 from Lyons:

'I know not when this letter will reach Your Magnificence, but I write to thank you for yours which I received from Francesco, who joined me here in Lyons, where I arrived safely and well, thank God, and am spending four days to rest the horses, which had suffered a little from the journey across the mountains. To-morrow, if it pleases God, I shall set out again on our journey. I am very glad to hear that M. Tommaso has recovered, but very sorry for M. Jacopo and M. Polissena. They, too, must bear these inevitable troubles with patience. I know not what comfort to give you as to the things which have happened at home, except to beg you not to distress yourself; for if Fortune is as changeable as men say, surely we may look for some prosperity before long. I commend myself with all my heart to you, and so do my companions, and I beg you to try and keep well and commend me to all our family, most of all to Suor Laura.'[1]

The dangers of this distant journey to unknown lands may well have filled Madonna Luigia with alarm, and the passage of the Channel in winter was dreaded by every traveller. Pope Julius himself, while still Cardinal di S. Pietro in Vincula, had intended to visit England during his exile in France, but on reaching Calais, he abandoned his intention because of the roughness of the Channel. Only a few months before, King Philip and Queen Joanna of Castile had been shipwrecked off Portland on their way from Zeeland to Spain, and had been forced to wade to shore, up to the waist in water! King Henry had immediately sent Cardinal Adriano

[1] Cod. Vat. Lat., 8210. Appendix VIII.

Castellesi, the Italian Bishop of Bath, with money and clothes to the help of his dear cousins, and had entertained them for a week at Richmond—indeed, as Philip wrote to the Emperor Maximilian, he could not have done more for them if he had been their father.   But this was poor comfort to the Venetian Ambassador, Vincenzo Querini, who, after undergoing unspeakable terrors for two days at sea, found himself stranded at Falamona (Falmouth), a wild and lonely spot, on the extreme point of the island nearest to Spain, and 250 miles from Antona (Southampton), where the sole human beings to be seen were a few barbarous natives, whose language and customs were entirely different to those of Londoners.[1]

Since it was impossible to procure horses, the Ambassador was compelled to wait until he was joined by the King and Queen, who declared they would rather stay at Falmouth six months than set sail again in bad weather ! Twice over the royal travellers and the terrified Venetian tried to start, but had to put into port again, and it was not till the end of April that they finally set sail for Spain, and were able to perform their vows at S. Jacopo's shrine.

All this had reached Castiglione's ears through Querini's friend Bembo, and the story of the Venetian ambassador's miraculous escape from drowning by the special intervention of St. Peter and St. Paul, to whom he cried in his distress, had been repeated in all the courts of Italy.   Fortunately, the Duke of Urbino's envoy fared better.   He crossed that ' dangerous sea, the Channel of England,' in safety, and landed at Dover on October 20.   Here he was

[1] Sanuto, vi. 295, 315, ' Calendar of State Papers in Archives of Venice,' edited by Rawdon Brown, i. 311-314.

met by Sir Thomas Brandon, whom the King had sent to receive him in His Majesty's name, and bring him to London.

'Heretofore,' writes Ashmole, the seventeenth-century historian of the Order of the Garter, 'the Soveraign hath caused the Proctor of foreign Knights of the Order to be received with great state, for so, on the 20th of October, the twenty-second year of our soverain lord, King Henry VII., there landed at Dover a noble ambassador, Sir Balthasar Castileon, sent hither from the Duke of Urbin, whom Sir Thomas Brandon, with a goodly company of his own servants, well horst, met at the Seaside ; and thence continually kept company with him, till they came neer Deptford in Kent ; where by the Soveraign's command, he was met by Sir Thomas Dokara, Lord of St. John's, and Sir Thomas Wriothesley, *alias* principall Garter King-of-Arms. The said Sir Thomas Dokara had attending him thirty of his servants, all in new liveries, well horsed, every Gentleman bearing a Javelin in his hand, and every Yeoman a Bow and a sheaf of arrows, and so they conveyed him to his lodging. The next day they conducted him to London, and by the way there met him divers Italians, and Paulus de Gygeles, the Pope's Vice-Collector, to whose house he was conveyed and there lodged.'[1]

Polidoro Vergilio, who held the office of Vice-Collector of Peter's Pence at this time, and enjoyed the special favour of Henry VII., was a native of Urbino. He had accompanied his kinsman, Cardinal Adriano Castellesi, to England, and had been appointed to the rectory of Church Langton, in Leicestershire. Afterwards he became Prebendary of Lincoln and

[1] Elias Ashmole, 'Institution and Laws of the Order of the Garter,' 1692, Appendix, p. 440 ; J. Anstis, 'Register of the Order of the Garter,' 1724, vol. i. 257.

Archdeacon of Wells, but is chiefly known as the author of a 'Latin History of England, which was undertaken at Henry VII.'s suggestion, and dedicated to his successor. Before the author left Italy, he had dedicated a book on proverbs to Duke Guidobaldo, and was naturally delighted to welcome an envoy from Urbino. But there were many Italians in London at this time, and in Polidoro's house Castiglione found himself surrounded by compatriots. Henry VII. had always encouraged Italians to settle in England, especially Venetians and Florentine merchants, with whom he often conversed on Italian affairs, and who were full of admiration for his wealth and financial skill.[1]

' This kingdom,' wrote a Milanese envoy to Lodovico Sforza, ' is perfectly stable, first by reason of the King's wisdom, whereof every one stands in awe; secondly, on account of his wealth, for I am informed that he has more than six millions of gold, and saves 500,000 ducats yearly; which is easy for him, as his revenue does not merely exist on paper, but is a real and great thing. And, what is more, he never spends anything.'

Besides employing 'notable men in Rome,' such as Cardinal Adriano or Silvestro Gigli and Giovanni of Lucca, he liked to have Italians about his person. Pietro Carmeliano of Brescia was his secretary and court-poet, Polidoro his friend and adviser, and when Silvestro Gigli succeeded his uncle as Bishop of Worcester, Henry kept him at court to act as Master of Ceremonies and receive distinguished foreigners.[2] Castiglione, who had known the Bishop intimately in Rome, and had originally hoped to travel to

[1] P. Vergilio, 'Hist.,' p. 615.
[2] L. Einstein, 'Italian Renaissance in England,' p.181.

England in his company, must have rejoiced to find this friend at court, and was, no doubt, introduced by him to the royal presence, when, two days after his arrival, he went to see the King at the palace of Greenwich. Here he delivered his credentials, and offered His Majesty the presents sent him by the Duke of Urbino—the horses and falcons and Raphael's little St. George—in an eloquent Latin oration. Castiglione evidently made a very favourable impression on the King, who could himself speak Italian, and who not only received him very kindly, but invited him to repeat his visit the next day. Baldassare, on his part, was equally gratified at this cordial welcome, and at the interest which His Majesty showed in Italian affairs, even though he owned that he found them ' difficult to follow, because Italian powers were so changeable.' But the English monarch, as Castiglione soon discovered, was admirably well informed and thoroughly acquainted, not only with the general state of affairs, but also with the personal character and attributes of the different Princes who ruled over Ferrara, Mantua, and Urbino.[1]

In the midst of these absorbing occupations Baldassare found time to write a hurried note to his mother :

' I know that you are longing to hear from me, and I write whenever I can. You must know that on November 1 I arrived here in London, which is the capital of England, safe and well, thank God, and was most honourably escorted to this city. At the end of two days I was summoned to have an audience of His Sacred Majesty the King, who treated me with the greatest honour and kindness,

[1] ' Ven. Calendar of State Papers,' i. 260.

and does more for me every day. So I hope to
satisfy the wishes of my dear Lord, and also please
His Majesty, and return before long safely to Italy,
please God! Here I met an ambassador from the
King of France, who has given me a letter from you,
which I am very glad to have, although it is already
old, being an answer to mine which I sent from
Milan by Scaramella. I have nothing to say in reply,
but that I am very well indeed, which I know you
will be glad to hear, and I shall hope to hear the
same of you.

'LONDON, *November 6, 1506.*'

The next day Henry issued the following commission, which has been preserved among the Garter
records :

'Henry, by the grace of God, King of England
and France, Lord of Ireland, Soveraign of the Most
Noble Order of the Garter, to our Right Trusty and
Well-beloved cousins, the Marquis of Dorset, the
Earl of Surrey, Treasurer of England, and the Earl
of Shrewsbury, Steward of our Household, companions of the said Order, greeting. Forasmuch as
we understand that the right noble prince, Gwe de
Ubaldis, Duke of Urbin, who was heretofore elected
to be one of the companions of the said noble Order,
cannot conveniently repair unto this our realm personally to be installed in the Collegiate Church of
that Order, and to perform other ceremonies where-
unto by the said Order he is bound, but for that
intent and purpose hath sent a right honourable personage, Balthasar de Castilione, Knight, sufficiently
authorized as his proctor, to be installed in his name,
and to perform all other things for him, to the
statutes and ordinances of the said Order requisite
and appertaining : We therefore, in consideration of
the promises, will, and by these presents give you
licence, full power, and authority not only to accept

and admit the said Balthasar as proctor for the same
Duke, and to receive his oath and instal him in the
lieu and place and for the said Duke, but also,
further, to do therein as to the statutes and laudable
usages of the said Order it appertaineth, and this our
writing shall be to you and every one of you sufficient
discharge in that behalf.

'Given under the seale of our said noble Order
of the Garter, at our mannor of Greenwiche, the
7th day of November, the 22nd year of our reign.'

On the following day Castiglione rode down to
Windsor, along 'the faire causeway ' which King
Henry VII. had lately made between London and
that town, escorted by three noble peers 'and a
gallant equipage.' At Windsor he was entertained in
the Dean's lodgings, where a costly and sumptuous
supper was prepared at the King's expense. The
Dean who had the honour of being Castiglione's host
on this occasion was Dr. Christopher Urswick, the
King's Almoner, one of the most generous friends
of Erasmus, who dedicated his Latin version of
'Lucian's Dream' to his 'best and kindest Christopher, in gratitude for many civilities and favours.'
Since he had been made Dean, Urswick had entirely
rebuilt the Deanery, and a picturesque fragment of
his work is still preserved, while his arms are to be
seen on the fan-vaulted roof of St. George's Chapel.
The last foreign visitor to Windsor had been no less
a personage than King Philip of Castile, who, after
being wrecked off Portland, had been magnificently
entertained by Henry VII. and installed as Knight
of the Garter. The splendours of that occasion
were still fresh in the Dean's mind, and M. Baldassare was told how the Castilian monarch hunted in
the park and played rackets in the new tennis-court

with my Lord of Dorset, while King Henry looked
on and his daughter Lady Mary danced and played
the lute ; how he attended mass and heard a French
sermon at St. George's. After this His Majesty spent
the rest of Sunday in horse-baiting and masques, and
finally rode off by the river-side, 'all the children of
Eton standing along the barres of St. George's
Cherche-yard,' to see His Majesty's departure.[1]

The next morning Castiglione was led by three
Knights of the order through the door of the Chapter-
house, into the choir of St. George's Chapel, where
the blue velvet mantle with the red-cross shield and
the collar and George were laid on the stall assigned
to the Duke. Then the ' proxie,' as he is termed in
the Garter book, kneeling at the altar, took a solemn
oath on the Gospels in the name of the Lord Duke,
and vowed to keep the statutes of the order inviolable, and to defend to the best of his power ' all the
liberties and franchises belonging to the College of
Our Most Blessed Lady and the holy martyr George,
where this most noble order was founded.'

When the ceremony of installation was ended, the
' proxie ' was conducted by his brother Knights to the
Dean's great chamber, where a banquet was prepared
at the King's charge, and Castiglione sat in the place
of honour and was served alone, the other Knights
being seated at the end of the table. It was the
custom for the newly-made Knight or his ' proxie ' to
pay heavy fees to the priests, choir, vicar and vergers,
sextons and bell-ringers, of the College of Windsor,
and to give alms to ' poore Knights of the foundation'; but, fortunately for Guidobaldo and Castiglione, the fees of foreign Princes were paid by

---

[1] Ashmole, 153 ; Tighe and Davis, ' Annals of Windsor,' i. 434.

the King, and all the 'proxie' had to do on this
occasion was to bestow a largess on the college.
We do not hear how long Baldassare remained at
Windsor, or if his companions took him hawking the
next day in the Forest, and showed him some of that
great variety of sport which mightily pleased a French
Count who came to England not long afterwards
on the same errand for his King. But we know
that on his return to London he paid visits to
all the Knights of the order in town, as was the
custom, and was feasted and hospitably entertained
by each in turn. After this he was sent for by the
King, and went down again to the royal palace at
Greenwich.

This time he was welcomed with even greater
kindness than before, and the King seems thoroughly
to have appreciated the charm of his guest's conversation. Perhaps, like the Venetian Captain,
Vincenzo Capello, M. Baldassare was invited to dinner,
and heard the widowed Princess of Wales, Katherine
of Aragon, and her young sister-in-law, Lady Mary,
play the spinet. But it is certain that he was presented to Henry, the young Prince of Wales, and
was as much impressed by his talents and love of
letters as Erasmus, who came to England in this
same year. To this visit we owe the splendid compliments which are paid to Henry VIII. by the author
of the 'Cortegiano' in his chapter on good monarchs:
'Look,' cries Ottaviano Fregoso, 'at my Lord Henry,
Prince of Wales, now growing up under his great
father in every form of excellence, like a tender shoot
in the shade, a fruit-laden tree, to become even more
beautiful and fruitful in its time. For, as our Castiglione writes from England, and promises to tell us
more fully on his return, it seems as if in this prince,

Nature were bent on showing her power by collecting the virtues of many persons in one man.'[1]

As soon as the Christmas festival was over he left London, bearing friendly messages and letters for the Duke, as well as many valuable presents. The King gave Castiglione himself several horses and dogs, and, what he valued still more, a gold collar of SS links, such as was commonly worn by English judges, and is familiar to us in Sir Thomas More's portrait, bearing two pendant portcullises and the royal badge of the Tudor rose in gold and silver. This collar Baldassare treasured in after-life as his most precious possession, and finally left as an heirloom to his descendants. Then he set out on his homeward journey, having successfully accomplished his lord's mission and greatly increased his own reputation. On January 26, 1507, he reached Lyons, and sent his mother a short note, telling her that he was in the best of health and spirits, and hoped soon to tell her with his own lips all that he had seen and done.[2] By February 9 he was at Milan, and sent a servant to tell his mother of his safe return:

' You will have heard from Francesco that, by the grace of God, I have arrived safe and sound in Milan, and intend to spend a short time here. Now I send this messenger to ask you how matters stand, and if you think I had better come straight to Casatico without asking leave, or if I had better apply to the Marquis. For my part, I am inclined to think it might be as well to inform His Excellency of my return, and beg permission to visit my lady mother at Casatico, so as to show him due respect, and to see if His Excellency would allow me to come to Mantua. I enclose a letter which I have written

[1] 'Cortegiano,' iv. 38.   [2] Cod. Vat. Lat., 8210. Appendix IX.

to M. Tolomeo, begging him to inform His Excellency that I have reached Mantua, and, with his gracious permission, would gladly come to see you at Casatico. But I leave the matter to you. You might consult M. Gio. Pietro, and send Francesco to meet me at Crema.[1]

'MILAN, *February* 9, 1507.

'P.S.— If you do not think it well to give M. Tolomeo the letter, you need not trouble about it.'

Madonna Luigia delivered her son's letter to the powerful secretary at Mantua without delay; but either he proved a false friend, or else the Marquis was still obdurate and refused to allow Castiglione to do more than spend a few days at Casatico. On the 13th Tolomeo sent a note couched in his usual suave language :

'MAGNIFICO M. BALDASSARE,—I rejoice as much as any of your friends to hear of your safe and honoured return. Our Illustrious Signor's reply to your petition is that he is willing to allow you to go and spend a few days with your mother at Casatico as you desire. And I beg your lordship to give me your further commands in anything in which I am able to do you service, and to believe that I would more gladly serve you than receive the greatest favours from others.'[2]

The moment this letter reached Baldassare he hastened to Casatico, and Madonna Luigia had the joy of embracing her son once more She was not, however, allowed this pleasure long, and four days later he continued his journey southward.

[1] Cod. Vat. Lat., 8210.   [2] Cod. Vat. Lat., 8211. Appendix X.

On the 20th he reached Bologna, where he found his master the Duke in attendance on the Pope, and was able to give him a full report of his mission. Two days later the Duke left Bologna with the Holy Father, as Baldassare informed his mother:

'Your Magnificence will be glad to hear that, by the grace of God, I arrived here at Bologna safe and well, and found His Holiness the Pope as well as the Lord Duke. They have both left Bologna to-day, and I hope to follow them to-morrow, and fear I shall not be able to return to Casatico this Easter, as the Duke does not wish it. Meanwhile I should be grateful if you could procure me some money to pay the twenty-five gold ducats which I borrowed from Vismara, as well as some things which I bought of him. Then there is my debt to Monsignore of Ferrara, which I know you will be anxious to discharge.'

This was a sum of 200 ducats which Cardinal Ippolito d' Este had sent Baldassare, when he was at Milan on his way to England, with a kind letter wishing him a prosperous journey, and begging him to bring back some fine horses for his use. The young knight had apparently only spent fifty of the Cardinal's ducats, and was anxious to repay the remainder as soon as possible.

'Please send Francesco to Milan to pack up those bards which I left there, and give them to the Vismari to be sent to Mantua. And as the Duke wishes to give Cardinal Sanseverino the dogs called Mordano and Bombò, I wish Francesco to present them to His Illustrious Reverence with the enclosed note, and see that he puts the gold collar and silk leash on Bombò. As soon as he returns, I should like him to come here with the mules, leaving the sick one at home if he is not yet cured, and my three horses and the little Arab.   As to this last, I should like you to consult Sebastiano, and see if he ought to be bled after this long journey, but do not give him any fodder excepting corn and straw.   I also pray you to ask Master Francesco of the Scuola, or his son Jeronimo, if he knows a boy in the village who can write a good hand.   If so, I should like to have him to live with me, since I need a secretary badly, as I have often told you.'

'BOLOGNA, *February 22, 1507.*'[1]

Three days later Castiglione joined his lord at Forli, and wrote again begging his mother to send another of his dogs to Milan by Francesco as a present to Sig. Antonio di San Severino, the husband of his friend Madonna Margherita, after which the servant was to start as soon as possible for Urbino, bringing with him mules, horses, and dogs —'in fact, the whole great company!'   This was on February 25.   On the last day of the month Castiglione returned to Urbino with the Duke, and the arrival of the Ambassador from England was duly chronicled by the annalist among the chief events of the month.[2]

[1] Cod. Vat. Lat., 8210.   Appendix XI.   [2] Cod. Vat. Urb., 904

CHAPTER XIII

1507

Visit of Pope Julius II. to Urbino—Conquest of Bologna—Castiglione returns with the Duke to Urbino—Festivities in honour of the Pope — Illustrious personages assembled at Urbino—The dialogues of the 'Cortegiano'—Castiglione visits Camaldoli — Giuliano de' Medici and Bembo at Urbino — Bembo's carnival *stanze*—Roman scholars introduced in the 'Cortegiano'—Sadoleto's description of the court of Urbino.

GREAT events had taken place at Urbino during Castiglione's six months' absence. A few weeks after his departure, Pope Julius II., attended by twenty-two Cardinals and a great train of servants, arrived at Urbino on September 25, and spent three days at the palace as the Duke's guest. He came straight from Perugia, where he had received the submission of Gianpaolo Baglioni, and was on his way to expel the Bentivogli from Bologna. It was a proud day for the little city, and her chroniclers were careful to record every incident of the warlike Pontiff's visit.[1] They tell us how His Holiness halted at San Bernardino, a mile without the gates, and entered the church to see Duke Federico's grave, and walked in the shady garden and admired the beauty of the prospect. It was evening by the time that he reached the city gates, where forty-five youths clad in silk brocade were waiting to escort him to the Duomo,

[1] Cod. Vat. Urb., 904; Baldi, 'Vita di Guidobaldo,' p. 105.

and, after the custom of the time, seized his mule, which was afterwards redeemed for six ducats. The highest honours were paid him. The roads had been mended beforehand. The city gates were taken down and the keys handed to him in a gold dish; triumphal arches were erected, and the Host was borne before him on a richly-draped white horse through the gaily-decorated streets. The Duke presented him with 100 sacks of flour, as well as gifts of wine and meat, of corn and poultry, which the Pope gave to the hospital of the Misericordia. 'The streets,' writes our friend the diarist, 'were so thronged with Bishops and priests, protonotaries and officials from Rome, that you could hardly cross the Piazza, and it was indeed a beautiful sight!'

Within, the palace was adorned with the richest tapestries and most costly treasures of gold and silver plate, much of which had been brought from Ferrara and Mantua for the occasion. All night the windows blazed with torches, and a cross of glittering fire illumined the Rocca on the opposite heights. 'The whole air,' writes the chronicler, 'seemed full of lights. Very early on the morning of the 28th His Holiness left Urbino, and, after subduing all the castles and cities on his way, entered Bologna in great triumph on St. Martin's Day.'[1] The Pope's success was complete, the French King abandoned his allies, Giovanni Bentivoglio fled before the victor's approach, and the Pope, borne in a sumptuous litter presented to him by Queen Anne of Brittany, was hailed by the people of Bologna as a deliverer. 'Although it was winter,' wrote one spectator, 'the roses and flowers bloomed abundantly, and it was summer weather, so that all the Bolognese said,

[1] Cod. Vat. Urb., 904 ; Albertini, 'De Mirabilibus Urbis,' p. 72.

"Truly, Julius commands the heavens and the planets!"' Another witness—Erasmus—who was also present on this occasion, remarked : 'The Pope fights, conquers, triumphs, and, in fact, plays the part of Julius to perfection.'[1] Guidobaldo had accompanied the Pope on his expedition, although, owing to his ill-health, the actual command of the Papal forces was given to the Marquis of Mantua, and the unfortunate Duke spent most of his time at Bologna in bed. On February 20 the Venetian ambassador sent home a rumour which had reached him, that the Duke was actually dead. Two days later, however, he recovered, and hastened home to receive the Pope on his way to Rome. Castiglione, who, as we have seen, entered Urbino with the Duke, and gave him Henry's gifts and affectionate messages, was received by him with every mark of favour. Guidobaldo and his courtiers listened with the greatest interest to Castiglione's description of the splendour of the English court, and the wealth of these Northern people, as well as of the character and habits of the King and his court. 'The Duke,' he wrote to his mother, 'and these other lords have welcomed me most affectionately, and all show the greatest pleasure at my return.' Before half his story was told, the Pope arrived, on March 3. This time only twelve Cardinals accompanied him, the other half preferring to take the easier and longer road through Tuscany, and thus avoid the bad roads and bitter cold of the journey across the Apennines. But nothing could daunt the old Pontiff's courage or subdue his energy. He reached Urbino in the highest spirits, and was once more magnificently entertained by the Duke and Duchess. Fortunately, he only remained two nights

[1] F. M. Nicholls, 'The Epistles of Erasmus,' p. 421.

on this occasion, being impatient to reach Rome by
Palm Sunday, and set out early on the 5th to continue his triumphal progress. The Duke accompanied him as far as Cagli, and then returned to take
a few weeks' much-needed repose.

'Here,' wrote Baldassare on March 5, 'we have
had His Holiness the Pope for two days, so that we
have been exceedingly busy.' In the opening sentences of the 'Cortegiano' he gives a fuller account
of these memorable days :

'After Pope Julius II. had by his own presence,
and with the help of the French, reduced Bologna to
the obedience of the Apostolic Chair in the year 1506,
and was returning to Rome, he passed through
Urbino, where he was received and entertained with
as much splendour and magnificence as could have
been possible in any of the noblest cities of Italy, so
that both the Pope himself and all the Cardinals and
other courtiers were exceedingly well satisfied. And
there were some who, attracted by the charm of the
company, remained for many days at Urbino after
the Pope and his court had left, during which time
not only were the usual festivities and amusements
held, but every one tried to increase the merriment,
and fresh games and diversions were held every
evening.'[1]

This, we know, was the precise moment which
Castiglione chose as the date of the conversations described in his 'Cortegiano,' the first of which is said to
have taken place on the evening after the Pope's
departure. His repeated allusions to his own absence,
and to the letters which he wrote from England at
the time, were graceful fictions, invented to explain
the fact that he himself takes no part in these dis-

[1] 'Cortegiano,' i. 6.

cussions. Although the actual dialogues may not
have taken place on this occasion, most of the personages introduced were actually present at Urbino
during this memorable week. Pietro Bembo, the
Magnifico Giuliano, Count Lodovico da Canossa, the
young Prefect Francesco Maria, Cesare Gonzaga,
Gasparo Pallavicino, Cristoforo Romano, the Fregosi
brothers, Morello da Ortona, Roberto Pio, Lodovico
Pio, l' Unico Aretino, the gay poet Terpandro, were
all there. Several others who are mentioned in
Castiglione's pages, such as Alberto Pio, Bernardo
da Bibbiena, and Niccolò Frisio, were probably also
present. Four Cardinals, we learn, were among
the guests to whom the writer alludes as having
lingered amid the delights of Urbino after the Pope's
departure. Two of these, Elisabetta's brother, Sigismondo Gonzaga, and Galeotto della Rovere, were
nearly connected with the ducal family, while Luigi
of Aragon, as we have already seen, was a cousin and
intimate friend of the Este princes, and the French
Cardinal de Narbonne had been brought into close
relations with Duke Guidobaldo during the recent
campaign of Bologna. These four prelates, however,
were compelled to leave Urbino, sorely against their
will, in the following week, and join the Pope at the
gates of Rome to take part in his triumphal entry on
Palm Sunday.

Castiglione was unable to gratify his mother's wish
that he should pay her another visit that Lent, but in
Holy Week he rode as far as Tuscany on a pious
pilgrimage to Camaldoli. Among the monks of this
order there was a certain holy father, a Florentine
named Don Michele, whom Bembo visited in his cell in
the autumn of 1506, when the benefice of the neighbouring Badia of La Vernia was conferred on him by

Cardinal Giovanni de' Medici. This saintly man sent
the Duchess a rosary, which she valued greatly, and
Elisabetta in return employed a 'great master of
painting' to execute a devotional picture for the
hermit of Camaldoli. Unfortunately, the unknown
artist had delayed to begin the work, and owing to
the severity of the winter the colours took a long time
to dry, so that many months passed before the work
was completed. But when, during that Holy Week,
Messer Baldassare visited the hermit in the narrow
cell at Camaldoli, which seemed to him and his friends
the holiest spot on earth, he took a courteous message from the Duchess, and told the good father
how constantly she thought of his austere and
devout life, and how earnestly she begged to be
remembered in his prayers. Elisabetta herself frequently expressed a wish to visit both Camaldoli
and La Vernia, the holy mountain consecrated by
the presence of St. Francis, but was never able to
carry out her intention.[1]

Having paid his devotions at this shrine in the
heart of the Apennines, Castiglione returned to
Urbino for Easter, which was the occasion of
renewed festivities in the ducal palace. On April 6
news reached the Duke that his nephew, Federico
Fregoso, had been appointed Archbishop of Salerno
by the Pope, an event which was hailed with as much
joy by the citizens as by the court.

Bembo and Giuliano de' Medici both spent Easter
at Urbino, and shared the generous hospitality of the
Duke and Duchess. These were the happy days
described by Ariosto, that king of court-poets, when
Cardinal de' Medici was still an exile from Florence,
and his brother Giuliano was a guest at the Feltrian

[1] Bembo, 'Lettere,' i. 250, iii. 8.

court, together with the author of the ' Cortegiano '
and Bembo :

> ' Quando il suo Giuliano,
>   Si riparò ne la Feltresca corte ;
> Ove col formator del Cortegiano,
>   Col Bembo, e gli altri sacri al divo Apollo,
>   Facea l' esilio suo men duro e strana.' [1]

When Bembo's Venetian friends blamed him for
being content to live at the Duchess's expense, he
retorted by pointing to the Magnifico Giuliano, the
brother of a Cardinal, with an income of 10,000
florins, who came to Urbino with ten horses at the
time of the Pope's visit, and stayed on for many
months as the guest of the Duchess. The frequency
of Giuliano's visits and the splendid hospitality with
which he was entertained are proved by the fact that
the wing of the palace of Urbino containing the
suite of rooms which he occupied still bears the
Magnifico's name. It was during these years of exile
which he spent at Urbino that he carried on a secret
intrigue with a fair lady named Pacifica Brandano,
who in April, 1511, gave birth to a son, afterwards
the Cardinal Ippolito of Titian's magnificent portrait.
One Easter Eve a babe was found in the street
wrapped in white swaddling clothes with a silver
clasp, and taken to the Children's Hospital. During
two years the little foundling was nursed by foster-
parents, who in 1513 were suddenly ordered by the
Magnifico to bring their charge to Rome and were
handsomely paid for their trouble. From that time
the boy was recognized as his son, and brought up in
the Vatican during the pontificate of his uncle, Leo X.
Cardinal Giovanni himself was a frequent visitor at
Urbino, and his nephew, Piero's son Lorenzo, was

[1] ' Satira Terza.'

brought there as a babe by his widowed mother, Alfonsina Orsini, and tenderly nursed by the kind Duchess.

Bembo's residence at the court of Urbino was even more prolonged. 'Be of good cheer,' he wrote five-and-twenty years afterwards to his young protégé, Vettore Soranzo, who was groaning over his poverty and lack of opportunities, 'be of good cheer, and do not allow melancholy to oppress you, remembering that I went to Urbino with only forty ducats in my pocket, and remained there six years, and without ever receiving more than fourteen ducats from my family.'[1] After many storms and troubles, Fortune had at length brought him into a quiet haven. In May of 1506 he had written disconsolately to Elisabetta from Venice, saying that his father, who was bent on seeing his son embrace a political career, or at least take a rich wife, positively refused to supply him with sufficient funds to go to Rome, and begging the good Duchess to get leave for him to inhabit rooms in the Badia della Croce at Avellana, in the mountains near Gubbio. A few weeks later he was invited to Rome by his friend Bernardo da Bibbiena, now secretary to Cardinal de' Medici, and found a lodging under this prelate's hospitable roof until he came to meet the Pope at Urbino. He followed the Papal court to Forli, to present a petition from the Knights of Rhodes, after which he had intended to return to the Badia dell' Avellana. But Elisabetta declared that she could not allow him to spend the winter in so rigorous a climate, and insisted on keeping him as a guest in her own house.

It was in vain that his friends in Venice—his old father, who had grown grey in the service of

---

[1] Cod. Marciana, Cl. x., No. xxii., 52.

the Republic, and his friend the ambassador, Vincenzo Querini, who had risen to high dignities and faced peril and shipwreck abroad, reproached him with sacrificing his career and being content to spend his life in a gilded cage. In a long and eloquent letter to the ambassador Querini he sets forth the reasons which actuated him, and shows that his house is not, after all, built upon the sand.

'If,' he writes, 'at your return home from the Flanders embassy you had found me in possession of some fat abbey, you would no doubt have said that I had done well, and might perhaps have added that you, too, once thought of taking the same path, had Fortune been favourable. You would have repeated that nothing is better than to live for letters and to be lords of ourselves, and not the slaves of others, with many arguments of the same kind which I have heard you exalt to the skies with marvellous eloquence. But because my medlar has been slower to ripen, you reprove me, and say I am launched on the troubled waves of life with Fortune for my pilot, while your feet rest on the solid masonry of the Roman amphitheatre. You tell me that, even if the Duchess and Cardinal Galeotto love me, they can do little, and it is folly to pin my faith on them. To which I reply that one of the two has already a fortune of 40,000 florins, and the other has made her brother a Cardinal.'[1]

He goes on to dilate on all the benefactions and kindness which he has received from both the young Cardinal and the Lady Duchess, whose exertions on his behalf justify the prophecy of an astrologer who once told him that he should be better loved and helped more effectually by strangers than by any of his own kin.

[1] 'Lettere,' ii. 59-61.

To his brother, Bartolommeo, Bembo expressed himself with still greater frankness in a letter written on the same day, December 10, 1506:

'As to the surprise which all my family show at my remaining in Urbino, all I wish to say is that I wonder they should think me so mad as not to realize what I am doing. Know, then, that I do not stay here without good reason, and that if I could advance my interests better by going to Rome, I would do so. But let them say what they choose! They are fools who think themselves wise, and imagine they can manage the lives of others better than their own. If God grants me a few more years of life, and the world does not move out of its courses for a few more months, they will, I hope, see that I have acted wisely. And even if the Pope dies, and the face of the world is changed, I shall not be worse off than I am now. But keep your counsel, and let men say what they please. Most people cannot see further than their own feet. You need not be afraid lest the charms of these ladies should make me forget myself. I can assure you that I am not asleep. . . . And let this suffice you. As for the extravagance with which I am charged, do not disturb yourself. For I am not as great a fool as your Solomons would make me out.'[1]

There can be no doubt that Bembo knew his own mind and that he had chosen well. A typical humanist of his day, he saw that his only hope of obtaining an easy life and freedom from care was to attach himself to a noble patron, at whose court he could devote himself to the study of literature. This was his one great passion, and with all his faults and weaknesses he remained, it must be said to his credit, true to the Muse whom he had served from boy-

[1] 'Lettere,' ii. 17.

EMILIA PIA.
(IMPERIAL MUSEUM, VIENNA.)

To face p. 200, Vol. I.

hood. To the end of his life he was covetous of
wealth and honours, and left no stone unturned to
secure some fresh benefice or vacant bishopric, and,
unlike his more high-minded friend Castiglione, he
succeeded in amassing a vast fortune. But his love
of letters never changed, and in days of prosperity he
was ever ready to lend a helping hand in his turn to
needy scholar or struggling poet.

He was certainly exceptionally fortunate in the
patrons to whom he attached himself, and the confidence which he had placed in the Duchess's kindness
and in his own prospects was realized beyond his
wildest dreams.

Throughout the following winter he remained at
Urbino, only retiring to Castel Durante for a week
of solitude in Advent and Lent. At Elisabetta's
request he and Ottaviano Fregoso composed a
masque, in which they appeared as the ambassadors
of Venus, sent to the cruel ladies who reigned in these
regions, and whose hearts of adamant and steel were
proof against Cupid's darts. In these stanzas, which
were evidently inspired by Castiglione's pastoral play
of the previous year, the poet addresses the Duchess
and Madonna Emilia, a lady at once ' crudel e pia,'
and adjures them no longer to despise the joys of
love, by the memory of those sweet strains which
Catullus sung of Lesbia, and Tibullus of Delia ; by
Dante's love of Beatrice, and Petrarch's devotion to
Laura. 'Gather ye the roses while you may, for
spring passes and flowers fade. All too soon Winter
lays his cold, icy hand on the fields. Your own beauty
will decay ; your golden locks will turn white ; your
lovely brows will be seamed with the wrinkles of old
age.'[1] On the last day of carnival Bembo and Otta-

[1] ' Rime di Pietro Bembo.'

viano recited these verses in costume before the Duchess, Madonna Emilia, and the lords and ladies assembled in the great hall of the palace of Urbino.

At Ottaviano Fregoso's request the poem was afterwards printed, although Bembo modestly declared that carnival verses, written in haste at that joyous season, and recited in those brief intervals between dancing and feasting, when fun and laughter were general, could not bear to be read in cold blood, but, like fish out of water, would lose all their flavour and freshness. In complying with Fregoso's wish, he begged him to remember that he, the cavalier, was rich in glory and famed for valiant deeds of arms, while his friend the writer was poor and needy, and could not well afford to suffer loss of reputation.[1]

But in point of fact these verses are among the most graceful and spontaneous that Bembo ever wrote, and compare favourably with the more laboured sonnets and epigrams which excited the admiration of his contemporaries.

Bembo and his distinguished companions were in constant communication with their friends in Rome, and there was hardly a scholar of note in the Eternal City who did not contrive to pay a visit to the court of Urbino in the course of the year. One of Castiglione and Bembo's most intimate friends, who also plays a leading part in the 'Cortegiano,' was Cardinal de' Medici's secretary, Bernardo Dovizi, better known by the name of Bibbiena, his native city at the foot of the mountain of La' Vernia. This 'bel Bernardo' was a man of remarkable ability, whose personal beauty and ready wit endeared him to the court circle at Urbino, while the position which he held in Cardinal de' Medici's household enabled him to be of great use

[1] 'Lettere,' iii. 41.

to both Bembo and Castiglione. Like Bembo, he took
minor orders early; but this did not prevent him from
being involved in many love affairs, to which we find
frequent allusions in the letters which passed between
Rome and Urbino. But, in spite of his ambitious
and pleasure-loving nature, he was a man of strong
feeling, and capable of inspiring deep and lasting
affection. ' The days seem years till I see Bernardo
again,' wrote Bembo to a mutual friend, the Archbishop of Salerno, 'and can once more enjoy the
pleasant company and delightful conversation, the
wit, the jests, the countenance and love of that
man !'[1]   And certainly neither conflicting interests
nor the rivalry of political parties ever altered the
love which he bore to Castiglione.

Another distinguished man of letters, who was also
at one time secretary to Cardinal de' Medici—Filippo
Beroaldo the younger of Bologna—frequently visited
Urbino at this period, and was on intimate terms
with the author of the 'Cortegiano.' There is an
amusing letter among Bembo's Latin epistles, in
which he laughs at the foolish fears which had prevented Beroaldo from visiting Urbino that spring,
on his return from Bologna to Rome. The reports
which reached the humanist of the disturbed state
of the country and of the soldiers who infested the
roads had alarmed him so much that he regretfully
abandoned his intention of visiting Urbino, and took
the safer route through Florence.

'When I read your letter to those noble ladies,
Emilia, Costanza, and your Margherita' [Margherita
Gonzaga, for whom Beroaldo professed especial devo-
tion], and when they heard that you did not dare travel

---

[1] 'Epist. fam.' iv. 150.

along the Flaminian Way, the safest and most famous road in Italy, because you were afraid of meeting ten or twenty of our men-at-arms, it excited the greatest laughter, and I was quite sorry you had written, so great was the scorn and contempt which they poured upon your folly. But if women deride you thus, what do you think those strong and valiant knights, Ottaviano, Giuliano, Castiglione, and Cesare Gonzaga said when they read your letter ? I cannot tell you how much your own reputation and dignity have suffered, while I, who tried to defend your cause and say that you acted prudently, found myself overwhelmed with ridicule !'[1]

Beroaldo, however, could be witty at Bembo's expense, and the gay repartees which he wrote from Bibbiena's *camerino* in Rome were the delight of all the ladies of Urbino.

Another great favourite of theirs, the Petrarchist poet and musician, Antonio Maria Terpandro, was also at Urbino that summer, and many were the tears that were shed at his departure, and many the messages that Bembo sent him from these fair friends, begging him not to forget his promise, but to return very soon. Terpandro was deeply attached to Messer Latino Giovenale, another member of the Roman Academy which met in Cardinal Giovanni's house ; and when his friend's appointment to a canonry of St. Peter's reached Urbino, the poet, in Bembo's graphic phrase, 'jumped out of his skin for joy.'[2] Latino Giovenale, or Juvenale de' Manetti, was himself a clever verse-writer who was afterwards employed on important missions by Leo X. and Paul III., and who is often mentioned in the 'Cortegiano.'

[1] 'Epist. fam.,' iv. 145.   [2] 'Lettere,' iii. 33.

Closely connected with all of these Roman humanists, and through them with Castiglione and the court of Urbino, was Jacopo Sadoleto, the great Bishop of Carpentras, who, after being indispensable to two Popes, was recalled from his distant diocese to be made a Cardinal in his old age. A native of Modena, after completing his studies at Ferrara, Sadoleto came to Rome early in the sixteenth century in the service of Cardinal Caraffa, and became famous for his learning and holiness. He wrote Latin prose and verse as well as Bembo, and was said to be as eloquent as Chrysostom. A graver thinker and a finer spirit than any member of the group, Sadoleto cherished the remembrance of the good Duke and Duchess to his dying day, and the language in which he speaks of the court of Urbino is no small tribute to the society in which Castiglione moved :

'I suppose that nowhere else in the whole world, whether in ancient or in modern times, would it be easy to find so many distinguished men of genius and learning assembled in one place, as there are now in the glorious court of Urbino. Here, for instance, you have Pietro Bembo, a man justly famous for his great knowledge and attainments, whom we may truly call the father of ancient Latin prose and of the modern Italian tongue. Then there are the two brothers Fregoso, Federico and Ottaviano, both of them illustrious for their noble character and for virtues and learning which render them the light of Italy, as well as Baldassare Castiglione and Cesare Gonzaga, a distinguished pair, celebrated alike for their valour in arms and for their achievements in arts and letters. Wherefore I think this city is indeed the resting-place and home of the Muses to-day.'[1]

[1] 'De Laud. Phil.,' ii. 190.

CHAPTER XIV

1507

Castiglione proposes to exchange estates with Ercole Bentivoglio—
His debts and difficulties—Mission to King Louis XII. at
Milan — Meeting with old friends — Return to Urbino —
Illustrious guests at court—Castiglione and Bembo's poems
—Summer days at Urbino.

WHILE Castiglione was every day becoming dearer
to the Duke and Duchess, and more happily settled
in his home at Urbino, his friends at home still
cherished a hope of regaining the Marquis's favour
and bringing him back to Mantua. His mother, as
might be expected, looked out anxiously for every
sign of relenting on Francesco's part, and rejoiced
when, in March, 1507, her kinsman, Lodovico Canossa,
arrived from Urbino and was graciously received by
the Marquis. Baldassare heard the news with satisfaction, but when his friend Valenti suggested that
his former lord should be asked to find him a wife, he
indignantly rejected this proposal.

'As for Valenti's idea that, in order to arrange my
affairs,' he wrote to Madonna Luigia on March 29, ' his
brother-in-law should ask the Marquis to find me a
wife, it is, I am sure, very good of both these gentlemen to trouble themselves about my happiness ; none
the less, I think this course of action might not only

profit me little, but bring me harm and ridicule in the bargain! I would never in all eternity consent to such a thing. If God puts a good marriage in my way, I will gladly embrace the opportunity without needing any help from others; but it seems strange to me that one who has always tried to oppress me should suddenly change his ways. What little reputation I have acquired—if I can call it that —has certainly not been his doing! (I write thus freely, as I am sending this letter by hand.) And as a certain proposal, which in my opinion seems very favourable, has been lately made to me, I am going to tell Your Magnificence about it. What has troubled me most has been to find myself without sufficient fortune to live away from Mantua. Indeed, this has made me very unhappy, and still distresses me greatly. And although I should be sorry to give up my native country entirely, yet I should feel much safer if I could secure some means of subsistence elsewhere. What I wish to tell you is that Sig. Ercole Bentivoglio, who is now at Urbino, was never able to set foot in Bologna while the other Bentivogli were reigning, and since they have been driven out, he is less able than ever to go there, and despairs of ever returning to this his native city. So that he is anxious to find a resting-place for his declining years, and thinks that Mantua would suit him very well in many respects, more especially because his mother, who is said to be fonder of him than of any of her children, has much money and many jewels and good things, of which he thinks he would have a large share if he were near her. For this reason he has proposed to exchange his property at Bologna with mine at Mantua, giving me possessions which, other people tell me, are worth 700 gold ducats a year, and include payments from tolls and other sources which do not vary in time of plenty or scarcity, together with a good house at Bologna, and another at some distance from the town, with a very beautiful garden. I listened to his proposals, and we discussed them together and agreed to resume the subject after Easter, since he is desirous of consulting his friends at Bologna, and I wished to hear your opinion on the matter, as well as that of M. Gio. Pietro. He, I know, takes as warm an interest in my affairs as I do, so I hope that when I come and see you after Easter, we may arrive at some conclusion. But I should be glad if, before I come, you could let me have a word to say whether this idea pleases or displeases you. It certainly pleases me highly, because I feel that I should be able to keep some of my property at Mantua, where I always hope to return some day, and should not mind having possessions in both places, since Bologna is near to Mantua and the revenue is good. . . .'

In the same letter he alludes to another English hound which the Duke had sent to Sig. Antonio di San Severino, the husband of Margherita Pia, and begs his mother to pay special attention to the precious bards which he had brought from England, hanging them separately on the wall, and seeing that they are kept free from damp and dust.

'Some of our people,' he adds, 'are suffering from acute rheumatic pains in the side. I remember that you once told me of a certain remedy of boiled garlic, please repeat this in your next letter. But I have gossiped enough for once, and Alessandro will tell you much more by word of mouth.'

Ercole Bentivoglio was the son of a former ruler of Bologna, Santi Bentivoglio, by his marriage with Ginevra, daughter of Alessandro Sforza of Pesara. In 1465, three years after the death of her lord, Ginevra married his young cousin, Giovanni II., the rightful heir, who recovered the dominions which Santi had usurped, and reigned in Bologna until he was expelled by Pope Julius and forced to take refuge at Mantua. Ercole himself was a valiant condottiere, who spent many years in the service of the Florentines, but made his home at Urbino, where his unhappy relations with his wife, the beautiful and cultured Ferrarese lady, Barbara Torelli, at one time excited much attention. In 1501 he accused her of attempting to poison him, to the horror of the gentle Duchess, who sent for an able and trusted Mantuan lawyer, Silvestro Calandra, to defend the innocent lady, whose mother was her own relative and friend. The Duke was present at the inquiry which followed, and Madonna Barbara was triumphantly acquitted.[1] In spite of Castiglione's regard for his kinswoman, who is repeatedly mentioned in his letters from Ferrara, and who afterwards became the wife of his friend Ercole Strozzi, he remained on good terms with her husband, and seriously entertained his proposal for an exchange of estates. A month later he wrote again to his mother on the subject:

'Signor Ercole is sending a messenger to Mantua on his own business, and will be the bearer of this. Since he still wishes to exchange lands with me, I should be glad if you would allow his servant to see Casatico and the estates, so that he can judge of the air and situation and other particulars. So I beg you to have him conducted there, and to ask the steward to show him everything ; but please do all this quite privately, and say that he is a friend of mine who is travelling through the country. If anyone asks about him, he can give them this answer, and need not appear to be showing him the place for any other object, as I am very anxious to keep the whole thing

---

[1] 'Archivio storico Italiano,' appendice, i. 248.

a secret until it is settled. Directly Sig. Ercole has arranged his affairs, we will proceed with the business, because I have quite made up my mind to effect this exchange, and hope you will be content for the various reasons which I have already explained, all the more that we shall not have to leave Mantua entirely, but can live there again some day, please God!'

Here, however, the matter seems to have ended, probably owing to the sudden death of Ercole Bentivoglio a few weeks later. That it was a relief to Madonna Luigia we can hardly doubt ; but her son groaned under the load of debts and difficulties from which he saw no hope of escape. There is hardly a letter in which we do not find some allusion to this increasing burden. He sold several of his horses because of the dearness of corn at Urbino, pledged his family jewels, and found himself compelled, much to his distress, to pawn the gold collar and pendant which the King of England had given him. In his anxiety to redeem this precious jewel, he sent his mother the richly embroidered mantle which he had worn at the English court, begging her to take it to pieces and have the gold ornaments melted down and sold. But he was still in dire need of money, and was obliged to defer the execution of a scheme which he and his mother had long planned—the erection of a monument to his father and brother in the family chapel of S. Agnese at Mantua. At Madonna Luigia's prayer, however, Baldassare sent her the following Latin inscription in memory of his deceased relatives :

BALTESSARI . CASTILIONO . AVO
CHRISTOPHORO . PATRI . HIERONYMO .
FRATRI . BALTESSAR . PIENTISS .
OPERA . ALOVISIÆ . GONZAGÆ .
MATRIS . P. NEC. TOTIS . QUIDEM .
QUORUM . FAMA . INTER .
HOMINES . SPIRITUS . IN . SUPERIS .
VIGET . ANNO . MDVII . XX . OCTOBRIS .

' You might inscribe these words,' he wrote, ' on
the resting-place of those blessed souls, my grandfather, father, and brother, for the present ; some
day, if only, please God, the stars change their
contrary courses, I mean to erect an honourable
memorial, and then we might think of some better
words.   At present I am too much harassed ; but if
you like this inscription to be altered later, it shall be
done.'[1]

His pious intention, however, was not accomplished until after his death, when a stately tomb was
placed in the Castiglione chapel of S. Agnese by
Madonna Luigia.

A new and honourable mission was now entrusted
to Castiglione by the Duke of Urbino.   He was
sent to pay homage to King Louis XII. of France,
who was in the act of laying siege to the revolted
city of Genoa.   Both Alfonso d' Este and Francesco
Gonzaga had joined His Most Christian Majesty
with their forces, and the other powers of Italy in
their turn hastened to do him honour.   But when
Baldassare reached Bologna on May 19, he heard
that Genoa had surrendered, and that Louis was
on his way to Milan.   Accordingly, he decided to
travel by Modena to Milan, in order to be present at
the King's triumphal entry.   But, as usual, pecuniary
embarrassments stood in his way.

' I am greatly concerned at the prospect of going
to Milan without any money, and facing the Vismari
[the bankers who had lent him money] and the
Cardinal d' Este.   So I have written to Carlo da
Castiglione begging him to give you these 300 ducats,
and would be very grateful if you could send them
at once to Milan by a discreet and trustworthy

[1] Serassi, i. 30.

messenger. I do not fail to beg the Lord Duke for supplies, and have already written to him twice; and had I known I would have to go to Milan, I would have been so importunate that perhaps I should have brought the money with me.' [1]

This time, however, Madonna Luigia was unable to raise the necessary funds. Fortunately, Cardinal Ippolito, far from pressing for payment, accepted Castiglione's excuses with the greatest kindness, which, as he told his mother, only made him the more anxious to fulfil his obligations. On May 24 Baldassare once more rode into Milan in the suite of the victorious French monarch, whose entry he had witnessed eight years before. Our old friend Jean d'Auton waxes eloquent over the brilliant weather, the rich tapestries and bowers of verdure that decorated the streets, and the arches which Leonardo da Vinci is said to have designed. He gazed with wondering eyes on the procession of children bearing fleurs-de-lys in their hands, on the 300 Milanese armourers in glittering silver, and, above all, on the ladies, beautiful as a dream, clad in cloth of gold and crimson velvet, with jewels twined round their long coils of hair. This time three Cardinals—Ambrose, Ferrara, and San Severino—rode at the King's side, and the Viceroy of Milan, Charles d'Amboise, the stout old general, Gian Giacomo Trivulzio, and the young Duke of Bourbon, immediately behind him. Baldassare looked with interest on this tall and handsome youth, whose mother, Chiara Gonzaga, had been escorted by his own parents on her wedding journey to France, and who now met his Italian kinsmen for the first time. Little did the Duke of Urbino's envoy dream of the terrible doom which this courteous

[1] Serassi, i. 33.

and graceful lad was one day to bring upon Italy ;
little did the young Duke know that just twenty years
later he would die in battle under the walls of Rome.

There were others in that splendid throng whose
faces must have strangely reminded Castiglione
of his old days in Milan. Close in attendance
on His Most Christian Majesty, honoured by the
highest marks of his favour, was that hero of his
youth, the Moro's favourite, Galeazzo di San Severino,
now known as *il Gran Scudiero* (*le Grand Écuyer*),
with Jacques de Crussol, the gigantic captain of the
archers to whom Lodovico Sforza had surrendered
at Novara, just behind him. There, too, was the
Moro's chosen painter, Leonardo the Florentine,
now, like Messer Galeazzo, in the service of his
deadly foe ; and there was his old master, the
Marquis Francesco, whom he had never seen since
he first went to Urbino. After attending mass in
the Duomo, the King rode on to the Castello, and
here Castiglione was received by King Louis, together
with the ambassadors of Venice, Florence, and
Ferrara. A few days later he was present at the
giostra on the Piazza of the Castello, and saw
Messer Galeazzo distinguish himself in the lists after
his old fashion, and witnessed the great procession on
the Feast of Corpus Christi, when the Host was carried
through the streets by the Legate, under a canopy
borne by the chief French nobles, and followed
by all the clergy and choristers of Milan. He was
among the guests at the famous ball given by Gian
Giacomo Trivulzio, when eleven kitchens were used
to prepare the banquet, and a ball-room was built
for the occasion. The crowd was so great that
the halberdiers had to clear the way for the King's
passage, and dancing lasted from ten in the morning

until vespers.   Many fair ladies smiled on the young courtier from Urbino that evening.   Margherita Pia, the wife of his friend Antonio di San Severino and sister of Madonna Emilia, was there, and Trivulzio's daughter-in-law, the Contessa di Musocho,[1] as well as many ladies of his own kith and kin.   But no one greeted him more graciously than the Marchesa Isabella, who had arrived in hot haste from Mantua at King Louis's urgent entreaty.   This Princess was the cynosure of all eyes as she sat at the royal table at the banquet in the Rocchetta, and danced with exquisite grace at her royal partner's side in these same halls where Castiglione had often seen her in Duchess Beatrice's days.

A splendid banquet given by his friend Cardinal Ippolito concluded the festivities, and then Baldassare made his way back to Urbino, where he found the Duke and all his household in the best of health and spirits.   The arrears of salary due to him were promptly paid, his anxieties were allayed for the moment, and he could enjoy the company of his friends and the pleasant summer weather without a care.

That season was long remembered at Urbino. The severe winter was succeeded by great heats in the spring and summer.   Excepting on Easter Eve, when there was a violent storm, no rain fell during ten months.   'There was one season,' Ariosto sings, 'when Apollo seemed to have once more given Phaeton the reins of his coursers, and every well and fount in the land ran dry, and you could pass the most famous rivers without a bridge.'[2]   The bed of the river Foglia was dry all the winter, the mills could not work, and the peasants of Cesena brought

[1] Paola Gonzaga, half-sister to Alberto Pio.
[2] 'Satira Terza.'

their corn to be ground at Cagli. That year harvest
began on the 26th of May in the valley of La Foglia,
and, by the 1st of June, was in full swing throughout
the country. But no seed came up excepting a little
that had been sown in October; the barley and oats
and clover were a complete failure. The price of
corn rose to sixty ducats a bushel, and Castiglione
wrote to beg his mother to send a load of oats and
straw by boat from Mantua to Ferrara and Pesaro,
if the Marquis would give leave, since no forage
was to be had at Urbino. Soon the wells began to
fail, and water had to be bought in the town. By
June the well at the gate of Valbona was exhausted,
and on July 20 the great well on the market-place,
which had never been known to fail before, ran dry.
The meadows were burnt up, and the vintage was so
scanty that wine had to be mixed with three parts of
water, and cider and perry were largely drunk, pears
and apples being the only fruits that were plentiful.
Every one suffered, but none the less, adds the
chronicler, people 'were very well in health.'[1]

The fine weather lasted till Christmas. All through
November roses bloomed in abundance and attar of
roses was distilled from their leaves; strawberries and
mulberries ripened in December, to the wonder of
all who saw them. Fortunately the second harvest
was better than the first, and by the end of the year
the price of corn fell to its normal level.

It was also a memorable year at the court. All
through the summer distinguished guests came and
went. The Pope's visits had attracted universal
attention, and the eyes of all Europe were fixed upon
Urbino. Early in the autumn King Ferdinand the
Catholic and his new Queen, Germaine de Foix,

[1] Cod. Vat. Urb., 904.

came to Naples, and expressed a wish to visit the Duke and Duchess, but were unable to carry out this project. Another still more illustrious visitor was expected, as we learn from several passages in the letters of Elisabetta and Castiglione that autumn. This was the Emperor Maximilian, who had made great preparations for his Italian journey, and was very anxious to see the famous palace of Urbino. But the obstinate refusal of the Diet to allow the expedition, and his own habitual lack of money, frustrated his plans at the last moment, and His Cæsarean Majesty was unable to keep the promise which he had made to the Duchess. This decision was probably a relief to her, for in August, Guidobaldo had a serious illness, which, although fortunately of brief duration, left him in an enfeebled state of health and unfit to bear any fatigue. The frequency and severity of the fits of gout from which he suffered, only increased the anxiety of his wife and friends to amuse him by every means in their power. He often watched his courtiers playing at 'palla' in the new hall which he had built to take the place of the old ground under S. Domenico, where the marks of the players' balls are still to be seen on the Della Robbia lunette above the door. And he was never tired of reading and discussing his favourite classical authors with Castiglione and Bembo, or any of the distinguished scholars whom chance brought to Urbino for a few days.

Filippo Beroaldo and Latino Giovenale both visited Urbino that summer. Bernardo Bibbiena came in August with his master the Cardinal, and made himself so agreeable that every one lamented his departure, and, as Bembo took care to tell his friend,

neither the Duchess nor Madonna Emilia were ever
tired of expressing their regard for him. Lodovico
Canossa and Alberto Pio were there too, the latter
on his return from Rome, whither he had been
sent as Ambassador by the King of France. This
handsome and cultured Prince, the intimate friend
of Castiglione and Bembo, had a special attraction
at Urbino in the person of Margherita Gonzaga, whom
he courted for many years, and who is called his
affianced bride in contemporary letters. Bembo
speaks of this fair maiden as ' Madonna vostra con-
sorte ' in a letter which he addressed to Alberto
in August, when he was daily expected at Urbino.
Another correspondent describes him and his betrothed bride as the most devoted pair, who have no
eyes or ears for anyone else, and says that when the
hour of parting comes, so many tears are shed on both
sides, that every one pities them. But, in spite of this
mutual devotion, the lovers were never united, and
the misfortunes which befell Alberto, the loss of his
State and his long exile, put an end to his hopes of
marriage.

Terpandro, the gay and popular poet, lingered on
until late in the autumn, and was followed to Rome by
affectionate messages from all the ladies and many
entreaties to return speedily. In October Raphael
came from Florence, where he was at work on his
great Entombment for Madonna Atalanta Baglioni
of Perugia, and paid his respects to the Duke and
Duchess, and renewed his friendship with Castiglione,
whose affection for the painter was well known to
all the court—' Your Raphael,' as Gian Cristoforo
calls him in the dialogues of the ' Cortegiano.'[1]

Each one of these guests received the same gracious

[1] Book i., 50.

welcome from the Duchess, and felt strangely loth to go, when summoned elsewhere on public or private business. For the court of Urbino was not only, as Cristoforo Romano called it, in one of his last letters to Bembo, the 'blessed temple of all the virtues,' but, as Castiglione and Bembo described it, a 'home of joy and common brotherhood, a shelter and haven where troubled souls could find peace of mind and freedom from carking care.'

'Come here!' wrote Bembo to Luigi da Porto, who was lying ill at Venice and oppressed with strange melancholy. 'Everything invites you. We will laugh for a week, and drive away the blues, which, I see, have laid hold upon you. If you love me, be joyful and keep up your spirits, for this is the only way to live. Therefore come.'[1]

And in a letter to Latino Juvenale in Rome he writes:

'There is little to say of our doings here; but we laugh, we jest, we play games, we invent new tricks and practical jokes, we feast and study, and now and then we write poetry. If I had more time, which I have not to-day, I would send you a proof of this in a beautiful *canzone* which my dear M. Baldassare Castiglione has composed during the last few days. You shall have it another time. Farewell. On the 9th of September, 1507, in more than haste.'[2]

Probably this *canzone* was the poem beginning,

'Amor, poi chè 'l pensier,'

in which Dante's famous line,

'Amor ch' a nullo amato amor perdona,'

is introduced, and each verse, after the fashion of the day, ends with a line of Petrarch.

[1] 'Lettere,' iii. 107.   [2] *Ibid.*, iii. 33.

Again Bembo sends his old Venetian friend Trifone
Gabriele one of his latest productions, ' a new *canzone*
on an old theme—the death of my brother,' the lovely
poem beginning with the lines :

> ' Alma cortese, che dal mondo errante
> Partente nella tua più verde étà,
> Hai me lasciato eternamente in doglio,'

In the same letter he repeats how perfectly happy he
is at Urbino, and how fervently he thanks the fates
which have brought him safely into port after all his
wanderings :

' Here I will only tell you that every day I rejoice
the more to have taken the course for which all of
my friends blamed me more than you did, and am
confident that one day they too will praise the wisdom
of my choice.'[1]

One day he sends Lucrezia Borgia two sonnets on
the device of the Cardinal of Aragon, to remind his
old comrades at Ferrara of his existence.   Another
time he encloses what he describes as his latest
canzone to his ' valiant brother-in-arms,' Archbishop
Fregoso, and invites the criticism of his Roman
friends on these compositions.

Most of these poems were fugitive pieces, which,
as Bembo himself owned, owe much of their charm
to the circumstances in which they were produced.
Such, for instance, was the sonnet

> ' Io ardo, e la risposta invano,
> Come il gioco chieda, lasso aspettar,'

which an early commentator explains to be an
allusion to a game of *propositi*, or questions and
answers, that was played one evening, and in which

---

[1] ' Lettere,' ii., 28.

the poet gives vent to his mortification at the Duchess's refusal to reply to his protestations of devotion.'[1] But here and there we come across a really fine sonnet, especially among those composed by Castiglione, who was, without doubt, the best poet of the group.   The Latin elegies, in which he warns the nymphs of the perils of the treacherous flood and the dangers of the unknown shore, or recalls the cruel fate of Hippolytus; the verses on the Duchess singing Dido's lament to her lute—' De Elisabetta Gonzaga canente '—naturally excited the admiration of the court, but his finest poetry, we think, was written in the vulgar tongue.   His Italian *canzoni* and sonnets strike a deeper note than any of the elegant trifles which Bembo and his comrades turned out with so much ease and deftness.   They speak the language of strong and true emotion, and their tender melancholy and natural grace are inspired by genuine poetic feeling.

The air of Urbino was haunted with classical memories ; its atmosphere was genuinely literary, and the interests of courtiers and ladies alike centred in these subjects.   Every one brought something to add to the common fund.   Those who did not write could always listen or criticize.   The young Prefect himself, a born soldier, of coarser fibre than the Dukes of the Montefeltro race, took keen interest in Greek and Roman history, and could discuss Xenophon's retreat or the siege of Carthage with intelligence.[2]   Even Cardinal Galeotto and Giuliano de' Medici, as we have seen, wrote sonnets.   Letters from Veronica Gambara or Graziosa Maggi, Latin epistles in prose or rhyme, arrived by every post from

---

[1] Cod. Vat., 8825 ; V. Cian, ' Motti inediti di P. Bembo,' 91.
[2] Riposati, ii. 127.

Rome or Mantua, and were passed from hand to
hand. The pleasantries of Bibbiena or Terpandro,
the practical jokes that were played on the Aretine
and Fra Serafino, afforded the whole company infinite
amusement. One day a witty letter would arrive
from the Marchesana Isabella, recounting the splendours of her visit to Milan, or forestalling the pomps
and pleasures of a journey to France, and defying
Duchess Elisabetta to rival these triumphs. Then
Madonna Emilia and Bembo or Castiglione would
lay their heads together and help the Duchess to
compose a merry answer, couched in the same style
and exulting in the glories of the Holy Father's visit
to Urbino, and in the royal and imperial guests whose
arrival was shortly expected. Another time some
antique bust or cameo, a marble relief of Taurus or
an engraved gem of Victory, would be sent by Gian
Cristoforo or Bibbiena from Rome, and courtiers and
ladies would hasten to admire the new treasure and
write epigrams in its praise. Or else a little group
would gather round the wonderful Aretine, and listen
with rapt attention to his eloquent improvisations and
dramatic recitals. And every evening, when the sun
set behind the far Apennines, and the long ridge of
Monte Nerone turned to ever-deepening blue, courtiers
and ladies met in the rooms of the Duchess. Madonna
Emilia and Gaspare Pallavicini started a war of quick
sallies and lively repartees, or Castiglione and the
Magnifico entered on an animated discussion regarding
the rival merits of painting and sculpture. Then the
Aretine dexterously turned the conversation on poetry,
and recited a sonnet of his own invention. If Bibbiena
chanced to be present, he told witty stories, and
encouraged others to follow his example, until the
hall rang with joyous laughter. Finally Bembo

took up his parable, and descanted on the immortal
power of Love and its Divine origin, and the company
listened, spell-bound by his eloquence, until the short
hours of the summer night were wellnigh over and
dawn was breaking in the eastern sky.

'Then the windows being opened on the side of
the palace looking towards the lofty peak of Monte
Catria, they saw that a beautiful aurora of rose-red
hue was already breaking in the east, and that all the
stars had vanished save the sweet Queen of the realm
of Venus, who holds sway in the borderland of night
and day.   A gentle breeze filled the air with freshness, and began to waken the sweet voices of joyous
birds in the murmuring forests of the neighbouring
hills.   All the company rose, and, having paid their
reverence to the Lady Duchess and taken leave of
her, went to their rooms without the light of torches,
that of day being sufficient.'[1]

[1] 'Cortegiano,' book iv , 73.

CHAPTER XV

1507–1508

Murder of Gian Andrea by Francesco Maria della Rovere — Comments of Bembo and Castiglione—The Duke's failing health—The court moves to Fossombrone—Last days and death of Guidobaldo—Tribute of Bembo to his memory.

In spite of the complaints of Cupid and the reproaches addressed by the ambassadors of Venus to the cruel fair who dwelt on the banks of the Metaurus, the ladies of Urbino were by no means all of them proof against the winged shafts of the god of love. Madonna Emilia, it is true, preserved an inviolable fidelity to her dead husband, and Castiglione sought no reward for his wholehearted allegiance but a word or smile from the Lady Duchess. But there were others who were cast in less heroic mould. Even at the court of Urbino youths and maidens were human, and dances and games in the palace, as Castiglione owns, afforded plenty of occasion for lovers to reveal their secrets by meeting eyes and clasping hands. It was pleasant to sit apart in the deep recess of the high-arched windows on a summer night, and listen to whispered vows, when Jacopo di San Secondo's viol was pouring out its impassioned strains, or to linger at the side of a gallant cavalier, under the roses and jessamine of the pergola, when the moon rose above the triple peaks of San Marino and the cool ripple of running water fell with soft murmur on the midnight air.

Bembo might descant in eloquent periods of the mystic glories and Divine origin of Love, but its earthly side was none the less familiar to him, and his letters to Bibbiena abound in cryptic allusions to their respective mistresses. 'All men live for love,' he sang in one of his best poems, and he himself was no exception to the rule. Margherita Gonzaga did not turn a deaf ear to Beroaldo's praises when her betrothed husband was no longer at her side, and the Magnifico's relations with Madonna Pacifica were far from being of a Platonic nature. But there was one love affair that autumn which had more serious consequences, and ended in a tragedy that forms a dark and painful contrast to the peaceful joys which marked court life at Urbino.

There was a young squire of Verona, named Giovanni Andrea, who had been the Duke's companion in his midnight flight before Cesare Borgia, and had distinguished himself fighting under the Church's banner in the campaigns of Romagna. Three years before, Guidobaldo had conferred the honour of knighthood upon him, and had rewarded his devotion with a grant of the castle of Sascorbara and the lucrative mills on the Foglia. Although of humble birth, Gian Andrea's gallant bearing and polished manners made him a great favourite, not only with the Duke, but with all the people of Urbino, and he is mentioned among the chief ornaments of the court by more than one writer. But in an evil hour this squire of low degree dared to pay his addresses to the Prefect's sister, Maria Varana, whose husband had been murdered by Cesare Borgia, and who was

living at her uncle's court with her orphan boy,
Sigismondo, the young Lord of Camerino. 'Although
a widow,' remarks the diarist, 'Maria was still
young and beautiful,' and lent an all too willing
ear to this Veronese knight, who, brave and handsome as he might be, was no fit match for so
illustrious a lady. In spite of this barrier Maria
loved the handsome cavalier. During many months
an intrigue was carried on between these two, and
it was even whispered that the Duke's niece had
borne Gian Andrea a son, who was hidden safely
away in some obscure corner. As ill-luck would
have it, this rumour reached the ears of Francesco
della Rovere when he returned from Rome in
September, 1507. This fiery and ill-disciplined lad,
who was only seventeen years of age, had lately
quarrelled with his mother, the Prefetessa, over the
government of Sinigaglia, and appealed to his uncle
against her. Pope Julius, who was fond of his
nephew, and easily forgave the violent temper which
resembled his own, took Francesco's part, and warned
Giovanna not to interfere with her son. So the
young man returned to Urbino in high spirits. In
a letter of the 13th to his friend Bibbiena, Pietro
Bembo remarks significantly that the Prefect has
arrived, and is, not only remarkably well, but particularly amiable, especially to the Magnifico, with
whom he appears to be on the best of terms.
But before many weeks had passed the story of his
sister's dishonour reached Francesco's ears. In his
rage he vowed to avenge a wrong which only blood
could wipe out, and since Gian Andrea was the
Duke's favourite, and could not easily be publicly
attacked, he determined to have recourse to treachery.
It was the first week in November, but the weather

was as hot as August, and the roses were still in full bloom. The Duke, with Castiglione and a few others of his suite, was absent for a few days, and Francesco took this opportunity to invite Gian Andrea to dine in his rooms one Saturday evening and have a fencing-match, a sport of which the young Prefect was very fond, and in which his guest excelled. After dinner the young men took up their foils and were engaged in the contest, when suddenly two of Francesco's servants entered from behind and seized Gian Andrea by the arms, while the Prefettino himself stabbed his guest to the heart with a knife. After this his servants fell upon the unfortunate knight and finished their master's work. The body was left pierced with wounds on the floor of the room, while Francesco, telling his servants to keep the door barred, took horse and rode as fast as he could go to his own city of Sinigaglia.

Meanwhile the Duchess, hearing a noise, came to her nephew's rooms and knocked at the door. But no answer came, and when Elisabetta, filled with alarm, bade one of the servants open the door, he replied: 'Madonna, it is of no use, I have the Lord Prefect's order to keep the door fast; and if you could open it you would see a sight that would be very displeasing to your eyes.' The Duchess insisted, the door was thrown open, and at the sight of the dead body covered with blood the poor lady burst into a flood of tears. 'But the Prefettino was gone,' continues the Venetian envoy, who reported the ghastly tale, 'and that same evening he sent some of his servants to kill his sister's carver, who had been employed to bear letters to her lover.'[1]

Both court and city were filled with horror and

[1] Sanuto, vii. 194.

consternation at the cruel deed, and the Duke, who
returned immediately on hearing the terrible news,
was plunged in the deepest grief. 'And the next
day,' writes the Urbino chronicler, 'being the
Madonna's feast-day,[1] after vespers, the dead knight
was borne with the greatest honour to the Duomo,
followed by all the Duke's gentlemen and all the
citizens, men and women, great and small, all weeping
bitterly, because he was so handsome and so beloved,
and for many years past no one who died in Urbino
had been more widely lamented.'[2]

In strange contrast to these words are the curt
sentences in which both Castiglione and Bembo
allude in their private letters to the unhappy Gian
Andrea's assassination. At the end of a letter to
his mother, written on November 21, after giving
orders about some bards and horses' trappings which
he had left at Casatico, Baldassare remarked :

'There has been some disturbance here about an
unfortunate event in the ducal family [*in Casa nostra*].
However, things are settling down now, and the Lord
Prefect is here again, so I hope there will be no
further trouble in the matter.'

By this time news of the horrid deed had reached
Mantua, and Madonna Luigia wrote, full of concern
and dismay, to make inquiries of her son. All that
Baldassare, however, would say in reply was to beg
her not to vex herself about the inevitable.

'You need not distress yourself,' he wrote on
December 2, 'about the death of Gio. Andrea—
may God pardon him !—because these things, when

[1] Sunday after All Saints' Day which in the Roman calendar is
observed as the patronal festival of churches consecrated to the
Blessed Virgin.
[2] Cod. Vat. Urb., 904 ; Ugolini, ii. 141.

they are once done, cannot be undone. Everything has been arranged, thanks to the wisdom and dexterity of the Lord Duke, and the Lord Prefect is here again, and is restored to His Excellency's favour, and he who no longer lives is already forgotten.'[1]

Bembo's reference to the murder sounds even more cold-blooded and heartless in our ears. On November 13, barely a week after the deed which had sent a shudder through the court and city, he wrote to inform Bibbiena that he had just returned from a visit to Padua, and observed that he would hear the latest news from Count Lodovico Canossa, who was on the point of starting for Rome.

'The Count will tell you what has happened here, regarding which he has received full and minute particulars from Messer Cesare. So I will keep silence, and will only say this : he who might remain standing, and falls by his own fault, deserves to lie there against his will.'[2]

It is difficult to understand the confusion of moral ideas which could lead a scholar as refined as Bembo, and a knight as gentle and high-minded as Castiglione, to palliate so dark and treacherous an act. All that can be said in their defence is that, by the code of honour commonly accepted in those days, there were certain wrongs which only death could avenge. The situation was no doubt a very difficult one both for the Duke and Duchess. The perpetrator of the deed was not only their own nephew and heir to the crown, but the Pope's nephew and the affianced husband of Elisabetta's niece. Hence family as well as political exigencies led them to accept Francesco's excuses and forgive his crime. Under these circum-

---

[1] Serassi, i. 34.   [2] 'Lettere,' iii. 15.

CARDINAL BEMBO.
(BRITISH MUSEUM.)

CARDINAL ALIDOSI.
(BRITISH MUSEUM.)

To face p. 228, Vol. I.

stances silence seemed to be the only possible course
of action, and it became the duty of a loyal courtier
to avoid any reference to the subject. It is, however,
worthy of note that both the historians of Urbino,
Baldi and Leoni, abstain from the faintest allusion
to the murder of Gian Andrea,[1] and it is only the
unknown chronicler of the Vatican manuscript and
the Venetian archives which supply us with details
of the incident.   Abate Serassi, in his notes on
Castiglione's correspondence, owns himself completely
baffled in his researches to explain the mystery, and
confesses to complete ignorance of the events to
which M. Baldassare refers in the above-quoted
passages.

So the very name of the Duke's favourite was
never heard again, and Francesco Maria's crime was
forgotten, until four years later the murder of Cardinal
Alidosi recalled this violent deed to the memory of
his enemies. As for Maria Varana, the other victim
of her brother's vengeance, we hear no more of her,
and only know that she was still living at Urbino
from a casual reference to her in the letters of a
Venetian envoy, who mentions a report that she was
to marry one of the valiant San Severino brothers.
This was Gaspare, better known by his surname,
Fracassa, who spent some time at Urbino in the
spring of 1513, and accompanied Duke Francesco
Maria to Rome. But the idea was abandoned, and
Maria, as far as we know, never married again.[2] The
court soon resumed its wonted tranquillity. The

---

[1] Ugolini, ii. 143.

[2] Littà and Dennistoun both state that Maria Varana married
Galeazzo Sforza Riario, the second son of Caterina Sforza, of Forli
and Imola ('Famiglie celebri,' ii. 267), but evidently confuse the
lady with her cousin, Cardinal Galeotto's sister, Maria Sista, who
in 1504 became the bride of this prince.

Prefect returned to his old quarters in the palace, and
Castiglione and Cesare Gonzaga rode out with him in
masks through the streets that Christmas, and made
merry in their usual fashion.   Bibbiena wrote witty
letters as before from Rome ; we hear of one especially amusing effusion which was addressed to his
three companions, Bembo, Castiglione, and Cesare Gonzaga, and provoked the Duchess and Madonna Emilia
to much laughter.   But the death of the Prefettino's
youngest sister, Costanza, was a cause of fresh sorrow
to the ducal house.   She died in Rome in December,
at the age of eighteen, 'greatly,' writes Castiglione,
'to the Lord Duke's grief.   God wanted her for
Himself,' he adds, 'because she was good.'

Soon after this Messer Cesare's horse slipped down
one snowy night in January, when he and the Prefect
and Baldassare were masquerading in the street, and
this gay gentleman was laid up for some weeks with
a broken leg.   Baldassare nursed his cousin atten-
tively, and wrote frequent letters to Mantua to calm
his mother and uncle's alarms.

Nor was Madonna Luigia without her anxieties that
winter.   Her son-in-law, Jacopo Boschetto, was ill,
and worried his wife and every one with his bad
temper.   'God restore him to health !' wrote
Baldassare one day that he had received an unusually
disagreeable letter from Messer Jacopo.   'It seems
to me his brain is full of that cursed gout, and this
must have affected his mind.'   But these minor
troubles faded into insignificance when in the early
spring the Duke fell dangerously ill.

In January the weather, which had remained
singularly mild up till Christmas, turned bitterly
cold, and snow and frost set in with severity.   Guidobaldo suffered from a bad attack of gout, and, at his

doctor's advice, decided to move to Fossombrone towards the end of the month. But when he reached San Bernardino in his litter he became alarmingly ill, and was obliged to spend the night at the neighbouring convent. The next day he recovered sufficiently to continue the journey to Fossombrone, where, under the influence of a warmer climate and sea-breezes, his health improved considerably, and on February 4 Castiglione was able to give his mother an excellent report of his lord's condition.

Bembo had gone to Rome, where Bibbiena had secured him comfortable quarters in the Belvedere, close to Cardinal de' Medici's apartments, and where Cristoforo the sculptor and Beroaldo were eagerly awaiting him to join their merry circle in Bernardo's *camerino*. At the end of the year Giuliano de' Medici also left for Rome, while Cesare Gonzaga was still laid up at Urbino. But the Prefect and Ottaviano Fregoso, as well as his mother and sisters, accompanied the Duke and Duchess to Fossombrone, and Castiglione, faithful to the last, remained in constant attendance on his beloved master during these last weeks. Guidobaldo grew paler and thinner every day, and when April brought a renewal of frost and snow his strength failed rapidly, and it became evident to the loving eyes that watched him that he could not live much longer. His devoted wife hardly left his bedside day or night, and his nephews, Francesco Maria and Ottaviano, were unremitting in their attentions. Guidobaldo himself retained consciousness to the end, and gave his last orders with perfect composure and tranquillity. The friends who stood round his couch tried to cheer him with hopes of recovery, but he only shook his head, and said as he looked at their sad faces : ' Why, my dear ones, should you wish to deprive me of the good that I long for most? Is not death, which can deliver me from these cruel pains, the kindest and best of friends?' And, turning to Castiglione, he repeated these lines of Virgil:

> ' Me circum limus niger et deformis arundo
> Cocyti, tardaque palus inamabilis unda
> Alligat, et novies Styx interfusa coercet.'[1]

After that his voice failed, but his dying gaze rested on his wife's pale face, and the Duchess, taking his cold hand in hers, tried to console him with sweet and tender words. On April 11 he asked for the last Sacraments, which the Bishop of Fossombrone administered, and bade his nearest relatives farewell. He addressed his last counsels to the Prefetto, and charged him solemnly to govern his people well, to be just and clement, and to take his uncle, the Pope, and his noble grandfather, Duke Federico, for his models. Above all, he begged him to obey the Duchess in everything, and treat her with filial love and reverence. Last of all he turned to Elisabetta, calling her his '*sposa carissima e dilettissima*,' and implored her to guide and help his nephew in the government of the State, that he might prove worthy of his race. 'But I need give you no commands,' he added tenderly; ' you know better than I do what I wish, and I place all my trust in you.' When his heart-broken wife tried to hide the tears that she could not restrain, he begged her not to weep and disturb the peace of his soul, since he was passing to a blessed home. After that he never spoke again, but lay for some time with his eyes fixed on his wife's face and his hand in hers. At ten o'clock that evening Cas-

---

[1] ' Georg.,' iv. 478.

tiglione snatched a spare moment to write the following brief note to his mother:

' I only send these few lines in answer to the letter brought me by Fracassa because we are all in the greatest distress. His Excellency the Duke is sinking fast, and the doctors give little or no hope of his life. The loss is very great for every one of us, most of all for the poor Lady Duchess, whom I will never leave as long as she needs my services. God help us! I think the Lord Prefect will succeed peaceably to this duchy. M. Cesare is at Urbino, which is a good thing, as no one else of importance is in the palace, and we cannot tell what may happen.'

An hour later the end came. The dying Prince laid his right cheek upon his hand, composed himself to sleep, and, without the slightest struggle, passed away so gently that Castiglione and the others who knelt around hardly knew when he was gone. 'No one,' wrote Bembo to Vincenzo Querini, 'ever died more calmly and nobly and in a more Christian manner.'

Even the Venetian humanist's cold and calculating spirit was moved to tears at the premature death of this Prince, who was so precious to his family and friends, and so dear to his subjects, who had been trusted and honoured by the Pope, and whose life seemed necessary to the peace of Italy. 'We in Venice,' he reminds his friends, 'witnessed the courage, constancy, and goodness which he showed in the weary days of exile, when both he and the Duchess made themselves so dear to us that it was hard to say which of the two was the more beloved. . . . And so ends the life of the rarest Prince of our age—let others say what they will!'[1]

[1] 'Lettere,' ii. 65.

CHAPTER XVI

1508

The Pope sends Archbishop Fregoso to Fossombrone—Grief of the Duchess and lamentation in Urbino—Castiglione's letter to Henry VII. of England and funeral of Duke Guidobaldo—Castiglione sent to Gubbio—Bembo's treatise.

THE news of Duke Guidobaldo's dangerous illness was a cause of great sorrow to his friends at the Vatican. The Pope sent the Archbishop of Salerno and his own doctor, Arcangelo da Siena, to give him the Papal benediction and attend him in these critical moments. But when Fregoso reached Fossombrone, the good Duke had already breathed his last, and all that he could do was to comfort the stricken widow. Both Castiglione, who witnessed the Duke's death, and Bembo, who heard full particulars of that moving scene from Fregoso, tell us how bravely the Duchess bore up to the last. It was only when she saw that her husband was dead, that her courage forsook her, and, flinging her arms with a cry of agony round his neck, and kissing his cold brow, she exclaimed: 'Why have you left me, my beloved? Where are you going? At least let me die with you!' Then she fell fainting in the arms of Madonna Emilia, while every one in the room broke into tears and sobbing, and throughout the

GVIDVBALDVS I.MONFELTR' VRBINI | DUX III. S.R.E. VEXILLIFER, &c.&c.
Hic Ducis Federici, & Baptiste Sfortie Coniug. | Filius xvi. Kal Februar. An. 1472. in lucem editus
& xv. Kal. Octobris Anno 1480. | Ducatus Imperium. suscepit.
Princeps clementissimus, & mira in adversis | patientia preditus, quo auspice littere Urbini
adeo coaluere, ut inter ceteras accademias | pmum sibi locum merito vindicaverit, etate
An.36. Men n.Di. 18. Forisempronij suaviter animam | eslavit m.Id. Aplis An.1508., ejusque Corpus Urbium
delatum in Min.Ref. S.Bernardini Ecclesia extra | Urbis menia tumulo fuit conditum.
Frantius Antonius Rondelli Urbinas f. 1743.

Photo, Lieut. Simondi.

GUIDOBALDO, DUKE OF URBINO.

To face p. 234, Vol. I.

house nothing but the sound of weeping could be heard. For the next twenty-four hours fears for Elisabetta's life were seriously entertained, and a report reached Urbino that the Duchess was dead, as well as her lord, and excited a frantic outburst of lamentation. The first thing that roused her from the stupor into which she had fallen was the arrival of Archbishop Fregoso, who read a letter from the Pope, and begged her to think of the young Duke and help him, for the sake of the love which she bore her husband and the trust which he reposed in her. Francesco himself spoke affectionately, calling her his mother, and reminding her how much depended upon her at this moment. With a great effort she controlled her grief, and, drying her tears, gave the necessary orders for the funeral, and issued a proclamation calling on the late Duke's subjects to obey his wishes and acknowledge Francesco Maria as his successor.

On the evening of Wednesday, April 12, the Duke's body was borne on the shoulders of the *contadini* of Fossombrone, attended by the members of his household carrying lighted torches, over the mountain-passes. Castiglione, who rode at the head of the mournful procession, describes the weird sights and sounds of that sad journey—the weeping crowds who lined the roads, the howling of the dogs on the lonely hillside, and the darkness of the starless night. The Duchess followed some hours later in a litter with her ladies, and the Prefect, who had ridden on before, met the corpse at the church of San Bernardino, with the nobles and gentlemen of the court. All that day the greatest agitation had prevailed in the city, and, in spite of the snow which fell heavily, the market-place was crowded with people throughout the night.

A meteor was said to hover in the air above the ducal palace, and the gates of the Zoccolanti Church, in which Duke Federico was buried, were seen to open wide and close again. A dense throng of weeping men and women, many bearing their babes in their arms, and striking their breasts and tearing their hair in token of their grief, lined the streets, as the chief magistrates of the city bore their dead lord to the palace gates. Here his body was clad in the black damask vest, rose-red hose, and gold-fringed cap, which he had worn, it is said, when Raphael painted his portrait, and over all was thrown the blue mantle of the Garter, with crimson velvet hood lined with white silk. Thus attired the Duke was laid on a stately catafalque, hung with gold brocade and surrounded with blazing torches, in the centre of the great banquet-hall, and here during the next two days his subjects came in crowds to take a last look at their beloved Prince. On Thursday morning Duke Guidobaldo's will was read in the Duomo. His nephew was appointed his heir and successor, and the widowed Duchess was to govern the State and administer the revenues until he reached the age of twenty-five. This prudent proviso did much to allay the fears of the citizens, who were inclined to look with suspicion on Francesco Maria, and had deeply resented their favourite Gian Andrea's murder. But such was the love which the people of Urbino bore to the Duchess that no one would oppose her wishes, and, as Bembo told his friend, ' it is quite certain that, if she had chosen to dispose of the State in any other way, all the city and country and every man in the realm would have obeyed her word, partly because she held S. Leo and all the chief fortresses in the realm, but still more because of the

ELISABETTA GONZAGA
Moglie del Duca
le cui nozze si celebrarono
Morì in Urbino

GONZAGA
Guid Ubaldo I.
l'Autunno dell'An. 1489
nel Febraro del 1526

Photo, Lieut. Simondi.

ELISABETTA GONZAGA, DUCHESS OF URBINO.

To face p. 236, Vol. I.

incredible love which they bore her.'[1]   Then the new
Duke was solemnly proclaimed, and, after receiving
the keys of the city gates in a silver basin, rode
through the town in white satin robes, and with the
ducal cap and crown on his head, amid shouts of
'Feltre! Feltre! Duca! Prefetto!' According to
the usual custom, on his return to the palace, the
Duke's charger and robes were given up to the
citizens; but such was the excitement of the young
men on this occasion that his white satin mantle lined
with cloth of gold was torn to pieces, and, in order to
satisfy them, Francesco gave them another robe of
black velvet and a gold brocade cloak. When the
ceremony was ended, the chief citizens were received
by the widowed Duchess. In spite of her pale and
altered appearance, and of the tears that she could not
check, she made them what our friend the diarist
calls 'a most beautiful speech,' thanking them for all
their love and sympathy, and begging them to show
the same loyalty and devotion to the Prefetto as
they had shown to their last Duke. 'I have lost a
most beloved husband,' she said, with touching
simplicity. 'and you a devoted Prince and father.
You all know how much he loved you. But it is the
will of God, who tries those whom He loves best
most sorely.'   And she thanked them for obeying
his last wishes, saying that the sight of their love and
loyalty to his desires would be her husband's best
joy in heaven, and the greatest consolation she
could have.[2] At six o'clock the Bishops and priests
assembled in the great hall, where a solemn requiem
was held, and at eight all the citizens, with Francesco
Maria at their head and lighted torches in their hands,
followed Guidobaldo's remains to the church of

[1] 'Lettere,' ii. 66.   [2] Baldi, p. 235.

S. Chiara. Here the body lay in state all night, many women being among the watchers by the bier, and ' on Friday,' adds the chronicler, ' they bore him to San Bernardino, and laid him in a coffin covered with gold brocade, opposite that of his father, as he had willed, and it rained torrents all the while.'[1]

In her deep sorrow Elisabetta showed a wisdom which excited the admiration of soldiers and states-men alike. Both Bembo, who was in Rome at the time, and her warlike brother, Giovanni Gonzaga, who had hastened to Urbino on hearing of Guido-baldo's death, praise her care and forethought in sending trusted councillors to the chief cities of the duchy to ensure the young Duke's peaceful succes-sion, 'thus showing herself,' wrote Giovanni, 'to be the wise and prudent lady that she is.'

Castiglione was sent to Gubbio, where the citizens were inclined to be unruly and disaffection was chiefly to be feared, and discharged his errand with complete success, as he informed his mother in a letter of April 29 :

'It is many days since I have written to you, because I have been so much occupied lately owing to the great and bitter loss we have suffered in the death of my dear lord and master. If the loss of so excellent a Prince is grievous for the whole of Italy, it is far worse for us here. The Lady Duchess is still in the deepest distress, but even she must take comfort in time. I certainly think Her Excellency's fate will be a sad one. If you have written to her, it will be a very good thing. I have just returned from Eugubbio, because there was some fear that this change of rulers would excite a tumult, as the city is full of powerful men and much enmity. But God has not allowed anything of the sort to happen. Everything

[1] Cod. Vat. Urb., 904.

has gone gone off well, and all the chief citizens were most obedient to my orders. Now I have returned to Urbino, to find the same tears and darkness everywhere. As for my future, I think I shall remain in the new Duke's service on the same conditions as before, because His Excellency seems very glad to have me near him, and it appears that His Holiness the Pope also desires that M. Cesare and I should stay with him. Meanwhile I shall not cease to do my duty towards the Lady Duchess and the Duke. Anyhow, you need not be anxious about my prospects, for at least I am out of swaddling bands and can look after myself.'[1]

The Gonfaloniere was sent to Rome to inform the Pope formally of Duke Guidobaldo's death and thank him on behalf of the Duchess for his kind offices. Both in public and private Julius II. expressed the deepest grief for the death of this Prince, whom he had loved and trusted more than any other man, as well as the most sincere regard and admiration for the Duchess.

He sent the Gonfaloniere back with a Papal brief in which he condoled with the faithful people of Urbino on the loss of their beloved Duke, and desired them to pay the same allegiance to his nephew, Francesco della Rovere, rejoicing that one of his own flesh and blood should now reign over them. With him came Giuliano de' Medici and Bembo, as well as a number of ambassadors and deputies from all parts of Italy, to bear condolences to the Duchess and attend the solemn funeral which took place on May 2. The Duomo was hung with black, and a stately catafalque, surrounded with 500 wax candles, was erected in the centre of the nave, immediately before the high altar. This funeral pile, with its

---

[1] Serassi, i. 39.

architectural and heraldic devices, its rows of columns and arches, its shields decorated with the arms, titles, and portraits of the Duke and Duchess, with paintings of Guidobaldo's deeds in war and peace, inscribed with appropriate legends, was the work of the court architect and painter, Girolamo Genga and Timoteo Viti, and excited general admiration. On the summit of the bier the mantle and insignia of the Garter, the sword and ducal cap, were laid, a sight which reminded Castiglione painfully of the joyous day when the Duke was first invested in these robes, and all Rome rejoiced with him.

The dead Prince's sister, Gentile Fregoso, with her daughter, Madonna Emilia, and all the ladies of the court, were present at the funeral ceremony in long black veils. Francesco Maria, as chief mourner, was attended by the court officials, the Papal nuncio, magistrates, foreign representatives, and more than 800 persons in mourning cloaks and hoods. An elegant Latin oration, full of classical allusions and invocations of the immortal gods, mingled with pious Christian sentiments, was pronounced by the Duke's old tutor, Lodovico Odasio.[1] This discourse, as both the diarist and that honest soldier, Giovanni Gonzaga, remark, lasted fully an hour. The latter, however, does not presume to pass any judgment upon its merits, but says that it was ' pronounced to be very fine by persons who understand these things better than I do.' The crush at the doors was so great that it was impossible to move, and as many as 10,000 persons passed by the bier. All those who were present agreed that so sumptuous a funeral had never been seen in Italy, and that no Prince had ever been more deeply and widely lamented. Elisabetta

---

[1] Bembo, ' Lettere,' ii. 69.

was determined to leave nothing undone that her
love and sorrow could suggest. By her desire
10,000 masses were said for the repose of her
husband's soul, and arrears of her dowry, amounting
to some 400 gold florins, which were sent her that
week from Mantua, were entirely devoted to this
object.[1]

'When the Duke's funeral was over,' writes Castiglione, 'all thoughts turned towards the Duchess '—
an infinitely pathetic figure in her silent and inconsolable sorrow.

'No eye could remain dry that saw her,' wrote
Bembo to Vincenzo Querini; 'no one could come
near her without being overcome with the deepest
compassion. How profoundly and bitterly she grieves
now that so many days have passed I can hardly tell
you, and you could scarcely believe. Whenever she
sees anyone fresh who has come to condole with her,
she bursts into floods of scalding tears, as if she had
never wept before. When I returned from Rome
some twenty days after the Duke's death, and came
to pay her reverence, no sooner did she catch sight
of me than she burst into tears, so that, instead of
consoling her, I found myself unable to speak a word,
and began to cry myself, and for some time we did
nothing but lament together, until I was obliged to
leave her lest she should weep the whole day. Thus
this unhappy lady remains in continual lamentation,
leading the hardest possible life, and never leaving a
closed chamber hung with black, in which both day
and night the only light is that of one little candle set
on a corner of the floor, so that this room seems to
be a dark and gloomy dungeon rather than a ducal
chamber—a home of the dead rather than of the
living.'

[1] Cod. Vat. Urb., 904; Luzio e Renier, 'Mantova e Urbino,' 185

At the same time he recognizes with wonder and admiration how wisely and well the bereaved lady has discharged the task assigned to her by her lord—how reluctantly, but with what ability and wisdom, she has taken up the reins of government, to the infinite satisfaction of all her husband's subjects, and to the great and lasting benefit of the State. The Prefettino, he owns, although a mere boy, pays her the utmost honour and reverence, and obeys her wishes in every particular. Madonna Emilia, he adds, being herself experienced in sorrows of this kind, has once more given proof of that admirable discretion and greatness of soul for which she is noted, and has been throughout the Duchess's most steadfast helper and companion. Finally, he informs his friends in Venice that it is the good Duchess's pleasure that he and his companions who had made their home at the court of Urbino during her lord's lifetime should remain there still.

' Not only is it greatly for the benefit of her own subjects that this excellent lady still remains in power, but for that of the foreign gentlemen who lived at her husband's court, who will, I believe, all, or almost all, continue in the new Duke's service at her request, since she feels that, out of respect to her lord's memory, this honourable company which served him should not be broken up.'[1]

Accordingly, Bembo and Castiglione, Giuliano de' Medici, and most of the courtiers and scholars who had helped to shed lustre on Guidobaldo's court, remained at Urbino, and served the new Duke in their different capacities. And since nothing could please Elisabetta better, both Bembo and Castiglione

[1] Bembo, 'Lettere,' ii. 70.

Photo, Anderson.

ELISABETTA GONZAGA, DUCHESS OF URBINO.

BY CAROTO (UFFIZI).

To face p. 242, Vol. I

devoted their pens during the next few weeks to
the composition of treatises in honour of the late
Duke. Both of these memorials recount the chief
incidents of Guidobaldo's life, and give full details
of his death and funeral. Both are marked by
the same fine scholarship, while they have all the
charm of spontaneous production. The form they
took, however, was very different. Castiglione
addressed a Latin epistle to King Henry VII. of
England, informing him, as Sovereign of the Knights
of the Garter, of the Duke's death, in courtly language,
with distinct reference to the late Prince's member-
ship of this noble order, and repeated allusions to his
own visit to England. A copy of this letter, bearing
Castiglione's arms, encircled with the golden collar
of SS links which the King had given him, was
sent to Henry VII., and is mentioned by Anstis
in his history of the Order of the Garter. Five years
later it was printed at Fossombrone, in a folio entitled
'De Vita et Gestis Guidobaldi Urbini Ducis,' and
adorned with a miniature of the Duke, which is of
especial interest as being one of the few authentic
portraits of him in existence. He is represented in a
black velvet suit and ermine stole, with flowing locks of
brown hair, parted in the middle of his forehead, long,
thin features and a gentle, melancholy air that give
an impression of habitual ill-health. This miniature
bears a marked likeness to the fine portrait of Guidobaldo by Caroto, now in the Pitti, which was
evidently painted at the same time as the Veronese
master's picture of Elisabetta.

Bembo's 'De Ducibus' is written in the *lingua
volgare*, and is an admirable example of his mastery
of the Italian language, in which, as his friend

Sadoleto remarks, he was as great an expert as in the composition of Latin prose. In the simplest and most natural way he tells us how one spring day, soon after the Duke's death, while Pope Julius was absent at Ostia, he was walking in the Vatican gardens with Sadoleto and Filippo Beroaldo, when the Papal Secretary, Sigismondo Conti of Foligno, came up to them with letters from Urbino. In these dispatches the Archbishop of Salerno described Guidobaldo's last moments in touching language, and the three friends listened with tears to the sad story. Having read the letters aloud, Sigismondo Conti, the prelate whom Raphael afterwards painted kneeling at the Madonna's feet in his great Foligno altar-piece, turned to Bembo and exhorted him to show his love for this illustrious lord and his devoted wife by writing a record of their lives which might be read by persons who had never known them. Then Beroaldo, who had spent the last summer at Urbino, chimed in, recalling the gracious welcome which the Duchess had given him, and extolling Elisabetta as surpassing all other women in beauty of character and greatness of soul. 'Others I have known,' he concludes in a famous phrase, 'conspicuous for certain qualities, but none in whom all virtues and excellencies were combined as they were in her.' Suddenly the conversation of the four scholars was interrupted by the arrival of a messenger from Ostia. Sigismondo hastened to answer His Holiness's letters, Beroaldo and Sadoleto went back to their daily tasks, and Bembo was left alone, musing sadly over the good Duke whose loss all men were lamenting. A few days later, at the urgent request of his father and friends in Venice, who knew how intimate he had been with the lamented Prince, he wrote down this conversation with his three companions, and published it in the form of a dialogue, entitled 'De Ducibus,'[1] which remains one of his best works.

[1] 'Opera,' iv.

WINDOW OF BANQUET-HALL, PALACE OF URBINO.

(See p. 51.)

CHAPTER XVII

1508–1509

Castiglione in the service of Francesco della Rovere—His devotion
to the widowed Duchess — His private affairs, debts, and
difficulties—Marriage proposals made by Giuliano de' Medici
and by the Martinengo family—Castiglione at Bologna with
the Duke—His visit to Casatico—Failure of both negotiations
—Clarice de' Medici betrothed to Filippo Strozzi.

THE death of Guidobaldo was the first break in Castiglione's happy life at Urbino. For him, as for Bembo and Fregoso, the court was never again what it had been in the good Duke's lifetime. His successor, Francesco della Rovere, was a man of a different stamp, a brave soldier, with none of his uncle's refinement and love of letters, but with a certain honest manliness and warmth of heart that went far to atone for his fiery temper. He soon learnt to appreciate Castiglione's loyalty, and relied upon his skill and tact to steer him safely through his greatest difficulties. But the services which the new Duke required were of a more exacting order. Henceforth Baldassare's time was spent in active warfare or anxious diplomatic missions. Often in the full and crowded years that followed he sighed for the old days and yearned to be at leisure to cultivate the neglected Muse and devote himself to his favourite studies.

The summer of 1508, however, was spent in comparative tranquillity at Urbino. By degrees the Duchess recovered her habitual equanimity, and, since she could not die with her husband, resolved to live to carry out his wishes and make his subjects happy. The devoted friends who stood by her in these dark hours—Madonna Emilia, Castiglione, and a few others —strove by every means in their power to cheer and amuse her, and watched eagerly for the first signs of revived interest in old pleasures.

'The Duchess begins to console herself in some degree,' wrote Bembo to his friend Bernardo Bibbiena. 'Can I say console herself? for this is hardly true, but at least she does not make herself quite as miserable as she did, and this alone is sufficient to make us all rejoice.'

It was quite an event when, a few weeks later, she actually smiled at a passage in one of Bibbiena's merry letters from Rome.

'The letter which you sent to Signor Giovanni Gonzaga,' wrote Bembo, 'was read by your Giuliano and my Archbishop, or, rather, your Archbishop and my Giuliano, or, better still, our Archbishop and our Giuliano! O what a fine invention! You may imagine how they laughed! Last night the letter was placed in the hands of the said Signor Giovanni, and then was read by the future bridegroom [Francesco della Rovere], and to-day our Lady Duchess has actually read it herself, and, although she never laughs at anything now, she could not refrain from a smile. So that you may be proud to feel you have accomplished thus much. It is true that I had recourse to a small stratagem, which may have been partly the cause of this happy result. But you must not wonder if I, too, wish to have my share of glory.'[1]

---

[1] 'Lettere,' iii. 24, 28.

The writer was still better pleased when Elisabetta asked to see a French version of his 'Asolani,' and wrote off in haste to his friends at Venice to obtain a copy. But this was several months later.

The death of the Pope's favourite nephew, Cardinal Galeotto della Rovere, in September was a fresh cause of sorrow, and the premature end of this young and popular prelate was lamented as much at Urbino as in Rome. In a letter to the Marchesa Isabella, Emilia Pia enclosed two sonnets written shortly before his death 'by that unfortunate S. Pietro in Vincula,' in one of which he foretells his coming doom. With a thoughtfulness which Isabella, of all others, appreciated, she adds that she has already written to ask Bernardo da Bibbiena if any of the late Cardinal's beautiful antiques are for sale, and promises to let Her Excellency hear about them.[1] The sculptor Cristoforo, who came to Urbino that autumn, brought word that the collection was to be sold to pay the Cardinal's debts, which, in spite of his large revenues, amounted to upwards of 90,000 ducats. If Isabella was eager to secure the dead man's antiques, Bembo was equally keen to obtain reversion of his benefices, and even before his death had written to Bibbiena, begging him to ascertain their exact number and value.

Castiglione, we find, often acted as secretary to the Duchess at this time, and many of the letters which she wrote to Mantua are in his handwriting. In his own letters to his mother we come across frequent references to Elisabetta and Emilia Pia, and he was evidently drawn into close and intimate relations with both these ladies.

'I think I must have told you before,' he writes on June 15, 'that the Lady Duchess continues to govern

[1] V. Cian in 'Giorn. st. d. Lett. it.,' ix. 115.

this State and enjoys the Holy Father's goodwill and favour in the highest measure, and is treated with the greatest reverence and attention by the new Duke. The Duke of blessed memory left her 14,000 ducats besides her dowry and allowances for the maintenance of her establishment on a suitable scale. So Her Excellency has 18,000 ducats, which have been paid in successive instalments from Mantua, secured to her, as well as this other 14,000 ducats and several other gifts which the Duke made her in his life-time. The Pope is very anxious for the Mantuan marriage, and has sent our Messer Alessandro here on that account. I think it will soon take place. M. Cesare and I remain in the new Duke's service with the same salary that we had before. I hope you will be satisfied this time, and think that I have written enough. The truth is, I do not care for the trouble of letter-writing, but when I have a secretary I will write to you so often that you will be tired of my letters! I grieve more than I can say for the death of our poor M. Ercole Strozzi. May God receive his soul! And I am also very sorry for Leonora's poor child, and beg you to offer my condolences to both parties, for indeed I feel the greatest compassion for them both.'

Serassi[1] adds a note explaining that this Leonora, who had lost her child, was a sister of Ercole Strozzi, whose assassination in the streets of Ferrara close to his own home had excited a great sensation. Castiglione, as we have already seen, was much attached to his charming kinswoman, Barbara Torelli, who soon after the death of her first husband, Ercole Bentivoglio, had become the wife of this accomplished Ferrarese poet, to whom she had lately borne a child. The name of the assassin remained unknown, and the rigid silence that was preserved on the subject at the

[1] *Op. cit.*, i. 43.

courts of Ferrara and Mantua leave little doubt
that Duke Alfonso was the perpetrator of the
crime, whether he was moved by jealousy of Ercole
Strozzi's intimacy with the Duchess Lucrezia, or
by his own passion for the unfortunate Barbara
Torelli.   Castiglione himself stood loyally by the
desolate widow, and eventually married her cousin
Ippolita.

Although Messer Baldassare's letters contained a
few allusions to public events, his correspondence
during this year was almost entirely occupied with
his private affairs.   Two subjects appear to have
engrossed his own and his mother's attention : the
one was his pecuniary embarrassments, the other his
marriage.   Castiglione, as we have already seen, was
far less skilful in the management of his own affairs
than in those of the princes whom he served.   No
doubt he often felt sadly hampered by the limited
means at his disposal, and was of too fastidious and
sensitive a nature to be easily pleased ; but he seems,
in his own words, to have been singularly unlucky in
servants.   One was an idler and incapable, another a
thief; one loitered by the way when the dispatches
entrusted to him were of the utmost importance,
another left Rome or Urbino without ever taking his
master's letters.   There was a certain hunchback,
Il Gobbo, a protégé of Madonna Luigia, who tried
his patience sorely, and was actually afraid to go
from Poggio to Mantua alone.   'I have forgiven him
this once,' wrote the young knight, 'because you
have taken him under your protection.   If it had
not been for this, I should have sent him about his
business long ago.'[1]   Then there was Antonio, the
secretary whose arrival he had impatiently awaited,

---

[1] Cod. Vat. Lat., 8210, fol. 101.   Appendix XII.

and who proved to be so ignorant that he could hardly read, far less write from dictation, and could not even be trusted to deliver a message correctly, but forgot half of his master's instructions before he reached Mantua.

'Some days he is impertinent to every one; at other times he will not even open his mouth to eat. He cannot read Pulci's "Morgante" or the "Cento Novelle" without help, and yet he gives himself grand airs. For God's sake, never let him come back here. He is a simpleton, and I cannot afford to keep servants who are absolutely useless.'[1]

This troublesome boy was the son of an old retainer at Casatico, and Castiglione was genuinely sorry to send him home in disgrace, and wrote to tell his father that he expected to be sent to Rome, and felt it would be a pity to leave the lad to waste his time at Urbino. But if Antonio was a failure, his successor, Bartolommeo, turned out still worse. From the first day of his arrival Castiglione complained of his laziness and ignorance, although, in his anxiety not to be constantly changing servants, he determined to give the man a trial. But the new secretary never ceased grumbling, and when, on one occasion, his master sent him to Urbino from Fossombrone, he made noise enough to bring the house down. Another time Castiglione heard him complain of the excessive labour and hard treatment which he had to endure in his service, and even venture to assert that he was indispensable to his master, who did not dare to dismiss him. This last statement was too much for Baldassare, who sent for him on the spot and gave him notice to leave the next day. But, since

[1] Cod. Vat. Lat., 8210.

Bartolommeo was a liar as well as an idler, Castiglione felt obliged to give his mother a full account of his reasons for dismissing the man, adding sadly: ' I have had so little good luck in my servants that I hardly know what to do next, but I must try and get along as best I can.' A certain Smeraldo, however, and two or three others, Scamarella, Giovanni Martino, and Alessandro, seem to have remained a long time in his service. Early in 1512 we first hear of Cristoforo Tirabosco of Asola, who was sent to him from Mantua with letters, and who in after-years became a confidential servant in whom he placed the utmost trust.

Next to servants, horses were his great anxiety. He needed handsome and well-groomed chargers for his duties at court and on parade, and was constantly sending home for fresh ones, and complaining that the grooms at Casatico did not feed and exercise his colts properly or turn them out to his satisfaction. If there was one thing on which he spent more ducats than he could afford, it was on horses. He had a keen eye for all their points, and never could hear of a remarkably good steed without desiring to acquire it by purchase or exchange. Many of his favourite horses are mentioned by name in his letters. There was Frisone (bullfinch), Carpegnolo, Buffone, Pappagallo (parrot), Il Magno, and, above all, the Shetland pony which His Majesty of England had given him, which he describes as both ' *bellissimo e bonissimo.*'

Another fertile cause of annoyance was the difficulty of conveyance between Mantua and Urbino. When Baldassare returned from England, he had left some painted bards and armour at Milan. These he begged his mother to send him by boat in the following autumn, together with other clothes and goods which he required, in charge of a trustworthy servant.

After much difficulty he obtained the necessary passes from the authorities at Mantua and Ferrara, and from the Signory of Venice, which held sway over the cities of Romagna, and the goods were safely landed at Rimini early in January. By this time the roads over the Apennines were so bad that Castiglione found it impossible to send for them, and, hearing that Rimini was full of thieving soldiers, ordered the greater part to be sold on the spot. But when the servant Giovanni Martino, whom he sent on horseback from Urbino to take charge of his property, reached Rimini, he found that most of the goods had already been stolen by a Mantuan servant, who turned out both a thief and a liar. 'This time I really think,' he wrote home, 'I am cured of having things sent from Lombardy!'

All these domestic worries were a source of perpetual vexation to Castiglione's soul, and he fretted over them, as poets will. But what troubled him far more than any of these minor annoyances were the debts that he could not pay, and which, as he told his mother, were like a 'worm gnawing continually at his heart.'[1] Ducats were still more scarce under Francesco Maria's sway than during the last Duke's reign. Castiglione's salary was generally in arrear, and his expenses, as he often told his mother, were always increasing. In spite of his efforts, he had been unable to pay his debt to Cardinal Ippolito d' Este, and still owed him 150 ducats. His letters during this winter contain repeated requests for help in this matter.

'I still owe that debt to Monsignor di Ferrara,' he wrote from Fossombrone during Guidobaldo's last illness, 'which oppresses me beyond measure for a

[1] Cod. Vat. Lat., 8210.

thousand reasons, principally because I am so anxious to retain his friendship, which, as you know, is extremely valuable to me. But it is impossible that I should pay this out of my salary, which is too small to defray my heavy expenses here. Once more, would you be so good as to tell me if there is any hope of your being able to let me have money from home, either now or later, because this debt lies heavily on my heart.'[1]

Three months afterwards, in June, 1508, he returned to the charge, and offered to try and raise 50 ducats out of his slender resources, if his mother would provide 100, or at least another 50, so that by paying Ippolito d' Este 100 ducats he might at least give him a proof of his good intentions. 'I would not for all the world,' he adds, 'that the Lord Cardinal should have to ask me for this money!' At length, in August, Madonna Luigia was able to grant his request, and 100 ducats were sent to Monsignore di Ferrara with Baldassare's most courteous excuses and expression of thanks. But by the end of the year Castiglione once more found himself in debt and was begging his mother for advances of money to satisfy his creditors at Urbino.

Under these circumstances a wealthy marriage seemed to be the best way out of his difficulties, and it was not surprising that Madonna Luigia once more pressed this course upon her son. Hitherto Baldassare had shown little inclination to take to himself a wife. When, in 1504, his mother had suggested a suitable alliance, and when three years later the Marquis of Mantua offered to find him a well-dowered bride, he firmly declined these proposals, saying that there was plenty of time, and he could find a wife for

[1] Serassi, i. 38.

himself when he chose. But although he had good reason to resent Francesco Gonzaga's interference, there can be no doubt that he was seriously contemplating the idea of marriage on his own account. In August, 1507, he wrote to assure his mother that a rumour of his betrothal, which had reached her, was unfounded.

'Your Magnificence might have known me better than to think that I could be so thoughtless and so much wanting in reverence as to enter on negotiations of this kind without your knowledge and permission. It seems to me that I have not conducted myself in such a way in other respects as to give you so bad an opinion of me.'[1]

But in the same letter he alludes to a possible alliance which has been suggested to him by Messer Bernardo da Bibbiena, and promises to let Madonna Luigia know if anything more should come of it. The bride whom Bibbiena proposed to his friend at Urbino was no less a person than Cardinal Giovanni de' Medici's niece Clarice, the daughter of Piero de' Medici and Alfonsina Orsini, who was living with her mother and brother Lorenzo in Rome. Both her uncles, the Cardinal and Giuliano, warmly approved of the proposed marriage ; but Alfonsina, it is plain, had more ambitious plans for her daughter, and returned evasive replies. 'For the present nothing can be decided for several reasons,' wrote Castiglione on September 18. 'None the less, you might try to find out the amount of the dowry and other conditions which are proposed. For the rest, may God be our guide!'[2]

---

[1] Codex Vat., 8210. [2] *Ibid.*

In January, 1508, a certain Mantuan lady of the Gambacorta family, who had incurred the Marquis Francesco's displeasure, and had been forced to leave the court and take refuge at Naples, paid a visit to Urbino, and brought Messer Baldassare fresh proposals from Alda Boiarda. This lady, however, particularly wished that her name should not appear in these negotiations, and, instead of addressing herself to Madonna Luigia, sent messages first by ' la Gambacorta,' and then by Pietro da Barignano, a Brescian poet whose name Ariosto has celebrated in his ' Orlando,'[1] and who visited Bembo at Urbino in February. The maiden in question was a daughter of Messer Giulio da Martinengo of Brescia, whose dowry of 14,000 ducats made her a prize in the marriage - market. The prospect was sufficiently alluring to make Baldassare propose to meet his mother at Ferrara or Poggio and discuss Madonna Alda's suggestion. But the death of Guidobaldo compelled him to defer his journey, and his friends at Urbino urged him to keep to his former intention, and conclude a marriage with Clarice de' Medici.

On May 13 he wrote to his mother :

' Your Magnificence remembers that I spoke to you some time ago about a marriage with a lady of the house of Medici. After a while the thing appeared to have cooled down because the mother had quarrelled with her other relatives, and was not inclined to allow her daughter to go as far from Rome as Mantua. But all along both Monsignore and the Magnifico Giuliano have been anxious for this marriage. Through their exertions the negotiations have so far advanced that yesterday Bernardo wrote to the Magnifico, saying that the mother and all the

[1] Canto xlvi. 16.

family were now favourable to the proposal, and had
empowered him to conclude the affair with me. For
the sake of their honour they would like the proposals
to be made through the Marquis or Cardinal Gonzaga
and the Lady Duchess, which would please me
greatly. Bernardo does not specify the amount of
the dowry, but says that it will be such as to satisfy
me amply. On hearing this I told the Magnifico
that I was very anxious to arrange the matter, but
must first write a line to you, and could not say
anything definite until I knew what you felt.
M. Cesare is gone to Rome on business for the
Duchess, so I will write and ask him to find out the
exact amount of the dowry, and, if possible, see the
lady. This is how things stand. You can confer
with M. Gio. Pietro and any other of our friends
whom you may think advisable, keeping this quite
secret for the present, and let me know what you
think I had better do.'[1]

Madonna Luigia's reply was entirely favourable,
and on the 23rd, Baldassare, who was in the act of
taking horse to ride to Gubbio, sent a few lines back
to say that ' a loving friend,' the kind Duchess, had
herself undertaken to ascertain the amount of Clarice's
dowry without delay. The answer, however, proved
somewhat disappointing. All that Alfonsina would
promise was a sum of 4,000 ducats to be paid down
at the time of the marriage.

' It is true,' explained Baldassare, ' that there will
probably be a good deal more eventually, but this is
all that is certain. And since I am entertaining these
proposals chiefly to please Your Magnificence, I await
your commands, and will do whatever you desire. No
doubt the match has many distinct advantages : the
family is noble on both sides, the uncle is a Cardinal, and

---

[1] Cod. Vat. Lat., 8210.

there is every prospect that they will soon be restored to their rightful home in Florence. But I am above all anxious that the tying of this knot should deliver me from other troubles, which, as you know, oppress me sorely. I beg you to think over these matters seriously, and send me word by this messenger what is your advice and that of M. Gio. Pietro and M. Jacopo, and anyone else whom you choose to consult. Once this is settled, it will be easy enough to find the best way of making the proposal. And since I have heard again on the subject of the Martinenga, you might try and learn some more about that business.'

Madonna Luigia, it is plain, was very anxious to see her son married, and urged him to lose no time in concluding an alliance with the Medici. Baldassare, however, still hesitated. Marriage in his eyes was purely a way of escape from burdensome debts, a means by which his fortunes might be advanced; and the cool way in which he discussed the whole question showed how little his heart was concerned in the matter. In a letter of June 15 he thanks his mother for her prompt reply, and owns that he is quite alive to the advantages of the Medici connexion, but still thinks the small amount of the dowry a great drawback.

'The dowry,' he writes, 'seems to be very small, and would not even suffice to relieve me of my present burdens, which you know vex me sorely. But if I found myself encumbered with a wife into the bargain, they would vex me much more, for the rooms that do for me now would no longer be suitable then; and as to being content to live with a single servant and mule, that I have never done, and never mean to do. I say this because you exhort me to regulate my way of living and expenses : and I have, in point of fact, reduced them to as fine a thread as possible. On the other hand, I have been much urged to delay these negotiations until I receive an answer from the Martinenga, because, if her dowry is 14,000 ducats instead of 5,000 or 6,000, and she, too, belongs to a good family, and is an only daughter, living in an important city near to our own, I should by this means secure a safe and comfortable home and sufficient fortune to free me from all anxieties. So I have decided to keep the thing in suspense a little longer until we see how matters stand. I beg you once more to find out whatever you can on the subject, and let me know any particulars which in these cases are not to be despised. May God inspire us to act for the best!'[1]

The next day Madonna Alda wrote to say another proposal had been made to Count Giulio Martinengo for his daughter's hand, and that he had decided to accept it. This being the case, Baldassare had no excuse for further delay with regard to the proposals of the Medici, and in his letters to his mother alludes to the marriage as definitely arranged. 'I hold the Medici marriage to be quite settled. God grant that it may prove a happy one!' he wrote to his mother on August 9. A few days later he begged her to get as many of the family jewels as possible out of pawn, 'as now we are making this marriage it will be well to show the Medici that we are not quite destitute.'[2] But he was anxious to see her and discuss the best means of raising the necessary money for the wedding expenses, and, if possible, make sure of the Marquis Francesco's approval before the final arrangements were concluded.

Francesco Maria had long wished to pay a visit to

[1] Serassi, i. 42.   [2] Cod. Vat. Lat., 8210.

his bride, Leonora Gonzaga, whom her uncle Giovanni
described to him as the prettiest girl in Lombardy,
and worthy to be ranked in point of beauty and
excellence with her father's famous racehorses! On
August 7 he started for Milan and Mantua, travelling
incognito, and only accompanied by Giuliano de'
Medici, Cesare Gonzaga and four servants, as the
Marchioness Isabella had lately given birth to a
daughter, and was unable to receive him with due
honour. But he paid a flying visit to the Castello at
Mantua on the 25th, and embraced Leonora, who was
by this time a lovely girl of fourteen. Castiglione
hoped to be able to come to Casatico, where his
mother was anxiously expecting him, but was delayed
by an unexpected incident. The Pope sent his nephew
sudden orders to hold a review of the Papal troops at
Bologna, and Castiglione, having with some difficulty
collected the Urbino contingent, joined his lord in
that city towards the end of September. On
Michaelmas Day the Papal Legate and that same
Cardinal Alidosi who three years later was to die by
Francesco's hand, celebrated high mass in the
Duomo, and solemnly invested the young Duke with
the sword and bâton of the Church as Captain of the
Papal forces. 'I suppose,' remarked the Venetian
envoy, alluding covertly to Francesco's well-known
dislike of the tyrannical Legate, 'that this feast-day
was chosen because it is the Archangel Michael's
office to drive away devils from men's souls, and the
Duke has already shown himself well disposed to
help the people of Bologna in this fashion.'[1]

The review, however, did not take place until
November 22. Both men-at-arms and horses were
in the finest order, but the magnificent sight was

[1] Sanuto, vii. 683.

unluckily marred by the rain, which fell in torrents and ruined the splendid uniforms of the men and rich trappings of the horses. As soon as it was over the troops were disbanded. The Duke returned to Urbino, and gave Castiglione leave to visit his mother at Casatico.

He had already sent a letter to the Marquis by M. Cesare in August, humbly asking for leave to come to Mantua and pay his respects as a dutiful servant. But no reply had been vouchsafed him, and he wrote sorrowfully to his mother :

'That letter which M. Cesare took to the Marquis has borne no fruit, saving that it may have broken the ice a little. We must try and follow it up, and I hope all may yet be well. I marvel at those who wonder why I do not come to Mantua, for if the truth were known they would see that it is no shame on my part to obey one who is my lord.'[1]

On October 12 he wrote from Bologna to tell his mother that the Marquis had refused to allow him to visit Mantua; and on the 20th he addressed a letter to Tolomeo Spagnoli begging him to obtain leave from His Excellency to visit his mother at Casatico as soon as the review was over. Still he received no answer, and as a last resource Madonna Luigia begged her brother, M. Giovanni Pietro, to ask M. Tolomeo, in well-chosen words, to obtain leave for her son to visit her at Casatico, in order that he might confer with her regarding his intended marriage. Even then, if Tolomeo's version of the affair is to be trusted, the secretary had great difficulty in obtaining a favourable answer. In a letter to his sister, M. Gio. Pietro describes how three times over in one day M. Tolomeo

[1] Cod. Vat. Lat., 8210.

approached his lord on the subject. First of all he ventured to remind His Excellency that his cousin, the Magnifico Gio. Pietro, had written to him on the subject ; secondly, he observed that Madonna Luigia had repeatedly made the same request ; and, thirdly, in the evening he informed His Excellency that Messer Gio. Pietro had sent to beg for an answer to his former application. Each time the Marquis turned his back upon him without a word. At last Baldassare's uncle himself went to see M. Tolomeo the next day, and insisted on obtaining an answer to his request, upon which the Marquis bade his secretary tell M. Gio. Pietro that, for love of him, he would allow M. Baldassare to spend four days, but no longer, with his mother at Casatico.[1] As a result of this ungracious message, Castiglione came to Casatico directly the review at Bologna had taken place, and spent a few days with his mother and family.

By December 5 he was back at Urbino, and three days later sent his mother a note to say he had spoken to the Magnifico of his affair, and was now only awaiting the answer from Rome in order to conclude the marriage. But he reckoned without his host. On the 20th he told his mother that no doubt his marriage would be arranged directly the Christmas feast was over, but confessed that the latest news from Rome was not altogether favourable, and that he was doubtful whether this was due to political causes or to any of M. Bernardo's tricks ! In spite of Castiglione's affection for Bibbiena, it is evident that his friend's wily nature had already inspired him with suspicion. What-ever the cause might be, he added : ' I do not feel much concerned, and shall not be greatly distressed if the whole thing should end in smoke.'[2] This letter

[1] Cod. Vat. Lat., 8212.　　　　[2] Cod. Vat. Lat., 8210.

was probably intended to prepare Madonna Luigia for
the disappointment in store for her.   On January 10
he wrote a letter chiefly relating to home affairs.
After telling his mother that he had spoken to the
Cardinal of Pavia's secretary about a benefice for
her confessor, a certain Fra Lodovico, and that the
Duke is preparing to come to fetch his bride from
Mantua, he adds:

'I have left for the last a piece of news which will,
I fear, vex you as much as it displeases me.   Our
marriage negotiations are, I think, quite broken off,
according to the letters which the Magnifico has had
from Rome.   The reason is that Monsignore has
received proposals from one of the Strozzi in Florence,
by whose means they hope to strengthen their party
in that city ; and so, although our mutual troth was
almost pledged, the prospect of these important advantages has induced Monsignore to conclude this
contract without saying a word to the Magnifico or
Bernardo.   However, I have given my mind by
word of mouth and letter to both my friends, for
throughout these negotiations I had not failed to
keep the thing alive and make the necessary promises
and solicitations.   I beg you not to grieve too much,
because God orders these things, and often what
appears to be most for our advantage proves the
contrary.   And I believe firmly that this, too, will be
all for the best.'[1]

But although he put a brave face on the matter,
Baldassare himself was considerably disappointed at
the failure of his hopes, and in a letter written a
fortnight later he remarks:

'We certainly had some cause of complaint, as on
both sides troth had been plighted by word of mouth.
However, the contract with this Florentine is entirely

[1] Serassi, i. 45.

settled and concluded. I think important reasons
and questions of peculiar gravity moved Monsignore
to act as he did ; for he certainly has not changed his
mind with regard to my suit, as you will see from the
enclosed letter which he wrote to me with his own
hand. But God be praised for all ! I beg you not to
distress yourself, for perhaps the thing would have
turned out quite differently from what we expected.
M. Cesare will tell you all about it when he comes to
Mantua.'

We see by this letter that Castiglione bore no
grudge either to Cardinal de' Medici or to Bibbiena,
who were apparently the chief promoters of the
Strozzi marriage, and by this means certainly succeeded in gaining a new foothold in Florence. As
for the Magnifico, Baldassare would not allow any
blame to be imputed to him, and told his mother
that, far from Giuliano having had any share in
breaking off the marriage, it had annoyed him ex-
cessively. 'And now,' he adds cheerfully, 'Your
Magnificence must try and find me another wife.'[1]

[1] Cod. Vat. Lat., 8210.

CHAPTER XVIII

1509–1510

War against Venice—Campaign of Romagna—Victories of Francesco Maria — Capture of Ravenna — Castiglione's illness — Fresh marriage proposals—The Duchess goes to Mantua—Madonna Luigia returns with her—The young Duchess Leonora —Visit of the Duke and Duchesses to Rome—Castiglione and Raphael.

WITH the New Year, the clash of arms and tumult of warlike preparations came to disturb the peace of Urbino. The Pope's long-cherished schemes for the overthrow of Venice were at length to be put into execution. On December 10, 1508, the League of Cambray was signed between Louis XII. and Maximilian, and in March the Pope publicly announced that he had joined the confederacy against Venice. The Duke of Urbino was hastily recalled from Mantua, where he was paying a brief visit to his bride, to take command of the Papal army. Castiglione forgot his matrimonial hopes and disappointments in the task of equipping his company of fifty men. As usual, he was sorely in need of money, and his letters to his mother abound in requests for horses, arms, and ducats. ' I find that I have several debts here,' he wrote at the end of January, ' and although they are none of them large, the whole amount to a considerable sum, so that I must ask you to send me sixty ducats without delay.'

On March 16 he repeats his request in still more urgent terms :

'We are expecting to take the field directly ; here every one is stirring, and I expect it is the same with you, and war will break out very soon. The more quickly you can send me the money, the better shall I be pleased, because owing to this prospect I have been compelled to pledge my next quarter's salary to my creditors and am without funds. I shall be glad if you could send me at least fifty ducats, for I am in need of a thousand things, and most of all of a horse, for my Buffone is hardly fit for the work. I am also impatiently expecting those blessed pieces of armour, and if they have not yet reached Mantua, I hope you will write to M. Gio. Angelo Vismara, begging him to send them to Bologna, to the care of Signor Lodovico da Carpi, and he will pay the carriage, which may be easier than to send them from Milan to Mantua.'[1]

This armour had been ordered from Missaglia of Milan several months before, and Castiglione, who needed it greatly for the coming campaign, was naturally indignant at the prolonged delay. But Madonna Luigia was overwhelmed with home troubles and losses, and could not always satisfy her son's demands as promptly as he expected. Early in January her son-in-law, Jacopo Boschetto, died, after a long illness, leaving a widow and one unmarried daughter.

'By letters from my lord Giovanni Gonzaga,' wrote Baldassare on January 23, ' I have heard of the death of our poor M. Jacopo, which grieves me, owing to the brotherly love which I bore him. We must have patience, and may God give him a happier life in another world ! I have written a line to Madonna Polissena, who must be plunged in grief, and

---

[1] Serassi, i. 47.

AUTOGRAPH OF BALDASSARE CASTIGLIONE.

(VATICAN LIBRARY.)

To face p. 266, Vol. I.

beg you to give me particulars of his death and to tell me what Polissena will do, and if a husband has been found for Anna. . . .' And in a postscript he sends the Duchess's sincere condolences to both his mother and Madonna Polissena.

On April 27 the Bull of excommunication against Venice was published, and the Duke invaded Romagna at the head of several thousand men. Castiglione's letters give an excellent account of the short and successful campaign that followed. The first was written from Brisighella on May 1 :

' Although I do not know how this letter is to be sent, I write on the chance to tell you that I am safe and well. Yesterday, being Wednesday, we arrived here at Brisighella, a town at the head of the Val di Lamone, and found that the city had already sur-rendered to our forces, and that the citadel was being besieged. This has now been taken, together with the persons of Sig. Gio. Paolo Manfrone and two other leaders, also the Provveditore and Castellan. The town has been sacked, because it was taken by one of our Spanish companies, and so without any trouble we have conquered the whole Val Lamone, which is a great acquisition, and, what is of still greater importance, have made Manfrone prisoner. Before long I think we shall march on Faenza, and I hope, with God's help, soon to gain fresh glory. Please send Pietrone here as soon as possible, for I am in great need of servants ; and if you have any kind of horse, I should like him to bring it with him, but if not, let him come as best he can, and we will find him a mount at once. He had better come to Bologna, and there he can find out where our camp is. I should be glad of particulars as to the sire and breed of Carlo degli Uberti's horses ; I want some badly, all the more that my poor Buffone has run a nail into one foot and will not be fit for work for several days.'

Castiglione's next letter bore the following Latin inscription : ' *Ex felicibus Castris S. R. Ecclesiæ apud Granarolum die* 7 *Mai. MDIX.*'

' Yesterday, just when I received your letters, a fierce assault was being made on a strong fort of Faenza called Granarolo. Many of our brave men were killed, but the enemy surrendered at discretion, and there has been no slaughter of the prisoners. We hope our arms will prosper, as we fight in a good cause and are a fine company. God guide our steps into a good path ! We are all well and happy. Please send Pietrone as soon as possible. As for M. Carlo's horses, I do not think they are what I require ; for I am not in need of young horses, but want a trained horse which would have some brains.'[1]

Once more, on May 18, the young knight wrote in high spirits :

' Yesterday Pietrone arrived, and I thank you for sending him.   I will send back his horse when I have an opportunity, and should be very glad to know what my colts are doing. We have been here, before Russi, a fortified city, for the last eight or nine days, and the day before yesterday were preparing for an assault, when 300 horsemen and 2,000 infantry sallied out from Ravenna, which is ten miles off, and attacked us to make a diversion.   Our light horse rode out to meet them, and behind them our Signor with no more than eight gentlemen, followed by Gio. Vitelli and his brother Chiappino, two youths with sixty men-at-arms. We pursued the enemy, and, although they were in a very strong position, attacked them so furiously that we broke their ranks, and some of our cavalry rode right into Ravenna. We made 300 foot and 50 horse prisoners, as well as much cattle, and won a great victory, much to the honour of our most illustrious Signor. Yesterday morning Russi surrendered, on

[1] Serassi, i. 49.

condition that the lives and property of the citizens
should be spared, and this evening the citadel has
done the same. I think we shall soon march on
Faenza. Under Ravenna our poor Bedino was mortally wounded in the throat by a pike. We carried
him back to the camp, but the poor fellow died in the
night, which grieves me very much. God grant him
pardon! M. Cesare went to Rome yesterday on an
honourable mission from the Duke and Legate [Car-
dinal Alidosi]. You might tell his mother this and
make my excuses for not writing. If you could send
me a few ducats, it would be a singular satisfaction ;
whether they are few or many, nothing will come
amiss, and please send them as soon as possible.'

On the last day of May, Baldassare wrote again
from the camp before Cervia. Once more he repeats
his tale of victories, but this time he writes in a sadder
strain. The miseries which war entailed, the wanton
bloodshed and human suffering inflicted by his own
soldiers, oppressed his heart, and he turned away
sickened by the sight.

'I have received a letter from Your Magnificence
by Catanio, together with the money, which could not
come more conveniently, and thank you infinitely for
all. Our campaign has been exceedingly successful so
far, and with little trouble we have conquered the
whole of Romagna. The repulse, which, as I told
you, we inflicted on the enemy from our camp near
Ravenna, terrified that city, although it was held by
a garrison of 5,000 foot and 300 horse. God orders
all! A secretary was sent by these Venetian lords,
offering to surrender Ravenna, Cervia, and Rimini,
on condition that the lives of the citizens and garrison
should be spared, and that the artillery and ammunition should be retained by them. These terms were
accepted, and now we have taken Ravenna, and are

going to take Cervia and Rimini, and in a short time
our campaign will be over, and we shall, I hope, be
back at Urbino. I should be glad to know if His
Most Christian Majesty has reinstated our Lord
Marquis in his possessions in Venetian territory, and
how things are happening over there. We have done
terrible damage and injury to the country round this
poor Ravenna, but the city itself has not suffered. I
did as little harm as I could, and see that every one
but myself is enriched. But I do not repent. I
cannot tell you how much I grieve over the death
of poor Uberto [his brother-in-law Tommaso degli
Strozzi's brother], for many reasons, but most of all
for the sake of his poor wife, whose family, whether
living or dead, bring her nothing but trouble. You
will kindly condole with M. Ludovico and with her.
I cannot write, as I have no time, and will only commend myself to you and my sisters, and all of ours.

   ' Ex Castris, ultimo Maii, 1509.'[1]

The victories of the French in Lombardy and the
crushing defeat of the Venetians on May 14 at the
Ghiar' Adda had made Louis XII. supreme in North
Italy, and after the conquest of Rimini, seeing there
was nothing more to gain, Julius II. ordered the
Duke to disband his forces. By the end of June
Castiglione was back at Urbino; but the hardships
and fatigue which he had suffered in the campaign
had told on his never robust frame, and he was
seriously ill for some weeks in August. Both the
Duchess and Madonna Emilia showed him the greatest
kindness during his sickness. 'If I had been their
son or brother, they could not have done more.'
Emilia Pia's waiting-women nursed him with the
utmost devotion. But it was many weeks before
he recovered his strength, and he still complained in

   [1] Serassi, i. 50,

September that he felt very weak and that health did not come as quickly as illness. By way of raising money to meet the expenses of his illness, he sold his old horses at the fair of Recanati, and sent for others from Casatico.

Here his mother was still busy making new plans for his marriage, and some half a dozen different brides were proposed to him during the course of the year. While the union with Clarice de' Medici was still in the air, Madonna Luigia received proposals from a Count Lodovico Visconti who had a marriageable daughter, and when the negotiations with the Medici were finally broken off, Duchess Elisabetta suggested one of Count Borromeo's daughters as a suitable bride, and in the kindness of her heart wrote to ascertain the amount of her dowry. For some reason the Visconti marriage did not attract him, but he was quite inclined to entertain the idea of an alliance with the Borromeo family. His friend Madonna Emilia's brother, Lodovico Pio of Carpi, who came to Urbino on the Pope's business, interested himself in the matter, and assured Castiglione that all the members of the Borromeo family, men and women alike, asked nothing better than to form an alliance with him. But a malicious report reached him that the maiden in question was exceedingly ugly, and he at once recoiled from the plan. 'However rich she may be,' he wrote to his mother, 'I would not, for anything in the world, take a devil to be my partner.'[1]

This, however, seems to have been a calumny, and a year later, when he was at Bologna in June, 1510, we find him reverting to the idea and seriously contemplating the marriage. One Messer Visconti, who was related to the Borromei, had apparently re-

[1] Cod. Vat. Lat., 8210.

opened negotiations and come forward with satisfactory assurances as to the maiden's age and beauty, so that, if the dowry were really as good as it sounded, Baldassare was quite willing to conclude the agreement. But as usual he left the decision to his mother and uncle, and as usual, before many weeks, the matter was allowed to drop.

Other proposals, however, reached him from different quarters. We hear of a daughter of Conte Giovanni Boiardo, and of another maiden of the Stanga family of Cremona, a daughter of Lodovico Sforza's favourite Marchesino. Then the Bishop of Asti had a niece of his own to recommend; while Lodovico Pio had seen a Ferrarese damsel of the Cavalieri family, who was not only tall and well educated, but, what was more to the purpose, had a dowry of 6,000 gold ducats, besides considerable expectations from her mother. Baldassare himself was more attracted by the account which he heard of one of Giberto da Correggio's daughters, whose stepmother, Veronica Gambara, was the Marchesa Isabella's god-child and Bembo's intimate friend. The maiden herself was fourteen years of age, well brought up, tall, and very beautiful, and her dowry was reckoned at 10,000 ducats, so that in every way the match seemed a most eligible one. But in this as in other cases some difficulty arose in the course of negotiations, and, after dragging on for many months, the matter ended in smoke.[1]

It must be owned that Castiglione was a very negligent suitor, and his own coldness and lack of interest in the subject may explain many of these

[1] Cod. Vat. Lat., 8210. See also V. Cian's pamphlet, 'Candidature nuziali di B. Castiglione' (Venezia, 1892), now unfortunately out of print, for a detailed account of these various proposals.

failures. All through we realize that he was perfectly content to live at Urbino in the Duke's service and in the company of the Duchess and Madonna Emilia, and that he only listened to the importunities of the friends who begged him to marry, because of his anxiety to be free from debt.

Meanwhile war in Lombardy between the League and Venice was still being waged with varying results. The Venetians had succeeded in recovering Padua, and the capture of the Marquis Francesco, who was surprised and made prisoner at a farm near Legnago on August 9, had filled both the courts of Mantua and Urbino with consternation. While the Pope 'blasphemed horribly,' and Isabella moved heaven and earth to obtain her husband's release, the Duchess Elisabetta was hardly less distressed. 'This capture of the Lord Marquis,' wrote Bembo to his father, the old Venetian patrician, 'is the most fortunate thing that could have happened ! It has troubled the Duke greatly, and more than anything else has grieved the Duchess, who is distressed beyond measure to think of her brother's confinement.' He proceeds to tell his father how the Duchess's sympathies have been with Venice all through the war, since she never forgets the kindness which she and her beloved lord received from the Republic in the days of their exile, and 'now weeps over these misfortunes.' 'And although it is true,' he continues, 'that the Pope is by nature very hard and intractable, he loves his nephew tenderly, and looks on him as the one remaining branch of the old oak, while there is no living person for whom he has so much regard as the Lady Duchess.[1] As yet, however, 'the first cause of all our troubles,' as Bembo calls the

[1] P. Bembo, 'Lettere,' ii. 528.

fiery old Pope, remained immovable. When the
Duke begged leave for an audience, he sternly bade
him remain at Urbino, and not stir from his State
without express permission, and when Francesco
Maria started incognito to visit his bride, he promptly
ordered him to return, although he had already got
as far as Carpi.

Under these circumstances, both Isabella and her
sister-in-law felt that their best policy was to hurry on
the Duke's marriage, and bring the influence of Leonora
and her lord to bear upon the Pope. The Marchesa
especially staked all her hopes on this union, which
Julius II. had always favoured, and the good Duchess,
yielding to her sister-in-law's prayers, agreed to undertake the long journey to Mantua in the dead of winter
and herself bring home the bride.

During the past summer M. Baldassare repeatedly
expressed his intention of coming to meet his mother
at Ferrara or some neighbouring spot, and arranging
these matters. 'I mean to go on a pilgrimage to
Loreto,' he wrote on August 21, 'and then, if God
will, meet you in some place where we can discuss
these different marriages.' But his illness interfered
with these plans, and when, at the end of November,
the Duchess went to Mantua to fetch the Duke's
bride, she kindly proposed that Madonna Luigia should
return with her to Urbino. Castiglione gratefully
accepted this gracious offer, and sent his most capable
and trusted servant to escort his mother on the
journey.

'As my illustrious Signora is coming to Mantua,
I thought I would send my servant to help you on
the journey, knowing that you will be well served
by him. If I could have found a good horse, I would
also have sent it for your use, since we know that you

will be asked to return here by the Lady Duchess. I wish you could procure me an answer from Lodovico Mantegna to a letter which I sent him lately. It would also be well if you would render infinite thanks to the Lady Duchess for the exceedingly great kindness which Her Excellency showed me during my illness, and the same to Madonna Emilia, for if I had been their son or brother they could not have done more ; and certainly the vows they made on my behalf will not be fulfilled for many a long day. I owe a great deal also to Madonna Emilia's women, and should like you to give a piece of linen or something more, for love of me, to the old one named Margherita, although I am really equally indebted to them all. I am sure you will pay them every attention and honour in your power, and need say no more. Please also give my servant cloth for a pair of shirts, and a cap of whatever kind he may prefer, because he really serves me most excellently, and I hardly know how I shall do without him ; but I wish you to have him to help you. I have given him several messages for you, and you will find that he is implicitly to be trusted. I should be glad if you can bring some money with you—as much as possible— for my affairs are in some confusion, owing to my recent illness.

'URBINO, *November* 19, 1509.'[1]

On the following day the Duchess, attended by a large and brilliant suite, set out for Mantua, and, after being splendidly entertained by Isabella during ten or twelve days, returned to Urbino with the young Duchess Leonora and Madonna Luigia in her train. The weather was terrible all over Italy that autumn. The poet Ariosto, who was sent to Rome at Christmas by his patron, Cardinal d' Este, to beg the Pope for reinforcements in the war against Venice, wrote that

[1] Serassi, i. 51.

it had rained every day since he left Ferrara, and that the floods were so high he should run the risk of being drowned if he were to start on his journey home.[1]

The Urbino party left Mantua in a dense fog, and, after wandering for hours in the dark, had to take shelter at the villa of Gonzaga. The roads were so heavy that mules and horses could hardly get along, and some of the ladies narrowly escaped drowning in crossing one river near Faenza. The poor Duchess suffered acutely from gout, and had to travel in the sumptuous gold and silver litter, borne by two handsome pages in liveries to match, which the Pope had sent for the bride. But courtiers and ladies alike kept up a brave heart and laughed over their adventures, and were hospitably entertained and amused by dances and banquets at Modena and Bologna, and wherever they spent a night.[2] By Christmas they reached their journey's end, and the Duke rode out from the gates of Urbino to meet his bride, and brought her back in triumph to the ducal palace. With him came Castiglione, who had the happiness of welcoming his mother, and Madonna Luigia forgot the perils and fatigues of the journey in the joy of embracing her beloved son.

That year Christmas was kept with great rejoicing at Urbino, and the halls of the Montefeltro palace once more rang with the sound of dancing and song. The Duchess forgot her own sorrows in the sight of her children's happiness, and Madonna Emilia, whose admirable judgment, Bibbiena remarked, was never at fault, commended Leonora's beauty and manners in the warmest terms. Bembo, who had been with

---

[1] A. Cappelli, 'Lettere di Lod. Ariosto,' iv.
[2] Luzio e Renier, 'Mantova e Urbino,' p. 194.

Elisabetta to Mantua, and the gay Messer Bernardo, who was spending the feast-days at Urbino, both wrote to tell Leonora's mother what an excellent impression the youthful bride had already made, and how much she was admired and loved by her new subjects. But what pleased Isabella more than all was to hear that Count Lodovico Canossa and M. Cesare Gonzaga had arrived from the Vatican with a congratulatory letter from the Pope, in which His Holiness desired the Duke to bring his aunt and his wife to spend the Carnival in Rome.

Accordingly, towards the end of February, the whole party travelled to Rome, where Carnival was celebrated with unusual splendour and a series of festivities were given in honour of the newly-wedded pair. Horse-races and bull-fights, theatricals and banquets, followed each other in splendid succession. From the palace of Cardinal Adrian Castellesi the Duchesses and their ladies looked on at a pageant in the Piazza Agone, in which, instead of the triumphs of the ancient Romans, the victories of the Papal forces in Romagna were represented. Leonora's cousin, Cardinal Luigi of Aragon, and the French Cardinal of Narbonne, who had been hospitably entertained at Urbino in past years, gave concerts and balls in honour of the bride, and one evening no less than four Cardinals and several Bishops joined in the dancing. The young Duchess's beautiful robes, carefully executed after her mother's designs by a skilful Roman tailor, excited general admiration. Some were of cloth of gold and peacock blue satin, others of black velvet, trimmed with white damask and gold lace, and adorned with big pearls and a variety of jewels, presented to her by the Prefetessa and other relatives. The goldsmiths' help had to be called in to

complete these elaborate toilettes, and 900 ducats of
the Princess's dowry were melted down to provide
gold ornaments for the black velvet robe worn by her
on the Sunday of Carnival. One evening Cardinal
San Severino gave a sumptuous entertainment, at
which a Latin comedy was acted before supper, and an
Italian play afterwards. The Duchess Elisabetta, the
Prefetessa, Madonna Emilia, and all the other ladies,
remained to the end, which was not till two o'clock;
but the Duke grew so tired of the performance that
he took his wife by the hand and rode home with her,
attended by one or two servants. The next evening
he scandalized the company still more by leaving
M. Agostino Chigi's palace immediately after supper
without waiting to hear the beautiful eclogue or the
thousand other *gentilezze* which the Siena banker
had prepared in honour of his guests. This was the
more indefensible because M. Agostino was at this
time paying assiduous court to the fair Margarita
Gonzaga, whose hand he sought in marriage, asking
no dowry, and promising to settle 10,000 ducats upon
her. But whether Margarita's heart was still given
to her old lover, Alberto Pio, who was now in Rome
as Imperial ambassador, or whether she shrank with
aversion from this elderly banker, it is certain that she
declined his offer, and M. Agostino himself frankly
owned that he had no wish to share his home and bed
with an unwilling bride.

The Pope was in high good humour, went everywhere, and would see everything. He gave suppers
and dances in the rooms of Pope Innocent, and
bull-fights in the Belvedere gardens, and presented
the bride with a costly gold chain and crown, as well
as a quantity of gloves and perfumes. When the
Marquis Francesco's horse carried off the *palio* in the

race, he listened with evident pleasure to the shouts of 'Mantua! Mantua!' with which the piazza rang. The two Duchesses took advantage of this occasion to beg him to remember their captive brother and father, upon which he said, with a smile, 'Have a little patience, my children.' But when the Duke in his turn tried to plead his father-in-law's cause, the Pope broke into a furious rage, and told him not to attempt to play the part of Valentino.[1] However, he consented to absolve the Venetian envoys who came to sue for pardon. On February 24 a strange scene took place on the piazza before S. Peter. The Pope, seated on a throne in the portico, and supported by the Cardinals, the Duke of Urbino, the foreign ambassadors, and a host of Bishops and officials, received the five envoys, who, clad in scarlet robes, knelt before him while the *Miserere* was chanted. After they had kissed his feet three times, His Holiness gave them absolution. Then the great church doors were thrown open, and the penitents were once more admitted into the sanctuary. Afterwards they visited the seven basilicas, and the household of the Pope escorted them home with great triumph and shouts of joy. There was nothing in the ceremony, wrote one of the five, but was honourable to the Republic; and since the alms offered at each church only consisted of five ducats, the envoys flattered themselves that they had obtained the Papal absolution at small expense.[2]

The gaieties of Carnival were followed by the services of Lent, and the Duchesses were assiduous in visiting the different churches, and attended a

---

[1] A. Luzio, 'Federico Gonzaga Ostaggio,' p. 58.
[2] Sanuto, x. 9, 71, 77 ; Alberi, Serie ii., v. iii. 36.

representation of the story of Lazarus in St. Peter's, which took place one Sunday in March, and was witnessed by over 12,000 persons. But the Pope, as one of the Venetians remarked, was never present at any long services. Castiglione found many of his old friends in Rome, and together with Bembo and Giuliano enjoyed the company of Sadoleto, Beroaldo, Bibbiena, Cristoforo, and the leading Cardinals. There was another friend from Urbino who welcomed his presence gladly. This was the painter Raphael, now in high favour with His Holiness, and engaged in decorating the Vatican *stanze* with his great frescoes. The Duchess and her nephew, who had been on friendly terms with the artist from his boyhood, naturally looked with especial interest on the works of the young master from Urbino; while according to an old tradition, repeated by an English traveller who visited Rome in the sixteenth century, Castiglione's advice was of great use to Raphael in designing his noble fresco of the School of Philosophy. The best proof we have of Castiglione's interest in the work is the introduction of his own portrait into the group on the left, close to Raphael himself. Here Baldassare appears in the character of Zoroaster, and stands looking towards the painter; while another native of Urbino, the architect Bramante, figures as Euclid in the foreground, and the young Duke appears in a corner of the composition. The portraits of both Castiglione and Francesco Maria must have been painted during this visit to Rome, while that of Leonora's brother, the curly-headed boy Federico, was added when he came to the Vatican as hostage for his father a few months later. When the Easter festival was over, the Duke and Duchesses took leave of His Holiness and their friends in the Sacred

Photo, Anderson.

PORTRAITS OF CASTIGLIONE AND RAPHAEL.

BY RAPHAEL (VATICAN).

To face p. 280, Vol. I.

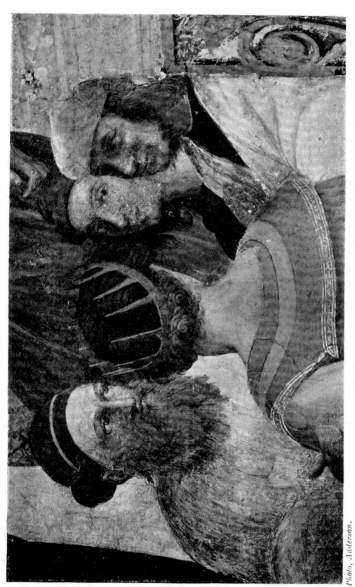

Photo, Anderson.

PORTRAITS OF CASTIGLIONE AND RAPHAEL.

BY RAPHAEL (VATICAN).

To face p. 280, Vol. I.

College, and returned to Urbino. A letter was
addressed to Lodovico Brognolo, the Mantuan
ambassador in Rome, by Castiglione, acting as
Elisabetta's secretary, on April 10, from Gubbio,
and on the 15th, Bembo, who had lingered behind
with his friend Ottaviano Fregoso, wrote to give
Gaspare Pallavicino an account of recent events.
This young lord, whose wit and gaiety had so lately
made him the life of the court, the Benedick who
bandied words with Madonna Emilia and declared himself the foe and hater of her sex, was dying slowly of
a wasting disease at his home of Corte Maggiore, and
Bembo, in the kindness of his heart, tried to cheer
him with news of old friends.

'Our illustrious Lord Duke and Madonna the
Duchess and the whole court,' he writes, 'came here
this Carnival. They were warmly welcomed by His
Holiness and all Rome, and have been feasted and
visited and greatly honoured during these joyous
days and the following Lent and Easter. They
received costly presents from His Holiness and
several from very reverend Cardinals. Six days
ago they started in the best of health and spirits for
Urbino. The new Duchess is a beautiful child, who
makes herself every day more beloved, and whose
sweetness of nature, tact, and gentleness are beyond
her years. Our own gracious lady and Madonna Emilia
are quite as well as usual, and so are all the other
gentlemen of the court. I have stayed in Rome a
few days for affairs of my own, and shall soon return
to Urbino.

'Near St. Paul beyond the Tiber, *April* 15, 1510.

'I beg of you, dear Signor Gaspare, let me hear
often how you are in health, for few hours pass in
which your memory is not present to my mind, and

it grieves me when the accounts I have of you are not those which I should like to hear.'[1]

A year after Bembo wrote this letter, Gaspare Pallavicino died at the age of seventy-five, and Castiglione paid a splendid tribute to his friend in the fourth book of the ' Cortegiano.'

Early in May, Madonna Luigia, who had accompanied the Duchesses to Rome, and returned with them to Urbino, started on her journey home, taking with her many affectionate messages to the Marchesa, and the following note from Elisabetta :

To my Dearest Sister.

' As Madonna Luigia da Castiglione is returning to Your Excellency, and can give you full information concerning our affairs, I will not try to speak of them. I send you a little oil of citrobe and wood of aloes which I brought from Rome, and hope you will accept for love of me, hoping soon to be able to let you have the news from Rome which I expect.'

On the 24th Isabella replied :

' I am greatly consoled to hear from Madonna Luigia da Castiglione that Your Highness has returned safely from Rome with the Duke and our darling child, and make use of the return of the bearer who came with Madonna Luigia to tell you that I am well, but have no news of my lord as yet.'[2]

At length, on July 17, the Marquis was released in compliance with the Pope's repeated demands. ' The Holy Father has ordered the Signory to set my lord free,' wrote Isabella joyfully, and the most heartfelt congratulations were sent her from Urbino.

[1] ' Lettere,' iii. 41.
[2] Archivio Gonzaga, Carteggio di B. Castiglione.

CHAPTER XIX

1510–1511

War of the Pope against France and Ferrara—Castiglione serves with the Papal forces at Bologna—Capture of Modena—Siege of Mirandola—The Pope in the trenches—His fury with the Duke—Castiglione's elegy on Mirandola—Capture of Bologna by the French—Rout of the Papal forces—Murder of Cardinal Alidosi—The Duke excommunicated and tried by the Sacred College—Illness of Julius II.—Absolution and restoration of the Duke.

EARLY in June Castiglione was sent to Bologna by the Duke on military business, and remained there for five or six weeks. His letters to his mother were full of the customary complaints about his servants and of discussions over the ever-recurring theme of possible marriages, the Borromeo bride at that moment being to the fore. But the necessity of laying out a few hundred ducats to begin with proved, as usual, an insuperable difficulty, especially, as he remarked, the thing might fall through and leave him worse off than he was before. Only the day before he had to give Evangelista, the Mantuan trainer, forty ducats for horses, and to advance the same amount to some troops who were ordered to Florence, so that he must beg Madonna Luigia to send him further remittances to satisfy his present needs. The few ducats which had been paid him for a horse that he had lately sold were not sufficient to meet these demands.

'At the same time,' he adds, 'one must have bread
to eat! Here at Bologna my expenses and the keep
of my horses cost little less than a ducat and a half a
day, so that I cannot afford to forget those who on
their part owe me money.' At the same time he
warns his mother that war is very likely to break out
before long, and begs her not only to send Cristoforo
and Smeraldo with his horses before the passes are
guarded, but also to employ every available labourer
at Casatico to get in the harvest, since he foresees that
there will soon be trouble at Mantua.[1] The reports
which reached him from Rome were indeed ominous.
The Pope's wrath against Venice had hardly been
assuaged before his fury was directed against his former
allies—France and Ferrara. He had an old quarrel
with Louis XII. over the nomination of French
Bishops, and resented the high-handed measures of
the French monarch in North Italy, while he had
long looked enviously on Ferrara as a fief of the
Church, and could not forgive Alfonso's close alliance
with France. 'The Pope is old and gouty,' wrote
Trevisano from Rome in April, 'but he is determined to be master of the world's game.' When, in
May, news reached the Holy Father that Bishop
Schinner had concluded a treaty with the Swiss, he
exclaimed joyfully : 'Now we shall be able to drive
the French out of Italy.' He could not sleep, he
said, because of the Frenchmen, and spent the night
pacing up and down his room, brooding over his warlike designs. Every one felt that there was trouble
in the air. 'The French in Rome look like corpses,'
wrote the same envoy a few weeks later, 'and His
Holiness is even more violent in his language against
them than he was against us last year.' The Duke

[1] Cod. Vat. Lat., 8210, fol. 101.

of Urbino was now ordered to prepare for an immediate advance on Ferrara. In the middle of July Castiglione was sent to Rome to give the Pope a minute account of the strength and position of Alfonso's forces previous to the opening of the campaign.[1] At the same time the Marquis of Mantua was released from his long captivity. Marino Sanuto relates how, on July 14, he himself, together with three other members of the College, were sent to bring His Excellency out of prison, and how the next morning the Marquis set sail for Rimini in a Venetian galley.[2] Here he found the two Duchesses waiting to welcome him, and proceeded in their company to Bologna, where he saw his little son Federico on his way to Rome. The boy, who was to remain in the Pope's charge as a hostage for his father's good behaviour, arrived at Bologna on the 25th, and before Elisabetta returned to Urbino she was able to tell her sister-in-law that she had kissed her darling Federico, and left him well and happy in his father's company. Unfortunately, both Castiglione and the Duchess suffered from the heat and malaria of this unhealthy season, and were attacked by fever on their respective journeys. Baldassare fell ill first in Rome, and afterwards at Viterbo on his way back to Urbino. On August 12 he wrote to tell his anxious mother that he had reached home safely, and had almost shaken off the fever. 'I am hoping soon to find myself in camp, but mean to get quite strong first. The Lady Duchess is not over-well, either; let us trust in God that her indisposition may not be grave.' A month later Elisabetta became dangerously ill, and her condition was a cause of grave anxiety through the autumn. Castiglione re-

---

[1] Sanuto, x. 883.   [2] *Ibid.*, x. 820, 824.

covered more speedily, and by the end of August was able to join the Duke in the camp at Finale.

By this time war had begun in good earnest. On August 9 the Pope launched a Bull of excommunication against Alfonso, denouncing him as a son of perdition, a traitor and rebel against the Vicar of Christ, and appointing the Marquis of Mantua Gonfaloniere of the Church in his stead. The Duke of Urbino advanced into Ferrara and Romagna, and made an easy conquest of the principal towns in this district. On the 20th Modena surrendered, chiefly owing to the action of the powerful Count Girardo Rangone, who declared himself for the Pope. But the capture of Ferrara itself was a more difficult matter. Alfonso and his subjects prepared for a vigorous defence, and the valiant captain Federico Gonzaga, one of Castiglione's Bozzolo neighbours, succeeded in fighting his way through the enemy's ranks, and joined the Duke within the walls. Although the Marquis of Mantua had been appointed to the chief command of the Papal forces, he delayed to take the field, and there can be little doubt that the Marchesana secretly used her influence on her brother's behalf. ' Here we are told of intrigues in Mantua which surprise us greatly,' wrote Castiglione to his mother from Modena on October 16 ; ' if you could find out the truth about what is really taking place, I should be very grateful.

His letters from the camp during this autumn and winter certainly give the impression that the Pope was justified in complaining of his general's dilatory measures.

'Our life in camp,' he wrote on September 21, ' seems to consist in lodging in the open air in the fields. The rains have been very heavy and are quite incessant, and how long we have to remain here no one can imagine. But the Pope will be in Bologna to-morrow, and then I expect we shall soon have our marching orders.'[1]

Through torrents of rain and a sea of almost impassable mud the indomitable Pope made his way to Bologna, accompanied by several reluctant Cardinals and a body of 400 men. The light-hearted Romagnese went into fits of laughter when they saw the long train of mules and servants bearing litters, struggling along the heavy roads in detestable weather, and forgot to kneel before the Holy Father as he passed. But the fatigues of the journey and the perils that threatened him at Bologna from the advance of the French army and the disaffection of the citizens, brought on a violent attack of fever, and for a few days the Pope's life was in danger. Even then his strong will asserted itself, and he insisted on being carried to the balcony to bless the citizens who rose in arms against the hated Legate, Alidosi, but were quickly pacified by the sight of the Holy Father. In spite of successive relapses, he rose from his sick-bed to say mass on Christmas Day, and, to the intense amazement of Cardinals and generals alike, he announced his intention of joining the camp and conducting the siege of Mirandola in person.

During the autumn months the combined Venetian and Papal forces had been encamped between Modena and Reggio, chiefly engaged in plundering the country round and skirmishing with the garrison of Ferrara. On December 11 Castiglione sent Cristoforo with his horse Pappagallo back to Casatico, begging his mother for money and white cloth, of which he was in great want, and told her that the Duke had been suffering

---

[1] Serassi, i. 54.

from fever for the last few days, and was going to Bologna for rest. 'We others, eight or ten of us, are going with His Excellency. The rest of the camp is moving towards La Mirandola.' Mirandola was now the point upon which the eyes of all Europe were fixed. The strongly fortified city was defended by a valiant Countess, Francesca Trivulzio, daughter of the old Marshal and widow of that Lodovico Pico whose head had been blown off by a shell a year before, when he was fighting on the Pope's side against Venice. This brave lady, supported by her cousin, Alessandro Trivulzio, and a troop of French cavalry, refused to surrender, and held out gallantly against the assaults of the Papal and Venetian troops. It was then that the Pope, declaring that his captains were either fools or traitors, put himself at the head of his forces and led the attack on Mirandola. The weather was bitterly cold, the snow lay thick on the ground, and the wind raged violently. The moat under the walls was frozen over, and the gunpowder was ruined by the torrents of rain and sleet, but nothing could daunt the lion-hearted old man.

'The Pope has appeared, to our great surprise!' wrote the Venetian envoy, Hieronimo Lippomano. 'He hates the French more than ever, and says nothing but " Mirandola! Mirandola!" until it is impossible to help laughing. He heeds neither cold nor snow, and has the strength of a giant. But his people do not support him. The court officials only care for money, and are longing to get back to Rome.'

This apathy on the part of his captains infuriated the vigorous old Pontiff. When the Duke of Urbino tried to make excuses for his delay in planting the artillery against the walls, he shouted out: 'Hold

your peace ! it is too late for words ! Let us attend
to facts, and act at once.'

'The Pope,' wrote Lippomano, 'is in a furious
rage. He blasphemes and curses all his captains in
turn, most of all the Duke of Urbino, who will not
go near him. And he swears by the body of Christ
that he will drive out these barbarians, cut the
garrison to pieces, raze Mirandola to the ground, and
then go to Ferrara.'[1]

On January 6 the Pope took up his quarters in
a convent close to the beleagured city, and lived in
the kitchen, while the Cardinals of Aragon and
Cornaro and the Venetian envoy shared the adjoin-
ing stables. Luigi of Aragon shivered with cold in
this unwonted abode, and envied Castiglione the
warm quilt of feathers which his careful mother had
sent him from home. Roberto of Bari fell ill in
camp, and had to seek shelter at Mantua. On the
15th Castiglione wrote a hurried note to his mother,
begging her to prepare a room in her home for this
friend, whom he loved as a brother, adding : ' We
are here in much discontent, as may be expected,
and in some danger, but hope that we may soon be
successful.'

But the Pope's health and spirits never failed.
One night a shell struck the bedroom where he was
sleeping and wounded two of his servants. He sent
the cannon-ball as a trophy to the shrine of the
Virgin at Loreto, where it is still preserved, and
returned to the trenches to direct the bombardment.
There he stood all day in the blinding sleet, wearing
trooper's boots under his pontifical robes, and looking
like a Polar bear with his long beard white with

---

[1] Sanuto, xi. 723, etc.

snow.   When he dismounted in the midst of a heavy
snowstorm, he had a big fire made, and asked for a
drink, which he shared with the common soldiers.
'Monsignore,' said Messer Hieronimo to Cardinal
Alidosi, as he watched the strange sight, 'it should be
recorded in all the histories of the world that a Pope,
lately recovered from dangerous illness, has himself
come into the camp in January in bitter cold and
snow.'   To which the Cardinal, who had none of the
Pope's military ardour, and was suspected of secretly
plotting with France, replied curtly: 'It is a great
event.'[1]

The wonder with which Christendom beheld the
scene is reflected in the witty Latin dialogue of
'Julius II. Exclusus,' which was published anony-
mously in Paris in 1513, but promptly recognized
as the work of a well-known scholar—' Aut Erasmus,
aut diabolus.'   Here the fighting Pope, wearing a
cassock over his blood-stained armour, and attended
by thousands of soldiers who fell in his battles, is
represented as thundering in vain at the gates of
Paradise, which St. Peter refuses to unlock, since he
cannot recognize in him any marks of the Vicar of
Christ, the pure and lowly Master who loved the
poor and gave His own life for mankind.   But this
famous dialogue was not the only composition inspired by the siege of Mirandola.   In these same
frost-bound trenches, where he spent day and night
directing the movements of the artillery, Baldassare
Castiglione conceived the idea of his noble dramatic
elegy, 'Prosopopoeia Ludovici Pici Mirandulani,' the
only poem which can be definitely ascribed to these
troubled years of his life.   In these fine Latin verses
he describes how, as he watched under the walls of

[1] Sanuto, xi. 745.

the beleaguered city, and the white moonlight shone on the glittering snows, the ghost of Lodovico Pico suddenly appeared before him, with bloody brow and sad face, gazing on the camp bustling in warlike array, and appealed in pathetic language to the Pope as the Father and Shepherd of the nations, the great Arbiter of the world, to whom God Himself had given power over heaven and hell. 'What have I done,' the pale ghost asked, 'to bring such ruin on my race and home?' and, pointing to the wounds which he had received in the Pope's service, implored the Holy Father to have compassion on his unhappy wife and innocent children, and on the ruined houses and desolate vineyards of the miserable peasants whose homes were laid waste by the cruel scourge of war. But while the hero spirit poured out his mournful complaint, the sound of roaring guns broke upon the air, shaking the earth with their fury, a sudden blaze of flames lit up the burning city, and with a groan, the sad spectre vanished into darkness.

Both the dead Lord of Mirandola and his wife had been Castiglione's friends, and the sight of the wrongs inflicted on an innocent race appealed to his poet-soul, rather than the triumphs of the warrior Pope, upon whose side he fought. But, as he and all the world knew, it was a lost cause. Chaumont, who with the French army was encamped hard by, between Rubiera and Carpi, did not move a hand, and the beleaguered town was left to its fate.

On the 20th a breach was made in the walls, and both her ammunition and provisions being exhausted, the Countess surrendered, sending word to the Pope that he might do his worst, but that she and her children would return to their own some day. This message, we are told, pleased the Pope so much that he sent the lady an escort, and gave orders that she should be allowed to leave the city with all the honours of war.[1] He himself would not wait till the drawbridge was restored and the walled-up gates opened, but climbed up a ladder and entered through the breach, a feat which, as the Venetian envoy remarked, the gouty old man only accomplished with some difficulty.[2] The next day he was carried on a litter round the walls, where he gave directions as to the necessary repairs, and appointed Lodovico Pico's brother Gianfrancesco Governor of the conquered city. 'Now,' he said exultingly, 'we will go on to Ferrara.' But he saw with annoyance the quarrels of his own captains, and the ever-growing hatred between Cardinal Alidosi and the Duke of Urbino. He stormed at them all in turn, told them they were dolts and cowards, and swore that he would hang the one and quarter the other.

'This Pope is exceedingly strong-willed and exceedingly difficult to manage,' remarked Lippomano, who had ample opportunity of forming an opinion. 'No one knows what he will do next; he has a brain of his own, and a spirit which is terrible in all things.

Even Castiglione came in for a share of these amenities, and experienced what Ariosto has finely called '*la grande ira di Secondo*'—the great wrath of the second Julius.[3] On January 24 he was sent to the Rocca by the Duke, who would not venture himself into the presence of the irascible Pontiff, to bear him his congratulations on the successful occupation of the city and ask his pleasure regarding the movements of the cavalry. But at the sight of

---

[1] Luigi da Porto, 'Lettere,' p. 231.　　[2] Sanuto, xi. 770, etc.
[3] Satire i. 152.

Castiglione the Pope flew into a violent rage, and
before this most courteous and polished gentleman
could utter a word, sprang from his chair and bade the
envoy be gone from his presence, crying in jeering
tones : ' You have behaved finely, and now you may
go your own way !'[1]

This outburst, which scandalized the Cardinals and
Venetian envoys who were present at the interview,
is partly explained by Castiglione himself.   In a letter
written from Sinigaglia eight months later, he tells his
brother-in-law, Tommaso Strozzi, that the Pope had
long suspected him of being on friendly terms with
the French King, and that this false impression was
due to the calumnies of Count Gio. Francesco della
Mirandola, who hated both himself and the Duke of
Urbino.   But we find no allusion to the Pope in the
short letters which he addressed to his mother from
Mirandola.   These only contained requests for furs and
clothes, as well as an intimation that he was sending
her several mules laden with baggage belonging to
Count Alessandro Trivulzio, who was now the Pope's
prisoner, and begged her to keep them for the present.
Baldassare's next letters were written from Finale,
where the Papal forces remained encamped until the
end of April, and hostilities were either languidly
carried on, or else suspended for a time.   The account
which he gives of his men's destitution and of the
difficulty of obtaining provisions shows the straits to
which the Papal forces were reduced during this long
and tedious campaign.

' We are in want of everything,' he wrote on
March 20, ' and we certainly ought by this time to
have taken La Bastia [a strong fortress command-

[1] Sanuto, xi. 773.

ing an important position on the banks of the Po]
and ask nothing better than to try our chance in
a battle, if only to get out of these miseries. All my
men and I myself are worn out by these long marches,
and our clothes are in rags. I wish you would try
and procure me some blue and tan cloth to make my
servants new vests, and some blue satin for a tunic
for myself, and I will let you know how much I
require. As for our next movements, I can only tell
you what every one knows. We are very near the
enemy, and are obliged to protect our flanks as well
as we can. We are at Finale, Bondeno, and Massa,
and the enemy at La Stellata and Sermeto. The
Pope was very anxious to take La Bastia, but every
one else expects great things from this conference at
Mantua.'

Again, on April 7 he wrote:

' Our labours are continual, and the famine increases
every day. There is hardly a feed of corn left for our
poor horses, and I have told the present bearer, Aurelio,
to ask you to send me 18 or 20 bushels of oats by a
means of conveyance that he will explain, and which,
I hope, you will be able to manage, as we certainly are
in a bad case. In two days I will send for the blue
and tan cloth of which I wrote, to clothe my poor lads,
who are reduced to a state of absolute nakedness.
I should also like to have two sacks of wheat, as not
a grain of corn is to be had here, and bread costs as
much as an eye !'

Still more pressing was his letter of the 9th, in
which he repeats his request for suits of blue and tan
cloth for Smeraldo, his secretary, and white cloth to
make a tunic for Gianpietro, and three pairs of fur-
lined boots. ' All of these I want as soon as possible,
for our clothes are all torn to bits. And I beg you
to send the corn at once, as the horses are in dire

necessity and have eaten the grass close down to the ground.'[1]

This time good Madonna Luigia bestirred herself in earnest, and on the 27th Baldassare wrote gratefully to thank her for the corn, eggs, and vegetables which had been sorely needed. In the same letter he laments the failure of the negotiations to which he had referred above.

This was the conference of foreign envoys whom the Marchesana, in her anxiety for peace, had invited to Mantua, where Maximilian's favourite, Matthæus Lang, Bishop of Gurk, met the ambassadors of France, Spain, and England, and amused himself flirting with Isabella's maids of honour in the intervals of business. On April 10 Bishop Lang was sent to treat with the Pope at Bologna, and behaved with such unmannerly arrogance and insolence that even the Venetians were disgusted, and could not wonder that Julius refused to come to terms with him. The Pope replied by excommunicating the Duke of Ferrara and all the allies of France, and on the 25th the Bishop left Bologna hurriedly with an angry countenance, which boded ill for all parties.

'You will have heard,' wrote Castiglione to his mother two days afterwards, 'that the Ambassador of His Cæsarean Majesty has parted from our Lord the Pope in anger, so that we expect war rather than peace. God send us what is best.'

At this critical moment a new French general appeared on the scene in the person of the fine old Marshal Trivulzio, who was sent with fresh reinforcements to take command after the death of Chaumont. His first step was to make a dash on Bologna, and on

<hr>

[1] Serassi, i. 56-58.

May 15 the Pope left hurriedly for Ravenna to avoid the risk of falling into the hands of the hated French. But hardly was he gone before the people of Bologna rose in arms against Cardinal Alidosi, who fled in disguise to his home near Imola without making any attempt at resistance. The Duke of Urbino, whose army was encamped in the neighbourhood, promptly ordered his men to retreat, and they were pursued and defeated with heavy losses by the French. The flight soon became a rout, and the ducal standard, together with twenty guns and all the baggage, fell into the enemy's hands, and on the 23rd Trivulzio entered Bologna in triumph. The Bentivogli were restored, the citadel which Julius II. had built was destroyed, and Michelangelo's bronze statue of the Pope was broken in pieces and melted down by Alfonso d' Este, who made it into a cannon, which he named La Giulia—an insult which the Pontiff never forgave.

Thus in a few days the old Pope saw himself deprived of all his hard-won conquests. But his courage never quailed. On Friday, May 23, he summoned the Cardinals into his presence at Ravenna, and told them that Bologna had been lost, not, as some men said, by the fault of the Legate, but by the revolt and treachery of its citizens. He asked for Alidosi, and, hearing he had fled to Imola, remarked that perhaps he felt safer there than here. Then he vented his fury on the Duke of Urbino, calling him a fool and a traitor, and saying that if Francesco fell into his hands he should be drawn and quartered, as he richly deserved. Early the next morning he sent for his nephew, and at the sight of the Duke broke out into a torrent of violent reproaches, telling him that his delays and irresolution had been the cause of all these calamities. As Francesco left the Pontiff's presence, burning with shame and anger at this treatment, he met Cardinal Alidosi near the church of S. Vitale, on his way to visit the Pope. The Legate, who was riding on his mule in a Spanish habit, accompanied by a troop of horse, saluted him with a smiling countenance, upon which Francesco sprang to the ground, and, rushing furiously at him with his sword, wounded him mortally, and crying out, ' At last I have thee traitor ; take that which thou hast deserved !' struck him on the head. The Cardinal's followers, paralyzed with horror, stood by speechless, while two of the Duke's servants dispatched the victim, and Francesco himself made his way through the gathering crowd and rode off to Urbino.

The murdered man was carried into S. Vitale, and lay there till Sunday evening, when his body was buried in the Duomo.

' A terrific storm broke over Ravenna,' writes the Venetian envoy, ' just after the fatal deed was done, and lasted all Saturday and Sunday, so that the whole city was flooded when the dead Cardinal was borne to the grave. It seemed as if the Day of Judgment had arrived, and the rain never ceased till he was laid under the ground.'[1]

At one o'clock that afternoon the news of his favourite's assassination was brought to the Pope. Filled with grief and horror, he gave way to the most passionate sorrow, and, refusing to take food in he city which had been the scene of so great an outrage, left immediately for Rimini. Here he fell seriously ill, and could only travel by slow stages to Rome, where he arrived on June 26, broken in health,

---

[1] Sanuto, xii. 201.

but still strong in courage and firm of purpose. His coolness and resolution in the face of overwhelming dangers amazed every one. A group of rebellious Cardinals, supported by Louis XII. and Maximilian, had summoned a General Council at Pisa, and cited the Pope to appear before this assembly. Julius retorted by issuing summons for a universal Council to meet at the Lateran in April, 1512, and pronounced the edict issued by the revolted Cardinals to be null and void. At the same time he fulminated excommunications against Bologna, and began to negotiate a league against France with Ferdinand of Spain, Henry VIII., and Venice. His enemies were divided and irresolute. The Council of Pisa proved an utter failure. Louis XII., fearing to proceed to extremities against the Head of the Church, ordered his troops to retire to Milan, and entered into negotiations for peace.

Meanwhile Castiglione had returned with the Duke to Urbino. He had lost everything in the rout of the Papal army, but held himself fortunate to have escaped with his life from this disaster. On June 1 he sent a brief note to inform his mother of his safety :

' By different ways you will have heard that we reached Cesena safely. This bearer will tell you that we are at Urbino, safe indeed, but utterly destitute. I have lost all my horses and everything that I possessed. However, I am not greatly concerned about this, since, thank God, I am safe and unharmed. I should be glad if you could send me a few necessary clothes, shirts, handkerchiefs, caps of gold cloth, and other things of this kind, for I have been stripped bare of everything.'[1]

We do not know if Castiglione was in Ravenna with the Duke and witnessed the murder of Alidosi,

[1] Serassi, i. 59.

but as no allusion to the event appears in his letters, it is more probable that he remained at the camp near Cesena endeavouring to collect the remnants of the army. It was, however, as usual, to him that Francesco turned for help in his hour of need. His influence counted for much with his lord, and both the Venetian envoys and the Mantuan correspondents speak of him as the Duke's chief minister and favourite—'the one who can do everything with him.' Castiglione, on his part, seems to have become attached to his young master, and was too loyal a servant to say a word against him even in private letters.

On July 21, three days after promulgating the Bull convoking the Lateran Council, the Pope summoned his nephew, the Duke of Urbino, to appear before the Sacred College to answer for the murder of Cardinal Alidosi, and declared him to have forfeited all his dignities and possessions. At first Francesco hesitated to obey the summons, but yielding to the counsels of his aunt, the Duchess, and his more prudent friends, he came to Rome with Castiglione on August 9 and presented himself at the Vatican.[1] The Pope ordered him to remain under arrest in the Duchess Elisabetta's house in the Via Lata, while his trial was referred to a commission of six Cardinals. Fortunately for Francesco, the chief of this tribunal was Giovanni de' Medici, a Cardinal closely connected by ties of friendship and gratitude with the ducal family, and whose brother Giuliano and secretary Bibbiena, as we know, were intimate alike with the Duchess Elisabetta, Bembo, and Castiglione. The Duke's defence was confided to another member of the same circle, Filippo Beroaldo, who pleaded Francesco's cause with a power and ability

[1] Sanuto, xii. 371.

that excited general admiration. The proceedings were long and involved, and fill a thick parchment volume, which is still preserved in the archives of Urbino, while Beroaldo's able and eloquent oration is among the manuscripts of the Vatican library.[1] It rests almost entirely on the crimes and treason of the murdered Cardinal, of which many substantial proofs could be produced, and, after a long recital of Alidosi's numerous acts of violence and treachery, his secret understanding with the French, and final betrayal of Bologna, ends by declaring that the Duke had rendered the Pope and Church a great service in delivering the world from this monster of iniquity. In a fine peroration the advocate appealed to the judges to spare a young Prince whose life was precious to so many illustrious and virtuous Princes, such as the Duchess of Urbino and the Marquis and Marchioness of Mantua, and whose sword was sorely needed for the defence of Italy.

These sentiments found a quick response in the popular feeling, both in Rome and in the rest of Italy. After the first shock of horror at the murder, there was a general revulsion in favour of the man whose hand had slain this hated villain. No one but the Pope grieved for Alidosi. The other Cardinals expressed their satisfaction openly. Paris de Grassis, in his diary, returned solemn thanks to Almighty God for having delivered the world from so odious a man and so notorious a traitor. The people in the streets of Ravenna rejoiced over the tyrant's fall, and a voice was heard calling down blessings on the Duke, whom God had chosen to be the avenger of their wrongs.

But in the midst of these proceedings the Pope

[1] Cod. Vat. Urb., 924.

suddenly fell ill. On August 17 he was attacked
with fever, which three days later returned with such
violence that his doctors gave little hope of recovery,
and the news spread through Rome that he was
dying. On the 22nd he became unconscious, and
the next day Cardinal de' Medici told our friend
Lippomano that the Holy Father could not live
through the night.

There was a tumult in the Capitol: the young
Romans rose in arms, the Cardinals began to prepare
for the conclave, and the chances of the most popular
among them were freely discussed. But the indomitable will of the old man still asserted itself.
After remaining unconscious during several hours, he
suddenly asked for a drink of wine, and when the
doctors refused threatened to send them to the
dungeons of the Castello. Then he remembered his
nephew, and with a touch of old affection for the
boy whom he had always loved, sent for the Duke
to his bedside, and gave him absolution and a present
of 12,000 ducats. On the 24th he received the
Viaticum, and dictated his last wishes to his daughter
Felice and Cardinal Riario. After that he ate an
egg, swore at all his doctors in turn, and asked for
olives and peaches. Three days later the fever
suddenly left him, and on the 28th the Venetian
envoy wrote that he was out of danger.[1]

As soon as the Pope was convalescent and able to
transact business, the Duke of Urbino left Rome and
returned to his own home. By an act of the Papal
Consistory, bearing the date August 22, 1511, he
was formally absolved from all ecclesiastical censures
and restored to his dignities and dominions. The
Pope's sentence was confirmed by the Cardinals, and

[1] Sanuto, xii. 441, 449, 450.

the full particulars of their decision were afterwards
embodied in a Bull signed by His Holiness and
eighteen Cardinals, and dated December 9, 1511.

On September 27 Castiglione wrote joyously from
Urbino to tell his mother that their anxieties were
happily ended:

' We have, thank God, returned safely from Rome,
bringing with us the absolution and restoration of my
illustrious lord to his state and honours, after passing
through infinite troubles and more anxieties than I can
describe. The worst of all was the very dangerous
illness of His Holiness, who has been saved, as it
were, by a miracle from the jaws of death to ensure
the safety of our Duke and of the whole Church of
God. For if he had really died, both the state and
person of the Duke would have been in the utmost
danger, and might have been exposed to great risks
at the hands of the Sacred College. Many indeed
were the perils that could already be foreseen. But
God be praised ! When I was in Rome I sent you a
letter by a messenger of the Lord Marquis, but do
not know if it ever reached you. In that letter I
begged you to send me fifty ducats to pay some of
my debts, which I have been forced to incur owing to
our misfortunes this year. As soon as I have received
the money I will set out on my journey and come
and see you. Meanwhile I am going to Our Lady of
Loreto, to whom I owe a vow. I cannot write more,
as my hand is very tired ; and although I can use
it to write, it is still weak, and only improves by slow
degrees.'[1]

Baldassare had suffered in body as well as in mind
by the calamities of the past year. He complained
repeatedly during the disastrous campaign of severe

[1] Serassi, i. 60.

pains in his side, which disabled him from active service, and now he suffered from sleeplessness and weakness of limbs. But the perils from which he and his lord had escaped were so much worse that he could only thank God as with a grateful heart he set out on his pilgrimage to Loreto.

CHAPTER XX

1511–1512

Marriage proposals renewed by Count Martinengo, and suddenly broken off—The Pope suspects Castiglione of intrigues with the French—The Duke of Urbino refuses to serve under another general—Incurs the Pope's displeasure anew—His offer of service accepted after the defeat of Ravenna—Campaign against Ferrara—Death of Cesare Gonzaga.

AFTER all the dangers and anxieties of the past year, Madonna Luigia was naturally anxious to see her son. She had also many things to discuss with him—above all, the eternal marriage question, which as yet remained unsettled. The pertinacity with which she met all rebuffs, and continued her exertions to find Baldassare a suitable and well-dowered bride, was altogether admirable; but it is hardly surprising if the knight himself began to grow tired of her importunities. Even when he was engaged in active warfare she sent him fresh proposals. From the camp at Finale he wrote on April 27:

'As for Madonna Bionda's offer, I leave it to you; but I fear the lady's father is not of gentle birth, a thing which I count of great importance; and I do not see that the other conditions are sufficiently good to counterbalance this drawback, or that, for instance, we can expect a large dowry, high position, or any other advantages.'[1]

[1] Serassi, i. 58.

On his return to Urbino in June, he wrote that he must put an end to these tiresome discussions, and marry either Count Giberto of Correggio's daughter or the maiden of the Stanga family. 'The fact is,' he adds, 'I am sick of the whole thing. Still, if you wish to entertain one of these proposals, it may perhaps not turn out badly. Anyhow, I would gladly settle the matter at once if it must be done, and may God prosper us!'

But after his return from Rome, the old idea of a marriage with Count Giulio Martinengo's daughter, which had been entertained three years before, was revived. The girl remained unmarried, and her family evidently realized the advantages of a connexion with a personage of Castiglione's importance, while he on his part was quite inclined to renew negotiations.

On October 13 he was concerned to hear that his mother had been seriously ill, and had written him a letter which had unfortunately been lost. This prompted him to send her a letter of affectionate inquiries, and express his regrets at being compelled to delay his visit:

'The reasons which hinder me are of such a nature that I cannot write them, so I will only say that I will come as soon as possible; for I am extremely anxious to conclude this business, which I now regard as settled. It is true, as you may remember, that a larger dowry was originally promised, but I do not wish to make a point of this. But I wonder why they should object to keeping the thing private for a little longer, as, once it is settled and promises are exchanged, I do not see that it can matter if it is announced a little sooner or later. However, I should like it to be kept private until my arrival, for the reason which I mentioned to you, unless you

think there is any risk in this delay. These ladies
[the Duchesses] all commend themselves to you, and
Madonna Emilia asks me constantly what she owes
you for the cloth, but I cannot tell her, as the letter
on this subject reached me in Rome ; I have lost it,
and cannot remember.'

Unfortunately, this time Madonna Luigia was not
only sorely disappointed, but seriously vexed with her
son for what she considered his neglect, and both
her widowed daughter, Polissena, and her son-in-law,
Tommaso Strozzi, wrote to inform Baldassare how
much she had taken his conduct to heart. Their
letters arrived at Urbino after he had started on his
pilgrimage, and only reached him at Sinigaglia on his
way back from Loreto.

'The day before yesterday,' he wrote on November 6, 'I received a letter of yours written on
October 19, which caused me the greatest vexation,
and such indeed as I have not experienced for a long
time ; and this because I see that you do not believe
me, and think that I am less obedient and loving than
I am and have always shown myself to be in all my
actions. I cannot think that what I have done is
serious enough for you to take it to heart in such a
way as to make yourself ill, as M. Tommaso and
M. Polissena tell me. What cause of complaint
have you? Have I ever said that I would not consent to this marriage or delay its conclusion without
good reason? If I had been unwilling to agree to this,
I should not have given you leave to make the contract as you have done, with my entire approval and
to my great satisfaction. If I have had to defer my
visit for a little while, this does not seem to me to be
so great a wrong, since this delay is only due to
imperative and most urgent reasons, which I would
have explained in writing if they were not so grave ;

for if the letter were to fall into other hands it might do much harm, now that the roads are so unsafe and are closely watched by the Pope's enemies. All the same, I will venture to tell you the cause now, lest you should take it to be other than it is. The Duke refused to give me leave to come to Mantua, and as it would take a long time to explain his reasons, I am writing another letter to M. Tommaso, who will repeat its contents to you, so as not to give you the trouble of reading them. Only I do beg you, if you wish to please me, not to distress yourself, because I do not mean either to delay or break off these negotiations. I trust that you will calm your spirits, and if you really wish for my happiness, try to get well and be of good courage ; for I promise and swear to come as soon as possible, and hope in any case this may be very soon. Meanwhile, if you hear again from Brescia, I am quite content that you should announce the marriage and conclude the contract as you may think best. I have nothing more to say, but that I do hope you will be cured quickly and keep up a good heart, for there is nothing that I more earnestly desire than to see you well and to be with you. And you will certainly not require the medicine that you say you would like to take !'

The following was the letter which he enclosed for his brother-in-law :

'*To the magnificent Cavalier and my most honoured Brother, M. Tommaso Strozzi.*

'I have been very much vexed to hear from you how bitterly Madonna our mother complains of me, God knows with what injustice, since I have never had a wish on earth excepting to obey and please her. The reasons of my delay, which I could not write by Pietrone, I now send you, so as not to give her the trouble of reading them, hoping you will either read or explain them to her by word of mouth.   I also beg you to show this letter to our Mag. Gio. Pietro, and to M. Polissena, and hope that you will all beg of her not to compel me to incur the Duke's disgrace for the sake of these few days, which would certainly be a great pity, as I have already fully explained, especially as the affair is so far settled that there can be no thought of drawing back now.   I beg of you kindly to go to Casatico at once and see her, and then send me a messenger to tell me how she is, for I am so much disturbed that I hardly know what to do.

'SINIGAGLIA, *November 6, 1511.*

' Since the beginning of these wars, the Pope has always thought and said that the Duke not only failed to do his utmost against the Duke of Ferrara and the French, but was in secret communication with them, and has often declared that he was a traitor and should be drawn and quartered, and many similar words, which he has repeated a thousand times and now maintains more strongly than ever. Now that the campaign against Bologna is to be undertaken, he has reduced the Duke of Urbino's old company by sixty men-at-arms, and has given the Duke of Termini[1] a force of 200 men-at-arms, and light cavalry, with the title of Lieutenant, which is greater than that of Captain, so that the Duke would have to serve under the Duke of Termini, and declares that he will rather die than submit to such an insult, for a thousand reasons which would take too long to tell.   Our Lord Duke has always tried, and is still trying, to remove the Pope's suspicions and prove his innocence, as the best way of recovering His Holiness's favour.   The Pope has repeatedly declared that I was the medium through whom the Duke kept up correspondence with the French, having received this impression from one who bore me no goodwill—*i.e.*, Count Gio. Francesco of Mirandola—

[1] A Neapolitan general in the King of Spain's service.

and was confirmed in his suspicions because, when I was sent to Parma to escort Captain Peralta—whom God pardon—these French lords treated me with the greatest courtesy and honour. The Pope said one day to the Bishop of Trirarico [Count Lodovico of Canossa] that he knew for certain that I had been at Mantua when the Bishop of Gurk was there to treat with him on behalf of the French, and no power on earth could induce him to believe this to be false, until the Bishop brought forward three or four witnesses to prove that I could not have been at Mantua at that time. This being the case, when I asked the Duke for leave to come to Lombardy, he refused, for fear of giving the Pope any ground of suspicion, and begged me to wait until His Holiness had decided what he would do for him; for undoubtedly, if the Pope had heard of my journey, nothing in the world would have persuaded him that I had not gone on some mission to the French. The Duke's affair with the Pope is still pending, and may be settled at any moment, and we hope it will end well. To me these reasons seem to be sufficiently grave, and it would, I think, be a great pity to throw away the service of so many years, especially in these times, when if I am held of any account it is for the Duke's sake. This need cause no interruption in our affair, which I consider to be settled and done, for it can make no difference if the actual contract be concluded a few days earlier or later. This, then, has been the reason of my delays, which I beg you not to ascribe to my own reluctance. Now I am here at Sinigaglia, and as soon as I get leave from the Duke I shall come. The Lord Duke is expected here to-morrow, and I, having gone to settle some differences at Fano, found His Excellency had left for S. Maria di Loreto.'[1]

This letter throws light on the renewed displeasure with which Julius II. regarded his nephew during the

[1] Serassi, i. 62-64.

next few months, openly accusing him of carrying on
intrigues with Louis XII., and declaring him to be a
rebel by a Bull issued only a few days before the battle
of Ravenna. Guicciardini alludes to the suspicion
with which the Pope regarded Castiglione, whom he
unjustly believed to be in correspondence with
Gaston de Foix, the young captain whose short
career was closed on that hard-fought field, where
he and Alfonso d' Este obtained so brilliant a victory
over the combined Spanish and Papal forces. But
although neither the Duke of Urbino nor Castiglione
were present at the battle of Ravenna, the Urbino
contingent, led by Domenico di Genga, fought under
the Pope's banner on that occasion.[1] As soon as the
disastrous result of the battle was known, Francesco
hastened to Rome and offered his services to his
uncle, who gladly accepted them, and once more
invested him with the chief command of the Papal
forces.

Under these circumstances Castiglione felt that it
was impossible for him to gratify his mother's wish,
and abandoned all idea of a visit to Mantua for
the present. The proposed marriage with Count
Martinengo's daughter, which had been the most
pressing cause for the journey, was suddenly broken
off owing to political reasons. Agostino Gonzaga,
who was sent to Urbino by the Marquis in December,
brought Baldassare some private information on the
subject, to which he refers mysteriously in a letter to
his mother of December 22:

'M. Agostino spoke to me about this intended
marriage, and told me a thing that I could never

---

[1] Guicciardini, x., c. 5; Ugolini, ii. 188; Dennistoun, ii. 330;
Brosch, ' Julius II.,' 245, 251.

have imagined, and which ends the matter. Since the affair was so far settled, and my mind was quite made up on the subject, I regret this deeply—for many reasons. But we must have patience, for this is the work of Fate. I am also grieved to think these gentlemen may not realize the true nature of my reasons, and I beg you to make them understand very clearly that this distresses me most profoundly. May God direct our course! for indeed I see great ruin hanging over this city, and above all over this unhappy family. At least it is something to feel that in this instance our lord has shown that he partly realizes how loyal a servant he has in me. But I will say no more about this. We often do not know what is our true gain or loss.'[1]

The unfortunate city to whose doom Castiglione alludes in words of prophetic warning, was clearly that of Brescia, which was besieged and taken by the Venetians in February, and retaken and cruelly sacked by Gaston de Foix a fortnight later. Before these disastrous events Count Giulio Martinengo, the father of his destined bride, was put to death with his two brothers for conspiring to give up the city to the Venetians. Some intimation of the plot, in which the Count was engaged, had evidently reached the Marquis of Mantua, who sent Castiglione this friendly warning by his kinsman Agostino Gonzaga. But the satisfaction which this token of renewed good feeling gave Baldassare was clouded by an unkind report which some malicious tongue repeated in his hearing.

'I am a good deal vexed,' he wrote on January 29, 'by a rumour which has reached me by a secret channel, to the effect that the Lord Marquis has

[1] Serassi, i. 64.

lately said certain things about me which show that some slanderous tongue has more influence with him than my true devotion to his service. If any trustworthy messenger is coming this way, I should be glad if you would tell me anything that you know about this.'

The bearer of this letter to Mantua was Bernardino Missaglia, one of the famous Milanese armourers. Castiglione proceeded to inform his mother that he had given Missaglia an order for a thing which he had longed to have for years past—a suit of German armour—and begged her to find sixty florins to defray the cost, since, if he could have nothing else, he meant at least to be well armed. After this came a modest request for two black caps made in Italian fashion, of double thickness, with two folds and low crowns, but no brims.

'I will do my best to ask for no more money at present, and will keep the bearer of your letter, Cristoforo da Asola, in my service. I will only add that I am very well, thank God, and anxious to have news of you and all of ours. I trust that things will settle down, so that we may see each other once more.'

Three months later the Duke of Urbino once more took the field at the head of a Papal army, and succeeded in recovering Romagna in the course of a short campaign. Castiglione, who remained in close attendance on his lord, wrote on May 12 from Rimini to Madonna Luigia :

'I have not written for some time, for lack of messengers, the roads being so unsafe ; but to-day I have found a bearer, and send this by him. We are still at Rimini, which we have retaken for the Church as well as the Rocca. We shall soon occupy the rest of Romagna without much opposition. We are all well, thank God. Monsignor di Gonzaga [Cardinal Sigismondo] is now our Legate, and is here with us. I am greatly in want of the armour which I have so often mentioned, and enclose a letter to Bernardino Missaglia. I beg you to give it him, and make Camillo and Filippo ask every day if it is ready, as I need it greatly. I also wish Camillo would write to me about our affairs. A report has reached us that there is plague at Mantua, which God forbid! I think the roads will be safe now from Ferrara to Rimini, and should be glad if Cristoforo would bring me Pappagallo. He can travel safely by Ferrara, but had better obtain a safe-conduct from the Duke. This I leave to Your Magnificence.'[1]

On the 26th he sent another short note by a young Mantuan merchant, who promised to visit Madonna Luigia himself, once more begging for the armour which he required so urgently, as well as for fresh supplies of money. A week afterwards he returned to Urbino for a few days with his lord, and wrote to say that he had left Rimini before Cristoforo's arrival, and was sending back a young horse to be trained and exercised at Mantua. The suit of armour, he heard, was at length ready, and full directions were given to Camillo, who was to pack it carefully in a box to keep out damp and rust, and bring it by water as far as Ravenna, where the Castellan would send it on to the camp. Another thing of which he stood greatly in need was a new tent, and since there were good tent-makers at Mantua, he begged Madonna Luigia to have one made for him of good tan and blue cloth, and not too large or heavy to be carried on the back of a mule, together with the stakes belonging to it.

[1] Serassi, i. 66.

On June 13 the Duke of Urbino entered Bologna, which once more shook off the yoke of the Bentivogli and acknowledged the Papal rule. At the same moment Pavia surrendered to the Swiss invaders, who had descended upon Lombardy under Cardinal Schinner. On the 20th Ottaviano Sforza took possession of Milan in the Pope's name. The French Bishop retired in confusion across the Alps. The triumph of Julius was complete. He celebrated the deliverance of Italy with solemn thanksgivings, a procession, and fireworks, and gave the Duke of Urbino renewed orders to press on against Ferrara. Duke Alfonso, finding himself deserted by his allies, was induced by the Gonzagas and Colonnas to come to Rome and throw himself on the Pope's mercy. On June 23 he left Ferrara, provided with a safe-conduct from the Pope, which his sister Isabella brought him with her own hands, and reached Rome on the evening of July 4. He paid a brief visit to his niece, the young Duchess of Urbino, on his way, as we learn from a letter which Castiglione wrote to his mother a few days later :

'I am here at Urbino, where I have been since the Lord Duke of Ferrara passed through on his way to Rome. But I expect we shall soon return to Bologna. All my household is there, and I have only a single servant with me here.'

Baldassare had evidently been sent on a confidential mission from his master to Alfonso, whose dominions he was invading in the Pope's name. Throughout the war the Marchesana Isabella, who left no stone unturned to help her brother, besieged her son-in-law with entreaties not to proceed to extremities against Ferrara, and her championship

of Alfonso's cause frequently excited the wrath of
Julius, who threatened to send his army against
Mantua, and put her boy Federico in the dungeons
of the Torresella of Venice.   In Rome the Duke
was lodged in Cardinal Gonzaga's house, and received
a cordial welcome not only from his nephew Federico,
but from the Pope's daughter Felice and Fabrizio
Colonna, whom he had generously released after his
defeat at Ravenna.

On the 9th the Colonnas escorted him to the
Vatican, where he received absolution from the Pope
and visited young Federico, who gave his uncle a
banquet in the Belvedere, and took him to see
Michelangelo at work on the vaulting of the Sistine
Chapel.   But it soon became evident that the Pope
would be satisfied with nothing but the surrender of
Ferrara, and Alfonso, being determined not to yield,
escaped from Rome on the 19th, with the help of the
Colonnas.   During the next two months he remained
hidden in the castles of these powerful friends or
wandered about the Campagna, disguised by turns
as a soldier and a friar, until, on October 14, he at
length reached Ferrara in safety.

Meanwhile Reggio opened its gates to the Duke
of Urbino, and on September 29 Castiglione wrote
from Ravenna to his mother:

'We are here, on our way to attack Ferrara.   May
God order our doings! I cannot employ my secretary
to write,' he added, 'for I have none.   Last night
our Camillo attacked Giovanni while he was asleep,
and struck him six times with his sword, and ran
away.'

All the same, like the good son that he was, he
proceeds to give his mother directions about the

new dovecot that she is building, which he wishes
to be square and partly enclosed in the courtyard.
And he inquires about another Brescian lady, a niece
of the unfortunate Count Martinengo, who has been
recommended to him as a possible bride. A week
later he wrote from Modena, where he was staying
with his kinswoman, Costanza Rangone the fair and
accomplished daughter of Bianca Bentivoglio, and
who had lately taken Cesare Fregoso as her second
husband. This time he had been sent by his lord
to meet Bishop Matthäus Lang, the imperial envoy
who had lately been present at the conference of the
Powers held at Mantua, and was now on his way to
attend the Lateran Council. What was Castiglione's
precise errand on this occasion we do not learn, but
there can be little doubt that its object was to plead
the Duke of Ferrara's cause with the Emperor's
powerful favourite. At the same moment he received a personal appeal from the Marchesana
Isabella, who told Cardinal Ippolito that she heard
Castiglione had more influence than anyone else with
the Duke of Urbino, and could be counted on as a
good friend. According to her account, Castiglione
assured the Marchesana that the Duke was conducting the campaign against Ferrara with the utmost
discretion, and intentionally creating difficulties and
delays.[1] The manner in which the war was pursued
that autumn goes far to prove the truth of her words.
The Pope, so the Venetian envoy in Rome reported,
was more eager than ever to press on the war, and
complained that the Duke's delays were interminable.[2]
When, at the end of September, boats and bridges
for the passage of the Po were prepared, Francesco

[1] Luzio e Renier, 'Mantova e Urbino,' p. 206.
[2] Sanuto, xv. 121.

declared that the violent sirocco gale and heavy rains made it impossible to proceed, and retired into camp at Lugo. Castiglione's own sympathies were no doubt on the side of the Duke of Ferrara, whose family was bound to his own by so many ties, and whose niece Leonora—the ' Duchessa giovane ' of his letters—was constantly sending messages to his mother and sister Laura.

Meanwhile a diversion was created by the death of Giovanni Sforza's little son, Costanzo, and the consequent reversion of the fief of Pesaro to the Church. Galeazzo Sforza, a natural son of the infant Prince's grandfather, promptly asserted his claim to the succession, and seized the Rocca, upon which the Pope recalled the Duke of Urbino, and ordered him to lay siege to this fortress. On October 30 Galeazzo surrendered, and retired to Milan after giving up his own lands in Pesaro to the Duke on payment of 20,000 ducats and a yearly pension of 1,000 ducats.[1] Cardinal Gonzaga took possession of the city in the Pope's name, and Julius openly declared his intention of investing his nephew with the vicariate of Pesaro as compensation for the arrears of salary due to him and the expenses which he had incurred in the service of the Church. The Duke was naturally much pleased by this sign of restored favour on his uncle's part, and in his gratitude to Castiglione for his past services promised to give him a castle and estate in his new dominions. After so many trials and disappointments, this piece of good fortune was very welcome to Baldassare, who alludes to these events in a letter which he wrote to his mother from Lugo on October 17. Poor Madonna Luigia had been greatly alarmed to hear of his secretary Camillo's

[1] Sanuto, xv. 319.

escapade, and was filled with fears, which her son did his best to dissipate.

' As for what you write about the ill-conduct of my servants, I thank you warmly for what you say, as I know it comes from your heart ; but I beg of you not to distress yourself about these matters, for, thank God, I am not in want of good servants, and can get as many as I desire. For the rest I trust in God, who will guide and protect me from danger, as He has done till now, thanks to the prayers of holy persons. I am rather puzzled to understand why you beg me to be careful as to whom I allow to sleep in my room, for I am not aware that I have any secret enemy. With regard to my secretary- ship, as I wrote before, I want a man accustomed to a hard life and who can write well. As long as he can do these things, you may send me anyone you choose. With regard to a bed-hanging that is not too large, I should be very glad to have one such as you describe to keep out the wind. But no one can tell what our future movements may be. How- ever, as far as I can see, we shall be able to do little more this winter. The bearer of this is a Spanish officer, a great friend of mine, who is coming to Mantua on business. I invited him to our house because he is a very pleasant and gallant gentleman. I think he will pay you a visit, and hope you will show him civility, and as far as possible amuse him, and if he likes a bed in our house I hope you will give him one. I will say no more, but beg of you to be of good cheer and trust in our Lord God, who will help us. And for your peace of mind I will tell you that the Lord Duke has been graciously pleased to give me a castle in his new State of Pesaro, which, from what I hear, is in a very fair and pleasant spot, in a fruitful domain, looking over the sea ; and although it may not be as fertile as our Lombard soil, yet it brings in quite 200 ducats a year, and is

surrounded by fine estates. The castle is called
Ginestreto, so that you may tell Madonna Polissena
to let Madonna Camilla know that I shall soon have
a castle and the 5,000 ducats she requires into the
bargain! If she is content with my proposal, we will
yet make a match.'[1]

Camilla Gonzaga, to whom Castiglione sent this
gay message, was the youngest and fairest of all
Madonna Antonia's daughters, who lived at Gazzuolo,
near Casatico, and whose wedding, five years afterwards, was celebrated by Bandello in one of his
novels.

[1] Serassi, i. 70.

CHAPTER XXI

1512–1513

Changes at the Court of Urbino—Federico Gonzaga visits his sister
—Death of Gaspare Pallavicino, Cesare Gonzaga, and Roberto di
Bari—Bembo and Canossa in Rome—Restoration of the Medici
—Count Rangone's daughter—Castiglione receives a grant of
the Castle of Novillara.

THE year 1512 brought many changes to the court of
Urbino. Up to this time the circle of Guidobaldo's
knights remained practically unbroken. Through the
tumult of wars that distracted Italy during the early
years of Francesco Maria's reign, we catch glimpses
of court festivities and many carnivals, which show
us that the old order was still unchanged. The
carnival of 1511 was especially gay, in spite of the
absence of the Duke and Castiglione in the campaign
of Mirandola. That February young Federico
Gonzaga, the Pope's hostage, who had accompanied
Julius to Bologna, and was the old man's pet and
plaything, paid a visit to his sister Leonora, and
remained at Urbino until April. His coming was the
signal for a round of balls, masquerades, banquets, and
concerts. Pastoral eclogues were recited, comedies
were performed, and Federico, after learning a few
lines from Virgil every morning to satisfy his tutor,
gave himself up to amusement. In the evening he
sang and played with his sister, the young Duchess,

FEDERICO GONZAGA.

BY FRANCIA (LEATHAM COLLECTION).

To face p. 320, Vol. I.

and entertained Leonora and her ladies, Margherita, Ippolita, and the fair Raffaella, at supper. The violinist Jacopo di San Secondo, Bembo, and the Magnifico Giuliano were generally of the party, as well as Count Alessandro Trivulzio, the hero of Mirandola, who had been released on parole after the surrender of that city, and stood high in favour with all the ladies. On the last day of carnival Duchess Elisabetta, who seldom left her rooms, joined the merry gathering, and was present with Madonna Emilia and all her gentlemen at the supper-party and masqued ball in the Marchesino's rooms.[1] In April Federico and his tutor returned to Rome, and Bembo went to Venice, not without a sigh of regret for the pleasant company that he was leaving.

'What are you all doing, I wonder,' he wrote from the shore of the Adriatic to Ottaviano Fregoso. 'How fares my Ippolita? Is she caught in the toils of San Secondo or Trivulzio? O fool that I am to leave my beloved a prey to men of war, and linger here on a sandy shore, more dull and useless than the very shells at my feet! A thousand greetings, I pray you, to both their Excellencies, as well as Emilia and the lively Margherita, and to Ippolita the adored, and to my rival, Alessandro Trivulzio.'[2]

The Muses had not yet deserted that court which Sadoleto praised as the Parnassus of the world. Castiglione still wrote matchless verses in Latin and Italian. Cesare Gonzaga sent madrigals to Isabella d' Este from the battlefield, vowing that, if his sword was pledged to the service of Mars, his heart belonged to the Queen of Love. Bembo and Bibbiena still addressed witty epistles to the Marchesana, and

---

[1] Luzio, 'Federico Gonzaga Ostaggio,' p. 16.
[2] 'Epist. fam.,' iv. 155.

helped her to play tricks on Mario Equicola or l' Unico Aretino. But a change was passing over the court where Guidobaldo had reigned of old. Elisabetta, the Duchess-widow, as she is called in the correspondence of these days, was slowly retiring into the background and fading out of sight. By degrees she gave up the reins of government to her nephew and his councillors, and only appeared in public when her generous help or gentle influence could avail to loose captive chains or assuage the Pope's anger. She wrote fewer letters, and the short notes which she sent to Isabella were generally dictated to a secretary. Even Madonna Emilia's pen was less active than of old, and a letter from Urbino was hailed with pleasure at Mantua. For a few loyal servants, for Castiglione, and perhaps Bembo, Elisabetta might still be the woman above all women, but in the eyes of others the young Duchess began to take her place. Leonora's beauty and goodness were extolled with reason by all visitors to Urbino, and Castiglione brought his praises to swell the flowing tide. 'If ever grace, beauty, intelligence, courteous manners, gentleness, and charm, were united in one person, it is in the new Duchess, whose every motion is adorned by these qualities.'[1]

Leonora had not inherited her mother's brilliant gifts, or the incomparable charm of her aunt, and never played the same part in the eyes of the world ; but she was genuinely good and affectionate, as well as remarkably beautiful. Her conduct was irreproachable at all stages of her life, and her devoted attachment to the widowed Duchess is one of the most attractive features of her character. To Castiglione she proved a faithful friend, and her regard

[1] 'Cortegiano,' iv. 3.

for him no doubt had its effect in removing the unjust suspicions which her father had so long entertained. Before long, time and death began to make larger inroads on the once happy family. Gaspare Pallavicino, as we have seen, was the first to go, dying in 1511, in his Lombard home, at the early age of twenty-five, of lingering consumption.

' Being attacked by acute disease, and several times reduced to extremity, although his mind was so vigorous that for long it successfully resisted death and kept his body alive, a premature end finally closed his life, to the great loss not only of our company and his own family and friends, but of his own country and all Lombardy.'

The next death which Castiglione had to record was a still more grievous one—that of his beloved cousin and brother-at-arms, Cesare Gonzaga, the comrade of his daily life, who had grown up with him from boyhood and shared his home at Urbino. Cesare's brilliant career was cut short by a sudden attack of fever, which carried him off in a few days, in September, 1512, when he was serving with Baldassare in the Papal army at Bologna. Since the death of Falcone six years before, Castiglione had suffered no loss which he felt so keenly.

' Not long afterwards died Messer Cesare Gonzaga, whose death has left a bitter and painful memory to all those who knew him, because, since Nature, all too seldom, produces men such as he was, it would seem fitting that she should not deprive us of them so early. And certainly M. Cesare was taken from us at a time when he began to fulfil the rare promise of his youth and to be held in that high estimation which his admirable qualities deserved. He had already given proof of his excellence in many perilous and toilsome wars, and his noble lineage was further adorned by the knowledge alike of letters and arms, and by every exalted quality, so that his goodness, talents, and learning led us to expect still greater things from him in the future.'

Yet a third name is linked with these, that of Roberto da Bari, the youthful shepherd of Baldassare's pastoral, and the accomplished courtier whose dancing was the admiration of all. He never recovered from the effect of the hardships which he had undergone in the siege of Mirandola, and died soon after M. Cesare, regretted by a wide circle of friends, who lamented in him ' a youth of rare beauty and charm, full of mirth and gaiety, as prosperous and gallant a gentleman as you could wish to see.' ' So,' writes Castiglione, 'unfortunate Death deprived our house of these three rarest gentlemen at a moment when they were most prosperous and entertained the highest hopes of honour and renown.'[1]

To their names yet another must be added, that of Giovanni Cristoforo Romano, the accomplished sculptor and brilliant letter-writer, who died at Loreto in May of this same year 1512. He had been Castiglione's friend since his early days at Milan, and was as much lamented by Isabella and her ladies at Mantua as he was by the scholars of Rome and Urbino. But death was not the only dividing cause which helped to break up the joyous company of Urbino. While some good knights—the best and brightest of the number—died in the flower of their age, others went their way to seek new fortunes in other lands. Lodovico Canossa, Baldassare's other kinsman, who had been at Urbino for the last seven-

---

[1] ' Cortegiano,' iv. 1.

teen years, was made Bishop of Trirarico by Julius II.
in 1511, and went to live in Rome, where he had
already acquired renown by his diplomatic skill.
He had always been a bad correspondent, and when
his mother at Mantua applied to Madonna Luigia for
the latest news of her absent son, Castiglione sent her
word that as Bishop he remained what he had been
as a layman—very chary of letters.   Alberto Pio, that
other distinguished diplomatist who had often spent
the summer at Urbino in Guidobaldo's lifetime, had
now gone over to the Imperialists, and had forfeited all
claim to Madonna Margherita's hand by his resolute
opposition to the Duke of Ferrara.   In 1512 another
popular member of the ducal household, Ottaviano
Fregoso, left Urbino to play a leading part in the
revolution of his native city against the French, and
to become Doge of Genoa.   And in the same year
Bembo, who had made his home at Urbino for the
last six years, finally settled in Rome, and entered the
service of Cardinal de' Medici.   As he remarked to
Duchess Lucrezia : ' Whether it is best to be great
and serve others, or to be humble and free, I know
not, but I am quite sure that to be humble and serve
is worst of all.'[1]

The hour of restoration had at length sounded for
this exiled family.   *Si volge*, the motto which the
Magnifico had chosen for his device, had come true,
and Fortune had once more turned her long-averted
face towards him.   That summer both he and his
brother, Cardinal Giovanni, returned to Florence,
which had surrendered to the arms of the Viceroy,
Cardona, and his Spanish troops.   At the end of July,
Giuliano was still at Urbino, enjoying the company
of the Duchesses and Castiglione.   On September 1

[1] 'Lettere,' iv. 25.

he entered Florence in state, and once more took up his abode in the house of his fathers. Among the many congratulations which he received on this occasion, none were more cordial than those which reached him from the Duchess Elisabetta, who had been so good a friend to him in the past and whose kindness he never forgot.

But although so many of his friends were dead and gone, Castiglione remained loyal to his master. After the continual warfare of the last three years, he was glad to enjoy a few peaceful days at Urbino. But, as usual, he found himself very short of money—*leggierissimo*, his usual term for empty pockets—and complained that for six months he and his comrades-in-arms had not seen a farthing of the Pope's pay. Early in December he wrote that he expected to be sent by his lord to take part in Massimiliano Sforza's triumphal entry to Milan, after which he hoped to come and spend three or four days at Casatico and talk of many things—above all, of those tedious marriage negotiations, which, as he remarked, seemed alike doomed to end in failure. But by the end of the year he wrote that his journey to Milan had been given up, and that he saw no hope of coming home till carnival was over. A month later he wrote a long letter to satisfy his mother's impatient inquiries with regard to a proposal which she had received from Costanza Rangone some months before, and which he had refused to consider until the war was over. This lady, who was connected with his mother through the Uberti and Strozzi, had proposed Ginevra Rangone, the only daughter of the powerful Count Girardo, as a suitable wife for Baldassare, and had afterwards discussed the matter with her kinsman himself when he was at Modena.

' I told her,' wrote Castiglione to his mother, ' that I liked the idea, but that Count Girardo seemed to show some reserve in his offers, and that if he did not think me good enough for his daughter I had no wish to have her.   She replied frankly that the first proposal came from them, but that she had written to Count Girardo, who was in Rome.   When I returned to Modena, to meet Gurk, in October, she said that she had heard from the Count, who said that he liked me very much, but that he had other intentions for his daughter, and confessed that he wished to see her in a more exalted place, and that he thought of marrying her to Giovanni Vitelli if he lived.   So I begged our Madonna Costanza to tell you this, and, indeed, I was somewhat angry with her, and almost resolved not to mention the subject again.   But now the thing is done, I am content to await the answer. Only I beg you not to show too much eagerness in this matter; for whoever I may take for my wife, I desire that she should be given me as willingly as I take her, were she a King's daughter.   I certainly wish to put an end to these negotiations, as it seems time that I should marry, but I will not go down on my knees, with little honour to myself, before one who is no better born than I am.'

Having delivered himself of his feelings in these proud words, Castiglione turns to a pleasanter subject, and tells her of the castle and countship of Novillara, which had been lately granted to him by his lord.

' The Lord Duke has taken possession of Pesaro by the Pope's permission, but he has not yet received the investiture, which he hopes may soon follow.   I think he will go there the second week in Lent.   Our M. Amato has been already sent there as lieutenant. When we are at Pesaro, I hope to take possession of my castle, which is no longer Ginestreto, because I have exchanged it for another called Novillara, which the Duke is equally content that I should have, and which suits me a great deal better.   It is only two miles from Pesaro and five from Fano.   The air there is excellent, the view most beautiful over land and sea, and the soil very fruitful indeed.   There is a fine palace, which is now my own, and the revenues are equal in value to those of Ginestreto, or perhaps rather more, so that I am exceedingly well satisfied. God grant me grace to enjoy it in peace !   It is so near Pesaro that I may say I have a house there.'[1]

On January 1 the Duke entered his new city, which, from its command of the Adriatic shore, was an especially valuable acquisition, and Castiglione saw the fair house and domain which he was proud to call his own.   A tower had been built at Novillara by the Malatesta of Rimini in the fourteenth century, and the castle had afterwards been a favourite residence of the Sforza princes.   Unfortunately, the citizens of Pesaro objected to the alienation of a domain which had always belonged to their rulers, and in 1522, when Francesco Maria received his duchy after the death of Leo X., they induced him to withdraw the grant which he had made to Castiglione.   So Novillara only belonged to its first Count during a few years when his lord was in exile, and he never enjoyed this beautiful home.   But the ruined pile on the heights looking over the blue Adriatic and the far Dalmatian shores will always be associated with the name of the noble owner who had deserved so well of his lord, and whose services met with so scanty a reward.

[1] Serassi, i. 72.

CHAPTER XXII

1513

Carnival fête at Urbino—Bibbiena's ' Calandria ' performed under
Castiglione's direction—The Count's prologue—Other comedies
— Patriotic verses written by Castiglione — His letter to
Lodovico Canossa.

In this year of 1513, carnival was celebrated with
unusual splendour at most of the courts of Italy. At
Ferrara, indeed, there was little cause for rejoicing,
and the critical state of affairs made Alfonso and his
family listen anxiously to every fresh report of the
fiery old Pope's health that came from Rome. But
at Milan Isabella d' Este was present at the fêtes held
in honour of her nephew Massimiliano Sforza. The
Viceroy and his Spaniards danced with her fascinating
maids of honour, or looked on at pageants in which
the deliverance of Italy from the barbarians by the
great Pontiff, and the golden oak of the house of
Rovere figured largely, while French guns still
thundered from the Castello. At Florence artists
and sculptors, Pontormo and Baccio d' Agnolo,
designed a series of sumptuous triumphs in honour
of the house of Medici, and sang the return of the
Golden Age. Giuliano and his nephew Lorenzo led
the revels, and Bembo and Bibbiena were summoned
by their patron, Cardinal de' Medici, to join the
festive throng. In Rome a yet more splendid

329

pageant was devoted to the apotheosis of the victorious
Pope who had triumphed over all his foes. An interminable procession of chariots, containing emblematic
representations, paraded the streets, escorted by
Roman youths bearing the arms and names of the
ancient houses from which they claimed descent—
the Fabii and Horatii, the families of Scipio and
Camillus, of Torquatus or Manlius. First came Italy
bound and captive in the thrall of her foreign foes,
then Italy free and triumphant, with a palm of victory
in her hand, followed by the conquered cities—Bologna
and Reggio, Parma and Piacenza—and a grand car
representing the Council of the Lateran, with Pope
and Emperor in its midst. Last of all a giant oak-
tree appeared, crowned by an effigy of Julius, with
the monarchs of the Holy League, the Emperor,
the Catholic King, and Henry VIII. of England, at
his feet.[1]

But more memorable than any of these were the
festivities held at the carnival of Urbino. Here it had
been decided to celebrate the safe return of the Duke
from the war, and the annexation of Pesaro, by a
series of dramatic representations after the fashion of
those arranged by Castiglione and Bembo in former
days. Three new comedies, we learn from the
chronicle of the ducal librarian, Federico Veterani,[2]
were given on this occasion. The first was the
'Eutichia,' a comedy by the Duke's Mantuan secretary,
Niccolò Grassi, founded on an episode of the conquest
of Urbino by Duke Valentino, a theme certain to be
hailed with enthusiasm by the audience. The second
was the work of a youthful prodigy, a boy of fourteen,

[1] Luzio, 'Fed. Gonzaga Ostaggio,' pp. 73-78.
[2] Cod. Vat. Urb., 490, A. Vernarecci in 'Arch. Stor. per le
Marche,' iii. 181.

the son of Ruggiero of Reggio, a Ferrarese councillor. This piece was acted by children of his own age—a performance, Castiglione tells us, of really marvellous excellence. But the third and by far the most famous play, which was performed on Sunday, February 6, was an Italian prose comedy, written by no less a personage than Bibbiena, the witty 'Moccicone,' who was so great a favourite with the ladies of Urbino. The plot of 'La Calandria,' or 'The Follies of Calandro,' as this play was called, had evidently been suggested by the 'Menæchmi' of Plautus, a Latin comedy that was very popular at Ferrara and Mantua. But in Bibbiena's play, the absurd mistakes arising from the close resemblance of a twin brother and sister, supply the leading motive; while the blind jealousy of Calandro, the husband, and the tricks played upon him by his companions, give rise to much clever fooling. La Calandria, which was the first Italian comedy to attain any wide popularity, is described by Giraldi, not altogether without reason, as full of jest and merriment, but as wanting in the higher qualities of art.[1] It is, strictly speaking, a farce, full of comic situations and doubtful jokes, which appealed to the taste of an age that was not fastidious in these matters, and was distinguished, as Paolo Giovio remarks, by its author's genuine wit and talent for stage effects. As the work of the 'bel Bernardo,' the play was sure of a warm reception at Urbino. At first Bibbiena had intended to superintend the performance himself, but in January he was summoned to Florence by Cardinal de' Medici, and sent on by the Pope to Milan to urge the Spanish Viceroy to take active measures against Ferrara. Accordingly, the whole brunt of the preparations fell on Castiglione.

[1] 'De Poetis,' Dialog. ii.

From his boyhood the Count had witnessed similar representations at the courts of Milan and Mantua, and had probably accompanied the Marchesana to Ferrara for those carnival festivities on which her father, Duke Ercole, expended so much time and thought. He was certainly present at the famous carnival of 1501 at Mantua, when a magnificent new theatre was erected in the Castello, and the stage was hung with Mantegna's newly-finished Triumphs. On that occasion a series of comedies by Plautus, Terence, and Seneca were performed, and the scene was laid in a classical temple, with lofty columns and arcades. Count Sigismondo Cantelmo, the husband of Isabella's beloved friend Margherita, who wrote a full description of the stage scenery and management to his lord, Duke Ercolo, remarked that this representation surpassed all that he had ever seen in grandeur and excellence, and deserved to be studied by all who wished to encourage the performance of ancient or modern plays.[1] This experience had not been lost on Castiglione, and the stage scenery and decorations which he arranged for the representation of Bibbiena's comedy were in many respects similar to those which he remembered at Mantua, while in some ways they were even more splendid and effective. The task, as he confessed, was one after his own heart, and he devoted himself with his usual energy to the preparations. During the next four months his time was so fully occupied with artists, carpenters, decorators, actors, and singers, that, as he told his mother, he had not a moment's leisure, and could only write to her late at night. The court painters, Timoteo Viti and Girolamo Genga, were engaged in painting the scenery, and at Christmas Castiglione

[1] 'Isabella d' Este,' i. 183-185.

himself ordered the costumes, and sent to a well-known maker at Mantua for gold-embroidered caps. Bibbiena had promised to write a prologue, but his composition only arrived the day before the performance, too late to be learnt by heart by the reciter, and in its stead one written by Castiglione himself for the occasion was delivered amid great applause from the audience.   This prologue is printed in some old editions of ' La Calandria,' and deserves to be preserved, if only as a proof of the versatility of the author's talents :

'You are to-day spectators of a new comedy entitled "La Calandria," written in prose, not in verse, in the vulgar, not in the Latin tongue.   It is called "Calandria" because it is about Calandro—a personage whom you will find so foolish that perhaps it will be difficult for you to believe that any human being could ever make himself so ridiculous !   But if you remember others like him whom you may have seen and heard—above all, Martino da Amelia, the man who thought the moon was his wife, and imagined himself in turn a god, a woman, a fish, and a tree— you will not wonder that Calandro could believe and commit the follies that you will see.   Since this comedy deals with the familiar things of everyday life, the author did not think well to use verse, considering that prose and words unfettered by metre are better fit for ordinary use.   That it is not ancient ought not to displease you, as long as it is in good taste, because things new and modern always please, and are more agreeable than old and time-worn themes, which have become tedious by long use.   It is not in Latin, because the author, wishing to be understood by many who are not learned, and being above all anxious to please, has chosen the vulgar tongue, so that he may equally delight all his hearers. And, besides, the tongue which God and Nature

have given us should not be held in less esteem
than Latin, Greek, or Hebrew, to which languages
our own would, perhaps, not be inferior if we kept its
rules, and polished it with the same care and diligence
as the Greeks and Latins. Surely that man is his
own enemy who counts a foreign language to be more
worthy of study than his own. For my part, I hold
my own language so dear to me that I would not
change it for any other in the whole world, and I
think you will feel the same. Therefore you ought
to be grateful to hear the " Calandria " in your own
tongue—no, I made a mistake : in *our* own tongue,
I mean, *not* in *yours. You* will hear the comedy
which we have to recite, and while we speak it is
your part to keep silence. If anyone says the author
is a thief, who has stolen from Plautus, let him hold
his peace ; for old Plautus would be well content to
be robbed, and allow " Il Moccicone " to have the
use of his treasures, and does not think it needful
to keep them under lock and key. But the author
swears by the Cross of God that he has not stolen
from Plautus, but has rather tried to emulate his
work. And he further says that, if you search all
through Plautus, you will find that the Latin poet
has lost nothing that pertains to him. This being
the case, Plautus has not been robbed ; and if you
or any obstinate person still dare to call the author
a thief, at least I beg you not to call him names
or accuse him before the magistrate, but go yourself and whisper the secret into the ears of Plautus.
But here comes the actor with his argument. Prepare
to receive it well, and let each one open the door of
his ear.'[1]

In the brief argument which followed, the author
explained that Demetrius, a citizen of the Greek
city Modone, had twin children—a boy, Lido, and a
girl, Santille—who were so much alike that when

[1] 'Teatro antico italiano,' i. 195.

clothed in the same garb it was impossible to know them apart.

'Which you may believe,' he added, 'remembering those two noble Roman brothers, Antonio and Valerio Porcaro, who are so much alike that they are constantly taken for one another by all Rome. And as Italy is more worthy than Greece, so Rome is a nobler city than Modone. And so farewell. *Valete et plaudite.*'

We can well believe that a storm of applause greeted Castiglione's well-chosen words, and can imagine with what breathless interest the brilliant assembly, including as it did many visitors from Rome, followed every scene and detail of Bernardo's play, and laughed at his gay sallies till the hall rang again.

When it was all over and the guests had gone their way, Castiglione sat down and wrote a long letter to one of his dearest friends, Lodovico Canossa, in which he gave full details of the performance, and especially of the scenery and *intermezzi*, or musical interludes, on which he had bestowed so much pains. This letter forms so valuable a document for the history of the drama, and is so characteristic of the writer, that we make no apology for giving it in full, more especially as it is one of the few specimens of Castiglione's correspondence with Canossa which has been preserved:

'My dear and reverend Monsignore,

'It is some time since I received a letter from V. S., to which I did not reply at first, out of curiosity to see if you would become my debtor for more than one letter! At length I must confess that you have won the day, and in reply I will tell you that I cannot recollect the precise date on which I gave you those 100 ducats to send to Naples. But I know this, that it was when our two Lady Duchesses left Rome and I stayed behind for ten or twelve days, intending to go to Naples, and then changed my mind and gave V. S. the money, and returned to Urbino with the Cardinal of Pavia. Now you will remember the whole thing !

'I send you my Marine Elegy, which please pass on to M. Pietro Bembo. I beg V. S. to read it and give me your opinion on the poem. I know not if it is worth your perusal, but I know well that it cannot possibly equal your expectations or be worthy of your praise. As for my delays, V. S. is aware how many reasons I have to excuse them. Our comedies have gone off well, most of all the " Calandria," which was represented in a truly magnificent style, which I need not describe, since you will have heard full accounts from many who were present. But I will tell you this much. The scene represented was an outer street of the town, between the city wall and its last houses. The wall with its two towers was represented in the most natural way possible, rising from the floor of the stage to the top of the hall. One tower was occupied by the pipers, the other by the trumpeters, and between the two there was another finely constructed rampart. The hall itself, where the audience sat, occupied the place of the moat, and was crossed as it were by two aqueducts. The back of the wall above the tiers of seats was hung with the tapestries of the Trojan War. Above these was a large cornice in high relief, bearing the following inscription in large white letters on a blue ground, running the whole length of the hall :

'Bella foris, ludosque domi exercebat et ipse
Cæsar magni etenim est utraque cura animi.'

Both in wars abroad and in games at home, Cæsar displays his strength, for both alike are fit work for great minds.

According to the chronicler Veterani, on the closing day of the carnival, the last line of the Latin motto on the cornice of the hall was altered, and made to run thus, '*Cæsar, et hæc nostri est utraque cura Ducis,*' thus introducing a personal allusion to the Duke Francesco Maria, who figured in the final interlude as the deliverer of Italy.

' From the roof of the hall hung great bunches of foliage, almost hiding the ceiling, and from the rosettes of the vault wire threads were suspended, to which two rows of candelabra in the shape of letters were fastened, from one end of the hall to the other. These thirteen rosettes made thirteen letters, spelling the words " *Deliciæ Populi*," and these letters were so large that they held seven or ten torches, which lighted the hall brilliantly.

' The scene was laid in a very fine city, with streets, palaces, churches, and towers, all in relief, and looking as if they were real, the effect being completed by admirable paintings in scientific perspective. Among other objects there was an octagon temple in low relief, so well finished that, even if all the workmen in the duchy of Urbino had been employed, it seemed hardly possible to think that all this had been done in four months ! This temple was completely covered with beautiful stucco reliefs, the windows were made to imitate alabaster, the architraves and cornices were of fine gold and ultramarine blue, with glass jewels here and there, looking exactly like real gems ; there were roundels of marble containing figures, carved pillars, and much more that would take me too long to describe. This temple stood in the centre of the stage. At one end there was a triumphal arch about two yards from the wall, marvellously executed. Between the architrave and the vault an admirable representation of the story of the Horatii had been painted to imitate marble. The two niches above the pillars supporting the arch were filled with little Victories bearing trophies in their hands made of stucco. On the top of the arch stood a most beautiful equestrian statue of a figure in armour, striking a vanquished man at his feet with his spear. To right and left of this rider were two little altars with vases of burning flame that lasted to the end of the comedy.

' I will not describe everything, as I feel sure V. S. will have heard a good deal already; nor will I tell how one of the plays was composed by a child and recited by children, who perhaps put their elders to shame. They certainly acted marvellously, and it was a new thing to see little old men, not a foot high, preserving a gravity and severity of manner worthy of Menander. Nor will I attempt to describe the strange music of these comedies, played by minstrels who were all out of sight, and placed in different corners ; but I will come at once to our Bernardo's "Calandro," which gave the greatest pleasure. And since the prologue arrived very late, and the actor who had to recite it, could not learn it by heart in time, another which I had written was recited in its place, and met with general approval. Otherwise little was changed, only a few scenes which, perhaps, were not fit for recitation ; but little or nothing else, and it was performed exactly as it is written.

These were the *intermezzi*. First a *moresca* by Jason, who appeared on one side of the stage dancing in antique armour, looking very fine, with a splendid sword and shield. On the other came two bulls, so life-like that several of the spectators took them for real animals, breathing fire through their nostrils. The good Jason yoked them to the plough and made them draw it, and then sowed dragon's teeth in the furrows. Presently ancient warriors sprang upon the stage in a way that was, I think, excellently managed, and danced a fiery *moresca*, trying to kill

Jason all the while. As they were leaving the stage, they fell upon each other and were slain, without being actually seen to die. Then Jason appeared again, dancing exquisitely with the golden fleece on his shoulders; and this was the first interlude, or *moresca*. The second was a very beautiful chariot of Venus, with the goddess seated and holding a lighted taper in her hand. The car was drawn by two doves, who certainly seemed to be alive, and who were ridden by two Amorini with lighted tapers in their hands and bows and quivers on their shoulders. Four Amorini went before the car, four followed after, all bearing lighted tapers in the same manner, dancing a *moresca* and flourishing their burning torches. Having reached the end of the stage, they set fire to a door, from which nine gallants issued all ablaze with light, and danced another most beautiful *moresca*. The third *intermezzo* was a chariot of Neptune drawn by two sea-horses with fish scales and fins, wonderfully well imitated. Neptune himself rode in the car with his trident, attended by eight monsters, four before and four behind, all as well done as it is possible to imagine, and dancing a sword - dance with the chariot all aflame. These beasts were the strangest creatures in the world, but no one who did not see them can have an idea what they were like. The fourth was a car of Juno, also ablaze with light. The goddess, wearing a crown on her brow and a sceptre in her hand, appeared seated on a cloud which encircled the chariot, and surrounded by numberless heads blowing the winds of heaven. This car was drawn by two peacocks so beautiful and life-like that I could not believe my eyes, and yet I had seen them before, and had myself given directions how they were to be made. In front were two eagles and ostriches, behind two sea-birds and two large parrots, with gaily-coloured plumage. All of these were so well done, my dear Monsignore, that I am quite sure no imitation ever came so near to reality, and they all danced a sword-dance with a grace that it is impossible to describe or imagine.

'When the comedy was ended, one of the Amorini, whom we had already seen, appeared suddenly on the stage, in the same habit, and explained in a few verses the meaning of these *intermezzi*, which was a separate thing from the comedy itself.

'First of all there was the battle between earth-born brothers, when, as we see to-day, there is war between those nearest of kin, who ought to live at peace, as set forth in the fable of Jason. Then comes Love, who kindles first mankind and earth, then the sea and air, with his sacred flame, and seeks to drive away war and discord and join the whole world in blessed concord. This indeed, you will say, is rather a hope and devout aspiration, but the vision of war, alas! is all too real for our misfortune! I did not mean to show you the verses that Love sang, but yet I send them, and V. S. can do what you like with them. They were written in great haste, by one who was struggling all the while with painters and carpenters, with actors and musicians and dancers. When the verses were ended Love disappeared. The sound of hidden music, proceeding from four viols, was heard, and then four voices singing a verse to the strains of a beautiful melody, as it were an invocation to Love. So the *festà* ended, after giving the greatest satisfaction and pleasure to the spectators. If I had not praised the whole thing so much, I would have told you what share I had in it; but I will not do this, for fear V. S. should think that I flatter myself! It would be too great a piece of good fortune to be able to attend to matters such as these, and escape from business cares. God grant that I may one day do this! This letter is far longer than I intended to write, or indeed have written for more than a year. V. S. must not take this as a proof that I have become a good secretary, for I am quite tired out, and am hardly able to tell you that a marriage has been arranged between our Madonna Margherita and a Count of Correggio, who is noble, youthful, rich, and handsome. . . .'

This description of the elaborate stage scenery employed, of the singers and orchestra kept out of sight, and the hall hung with garlands and lustres, is curiously modern, and might almost refer to the Baireuth performances of recent years. As in Wagner's music-dramas, all the arts were combined in these Renaissance comedies, and the whole show ended in a glorification of ideal love. But the patriotic note introduced on this occasion was plainly due to Castiglione. In his modesty the Count omits all reference to the *intermezzo* composed by him for Niccolò Grassi's comedy, and repeated on the last day of carnival, when the children's play was given. Veterani tells us how Italy appeared in the figure of a sad and weary woman, with dishevelled locks and raiment, torn by the hands of barbarians, and so much oppressed with the burden of her sorrow that she could hardly utter the words of her complaint, and paused repeatedly, as if overwhelmed by grief. In pathetic language she lamented the ravages of Time and the vanity of human glory, and recalled the days when she was queen of the whole world, and captive kings and nations knelt at her feet. Now she was poor and miserable, shorn of all her splendour, and reduced to weep in solitude and chains over her lamentable fall.

> ' Hor vilipesa, serva, abbandonata,
> Mi trovo afflitta, misera et meschina,
> Poverella mendica et sconsolata,
> Piango la mia crudel alta ruina.'

Vainly she called on the heroes of old, on Cæsar, Fabius, Scipio, and all the pale ghosts of heroes who

throng the banks of Styx, to wake at her voice and
wield their ancient swords in her defence. No answer
came, and after uttering these piteous verses the sad
speaker disappeared from the stage, unable to utter
another word. But in the final scene the same figure
appeared again and called in impassioned strains on a
living hero to come to her help, bidding him unfold
the banner of the triumphant eagle, and win immortal
glory in her cause.

> ' Et tu amato Figliol, Duca d' Urbino,
> In cui vero valor rinascer sento,
> Fa vendetta del mio sangue latino,
> E del mio nome che è quasi in tutto spento,
> Rinnova l' ali del tuo ucel divino,
> L' insegna triumphal spiegando al vento,
> Ch' acquisterai in giovenil' etate,
> Cum tua gloria immortal, mia libertate !'

' Then from the opposite side of the stage,' writes
the old chronicler, ' there suddenly sprang to light a
figure of the Duke with a drawn sword in his hand,
looking as if he had driven out all the barbarians who
had stripped and plundered Italy. Now, returning
from the fray, he placed a crown on her head and
threw a golden mantle over her shoulders, and the
two danced a graceful *moresca* to the sound of unseen
music, and went out together dancing hand-in-hand.
Truly a most beautiful sight !'[1]

The fine verses recited by the warrior, with their
courtly allusions to the young Duke's triumph and
the deliverance of Italy from the barbarians, were,
there can be little doubt, composed by Castiglione,
and formed a fitting close to a carnival that was long
remembered at Urbino. It marked the end of a great
age. The brilliant assembly of lords and ladies, who
were present on this festive occasion, little dreamt

---

[1] Cod. Vat. Urb., 490.

that they would never meet again in the great banquet-hall which had witnessed so many joyous carnivals. Once more the doom of war and invasion hung over the Duke and his loyal subjects, and when, after years of exile, Francesco Maria returned again to his own, Pesaro, and no longer Urbino, became his capital, and was henceforth the seat of the ducal court.

CHAPTER XXIII

1513

Death of Julius II.—Conclave and election of Leo X.—His proclamation and procession to the Lateran—The Dukes of Urbino and Ferrara and the new Pope—Castiglione in Rome—His correspondence with the Duke and Duchess—Negotiations regarding Solarolo—Suor Chiara and the convent of Assisi—Madonna Raffaella—Influence of Bibbiena at the Vatican.

' It would be too good to feel that one might escape from the cares of business and devote the rest of life to these pleasures.' These words, in Castiglione's letter to Canossa, have a pathetic ring, when we find how rudely the writer was to be awakened from these happy dreams and how soon he was to be plunged into the turmoil of intrigue and discord, which his soul loathed. During the next three and a half years his life was spent continually in diplomatic missions and in political business of the most anxious and harassing description. Fortunately, he had two great consolations which never failed him—friendship and literature. These two powers played a great part in his life during the memorable period on which we are now entering, when Rome became, to a great extent, his head-quarters and the centre of his existence.

Twelve days after the last carnival festivities on Shrove Tuesday, Pope Julius II. breathed his last in the Vatican. The strong soul made a brave fight for life, and met death with a composure which surprised

344

those about him.   There was grief and consternation
in Rome when the news became known.   The crowds
who thronged St. Peter's to see the last honours paid
to the dead Pontiff were greater than had ever
been seen before at a Pope's funeral, and many
lamented the man who had saved Italy from foreign
invaders.   His enemies naturally rejoiced, and felt
that they could once more breathe freely.   Neither
the Duke of Ferrara nor his sister made any secret
of their satisfaction.   ' The Marchesana,' wrote the
Venetian envoy from Milan, where Isabella was keeping carnival with her nephew, Massimiliano Sforza,
' was filled with joy when she heard that His Holiness
was at the point of death'; and Lippomano wrote
home ' that it was a pity for Venice and Christendom
that the Pope had not died five years sooner.'[1]   But,
as Castiglione had foreseen, the death of Julius II.
was a grievous loss to the Duke of Urbino.   For all
his violent outbursts and suspicious temper, the old
man was fondly attached to his nephew, and his last
act, as he lay dying, was to summon a consistory and
confirm the investiture of Pesaro, which he had granted
to the Duke.   Two days afterwards he was dead.[2]

The Sacred College immediately sent 10,000 ducats
from the Papal treasury to the Duke, desiring him
to raise a body of 5,000 troops and come to Rome
at once.   But whether Francesco Maria found it
impossible to collect his forces, or whether he was
glad to delay his coming until a new Pope was
elected, he excused himself from obeying the
summons, and sent Castiglione to attend the late
Pope's funeral in his stead.   On his arrival the Count
found Rome seething with the usual intrigues rife

---

[1] Pastor, vi. 437 ; Sanuto, xvii. 6, xv. 261.
[2] Sanuto, xv. 560.

before a conclave. At first Cardinal Raffaello Riario di San Giorgio was the favourite. His claims as the wealthiest and one of the senior members of the College were strongly supported by the Marquis of Mantua, with whom he was intimate, and who begged his son-in-law to assist his exertions. But all the Duke of Urbino's interest and all Castiglione's personal influence were naturally employed in favour of Cardinal Giovanni de' Medici, who arrived from Florence on February 26 with his clever secretary, Bernardo da Bibbiena.

This Cardinal, to say the truth, was popular with all parties. His kindness and liberality, his genial and easy-going nature, the soft words with which he knew how to ingratiate himself with those who approached him, the frequent smile that lighted up the large bland face and heavy jaw with which Raphael's portrait has made us familiar, all helped to render him a general favourite. 'There is much talk of Medici,' wrote Foscari, the Venetian envoy, on March 7 ; ' he is very young for a Pope, but is as good a man as possible—worthy, learned, of exemplary conduct.'[1] Above all, Cardinal Giovanni was quiet and peaceable, and, after the warlike and turbulent Julius, there was a widespread feeling that peace and tranquillity were the most desirable things for Italy. It is true that he was only thirty-seven, and his youth, as the Venetian remarked, was against him ; but since he was said to be suffering from an internal complaint, and had to be carried in a litter to the conclave, and undergo an operation a few days later for fistula, there was good reason to believe that his life would not be a long one. On March 4 the conclave met in the Vatican, and at the first scrutiny only one

[1] Sanuto, xvi. 28, 30.

Cardinal, the Swiss prelate Matthias Schinner, gave his vote for Medici.[1] For a time the issue seemed doubtful. But soon the contest resolved itself into a struggle between the old and young Cardinals. First Luigi of Aragon, then Sigismondo Gonzaga and Marco Cornaro, actively espoused the cause of Medici. Without the walls of the Vatican, the hopes of his Florentine partisans who had hastened to Rome rose high. 'Those who have lived long at court here,' wrote Filippo Strozzi, Clarice de' Medici's husband, to his brother in Florence on March 9, 'say that never was there so much uncertainty as to the future Pope. The betting is now 18 on San Giorgio, 16 on Grimani, 16 on Medici; but it varies so much that one can count on nothing.' An hour or two later he added : 'Our hope does not diminish, although at the banks the odds have fallen from 25 to 16. Either he will come in first, or will sell his votes so dearly that in any case we shall be the gainers.'[2] But all doubts were set at rest when, at dawn of day on March 11, Cardinal Farnese publicly announced the election of Cardinal de' Medici, and proclaimed him Pope by the name of Leo X.

'The young Cardinals have won the day; the old are nowhere,' wrote a Venetian who watched the members of the Sacred College issue from the Vatican and take their places before the high altar of St. Peter's. 'Cornaro and the other Cardinal-deacons were laughing; San Giorgio and the Cardinal of England [Bainbridge] looked very much out of temper, while of the others, some laughed and others sighed. Every one in Rome is delighted; I hope things may not turn out badly for Venice.'[3]

[1] Sanuto, xvi. 82.
[2] F. Nitti, 'Leone X. e la sua Politica,' pp. 5, 7.
[3] Sanuto, xvi. 39, 40.

The Florentines, naturally, rejoiced most of all at the exaltation of Lorenzo de' Medici's son. The crowds who rushed to acclaim the newly-elected Pontiff filled the air with shouts of '*Palle! palle!*' and the partisans of the exiled house came in for a large share of rewards and honours. Bembo and Sadoleto were appointed Papal Secretaries; Bernardo da Bibbiena, to whose clever manœuvres during the conclave Leo's election was chiefly due, became Treasurer of the Pope's household. And although Francesco Gonzaga had at first supported Cardinal Riario's candidature, Leo X. did not forget how hospitably he had been entertained at Mantua when he escaped from his French captors after the battle of Ravenna, and told the Mantuan envoy that when he was elected Pope he was still wearing the clothes given him by the Marquis.[1] But of all the generous friends who had stood by the Medici in the days of their exile, none had deserved better of them than the Duke and Duchess of Urbino. Not only had Guidobaldo received the refugees in a tender and most hospitable manner, but Giuliano had spent many months at a time in the ducal palace, and the Pope himself had frequently been a guest at the court. No congratulations were warmer or more sincere than those which reached the new Pope from Mantua and Urbino, from the Marchesana Isabella and her son-in-law, Francesco Maria.

In a letter of March 14 the Duke thanked Castiglione for his full and detailed account of the conclave, and expressed unqualified satisfaction at Cardinal de' Medici's election:

'We cannot tell you how delighted we are to hear this good news, and hope that our services to this

---

[1] Luzio in 'Archivio storico Lombardo,' 1906, 114.

good and holy Pontiff will now receive recognition. You will commend us cordially to His Holiness, and assure him that we shall be no less zealous in his service than we were in that of our uncle, of blessed memory, and place ourselves absolutely at his disposal.'[1]

Castiglione now urged his lord to come to Rome and kiss the Pope's feet as soon as possible ; but the Duke still delayed, after his usual habit, pleading the cost and time necessary for preparations if he were to appear with suitable splendour at the approaching ceremonies. At length, on the evening of April 7, two hours after dark, he arrived in Rome with a body of 300 horse, and was received with due state by the Vatican officials. Fabrizio Colonna and many of the noble Romans rode out to meet him at Ponte Molle, and escorted him to the Duchess of Urbino's house in the Via Lata, behind the garden of the Venetian embassy. The Pope treated him with the greatest honour, and sent him a liberal supply of provisions, including large stores of barley, wine, salt meat, and 80 pairs of capons, 200 torches, 50 pounds of candles, and 100 boxes of confectionery.[2] When, on the morning of the 9th, Francesco Maria presented himself at the Vatican, he was most graciously received. His Holiness spoke affectionately of their old friendship, confirmed him in his office as Prefect of Rome, and renewed his appointment as Captain of the Church for another year. In this capacity the Duke, clad in black velvet and satin, and attended by a fine company of twenty-five gentlemen also wearing mourning for his uncle, appeared in the magnificent procession to the Lateran, which the Pope fixed for

[1] Cod. Vat. Lat., 8211, fol. 504. Appendix XIII.–XVI.
[2] Sanuto, xvi. 678.

April 11—the Feast of St. Leo and the anniversary of the battle of Ravenna.

On that memorable day, which recalled the triumphs of ancient Rome, when all the gods and goddesses of Olympus came to hail the Vicar of Christ, and the triumphal arches along the new Pope's route were adorned with images of the Virgin and Apostles on one side, and of Venus and Pallas on the other, the Duke of Urbino rode immediately behind the Roman nobles and foreign ambassadors, and in front of the tabernacle which held the Host. A tall and gallant warrior, Gaspare Fracasso di San Severino, clad in cloth of gold from head to foot, and mounted on a charger heavily draped with the same tissue, bore the banner of the Church before him, and at his side rode the Pope's nephew, that young Lorenzo de' Medici who was ere long to rob him of his crown. For the present, however, all went merry as a marriage-bell. The new Pope adopted a golden yoke as his device, with the motto *Soave*, which was embroidered on the rose-coloured liveries of his servants, and expressed the most friendly and peaceable intentions, even towards the Duke of Ferrara.[1]

Alfonso had arrived in Rome on April 4, and was immediately conducted by his cousin, the Cardinal of Aragon, into the presence of the Pope, who suspended the ecclesiastical censures which hung over him, and restored him to all his dignities, in order that he might take part in the Lateran procession. Isabella d' Este's secretary, Mario Equicola, who had been among the first to kiss the Pope's feet and offer his mistress's congratulations to her old friend, describes the cheers which greeted the Duke as he

[1] Sanuto, xvi. 160 ; Baschet-Reumont, ' La Jeunesse de Catherine de' Medici,' p. 242.

galloped across the Piazza, followed by thirty horse-men, and looking like Mars himself in his crimson vest and plumed cap, and tells us how the Romans ran after him, shouting ' *Duca ! Duca !*' whenever he appeared. On the morning of the procession Alfonso met his niece's husband, the Duke of Urbino, who only reached the Vatican when the Host was already placed in the tabernacle in the Papal chapel, and shook hands with him in the most cordial manner. Afterwards it was noticed that the Duke of Ferrara walked by the Pope's side along the steps of St. Peter's, talking and laughing all the way, and held his horse's bridle as far as the fountains on the Piazza, when, at the Holy Father's express command, he mounted his own white charger. The victor of Ravenna, a splendid figure in his glittering mantle of white and gold brocade, with a single diamond worth 10,000 ducats in his black velvet cap, attracted universal attention; and people in the crowd were heard to say that to-day Duke Alfonso had triumphed once more.

'Two days afterwards he had an audience with the Pope, which lasted over three hours, at the end of which he left the Vatican, looking very joyous, and saying that now he had only got to enjoy himself and see the pictures and antiquities of Rome.'[1]

The Duke of Urbino, feeling that he had nothing to fear, and being anxious to visit his new city of Pesaro, went home at the end of the week. But since various business matters regarding his salary and office had to be arranged, he decided to leave Castiglione in Rome for the present, knowing well that no one else would be as acceptable to Pope Leo and his servants. The new palace officials, indeed,

[1] Luzio, 460.

were Castiglione's most intimate friends. Bembo and
Sadoleto, as we have seen, were Secretaries, and the
Master of the Household was his kinsman, Canossa,
in whose house he lived as long as he remained in
Rome. Above all, Messer Bernardo, the gay comrade
and witty story-teller, whose comedy had been acted
at Urbino only a few weeks before under his own
direction, was supreme at court. Bibbiena's sunny
temper, his wit and readiness, his love of art and
literature, had long made him dear to Cardinal de'
Medici, and now he became indispensable to the new
Pope. All the envoys at the Vatican agree in describing
Bibbiena in these early years of Leo X.'s reign as the
Pope's confidential adviser—his *alter ego*—who dis-
pensed patronage, held the tangled threads of political
intrigue in his hands, and enjoyed his master's absolute
trust.[1] In his elegant suite of rooms in the upper
story of the palace, adorned with costly tapestries and
precious gems, with rare antiques and paintings by
the hand of his favourite Raphael, the new Treasurer
was the object of general envy and admiration,
courted and feared by all, but still beloved by his old
friends, such as Bembo and Castiglione. 'As for
Messer Bernardo,' wrote Equicola, 'it would fill four
sheets were I to try and describe his plate and
tapestries, the visits which he receives, etc. In fact,
he is Pope.'[2] And a Mantuan kinsman—one of the
Valenti—who wrote to congratulate Castiglione on
his good fortune, remarked that he knew prosperity
would never alter the love which he and Bembo bore
to their friends, but did not feel sure if he could
count on Bernardo.[3]

The first important business which Castiglione had

---

[1] Pastor, iv. 58, 59 ; Sanuto, xvi. 54 ; Bandini, 'Bibbiena,' 16.
[2] Luzio, 454.   [3] Cod. Vat. Lat., 8211.

to transact on his lord's behalf brought him into
direct contact with the new Treasurer. In the
autumn of 1512, Francesco Maria had borrowed
20,000 ducats from his wife's uncle, Cardinal Sigismondo Gonzaga, who was with the Papal troops as
Legate, in order to indemnify Galeazzo Sforza for his
rights on Pesaro. This sum he now sought to recover
from the Papal Treasury in payment of arrears of
salary and expenses incurred during the last campaign. Greatly to his surprise and indignation,
Bibbiena repudiated this claim, or, at any rate,
demurred to its justice. The letters which the Duke
addressed to Castiglione on the subject reveal his
ungovernable temper. No words were too bad for
what he called a flagrant breach of faith, or for
the Treasurer who was guilty of it. 'Of all men
in the world, we should have held our friend
M. Bernardo to be the last who would break his
word to us,' he wrote ; and in the same breath he
desired Castiglione to let him feel the full force of his
resentment. Even Baldassare, who in former letters
was invariably addressed as *dilettissimo e carissimo*,
was now treated with the barest courtesy, and made to
bear the brunt of the ducal displeasure. Fortunately
for all parties, Castiglione conducted this difficult and
delicate negotiation with so much skill and tact that
in the end Francesco Maria was satisfied. The Pope
already found it impossible to satisfy the hundreds
of needy suppliants from Florence who crowded the
Vatican, and agreed to indemnify Cardinal Gonzaga for
his advances by a grant of the Papal fief of Solarolo,
near Faenza, which, after prolonged negotiation, he
consented to accept. Considerable interest attaches
to this transaction, which explains how it was that
Sigismondo acquired the little town and principality

which, after his death, passed into the hands of the Marchesana Isabella.[1]

But these were only the most important of many matters which passed through Castiglione's hands while he represented the Duke of Urbino at the court of Leo X., in the absence of Francesco's ordinary envoy, the honest and faithful Orazio Florido.

The peaceable intentions of the Pope were shown by his efforts to avert war between France and the League, but he was powerless to restrain the ambition of Louis XII., who once more invaded Lombardy early in May. While Leo X. nominally remained neutral, he secretly helped Massimiliano Sforza with money to pay the Swiss, and strove persistently to detach Venice from the French alliance. The vacillating character of the Papal policy and general uncertainty are reflected in the following passage from a letter which Castiglione addressed to the Duke of Urbino from Rome on May 28 :

'The Pope cannot make up his mind whether to send troops to Parma and Piacenza, but will wait to see what the French do. It seems to me that Your Excellency must also await his decision, as it would neither be honourable nor desirable for you to go to the scene of action until war is openly declared. I will let Your Excellency know what happens, and what seems to be advisable. The Swiss promise great things, and talk of invading Burgundy with 8,000 men, besides descending upon Lombardy. The English are routing the French horse in large numbers. The Emperor is said to be preparing troops to attack the French and Venetians, and has relieved Verona and forced the Venetians to raise the siege. Madonna Margherita has proclaimed war against France throughout Flanders, and all the harm

[1] Cod. Vat. Lat., 8211. Appendix XVII., XIX.

that can be done to the French on that side will
be done. The Pope has had letters informing him
of all these things. God knows if they are true!
Every one speaks and writes according to his own
wishes.'[1]

When in June the Duke received a Papal brief
desiring him to be ready to march to Verona to help
the Emperor Maximilian against the Venetians, he
raised difficulties as to his own position, and bade
Castiglione ask that a guard should be given him,
and suitable provision made for the protection of his
person, declaring that this was the only way in
which he could ensure the obedience of the insolent
Spaniards and be safe from their attacks.[2] The
Pope, however, abandoned his intention of sending
troops to Lombardy, and the matter dropped. But
the Duke's conduct was afterwards remembered
against him, and a shadow darkened the good understanding between himself and the Pope, which Castiglione was doing his utmost to maintain.

Francesco Maria's quarrel with Giovanni Maria
da Camerino, who usurped the title belonging to his
nephew, young Sigismondo Varano, and tried to seize
his duchy, was another cause of contention which
called for all Castiglione's tact. Other questions
regarding the payment of troops, or the claims of
captains who had served under the Duke in the
last campaign; the settlement of loans which had
been advanced by the banking firm of the Sauli, or
of small bills sent in by musicians and actors, who
clamoured for a few ducats; requests for benefices
and pensions from religious communities or indi-

---

[1] 'Archivio di Stato di Firenze: Carte di Urbino,' f. 241; Martinati, p. 66.
[2] Cod. Vat. Lat., 8211, f. 511. Appendix XVIII.

vidual ecclesiastics—these and a score of minor
matters were all referred to the Duke's envoy. The
gentle Duchess Elisabetta, on her part, kept up an
active correspondence with her loyal servant during
his absence from Urbino. After her wont, she was
beset with suppliants and protégés, in whose favour
she constantly solicited Castiglione's good offices with
the Pope or other exalted personages. Now it was
her sister-in-law Chiara, the widow of Roberto Malatesta, who sought the Pope's intervention to enable
her to recover certain sums of her dowry in Rimini;
now an Urbino gentleman, who asked for a recommendation to His Holiness; then, again, a merchant
of Sinigaglia, who begged that Messer Agostino
Chigi, the rich Sienese banker, would renew the
lease of a shop to his daughter. Or else it is one
of her Mantuan connexions, M. Agostino Gonzaga,
who has visited Urbino on his way to Rome, and in
whose favour Elisabetta is eager to enlist the Magnifico Giuliano and the all-powerful Treasurer; and
the kind Duchess entreats her dearest and most
beloved kinsman Baldassare to deliver her letters
in person, and do his utmost to further M. Agostino's
suit. Then, again, it is Madonna Emilia who begs
the Count's help in some private business of her own,
and this time the Duchess feels she need make no
apology for troubling him, and is sure he will arrange
the matter with his wonted prudence. Many of
these letters are written with Elisabetta's own hand,
and abound in kind expressions of regard and affection
for M. Baldassare, and of earnest hopes that he may
soon be able to return to Pesaro, where the Duke and
Duchesses were spending the early summer.

From Pesaro on March 26, only a fortnight after
the Pope's election, Elisabetta addressed an urgent

letter to the Count on behalf of the gallant Captain
Gaspare San Severino, who, if report said true,
was about to wed her niece, the widowed Maria
Varana.

'It is the desire of my heart,' she wrote, 'if
possible, to help the said San Severino, because of
the relationship between us and the many obligations that I owe him. Therefore I beg you to show
this letter to His Holiness's Treasurer; and when
you have heard his advice, go to the Pope's feet and
commend San Severino to him most warmly from
me, employing all the means in your power, and
doing everything that you can imagine to bring this
to a good end. And let me know at once what is
the result of your efforts, that I may tell him how
far I have been able to help him, according to my
earnest wish.'[1]

After this Fracasso, as we have seen, came to
Rome, and bore the Duke's banner in the Papal
procession; but the Duchess's exertions do not seem
to have met with any further success. In June he
returned to Lombardy, and his marriage with Maria
Varana never took place. Some of Elisabetta's
wishes, it must be owned, were by no means easy
to gratify. Guidobaldo's widowed sister, Chiara, had,
on the death of her husband, Roberto Malatesta,
taken the veil in the convent of Poor Clares, founded
by her father, Duke Federico, at Urbino. She was
now greatly disturbed at the scandals which had
arisen among the nuns of Santa Chiara of Assisi,
and was anxious to bring them under the rule of the
reformed Franciscan community known as the Osservanti, to which her own convent belonged. Accord-

---

[1] Cod. Vat. Lat., 8211.

ingly, on June 10 she addressed the following letter
to the Count:

'MAGNIFICO BALDASSARE,

'As I am very anxious that the convent
of Sta. Clara of Assisi, where the glorious body of
this saint rests, should be brought under the rule
of the Osservanti, in order that it may be properly
governed, and that the present nuns, whose life, as
I have been told by many of the citizens, is anything
but honest and religious, may be removed. In the
days of Pope Julius I applied for leave to go to Assisi
and take charge of the convent, and bring it under
the rule of our Osservanti Order, which I had been
asked to do by many persons living in that city.
His Holiness graciously consented to my proposal,
and desired me to appoint a confessor to make a
visitation . . . but I declined this proposal, since I
was reluctant to leave this convent and the rule
under which I had made my profession. Thus the
matter remained undecided. But as I still cherish an
earnest desire that order and good living should be
restored in this place, I hope that His Holiness,
whose goodness and saintly living are well known,
will condescend to grant my ardent desire. I beg
you to speak to the Magnifico on this subject, and
make him unite with you in urging our Lord the
Pope to allow this convent to be brought under the
rule of our Osservanti Order, which, beside being a
holy work and most acceptable and meritorious in
God's eyes, would give me more pleasure than I
can say. And I beg you to keep this secret from
all but the Magnifico and the Holy Father, lest
the rival Order may get wind of it and oppose our
intention.

'FELTRIA SOROR CLARA.

'I beg with all my heart that you will obtain this
favour for me, and I entreat you to help me by the

love which you bore my brother of blessed memory.
I know, too, that you are a devout follower of the
glorious St. Francis and of Santa Chiara, and have
God and these two most blessed saints before your
eyes, as well as your own sister Suor Laura and all
the nuns who fight under the triumphant banner of
this glorious Virgin. And if you are able to arrange
that her body should be placed in the hands of those
who live according to her will, I doubt not that she
will give you a plentiful reward in this life and in the
next, while we of this community will pray God per-
petually for you. You will hear more fully on this
subject from my sister the Duchess Elisa, and I
commend the whole to you. Only, for the love of
God keep it secret, and give the enclosed to the
Illmo Giuliano. And do not forget my Rimini business,
either.'[1]

A month later the Duchess wrote asking her
dearest Baldassare if he had ever received a packet
of letters in which were two written by her most
reverend sister-in-law and herself with their own
hands, to which, much to their disappointment, he
had never sent any answer. In case the said letters
had miscarried, the Duchess repeated the tenor of
their contents. First of all he was to communicate
with the Magnifico Giuliano, because he was a devout
Catholic and inclined to favour pious objects, and then
go to His Holiness, and inform him how important
it was to bring the Convent of Sta. Chiara of Assisi,
where the blessed saint's body was, under the rule of
the Osservanti, so that in this holy place people should
lead a better life than they did at present and show
more fear of God. Since the scandalous lives of the
nuns were known to all, it would be a good and holy
deed on the part of His Holiness, and agreeable to the

[1] Cod. Vat. Lat., 8211.

devout nature of the Magnifico, to see that this change
were effected immediately, and send ambassadors to
the citizens of Assisi, who on their part declared that
they would no longer tolerate the present state of
things. 'And in order to incite you the more to prompt
action,' adds the Duchess, 'you must know that the
mighty spirit of Pope Julius had been so much
moved and softened by this our petition as to declare
it worthy to be granted.' Unfortunately, the crusade
on which these pious ladies had embarked was more
serious than they realized. After protracted discussion, the matter was referred to the office of the
Papal Datary, Lorenzo Pucci, whose secretary replied
curtly that it was not convenient that the Lady
Duchess should interfere in the administration of
convents outside her own territories. This reply,
which effectually crushed the hopes of Suor Chiara
and the good Duchess, was sent to Castiglione after
he left Rome by his old friend Terpandro, the lively
poet who had formerly been so great a favourite with
the ladies of Urbino, and who tried to soften the
effect of his refusal by cordial messages.

'Give my Lady Emilia,' he wrote, 'my sincere condolences on the death of her reverend brother [Enea
Pio], whose grief causes me more concern than the
death of His Highness, since he is probably better off
than we are. Commend me to Anna, and, if you are
bold enough, to Madonna Raffaella, as well as to
yourself.

'ROME, *August* 11, 1513.'[1]   Your TERPANDRO.

This allusion to the fair maid of honour, who kept
a soft corner in her heart for our hero, reminds us
that Raffaella honoured Castiglione with her especial

---

[1] Cod. Vat. Lat., 8211.   Appendix XX.–XXV.

favour, and herself occasionally wrote to him with her own hand. A short and ill-spelt letter which she addressed to her knight when he was absent at the camp with his lord, is still preserved in the family archives.

'It is many days since I have written to V. S., but this has only been from fear of troubling you. Now I write to remind you of me, and to beg you, if it is not giving you too much trouble, to deign to write to me in return. This would give me great and singular pleasure. I will not trouble V. S. further at present, but only commend myself continually to you.

'From one who longs to see V. S.,

'RAFFAELLA.'[1]

The cover is addressed: 'To my dearest Messer Baldassare da Castiglione, Knight, with the Most Illustrious Duke of Urbino.'

M. Baldassare not only appreciated the lovely maid of honour's attentions, but replied to her letters with his usual gallantry, and it appears, from another passage in his correspondence this summer, that Madonna Raffaella still considered herself to have a claim on his devotion.

'I showed that part of your letter which concerned her to Madonna Raffaella,' wrote the ducal Secretary, Cesare Minutolo, from Pesaro in May ; 'and although she would not allow me to kiss her white hand, I was presumptuous enough to aspire to her favours, but all in vain. She desired me to tell you from her that she eats well and drinks still better, amuses herself, has a good time and lives joyously. To say the truth, she does not seem to distress herself much at your absence, whether this arises from lack of affection

---

[1] Cod. Vat. Lat., 8211, f. 525.

or from her changeable and unfeeling nature, which
leads her only to think of her lover when he is present.
But I shall never understand her! You know how
much I like her and what attentions I pay her, and
the only rewards I get are constant rebuffs, bad
words, and cross looks. O ungrateful woman!

After describing the preparations for the tournament which is to take place at Pesaro, and the Duke's
feats of arms, the writer commends himself to
Monsignore Trirarico, and sends M. Baldassare warm
greetings from the whole court, and most of all from
Madonna Raffaella.[1]

The letters preserved in the Vatican show how vast
was Castiglione's correspondence during these early
months of Leo X.'s pontificate. Old friends at
Urbino and Ferrara, distant kinsfolk at Milan and
Mantua, comrades who had played with him when he
was a lad, or had more recently shared his campaigns,
alike wrote to congratulate him on his proud position
as envoy at the Vatican, and to remind him of their
existence. 'Venit post multas una serena dies,'
wrote Benedetto Valenti, when he wished his kinsman joy on the smiling face which Fortune, that
fickle dame, had turned to him, and prayed that he
might ever remain the same loyal and unchangeable
friend as of old. Others were less modest in their
demands. Some begged him to use his influence
with the Holy Father or the Treasurer on their
behalf or asked boldly for benefices and pensions.
One mother, who signs herself, Dorotea, daughter of
Messer il Priore da Castiglione, 'having heard from
your lady mother of the high favour which you
enjoy with His Beatitude Pope Leo,' begs him, for her

[1] Cod. Vat. Lat., 8211, f. 479. Appendix XXVI.

sake and for the honour of the family, to take her
son, a *zentil putto* of ten, into his service and allow
her to make him a present of the boy, which thing
she will count a singular grace. Another letter is of
interest as coming from Capino di Cappo,[1] a brave
Mantuan soldier whose devotion to Castiglione
endured to the end of his life, and of whom M. Baldassare invariably speaks with the deepest affection,
as one who was dear to him as a brother, and with
whom he shared the closest secrets of his heart.

To all of these appeals M. Baldassare replied with
perfect temper and invariable courtesy, although in
his secret soul he often groaned over the multitude
of his correspondents, and felt, with Bibbiena, that
begging favours for others was truly 'devil's work.'

[1] Cod. Vat. Lat., 8211.

CHAPTER XXIV

1513

Castiglione's friends in Rome—The early days of Leo X.—Scholars and poets flock to Rome—The Roman humanists—Colocci, Goritz, Sadoleto, Raphael—Castiglione's poems and sonnets—Giuliano de' Medici in Rome—Fêtes at the Capitol—Castiglione returns to Urbino—Fresh schemes for his marriage.

IN spite of the burden of diplomatic business and private correspondence under which Castiglione groaned, these months which he spent in the Bishop of Trirarico's house in the Borgo were very happy ones. It was a memorable and eventful time both in the history of Rome and in that of the Papacy. Never before had the Eternal City witnessed so great a concourse of scholars and poets as in these early days of Leo X. The accession of a Medici Pope, who, in his own words, 'had grown up in a library and loved the fine arts from his cradle,' attracted men of letters not only from Florence, but from all parts of Italy.[1] The poets who sang the praises of the house of Medici, and acclaimed Leo X. as a new Mecænas, found themselves lavishly rewarded. Ariosto, it is true, who had hastened to salute his old friend, was sent away unsatisfied, and driven to conclude that the Pope, having given up the use of his eyeglass, had failed to recognize him. But ducats were freely showered on smaller men, and crowds of poetasters

[1] Pastor, iv. 426.

364

and reciters, musicians and buffoons, swarmed around
the good-natured Pope, who laughed at their jokes
and allowed them to feed at his table.   Strangers
like Erasmus, who had once tasted the delights of
Rome, turned longing eyes towards the city which
they felt was their true fatherland.   In the fogs of
London and the fens of Cambridge, the Rotterdam
humanist pined for the noble libraries and delicious
gardens, where he had enjoyed the companionship of
men who were the lights of the world, and cried for a
draught of the water of Lethe that he might be able
to forget Rome.

'When I think of Rome,' he wrote to his friend
Cardinal Grimani, 'and all its charms and advantages, I repent that I ever came here.   Rome is the
centre of the world.   In Rome is liberty.   In Rome
are the splendid libraries.   In Rome you meet and
converse with men of learning.   In Rome are the
magnificent monuments of the past.   On Rome are
fastened the eyes of all mankind.'[1]

On St. Mark's Day, Pasquino, who had armed himself with a sword the year before, and cried, ' Fuor i
barbari !' with Julius II., now assumed the guise of
Apollo, and, lyre in hand, chanted the return of the
golden age, while the fountains at his feet ran with
milk and honey.   The phrase passed from lip to lip
and became a commonplace with poets and scholars.
Erasmus adopted it in his famous epistle to Leo X.,
in which he thanks the Pope for accepting the dedication of his book on the Greek Testament.   'Come to
Rome and see our golden age,' wrote Guido Postumo
Silvestri, the poet-doctor of Pesaro, to Isabella d' Este
at Mantua.   This bard, whom Ariosto pronounced

[1] Erasmi, Op., Ep. 136, 167, 168.

worthy to wear the double crown of Pallas and
Phœbus, had good reason to praise the new Pontiff's
liberality. For, as we learn from a letter addressed
by Tebaldeo to Castiglione, he received a gift of
200 ducats when he presented His Holiness with a
book of poems, and was enabled to rebuild his house
at Pesaro at the Pope's expense.

In this atmosphere Castiglione naturally found
himself at home. He was surrounded by old friends.
Bibbiena, Sadoleto, and Bembo were not the only
members of the Urbino circle whom he found among
the Papal officials. Beroaldo, Latino Giovenale, and
Terpandro, 'whose hilarity,' Bembo said, 'the gravest
affairs could not diminish,' were all employed in
different capacities at the Vatican. Guido Postumo
was secretary to Cardinal Ippolito d' Este; Tebaldeo,
the Ferrarese poet, dear alike to Raphael and Castiglione, to Bembo and Elisabetta, was among the
bards whom Leo rewarded with reckless liberality.
Accolti, the devoted slave of the Duchess, was constantly summoned to give his wonderful improvisations in the Vatican, where the Holy Father and the
Cardinals joined in the cry of 'Long live the divine
poet!' And there, too, Raphael of Urbino was busy
decorating the Pope's rooms, and painting Madonnas
and portraits for all the members of the Sacred College
in turn.

A whole troop of Mantuans came to Rome to
pay their respects to the new Pope, and Castiglione was surrounded by the familiar faces of his
youth. Cardinal Sigismondo, of course, had been
present at the conclave, and Federico of Bozzolo and
Baldassare's own cousin, Luigi Gonzaga of Borgoforte, arrived in time to take part in the Lateran
procession. Early in June another of his kinsmen,

Valenti, came in the suite of Luigi Gonzaga of
Castelgoffredo, who was sent by the Marquis on a
special embassy to the Vatican;[1] while Mario
Equicola found Rome so pleasant that he lingered
there till after Easter. One of the Pope's first acts
was to appoint the learned humanist and theologian,
Battista Spagnoli, a brother of Francesco's secretary,
Tolomeo, to the important post of General of the
Carmelites. Another distinguished Mantuan, the
doctor Battista Fiera, whose fine portrait by Lorenzo
Costa hangs in our National Gallery, was among the
poets who hastened to lay their tributes at Leo's feet
that summer. This worthy man had a house near
the church of S. Francesco, in the same quarter as
the Castiglione palace, and was an old friend of the
family. Several of his early poems were addressed to
M. Gian Pietro, and he had lately composed an elegy
on the death of Cesare Gonzaga. During his residence
in Rome he became much attached to Baldassare,
whose own death as well as that of his young wife he
was to live to commemorate in verse. To these we
may add the name of the protonotary Chiericati,
Cardinal Schinner's secretary, who, although a native
of Vicenza, had spent most of his life at Mantua, and
was connected by many ties with the Gonzaga princes.
A godson of Duchess Elisabetta and one of Isabella's
most constant correspondents, this able ecclesiastic
was brought into close relations with Castiglione
during the next few years, and in his letters to
Mantua is never tired of praising the Count's vigi-
lance and loyalty.[2] Nor must we forget to mention
Federico Fregoso, the good Archbishop of Salerno,
and Agostino Chigi, the princely Sienese banker,

[1] Cod. Vat. Lat., 8211.
[2] B. Morsolin, F. Chiericati, 159.

among the friends who helped to make Castiglione's
stay in Rome pleasant. Another house where he
found a warm welcome was that of his kinswoman,
Bianca Bentivoglio, the widow of Count Niccolò
Rangone, and mother of his especial friends Costanza
and Ginevra Rangone. This lady had generously
entertained Cardinal de' Medici at Modena after his
escape from captivity, and the Pope now requited
this service by inviting her to Rome and giving her
a house in the Borgo. Castiglione, as we have seen,
was already friendly with Bianca's daughters, and
two of her sons, the future Cardinal Ercole and
Annibale, afterwards Captain of the Papal Guard,
were among the most intimate friends of his Roman
days.

The Bishop of Trirarico's house, as might be supposed, was a meeting-place for the choicest spirits of
Leo X.'s court. There Castiglione met the foremost
members of the Roman Academy: Angelo Colocci,
the accomplished Papal Secretary and generous patron
of letters ; Inghirami, better known by his surname
of Phædra, the learned keeper of the Vatican library,
whose massive brow and squinting eye still live in
Raphael's picture ; the two accomplished Venetian
patricians, Agostino Beazzano and Andrea Navagero,
whose friendship the great master immortalized by
painting both their portraits on one canvas, and many
others whose names are barely remembered now.
The brilliant Count who came from Urbino with
so great a reputation, was an honoured guest at the
banquets and suppers where the Roman humanists
met in Colocci's lovely gardens near the ruins of the
Acqua Virgo, in the sumptuous halls of Chigi's
stately pleasure-house on the Tiber, or in Sadoleto's
humble villa on the Quirinal.

Long afterwards, when these fair regions had been laid waste by barbarian invaders, and most of this goodly company were dead and gone, Sadoleto, writing to his old friend Angelo Colocci, recalled these delightful meetings, when poems and orations were recited by the foremost intellects of the day, and paid a splendid tribute to Castiglione, calling him the noblest and most gifted of men.[1]

Ariosto, who had himself been in Rome that spring and shared for all too short a time in these delights, sighed in his remote provincial home, not, he tells us, for the flesh-pots of Egypt, but for the good company and intellectual converse of his absent friends.

'Tell me,' he cries, 'that I may once again visit the haunt of the Muses and wander singing in the sacred groves; tell me that I may every day exchange ideas with Bembo and Sadoleto, with the learned Giovio and Cavallo, with Blosio and Molza and Tebaldeo, and take one or the other for my guide over the seven hills. There, book in hand, I may look down on the regions of ancient Rome, and say, Here was the Circus Maximus, here the Roman Forum; on this side lay the Suburra, yonder the Sacred Way; here rose the Temple of Vesta, there that of Janus.'[2]

These were the pleasures which Castiglione actually enjoyed in the brief intervals that he could snatch from diplomatic business. We learn from Bembo's letters how he and M. Baldassare visited the anti-quities of Rome with Raphael, and made excursions in the Roman Campagna, seeing everything, both old and new, and enjoying the beauties of the early summer. Castiglione's own poems show us the close attention with which he studied the antiques collected

---

[1] Ep. i. 106. [2] Satire, vii. 112.

by Julius II. in the court of the Belvedere, and the latest frescoes painted by Raphael. The help that he gave the master in drawing up his famous report on ancient Rome is a proof, if any were needed, that he shared his friend's enthusiasm for the remains of the Eternal City, as well as his zeal for their preservation. And we know from Raphael's often-quoted letters how much he trusted Castiglione's judgment, and how proud the painter was of the praise which the Count bestowed on his beautiful Galatea in Chigi's villa.

These congenial surroundings, the intercourse with so many scholars and poets, naturally gave fresh stimulus to Castiglione's poetic powers, which had long been neglected in the stress of political cares and active warfare. Many of his best Latin poems and epigrams were composed during the months which he spent in Rome. As Sadoleto had sung the glories of the newly - discovered Laocoön, so now Castiglione celebrated the beauty of the Cleopatra [1] which had been brought to light and placed in the Belvedere by Julius II. He also contributed a Latin poem to the Coryciana, or collection of verses that were yearly placed on Sansovino's group of St. Anne in the chapel built by Cardinal Göritz, the white-haired Luxembourg prelate, whose gardens in the Forum of Trajan were a favourite haunt of Roman humanists. There can be little doubt that it was during these months in the Eternal City that Baldassare wrote the beautiful sonnet in which he invoked the seven hills of ancient Rome,

'Superbi colli e voi sacre ruine
Che 'l nome sol di Roma ancor tenete,'

---

[1] The statue in the Vatican now known by the name of Ariadne

and the pathetic *canzone*, 'Manca il fior giovenil de' miei primi anni,' in which he looks back on his lost youth and laments the vanity of earthly loves.

It was then, too, that the 'Cortegiano' grew into being. The first sketch of the work was hastily written 'in a few days,' the author tells us, soon after Guidobaldo's death, while the good Duke's happy times were still fresh in his memory. In the distractions of his busy life, the work was laid aside, and only resumed in Rome during these early days of Leo X. Then the sympathy and admiration of his literary friends encouraged Castiglione to take up his pen once more, and further develop that picture of the ideal court and perfect gentleman which he had begun at Urbino. The greater part of the work was completed during the following winter and spring, as we see from the allusions in the fourth book to the death of Roberto da Bari, Gaspare Pallavicino, and Cesare Gonzaga, as well as to the exalted position attained by the Magnifico Giuliano.

In the first week of May, Giuliano de' Medici arrived in Rome, and the Pope, who was sincerely attached to his brother, and had probably realized how unequal this amiable but pleasure-loving Prince was to the difficult task of governing Florence, determined to keep him at the Vatican, and send his nephew Lorenzo to take his place. The presence of Giuliano was an additional gratification to Castiglione, who found his old friend unchanged by prosperity, and full of affection. His arrival was the signal for renewed festivities, and his elevation to the dignity of Roman patrician was celebrated by one of the grandest and most sumptuous entertainments ever held at the Capitol. A spacious theatre, adorned with statues and paintings by Peruzzi and other excellent artists, was erected for the occasion, and a succession of banquets and theatrical representations was given by the Roman nobles, at which Giuliano and all the Cardinals were present. A marvellous array of symbolical figures welcomed the new citizen, and thanked him in flowery orations for the honour which he had conferred on Rome. The Virtues appeared to arm him with golden sword and shield, and, what delighted the audience more than all, the goddess Cybele offered the Magnifico a globe which burst open and displayed an infinite number of birds, which flew about the theatre, to the sound of exquisite melodies, sung by the Cardinal of Ferrara's musicians. The splendour of the costumes and jewels worn by the actors, the variety of the comedies and dances, and the crowds of people in the assembly, were described by many eyewitnesses.

'I think the "Penulus" of Plautus was never represented better in the days of Plautus himself,' wrote Chiericati to Isabella d' Este. . . . 'In the universal opinion, the Senate and Roman people have done themselves the greatest honour by this magnificent display, and have spent at least 6,000 ducats. And it is reckoned that there were at least 20,000 persons present at the spectacle.'[1]

Towards the end of August, Castiglione left Rome and returned to Urbino, where he was warmly welcomed by the whole court, including, let us hope, Madonna Raffaella. The Duke marked his appreciation of his envoy's service by investing him formally with the countship and estates of Novillara in a deed

[1] Harleian MS. 3462.

bearing the date September 2, 1513. The preamble of the grant speaks in glowing terms of the Count's scholarly accomplishments and warlike exploits; above all, of his unswerving fidelity and indefatigable labours in the ducal service. It records the long days and nights spent in unceasing toil, in distant and perilous journeys, and ends by promising him larger rewards, more fitting to his splendid services, in future days.[1]

No one was better pleased to hear of his safe arrival than his mother. Madonna Luigia had been apparently a good deal disturbed by her son's prolonged residence in Rome. While his family and friends all congratulated the Count on his elevation, and rejoiced at the signal marks of favour bestowed upon him by the new Pope, his mother felt as if her beloved son was slipping out of her hold, and was being carried farther from her every day. His departure from Urbino had been so hasty and unexpected, that for some time she was left in doubt as to his movements, and could only send her letters by the Duchess Elisabetta's seneschal, addressed to her son 'in Urbino, Rome, or wherever he may be.' When at length his letters reached her, they were short and hurried notes, in which Baldassare seemed hardly to have leisure to reply to her anxious inquiries or satisfy her curiosity about his new estates at Novillara. These last were a source of great concern to this active-minded lady, who had the deepest distrust of her son's business capacities, and never ceased begging him to send a trustworthy steward to take possession of his Castello and collect the rents due to him.

[1] 'De origine rebus, gestis ac privilegiis Gentis Castilionæ,' Matteo di Castiglione.

In a letter of April 6 she wrote:

'I have begged you several times to consider these affairs at Casatico, and not go to sleep over them, for no one can tell how long this Pope will live; so I must repeat this once more, and if you think me tiresome, remember this only arises from my anxiety to see you once for all set free from care, if this should please God! Many people in town are ill, and some are dying from what seems to be acute pain in the side, but I fear it must be a serious complaint. Take care of yourself for the love of God!... I hear from Carlo Bardellone that in Rome you find a much better kind of Rheims linen than is to be had here, so if you are in want of shirts, and like to send me some linen, I will have them made for you. But this must be as you like.'[1]

As usual, money was scarce, and Madonna Luigia urged her son to practise a rigid economy, and found it difficult to scrape a few ducats together, since the last harvest had been a bad one, and the peasants at Casatico would have died of hunger if they had not been fed at her expense.

On May 1 her nephew Luigi Gonzaga returned from Rome, and brought good news of Baldassare; but as Luigia herself was on the point of leaving Mantua for her country home, she complained that she had not much time for conversation with him. At length, however, towards the end of July, a certain Boccalino arrived from Rome, and Madonna Luigia was able to satisfy herself as to her son's welfare from one who had seen and spoken with him. He found her in bed with an attack of tertian ague, which had left her weak and melancholy, and Bal-

---

[1] Cod. Vat. Lat., 8211.

dassare complained, not without reason, of the querulous tone of her letters.

'In your last letter,' she wrote on July 28, 'you seem to resent my continual entreaties that you should attend to your own affairs. But I did not wish to vex you or expect you to do what is impossible, which would be folly. All I desire is to know that you are well and happy, which is the greatest joy I can have. It is, however, true that next to this I wish to see your affairs in a prosperous condition, and that I know no one can stay long in Rome without spending a great deal, and that being absent so long from your household must be the cause of innumerable disorders, since no one is left to govern your servants at Urbino. And I must once more repeat how necessary it seems to me, if this stay in Rome is to be so prolonged, that you should send a responsible person to occupy your castle. . . . All the same, I cannot pretend to understand these things, but can only turn them over in my mind and write to you. So, my dear son, take this as my excuse, and accept it with the same love which prompts me to write. God knows I would much rather tell you these things by word of mouth, if this were granted me, and then you might give me your reasons in return. It would of course give me the greatest joy if you could come to Lombardy, to some place where I might see you. Meanwhile I do hope you will try and find a thoroughly trustworthy man, or if possible two, one who may be always with you, and another who would attend to the management of your household and who could make himself feared and know how to act on his own responsibility, when occasion required. And do not be afraid of the expense, for he would certainly save you money in the end. . . . Our corn is not yet thrashed. It will give a much better yield than last year, but the price is very low. I cannot write more, as I am tired, although it has taken me two days to write this letter. Try and keep well, and commend me to our Bishop and to Messer Agostino, if you are still in Rome. And God keep you from all danger.

'Your mother,
'LUIGIA CAST.

'CASATICO, *July* 28, 1513.'[1]

Early in August the good lady came to Mantua to see her corn sold, but the crops were so abundant that in some fields the corn was not worth reaping, and the market was so bad that she could only raise 100 ducats. These she sent to Pesaro by a Mantuan merchant, as soon as she heard that M. Baldassare had arrived safely at Urbino.

Castiglione's first act on his return from Rome was to send his servant Bindo to Mantua, and by the time that the man was ready to go back, Madonna Luigia had succeeded in raising another 100 ducats, which she sent her son together with a stock of new clothes, bed-quilts, a wolf-skin cloak, some yards of fine white cloth, two handsome black velvet caps, and a supply of cheese and salt meat. At the same time she entreated him earnestly to come and spend a fortnight or more at Casatico, in order that the long-discussed question of his marriage might at length be settled.

The idea of an alliance with Count Girardo Rangone's daughter had been by no means abandoned, either by Madonna Luigia or Costanza Rangone, both of whom had repeatedly written to Baldassare during the past summer, urging him to come to a decision on the subject. But besides being too much absorbed in the cares and pleasures of Rome to think of marriage, Castiglione was obviously dissatisfied with

---

[1] Cod. Vat. Lat., 8211. Appendix XXVII., XXVIII.

the conditions proposed by the Modenese Count.
The dowry seemed to him too small; the bride herself
was apparently not altogether to his taste. 'I am
very sorry to hear that you do not like Madonna
Costanza's proposals, but for nothing in the world
would I urge you to conclude a marriage that is not
to your taste.' Messer Luigi Gonzaga, it appears,
brought the same report from Rome, and his aunt
thought it well to complain to Polissena Rangone
of the subtleties employed in the matter by Count
Girardo. At the same time Madonna Luigia owned
that it was difficult to see why her son had taken
five months to come to this conclusion, and begged
him to make his choice soon for the honour of
the family, and in order not to offend the proud
Rangone Count. But, with unwearied patience and
perseverance, she began to look about for other
desirable matches. First she proposed a grand-
daughter of Count Antonio della Mirandola, who was
being educated in a convent in Florence, and whose
marriage the Pope had undertaken to arrange. Then
there was one of the Gonzagas of Novellara, who
was said to be by no means ugly, and in all other
respects eminently suitable; while a daughter-in-law
of Bartolommeo della Rovere, 'young and well
dowered,' was recommended by one of Federico
Gonzaga's ladies, Maddalena. There seems to have
been another lady for whom M. Baldassare at this
time had an evident inclination—possibly the fair
Raffaella. If so, Madonna Luigia promptly dismissed
her in a contemptuous phrase as being 'poor and in
difficulties—two very bad conditions, to my mind.'
However, she hastens to add: 'You must do as you
like, but I think either of the Lombardy matches
would be better—the Modenese one, or her of

Novellara.' The best plan, she finally decided,
would be for Baldassare to visit both Novellara and
Modena on his way to Lombardy, and see 'the
merchandise,' as she terms the young ladies, not without some reason. This could easily be managed
in the case of the former, as Luigia heard from a
mutual kinsman, Francesco Gonzaga, that the girl
always took meals with her father, and Baldassare
need only stop a night at Novellara and see her. At
Modena his cousin Costanza would gladly welcome
a visit, etc., 'and so at length,' wrote the anxious
mother, 'we may touch land.'[1]

The Count's sister, Francesca Strozzi, now added
her entreaties to those of her mother, and sent him a
long and affectionate letter from Rovere, expressing
her satisfaction at hearing good reports of his health
and welfare, and begging him to marry and settle
down.

' I hear,' she writes playfully, 'that you have grown
fat, and have not suffered from the excessive heat of
this summer as much as we have. It has made us
all ill, and we had to leave Mantua because of the
heat. I was the first to fall ill, and, thank God, am
also the first to recover, and am able now to wait on
the others. My poor Messer Tommaso has been in
bed for three weeks with a tedious, but happily not
acute, tertian fever. He has lost his appetite entirely;
nothing can tempt him to eat; and if we were not
a whole day's journey from home, I would send to
Mantua for a bottle of our wine, as we hear it is so
good, and this might bring back his taste for food.
My little ones are all ill, and as soon as they are cured
we shall, please God, go to Mantua. I asked Bindo
if you had yet been to see your castle, and he said
no. I wish you would go there, for if we should come

[1] Cod. Vat. Lat., 8211.

into those parts we think of visiting you there, and if I had known the name of the patron saint of the village church when I was ill, I should have made a vow to go there. We all beg you to take a wife speedily, so that we may come to your wedding and take a journey for our pleasure at the same time. I begin to feel sorry that you have put this off so long, and fear that I shall soon be so old that I shall be ashamed to dance at your wedding. I will say no more, saving that M. Tommaso and I both commend ourselves infinitely to Your Magnificence, and long to see you and enjoy your company.

'Your loving sister,

'FRANCESCA STROZZA.'[1]

Castiglione's visit was now impatiently expected by his friends at Mantua, and Madonna Luigia began to send him her final directions before he started on his journey. She was especially anxious that he should redeem the gold collar which the King of England had given him, and which his usual pecuniary difficulties had compelled him to leave in pawn when he went to Rome.

'I implore you,' she wrote in September, 'to take your chain out of pawn, and bring it with you, and also any hangings that you may have which would be useful for the house. You know that, when I was at Urbino, you never would let me see the contents of your chests, and then in your absence people came and spoilt the stuffs; and it would surely have been much better for me to have brought the things home and put them to some good use in the house, than to have left them to those wretches.'[2]

In the same letter she informed him of the death of her cousin Lodovico degli Uberti, who was really

[1] Cod. Vat. Lat., 8211, f. 240.   Appendix XXXI.
[2] *Ibid.*   Appendix XXIX.

so infirm that his decease could hardly be a cause of regret, adding a characteristic postscript, in which she begged him to be sure to answer the relatives who had written to inform him of the sad event.

Again, a fortnight later, she renewed her entreaties, begging her son not to delay his departure longer:

'We all expect you with the greatest eagerness, and pray you not to delay any longer; for every day the weather gets worse, and the roads begin to show that we are near winter, as indeed we are. Do not forget to come by Modena and Novellara, that you may have something to tell me when you get here. And be sure to leave your house in proper order, and see that the things you leave there are in good hands, so that they may come to no harm; and do not forget to bring your chain, that I may take care of it for you. God keep you from harm! Be sure to tell me how soon you are likely to be at Casatico, because many persons are anxious to come and see you.

'Your mother,
'LUIGIA.'[1]

But, alas for the vanity of a fond mother's hopes! The next we hear of M. Baldassare is that he had left Urbino to perform a vow at Loreto, and his visit to Mantua was once more postponed to a more convenient season.

[1] Cod. Vat. Lat., 8211.   Appendix XXX., XXXI.

CHAPTER XXV

1513–1515

Policy of Leo X.—Ambitious designs of Alfonsina Orsini and the
Florentines—Bibbiena created Cardinal—Castiglione in Rome
— Papal briefs in his favour — Entry of the Portuguese
ambassadors — The Pope's elephant — Raphael's letter to
Castiglione—Visit of Isabella d'Este to Rome—Castiglione at
Mantua—His restoration to favour at court.

THE high hopes which had been entertained of the
new Pope were doomed to disappointment, and the
reign of peace, which his accession was to have in-
augurated, proved of short duration. 'As long as
Leo X. was a Cardinal,' wrote the Ferrarese historian
Pistofilo,[1] 'he dissembled so well that he was held to
be half a saint; but once upon the throne, he showed
himself to be quite the contrary.' The natural deceit-
fulness of his character became evident both in the
double game that he played with France and Spain,
and in his dealings with the Duke of Ferrara, who
never obtained the promised restoration of Modena
and Reggio. His avowed policy was never to break
off negotiations with one power when you had entered
into alliance with the opposite party, and, as he himself told Castiglione, he regarded bulls and briefs as
the best methods of deception.[2] Yet Leo X. was
neither ambitious nor warlike by nature. On the

[1] 'Vita di Alfonso I.,' cap. 58.
[2] Alberi, iii. 290; Martinati, 78.

contrary, he was indolent and pleasure-loving, pas-
sionately fond of music and hunting, and determined,
as he told his brother Giuliano, to enjoy the Papacy
which God had given him. 'The Pope is a good-
natured, liberal man,' reported Marin Zorzi, 'who
does not like either war or trouble, but is constantly
involved in these by the intrigues of his own family.'[1]

The friends and kinsfolk of the Medici, the greedy
Florentines who had flocked to Rome to have a share
in the spoils—above all, the ambitious and designing
Alfonsina Orsini—were bent on the aggrandizement
of the Pope's family. Their hopes were gratified
by his first creation of Cardinals, on September 23,
when the newly-appointed Archbishop of Florence,
Giulio de' Medici, the illegitimate son of Giuliano,
who had been murdered by the Pazzi conspirators,
was advanced to this dignity. Another member of
the family, the youthful son of the Pope's sister,
Maddalena Cibo, and two other of its stanch supporters, Lorenzo Pucci and Bernardo da Bibbiena,
shared the same honour, to the great satisfaction of
the last-named prelate's friends at Urbino.

Thus encouraged to expect new favours, the
gentlemen of Giuliano's household discussed their
ambitious plans freely, and talked seriously of seeing
the Magnifico King of Naples, and his nephew Lorenzo
Duke of Milan. The Pope himself was more modest
in his aspirations, and would have been content to
form a new state in Central Italy for Giuliano, of
whom he was really fond, and to secure a position in
Florence for his nephew, similar to that which had been
held by his father Lorenzo. At the same time it was
confidently reported that the Duke of Urbino was to
be deprived of his office as Captain of the Church,

[1] Alberi, iii. 51.

and that his bâton would be given to Giuliano.[1]
These rumours were sufficiently disquieting to render
Castiglione's presence in Rome advisable, and early
in the New Year he returned to the Vatican as ducal
envoy. The favour which he enjoyed at the Papal
court was greater than ever.

When, in September, 1513, a few weeks after his
return to Urbino, Bibbiena's services were rewarded
by the much-coveted red hat, the first letter which
the new Cardinal wrote to announce his elevation,
was addressed to Castiglione:

'MY OWN MESSER BALDASSARE,

'The depth and sincerity of our friendship
moves me to tell you, even before I write to my
brother M. Piero, of my last promotion, since it has
pleased the infinite Majesty of God, and His Beatitude,
more from his own clemency than for any merit
on my part, to make me and three other creatures
members of the Sacred College. Beside the rare
virtues which endear you so deeply not only to me,
but to all those who value the humanities and sweet
mutual affection, your love for me, independently of
so many other causes, will always make you first in
my heart. Rejoice, then, my own M. Baldassare, as
you love me. Be sure that my good fortune will
prevent any diminution of your authority, and live
happy in the knowledge that you can depend on me
and on all that I do, as surely as on yourself. I kiss
my dear Castiglione, on condition that he will keep
me in the good graces of the Lord Duke and of our
most illustrious ladies, and commend me to Their
Excellencies as well as to all my brothers, the gentlemen of their household. And I remain the same
" bel Bernardo " as of old.

'FR. BERNARDO DA BIBBIENA,
'*Cardinale di S. Maria-in-Portico.*'[2]

---

[1] Nitti, 18; Sanuto, xvii. 127.   [2] Serassi, i. 174.

So, in the exuberance of his joy, wrote the new Cardinal, who was ere long to be leading the Papal forces against this friendly state, and driving the Duke and Duchesses from the home where he had so long enjoyed their splendid hospitality. For the present, however, the house of Medici was on the most cordial terms with the Urbino princes, and a few weeks later, we find Giuliano addressing M. Baldassare as his dearest brother.

On his return to Rome in January, Castiglione found the Papal court given up to a life of dissipation. On the 9th His Holiness set off for Viterbo, with eighteen Cardinals, to take part in a great hunting expedition at Cardinal Farnese's beautiful country-house of Capo di Monte, and shoot pheasants and grouse, in the forests along the Lake of Bolsena. The sight of a Pontiff organizing hunting expeditions on this large scale was a shock to many of the faithful; but what scandalized his Master of the Ceremonies most of all, was the costume which the Holy Father adopted on this occasion. 'The Pope,' wrote Paris de Grassis, 'left Rome without stole or rochet, and what is still worse, in hunting-boots. What will happen if anyone wishes to kiss his feet? And when this was pointed out to him he only laughed, and did not seem to care in the least.'[1]

Next to hunting, music and comedies were Leo X.'s favourite pastimes, and during his absence from Rome fresh masques and fêtes were prepared for his return. 'Some fine comedies are to be acted when the Pope comes back,' wrote Chiericati to Mantua, 'and for this winter we need think of nothing but pleasure and amusements.'[2]

By the end of January His Holiness returned to

[1] Roscoe, iii. 520; Pastor, iv. 101, 410.   [2] Morsolin, p. 140.

the Vatican, and a gay carnival was followed by what
the same writer describes as a yet more splendid
triumph—the state entry of the Portuguese ambassadors. The Pope himself witnessed this imposing
ceremony from the Castell' Sant' Angelo, and the
Roman populace gazed with delight on the costly
presents and strange animals from India and Africa,
which King Emanuel had sent to His Holiness.[1]
Tristan d' Acunha, one of the leading explorers, who
had recently travelled in these distant regions, and
two other envoys in black velvet suits and hats
embroidered with pearls and jewelled chains, rode
through the streets, followed by trumpeters in scarlet
and servants in liveries of black and yellow satin. A
brilliant company of foreign ambassadors, Roman
nobles, Papal officials, and Swiss Guards escorted the
strangers, while the chief Portuguese envoy rode
between the Governor of Rome and Francesco
Sforza, Duke of Bari, the son of Lodovico Moro and
Beatrice d' Este, who had been sent to represent his
brother, Maximilian, at the Vatican. Persian horses
ridden by natives in Eastern costume, leopards and
panthers, parrots and guinea-fowls, were among the
royal gifts paraded on this occasion ; but what delighted
the Romans most of all was a white elephant ' six
year old, and as big as three bulls,' ridden by an Indian.
On his back was a silver chest covered with cloth of
gold, containing presents for the Pope—a richly chased
gold chalice and tabernacle for the Host, a set of
sumptuous vestments, and a marvellous altar frontal,
valued at 270,000 ducats. But all eyes were fixed
upon the elephant itself, no such animal having been
seen in Rome since Imperial days. Chiericati favoured
the Marchesana with a minute account of the strange

[1] Baschet-Reumont, p. 243.

animal, who was said to understand two languages—
Indian and Portuguese—and was as docile and intelligent as a human creature. 'These last days,' the
writer adds, 'he has wept much at leaving home;
but he is now quite consoled, and knows that he has
found a good home.' The secretary describes how,
when the procession halted at the bridge of S. Angelo,
and a salute of 100 guns was fired, the terrified elephant
nearly jumped into the Tiber. When the animal was
brought into the Holy Father's presence, he knelt
down and bowed his head three times, upon which
the Pope sent for a bowl of melons and confetti,
which he ate gladly. But both His Holiness and his
courtiers were still more delighted when the elephant,
after drinking from a pail set before him, threw up
his trunk in the air, and sent a shower of water over
the assembled spectators.[1]

From that day the elephant Amnone became the
pet and plaything of the Vatican. The Pope paid
him frequent visits in the garden, and laughed loudly
at his tricks. Raphael of Urbino painted his portrait
on a tower of the palace, and his effigy may still be
seen wrought in tarsia on a door of the Stanze.
Sadoleto extolled the elephant in an elegant Latin
epistle which he addressed to King Emanuel when
the Pope sent him the Golden Rose that Easter.
And when, at the end of two years, the poor animal
died of angina, the Papal chamberlain, Branconi
d' Aquila, placed the following epitaph upon his
grave :

'Under this mound, I, the great elephant sent to
Leo X. by King Emanuel, the conqueror of the East,
am laid. The Romans admired me for a while, and

---

[1] Harleian MSS. 3,462, p. 77.

recognized that human sentiments can live in the heart of an animal. But the Parcæ envied me my home in happy Latium, and would not suffer me to serve my lord three years. O ye Gods, I pray you, add on the years of which they have robbed me to the life of Leo.'[1]

That same March, amid the stir and noise of these carnival revels, the Pope thought fit to honour the Duke of Urbino's envoy with a mark of special favour. He addressed a letter to Castiglione, written in Bembo's hand, congratulating him in the most cordial terms on the grant of Novillara which he had received from the Duke, praising him for his learning, virtues, and loyalty, and expressing a hope that the Holy Father might some day be able to reward him in a manner more worthy of his merits. Two months later—on May 22—when Leo was enjoying a brief interval of repose at his favourite country-house of La Magliana, he issued another brief, written this time by Sadoleto, in which, as supreme lord of Pesaro, he formally confirmed the grant of Novillara, and exempted the Count and his descendants from all taxes and tributes to the Holy See.

But, in spite of these honours and compliments, there was an uneasy sense among the Duke's friends at the Vatican. At the end of March Francesco Maria himself came to Rome, on his way to Naples to answer a summons from the Catholic King, whose allegiance he owned as Duke of the principality of Sora. A charge was brought against him of having contributed to the victory of the French at Ravenna, two years before, by absenting himself from the Papal army, but it seems to have been soon dropped.

[1] Gnoli, 'Leo X.': 'Nuova Antologia,' 1898.

'Every one,' wrote the Venetian Lippomano, 'says that the Duke did wrong to come here, and will do worse to go to Naples. He has come to ask the help of the Pope and the Magnifico; but it is said that he will be deprived of his State by the Pope, who means to give it to his brother. And this is all the reward that he will receive for his goodness to the Medici.'[1]

Cardinal Bibbiena, however, came to see His Excellency at the Bishop of Trirarico's house, and after going in May to the shrine of Loreto to meet Bembo and Cardinal Gurk, he paid a visit to the Duke at Pesaro. But the Pope's duplicity began to excite suspicion on all sides. 'He plays marvellously with both hands,' remarked an English envoy—Richard Pace—who had some knowledge of Leo's ways; or as another contemporary puts it: 'The Pope never sails with one wind at a time.' And Cardinal Gurk, who left Rome highly dissatisfied with the result of his mission, in spite of Bibbiena's soft words, was heard to say: 'The Holy Father weaves everything into a labyrinth.'[2]

Unfortunately, there is a gap in Castiglione's correspondence at this period, and we have no certain information regarding his movements. But there seems little doubt that he spent the greater part of the year in Rome. The famous letter which his friend Raphael addressed to him in the autumn, proves that he had only lately left the Papal court. Often as this letter has been quoted, it is so important a document in the history of both these distinguished men that we cannot refrain from giving it here :

<hr>

[1] Sanuto, xviii. 68, 81.

[2] Brewer, ii. 1729; A. Verdi, 'Gliultimi anni di Lorenzo de' Medici,' 103.

'MY LORD COUNT,

 ' I have made several drawings of the subject which V. S. suggested, and those who have seen them appear to be well pleased, unless they are all base flatterers! But I confess that they do not satisfy my judgment, because, I fear, they will not satisfy yours. I send them, and hope V. S. will choose whichever is most to your taste. Our Lord the Pope has done me the honour to lay a great burden on my shoulders. This is the charge of the fabric of St. Peter's. I hope I shall not sink under the load, especially since the model which I have made pleases His Holiness and has been praised by several men of fine intellect. But my thoughts soar to greater heights. I long to find out more about the noble forms of ancient monuments, and I know not if my flight may not prove to be that of Icarus. Vitruvius has thrown much light on the subject, but has not shown me all that I want to know. As for the Galatea, I should count myself to be a great master if one half the kind things which V. S. finds in her were there, but in your words I recognize the love that you bear me. And I tell you that, if I am to paint a beautiful woman, I must see several, and have you at my side to choose the fairest. But since good judges and lovely faces are both rare, I make use of a certain ideal that is in my mind. If it has any artistic excellence, I know not, but I try hard to reach it. Let me have your commands.

 '*From* ROME.'

This letter, which was first published in 1554, must have been written after August, when Raphael's wooden model of St. Peter's had been presented to the Pope for his approval. From this we learn that Castiglione had asked the master for a picture, and had expressed the warmest admiration for the fresco of Galatea and her nymphs which Raphael had lately painted in a hall of Agostino Chigi's villa. The Count, who had himself sung the charms of the milk-white Galatea in his eclogue in honour of the Duchess Elisabetta, may well have helped the painter with his advice in the composition of this beautiful group, which is the very type of the Greek world as it appeared to the humanists of Leo's court. At least Raphael's letter proves how much he relied on M. Baldassare's fine taste, and how close and enduring was the intimacy which united them.

Another illustrious man was probably brought into closer relations with Castiglione during that autumn. This was the poet Ariosto, who came to Urbino in the train of Cardinal d' Este, on the way to Rome. The poet relates how the joyous party set out, and how, as ill-luck would have it, he fell ill in the Furlo Pass, and was laid up with fever at a little country town—Cagli or Fossombrone. Here he remained for several weeks, after which he went to Pesaro, and returned to Ferrara, without seeing Rome.[1] On this visit to Urbino, and during his enforced residence in the immediate neighbourhood, the poet probably renewed his acquaintance with Castiglione, who had frequently met him in Rome, and was intimate with his cousin, Alfonso Ariosto, and nearly related to another friend, Lodovico da Bagno. What is quite certain is that the poet was well acquainted with the author of the 'Cortegiano,' whom he mentions in his great epic, and to whom, we learn from his son Virginio, he actually dedicated a satire which was never finished.[2]

The Duke of Urbino came to Rome again in

---

[1] L. Ariosto, capitolo i. ; E. Gardner, 'The King of Court Poets,' 121.

[2] G. A. Barotti, 'Vita di L. Ariosto.'

August, and the Pope stood at the window of the
Vatican on one of the hottest days in the year to see
him make his state entry.[1] But it was the last time
that Francesco Maria appeared in Rome as Captain
of the Church. His term of office had already
expired, and it was an open secret that the Pope
intended to give the bâton to his brother Giuliano.
On January 8, 1515, the Magnifico was solemnly invested with the badge of office. At daybreak the
next morning, as we learn from an entry in Leonardo's
note-books, he left for Turin, to celebrate his marriage
with Filiberta of Savoy. This Princess, we are told,
was thirty years of age, and neither young nor
beautiful,[2] but gentle and attractive in manner, and,
what was of greater importance in the Pope's eyes,
closely connected with the French Royal Family
through her sister Louise, the mother of Francis I.
But on the very day that Giuliano left Rome, His
Holiness received the news of Louis XII.'s death.
This event relieved the Pope of his worst fears. Of
late he had lived in hourly dread of hearing that the
French armies had once more invaded Milan, and
had been seeking to avert this catastrophe by his
customary intrigues. Now he made no pretence to
conceal his joy, and went off to hunt at La Magliana,
where he killed fifty stags and twenty wild-boars in
one day.[3]

Alberto Pio, the Emperor's representative at the
Vatican, told the Mantuan envoy that he would
have given his best velvet suit for the French King's
life to have been prolonged another fortnight, by
which time the Pope would have been too deeply

---

[1] Sanuto, xviii. 426.
[2] 'The Writings of Leonardo,' by Dr. Richter, ii. 417.
[3] Sanuto, xix. 391.

pledged to an alliance with his master, to be able to withdraw.[1]

Bembo, who had been secretly sent on a fruitless mission to Venice, to try and detach the Doge from the French alliance, spent that New Year's Day at Pesaro with his old friends the Duchesses of Urbino. On January 1 he wrote to Cardinal Bibbiena saying that he had sailed from Chioggia in the roughest weather, and, after tossing about for two nights at sea, had reached Pesaro so worn out that he was compelled to spend two nights there.

' I arrived here on Saturday evening, it is true, but so tired and shattered and weary that I am confirmed in the opinion which I had already formed before leaving Rome, that travelling by post is not fit for old people. I had some fever last night, in spite of all the caresses and charms of my dear Madonna Emilia. I found our Lady Duchess in bed, owing to a shock which she received from an outbreak of fire here, but she is consoled for her fright by hearing that you, too, have suffered from the same fire and the same shock. Indeed, these ladies are proud to think they have had the Pope for companion in their misfortunes.'[2]

By a curious coincidence, it appears that on the night of December 22, there was a fire at the Vatican in Cardinal Bibbiena's rooms, exactly above those occupied by the Pope and his favourite chamberlain, Serapica, which did considerable damage. His Holiness seems to have been as much alarmed as the widowed Duchess, and was unable to hold any audiences the next day.[3]

' I can see you laughing,' continued Bembo, 'and saying, O what a fine invention ! I am sure that you

---

[1] Luzio in ' Arch. st. Lomb.,' 1906, 479.
[2] Bembo, ' Lettere,' i. 320.   [3] Sanuto, xix. 336.

think I am feigning sickness in order to spend some days here. But, by God and all the saints, my dear Monsignore, I am not talking nonsense. All yesterday I was so tired and exhausted and worn out, that I could hardly stand, and I began to be afraid that it would take me some days to recover. And knowing how sorry you would be for me, and how kind and thoughtful you and the Pope are for your servants, I decided to stay here to-day. To-morrow, if I am not worse, which God forbid, I will mount my horse and travel to Rome, not by post this time, but by slow stages on the horses which the Lord Duke has lent me.'[1]

That winter the Duke's mother-in-law, Isabella d' Este, spent some months in Rome, where she was fêted and entertained as no royal lady had ever been treated before. The Pope and Cardinals vied with each other in doing her honour. The Marchesana and all the members of her suite were the guests of the Cardinal of Aragon, and wherever she went she was attended by Monsignori and Roman nobles. Giuliano and Lorenzo de' Medici, Cardinals Bibbiena and San Giorgio, Luigi of Aragon or Ippolito d' Este, escorted her in visits to the Forum and Baths of Titus, to the crypt of St. Peter's, and the Coliseum. Comedies and musical parties, banquets and suppers, were given in her honour, and her ladies were buried under piles of confetti by the merry Cardinals and their retainers. The Pope himself gave a magnificent performance of Cardinal Bibbiena's 'Calandria' at the Vatican. At the first audience to which she was admitted, His Holiness raised her from the ground, touched her cheek with his own, and made her sit by his side in the presence of all the Cardinals.[2]

---

[1] Bembo, 'Lettere,' i. 320.
[2] Harleian MSS., 3462 ; Luzio, 468-474.

When Isabella went to Naples to visit Queens
Giovanna of Aragon and her daughter, Leo X. insisted that she should return for Christmas, and
induced the Marquis to allow her to spend the
carnival in Rome. That January she took part in
great hunting-parties at La Magliana and Campo
Salino, and was sumptuously entertained by Cardinal
San Giorgio and Agostino Chigi at their country-
houses. During the carnival, wrote the Venetian
envoy, she kept the whole city *en fête*, and masquerades, comedies, bull-fights, regattas, horse-races,
and dances succeeded each other daily.[1] Thanks to
the Marchesana, as Bembo said, this was the gayest
carnival ever known in the Eternal City. The Pope
took the greatest pleasure in her society, invited her
to the Castello to see the races on the Tiber, and
conversed with her on political affairs for hours
together. But all Isabella's charms and cleverness
could not prevent the Duke of Ferrara from being
treacherously deprived of Modena, or her son-in-law
from losing his office of Captain of the Church.
Throughout the winter Leo X. was playing his usual
double game. On the one hand, the newly-married
Giuliano paid assiduous court to his wife's kinsman, Francis I., and Canossa, the noblest of Italian
diplomatists, who had been sent to congratulate the
young King on his accession, tried dexterously to
obtain Parma and Piacenza, if not Naples, for the
Pope's brother; while, on the other hand, Alberto
Pio was closeted for hours at a time with His Holiness, plotting a new and powerful league against
France.[2]

Castiglione probably spent the whole of this winter

[1] Sanuto, xix. 391, etc.
[2] Baschet-Reumont, 245 ; Nitti, 61.

in Rome.   He may have been present at the representation of the 'Calandria,' for which Baldassare
Peruzzi painted the scenery, and which, by the
Pope's desire, as far as possible resembled the performance which he himself had arranged at Urbino.
But he certainly met the Marchesana during her visit,
and this meeting led to a renewal of their old friendship.   It was doubtless Isabella's regard for Castiglione, and the pleasure which she took in his
society, which led to the cordiality with which the
Count was received by the Marquis when he went to
Mantua that spring.

The important services which the Count had
rendered to his son-in-law, and the distinguished
position which he held at the Vatican, combined to
produce a marked change in Francesco's behaviour.
In the autumn of 1513, when the Count returned
from his first successful embassy to Rome, the Marquis sent him a present, accompanied by a cordial
message, through one of his old Mantuan friends.
This first token of recovered favour was soon followed
by others.[1]   Now at length the cloud was lifted, and
Castiglione felt that he could return to Mantua and
visit his old home without feeling himself an object
of suspicion and hatred in his lord's eyes.   So it
came to pass that in the pleasant May time, when
the Pope and Cardinals went to hunt at La Magliana,
the Count was able to take a brief holiday, and
Madonna Luigia had the joy of welcoming her
beloved son and of seeing him honourably received
at court.   Her friends and relatives were not slow to
hear the good news, and congratulations poured in
upon her from all sides.

[1] Cod. Vat. Lat., 8211.

' I have heard by persons who have come from Mantua,' wrote one of her Milanese cousins, Cecilia Malatesta, on May 29, ' that your son, the Magnifico Baldassare, has returned to Mantua. This news has given me the greatest possible pleasure and satisfaction, all the more that I hear he has been received with great favour by His Excellency the Marquis. Now that you have got him back, I hope you will be able to keep him and enjoy his company, and find him a good and beautiful wife.'

The writer concludes by saying that a certain maiden of the illustrious house of Beccaria, in Pavia, who had been suggested as a bride for M. Baldassare, was eminently suitable in many respects, but that on making further inquiry she regretted to find that the girl's dowry would be small, because she was one of a large family.[1]

One proof of the recovered favour which Castiglione enjoyed at court is seen in the numerous commissions with which he was charged by the Gonzaga ladies. On this occasion the young Duchess Leonora sent her brother Federico a set of balls, four large and nine small, for his favourite game of *palla*, which he had ordered from a Cagli maker. The receipt of these was acknowledged by the Marquis himself in a note addressed to M. Baldassare at Casatico, calling him his honoured friend and thanking him for his loving diligence.[2] The Marchesana next availed herself of this opportunity to ask the Count to do her a more important service. Since her return from Rome in March, life at Mantua had seemed intolerably dull and tedious. Although her bodily presence was in Mantua, her heart was in

---

[1] Cod. Vat. Lat., 8212.
[2] Archivo Gonzaga, Carteggio di B. Castiglione.

Rome, as she wrote to Cardinal Bibbiena. In the little rooms of the old Castello, Isabella thought with longing of the Vatican halls and the spacious palaces where she had been entertained by Cardinals and princes and His Holiness himself had made her welcome. Now she gladly rejoiced to meet a member of the brilliant society which she had left behind, and with whom she could talk freely of her distinguished friends in Rome. M. Baldassare found himself a frequent and welcome guest in the shady groves of the fair villa at Porto, where Isabella escaped as soon as the first summer days made it possible, feeling, as she wrote to a Roman friend, 'that in the solitude of the country it was easier to think of the delights of Rome than in the small and narrow society of Mantua.'[1]

On one of the visits which the Count paid her in these early June days, the Marchesana asked him to use his influence with his friend Raphael to induce him to paint a picture for her studio. When she was in Rome the great master had promised to gratify her wish, and had lately told Agostino Gonzaga that he hoped to begin the work soon. But, knowing how little trust could be placed in these assurances, Isabella begged Castiglione to second her request. Accordingly, on his return to Urbino he wrote at once to Raphael, and, when he saw him a few weeks later in Rome, was so urgent in his entreaties that the painter promised to put everything else aside, and went so far as to ask for the exact measurements of the picture that the Marchesana desired. But although Isabella sent the canvas, with full particulars of the size and lighting of the picture, by an express to Urbino, and her loyal servant lost

[1] Luzio, 179.

no time in forwarding these, Raphael's picture was still unfinished when Castiglione returned to Rome in 1519. A few months after that Raphael died, the contents of his studio were dispersed, and the fate of Isabella's much-coveted treasure still remains a mystery.[1]

[1] 'Isabella d'Este,' ii. 163, etc.

CHAPTER XXVI

1515–1516

LEO X. and the Cardinals who shared his confidence had flattered themselves that the French King would delay his intended invasion of Italy till the following year. But Francis I. was young and ambitious, eager for military glory, and impatient to recover Milan and Naples. In June, while Castiglione still lingered with his friends at Mantua, the French forces were gathering at Lyons, and a few weeks later they descended on Lombardy. The Pope, now really alarmed at the prospect of a foreign invasion, at length joined the League against France, and appointed Giuliano to the chief command of the Papal army.[1] Early in July the Magnifico left Rome for Bologna, where the forces of the Church were to be assembled, and stopped at Gubbio on his journey to visit the Duke of Urbino, and, according to the Venetian envoy, persuade him to fight for Italy and not for France.

[1] Pastor, iv. 76.

Francesco Maria came to meet him, and wished to take him back to Urbino ; and although Giuliano was unable to accept his offer, he met the Duke's advances in the most friendly spirit, assuring him that there was no truth in the rumours which he had heard of the Pope's designs against Urbino. He, for one, would never consent to such a crime, and would always hold the Duke as dear to him as a brother. For the time Francesco's suspicions were allayed. He promised to raise a body of men and join the Pope's banner if sufficient money and a suitable guard were allowed him. Leo X., on his part, was satisfied with Giuliano's assurances, agreed to the Duke's conditions, and sent him liberal supplies of money.[1] Unfortunately, Giuliano fell ill in Florence, and after prolonged delays the command of the Papal forces was given to his nephew Lorenzo, who had already been appointed Captain-General of the Florentines. The Duke of Urbino, who had professed his willingness to serve under Giuliano, now made fresh difficulties, and at the end of July Castiglione was sent to Rome to arrange matters.[2] His task was not an easy one. There was much irritation on both sides, and, after the treatment which Francesco had received from Leo X. and the persistent rumours that were circulated of the Medici's designs on Urbino, it can hardly be wondered that he began to look to the French King for help. On July 30 Castiglione was dismissed with peremptory orders to the Duke, and Cardinal de' Medici's secretary advised Giuliano to warn his friend that His Holiness's patience had reached its limits, and that if he did not march at once he was a ruined man.[3]

[1] Torrigiani MSS., 'Arch. st. Ital.,' xix. 238.
[2] Sanuto, xx. 383.   [3] Torrigiani MSS., xix. 244.

A fortnight later we find the Count once more in
Rome, trying to dispel the Pope's anger and to excuse
his master's delays. But on August 31 a Venetian,
who had seen Castiglione that day at the Vatican, reported that the Pope had ordered the Duke of Urbino
to march to Bologna, and that he had refused to go.
The impression that Francesco was secretly allied with
the French King evidently prevailed both in Rome
and at Venice, where the Duke was described as the
friend of France and the Pope's enemy.[1] Long
afterwards, Castiglione, who was in a position to
know the truth, told Federico Gonzaga that his
brother-in-law had lost his duchy solely because
he was too French in his sympathies. According
to Leoni and Ugolini,[2] the historians of Urbino,
he would not obey the Pope's orders himself, but
raised a body of men who refused to fight without
their Prince, and turned back when they reached
Cesena.

The rapid progress of the French arms soon cul-
minated in the victory of Marignano and the practical
annihilation of the Swiss forces. When the news of
this disaster reached Rome, the Pope saw that further
resistance was in vain, and exclaimed, ' We must throw
ourselves into the arms of the most Christian King
and beg for mercy.' Before the battle, Canossa,
who was in the French camp, had already done his
best to obtain good terms for the Pope, and when, on
October 11, Francis I. entered Milan in triumph and
received Maximilian Sforza's abdication, Lorenzo de'
Medici hastened to greet the victor. Francis, who
had no wish to drive the Pope to extremities, received
him kindly, and on the 13th a preliminary peace was

[1] Sanuto, xx. 450.
[2] Ugolini, ii. 199 ; Serassi, i. 27.

signed at Viterbo, by which the Pope gave up Parma
and Piacenza to the King, who in return promised to
maintain the Medici in the government of Florence.
From this moment the Duke of Urbino's situation
became critical.   Since the loss of Parma and
Piacenza precluded the formation of a kingdom in
Central Italy, the thoughts of Lorenzo de' Medici and
his ambitious mother turned towards Urbino. '*La
mira mia è in su Urbino*,' wrote Alfonsina Orsini to
her son on November 3—'My hopes are fixed upon
Urbino.'[1] Four days later Cardinal Giulio de' Medici
wrote from Rome: 'As to Urbino, the Pope's mind
is made up.   He does not wish to hear the thing
discussed, but it will be done without any more
words.'[2]

Francesco's refusal to serve under the banner of the
Church had given his enemies an opportunity of
which they were not slow to take advantage. The
Medici partisans with one accord began to denounce
his conduct and impute the worst motives to him.
The Pope, after some hesitation, determined to
punish his disobedient vassal, and at the same time
gratify the vanity and greed of his nephew. And
Giuliano, who alone of his family remained faithful
to his friends, and could not bear the thought of
depriving Francesco of his State, lay ill and helpless
at Florence. The Duke's only hope was in the
French King's friendship, and the news that Francis
had made peace with the Pope filled him with
dismay.

He began to make preparations for the defence of
his State, and sent his little son Guidobaldo to the
stronghold of S. Leo in the charge of the Pesaro

---

[1] Nitti, 71 ; Verdi, 20 ; Pastor, iv. 102.
[2] Giorgetti in 'Arch. st. Ital.,' 1881.

poet, Guido Postumo, who had arrived at Urbino in
July with a letter of recommendation from Tebaldeo
to Castiglione.[1] At the same time, he neglected no
means of awakening the French King to a sense of
his ally's danger. In the Papal envoy Canossa, who
stood high in that monarch's favour, the Urbino
princes already possessed a good friend, and young
Federico Gonzaga, whom his clever mother sent to
Milan to pay his respects to King Francis, lost no
opportunity of pleading his brother-in-law's cause
with the conqueror. But, as usual, it was on Castiglione's personal efforts that both Francesco and
Elisabetta depended.

Francis I. had expressed a strong wish to confer
with the Pope in person, and Leo X., who feared the
evil effects which might result from the presence of
the French in Florence, agreed to meet the King at
Bologna early in December. Accordingly, the Pope
travelled by Cortona and Arezzo to Florence, and
entered his native city in state on November 30,
accompanied by eighteen Cardinals and a splendid
train of ambassadors and Roman and Florentine
patricians. The reception which his fellow-citizens
gave him was magnificent. Ten triumphal arches,
decorated by the best artists of the day, adorned
the streets and bridges over the Arno, and bands
of musicians and choirs of children, stationed along
the route from the Porta Romana to the gates of
the Duomo, welcomed his presence. Leo took up
his abode in the Papal rooms at S. Maria Novella,
and attended mass in the Duomo. On Saturday,
December 1, he prayed at the shrine of the Annunziata, and spent the evening with his sick brother

[1] Serassi, i. 177.

Giuliano in the palace of the Via Larga.[1] On Advent
Sunday he celebrated mass in S. Lorenzo, and knelt
with tears in his eyes at the tombs of his ancestors.
Raphael had accompanied him from Rome, to
prepare designs for the façade of the parish church
of his family, and at the same moment, by a strange
coincidence, Leonardo arrived at Bologna in the train
of the French King. The next morning His Holiness left Florence, and on the 7th entered Bologna.
Here the coldness of the Bolognese formed a marked
contrast to the acclamations which had greeted the
Pope in Florence. No sumptuous decorations adorned
the streets ; no shout of ' Palle !' or ' Medici !' were
heard.   According to the Mantuan Archdeacon, Gabbioneta, the few arches which had been erected were
hideous, and the women, who in his opinion generally
formed the best part of the show, had the ugliest faces
in the world.[2] When, four days later, the French King
entered the city in state, he met with a better reception, but in the eyes of the Bolognese the procession
was a very shabby affair. The King himself was a
commanding figure, mounted on a spirited charger,
and wearing a magnificent cloak of gold brocade
and rich zibeline furs. Silvestro Gigli, the Bishop
of Worcester, describes him as tall and broad-
shouldered, ' with a handsome oval face, inclined to
corpulence, but very slender about the legs.' But
the spectators, who had expected to see a splendid
display of gold and silk and new fashions, ' in which
the French are said to be very clever,' were bitterly
disappointed. Nothing could be more squalid. The
archers of the guard looked like bargemen, with dirty
faces and greasy, threadbare coats They had not

---

[1] Chiericati to Isabella d' Este : Harleian MS. 3462.
[2] Pastor, iv. 91 ; Sanuto, xxi. 375, 391.

four gold chains, and hardly a suit of brocade,
among them, and the whole thing seemed more like
a city magnate entering on his office than a great
King coming in state to meet the Pope. Yet the
Italians complained that the French guards were as
rude and haughty as ever, and handled the Pope's
servants and Mantuan gentlemen so roughly that
young Federico Gonzaga's tutor thanked his stars
he had escaped with no bones broken.[1]

When the King entered the great hall where
the Pope was awaiting him in jewelled tiara and
glittering robes, the dense crowd swayed back-
wards and forwards so heavily, that the Bishop
of Worcester thought he would be trampled to
death, and some time elapsed before the Master of
Ceremonies could clear the way for His Majesty.
The Pope received him most graciously, kissed him
on both cheeks, and conversed in a friendly way with
him for some minutes, after which His Holiness
retired to take off his cope and tiara, which were so
heavy that he could hardly walk, and was forced to lean
on the monarch's arm. The King's demeanour, as all
the eyewitnesses agree, was perfect. He showed the
deepest reverence for the Pope, and conversed freely
with the Cardinals, especially with Bibbiena, whom he
treated with marked favour. His devotion at mass the
following day greatly edified the Holy Father. After
supper all the Cardinals retired, and Francis, who
lodged in the lower story of the palace, went upstairs
and spent two hours in private conversation with
His Holiness.[2] The same prolonged interviews were
repeated during the next two days, and, although
nothing passed in writing, the utmost secrecy regard-

[1] Brewer, ii. 341 ; Harleian MS. 3462.
[2] Harleian MS. 3462.

ing the subjects which they discussed was preserved. The main conditions of the Treaty of Viterbo were virtually ratified. Francis obtained the cession of Parma and Piacenza, and insisted on the restoration of Reggio and Modena to the Duke of Ferrara within two months, a promise which the Pope, however failed to keep. But when the King began to intercede on behalf of his ally the Duke of Urbino, the Pope was inflexible. The Duke, he insisted, had broken faith with the Holy See. Such open disaffection and acts of insolence plainly must be punished, and Lorenzo de' Medici, who was now bent on acquiring the duchy of Urbino, and had done his best to ingratiate himself with Francis, begged the King to leave Francesco Maria to his fate.[1]

Meanwhile the Duke made a last appeal to Francis through Castiglione. In November he decided to send the Count to Mantua to seek help from his father-in-law. Bologna lay on his way north, and when the meeting between the Pope and King was definitely arranged, it was easy for M. Baldassare to make this city his halting-place and deliver his dispatch to Francis. At the last minute his departure was delayed, probably in order that his presence at Bologna when the King arrived might not excite the Pope's suspicion, and he was still at Urbino on December 10. On that day the Duchess Dowager wrote to tell the Marchesana that she was sending her some gold-embroidered caps 'by the hands of M. Baldassare.'[2] So that the Count could not have reached Bologna until the King's first meetings with the Pope were over.

---

[1] Nitti, 73 ; Verdi, 21.
[2] Archivio Gonzaga, Carteggio di Castiglione.

Immediately on his arrival he was introduced into
the King's presence by M. Alfonso Ariosto, a gentleman of Ferrara and cousin of the poet, who was
related to Castiglione's kinsman, Lodovico da Bagno,
and was one of Bembo's intimate friends. This discreet
and charming youth, as our author calls him, was a
great favourite with the French monarch, as well
as a loyal servant of the house of Este, and did
his utmost to support his friends from Urbino. The
Count found another stanch ally in the person of
Felice della Rovere, who had hastened to Bologna
to meet the King, and had been among his first
visitors. Clad in peacock velvet and white ermine,
and attended by ten maidens in the same costume,
this gallant lady had ridden through the streets
of Bologna to pay her respects to Francis, with
Giuliano's wife, the Duchess of Nemours, and
had charmed the susceptible monarch by her fascinating ways. For a moment the Duke of Urbino's
friends took courage. Their hopes rose high when
they heard that Castiglione had pleaded his lord's
cause long and eloquently, and that the King had
spoken warmly to His Holiness in favour of the
Duke. But Archdeacon Gabbioneta did not share
their confidence, and on December 14 he added the
following ominous postscript to his letter to Mantua:

'As for the affairs of Urbino, things look bad; and
although the King has promised M. Baldassare Castiglione that he will speak to the Holy Father once
more on the subject, those who love the Duke fear
the worst.'[1]

That evening Francis supped with the Pope, and
the two were as merry as possible together. The

[1] Luzio in 'Arch. st. Ital.,' xl. 32.

next morning he took leave of His Holiness, and left
Bologna to spend Christmas at Milan. But neither
Madonna Felice's charms nor Castiglione's eloquence
could avail to save the ill-fated Duke from the Pope's
rancour and Alfonsina's ambitious designs, and before
Francis parted from Leo X., he had consented
reluctantly to the sacrifice of his ally. Castiglione's
mission, so far as its object was political, had
failed. But his first meeting with King Francis
was memorable from another point of view. This
chivalrous young monarch, whose genuine love of
letters had already captivated both Canossa and
Bibbiena, was charmed by the culture and art of
Italy. He had brought Leonardo to Bologna in his
train,[1] and had boldly asked the Pope to give him the
Laocoön, a request which Leo X. evaded by sending
the King a copy of the famous group by the hand of
Baccio Bandinelli. Now the courtly manners and
brilliant conversation of the accomplished Count made
a deep impression upon his mind. But what interested Francis above all was Messer Alfonso's account
of the book on the Perfect Courtier which Castiglione
had written, and which he begged the Count to complete without delay. This request, we learn from the
dedicatory letter to Alfonso Ariosto, which the author
originally intended to publish in his ' Cortegiano,'
was afterwards repeated several times by the King.
In this epistle,[2] which was suppressed when the
' Cortegiano ' finally saw the light, thirteen years later,
the author thus addresses his friend :

' I have long hesitated, dearest M. Alfonso, between
two courses, both of which are equally difficult—

---

[1] Müntz, ' Leonardo da Vinci,' ii. 206.
[2] Serassi, ii. 181.

whether to refuse the urgent request which you have many times made of me on the part of this illustrious King, or to undertake the task. On the one hand, it seems very hard to refuse so laudable a request made by a friend whom I love so well, and who loves me no less, when it is supported by the wish and command of so exalted and noble a Prince. On the other, it seems hardly right to attempt an undertaking which I am conscious that I can only carry out imperfectly.'

After a long dissertation on the difficulties of the task, he concludes by saying that it would be a crime to disobey so great and accomplished a King, and that, if His Majesty considers him sufficient for such a task, he will no longer hesitate, but will take confidence from the knowledge that this is the opinion of the greatest King who has reigned in Christendom for many a long day. There seems no doubt that this brief interview at Bologna supplied our author with the necessary stimulus, and induced him to complete his unfinished work in the quiet years spent at Mantua after his marriage.[1]

From Bologna the Count now continued his journey, probably by way of Modena, to Mantua, where his mother was awaiting his arrival with the utmost impatience. For the long-delayed marriage question, which had cost her so many years of toil and trouble, and had of late seemed more hopeless than ever, was now at length on the eve of solution. The very difficulties of the political situation, and the critical condition of affairs at Urbino, had helped to bring about this happy state of things by restoring M. Baldassare to his lord's favour, and the Marquis

[1] Cian in 'Giorn. st. d. Let. It.,' xvii. 120; Gaspary-Rossi, 'Storia d. Lett. Ital.,' ii. 97 ; F. Flamini, ' Il Cinquecento,' 369.

himself seems in this instance to have done all that was possible to promote his loyal subject's marriage.

In September Madonna Luigia had written to her son in great anxiety about the repeated journeys to Rome which he had been forced to undertake, in the Duke's service, during the great heats.

' I have been very anxious about you,' she wrote, ' since I heard that you had been twice to Rome in so short a time, and in this weather, which is hotter here than it was in July. And I see by your letters that you are unhappy, which grieves me for your sake. But you must believe that God is working for the best, and will do more for us than we know how to ask. . . . Only try and keep well, and never mind the rest.'[1]

After begging him earnestly neither to neglect his religious duties nor his health, she alludes to proposals of marriage which had reached her two months before through one of her cousins at Ferrara, Simona degli Uberti, the wife of the murdered Ercole's brother, Guido Strozzi. The bride suggested was Ippolita, the youthful daughter of Guido Torelli, a condottiere of note, and of Francesca Bentivoglio, one of the numerous daughters of Giovanni Bentivoglio and his wife Ginevra. The family of Torelli was one of the oldest and most illustrious in Ferrara, and had at one time disputed the lordship of that city with the house of Este. Branches of the Torelli had settled in Pavia, Naples and Guastalla. Ippolita belonged to the branch of Montechiaraguolo, a castle and fief near Parma, of which her father had been dispossessed by one of his cousins. Guido Torelli himself had died some years before. His wife, a spirited lady who had acquired

---

[1] Cod. Vat. Lat., 8211.

some notoriety by stabbing her first husband, the
faithless Galeotto Manfredi, in his sleep with her own
hands, was also dead, and Ippolita had been brought
up at Modena in the care of her aunts, Bianca Bentivoglio and Leonora Torelli, the wives of the Rangone
brothers, Niccolò and Uguccione. Thus the girl
was well known to M. Baldassare's intimate friend,
Costanza Rangone, and to many others of his own
kith and kin. Through her mother's family, Ippolita
was related both to the Este and Gonzaga princes.
Her uncle, Annibale Bentivoglio, had married
Lucrezia d' Este, Isabella and Beatrice's half-sister,
and her aunt, Laura Bentivoglio, was the wife of
Giovanni Gonzaga, the Marquis of Mantua's brother.
Her cousin, Barbara Torelli, Ercole Strozzi's widow,
had always been fond of Baldassare and his mother,
and Barbara's relative, Marco Secco, took an active
part in forwarding the marriage. This gentleman
now came to Mantua to see his relatives and condole with them on the death of an old and wealthy
ecclesiastic, Messer Carlo de' Uberti. Madonna Luigia
consulted him in her perplexities, and received the
most encouraging answer. He spoke not only in the
highest terms of Ippolita, but also promised to use his
influence with her guardians to bring the matter
to a speedy conclusion. 'Indeed,' adds Luigia,
'he considers the thing as settled, and only marvels
that there have been so many delays, as the head
of the family is in Lombardy and he knows how
highly esteemed you are by all of that house.'[1] This
last remark probably alludes to the girl's uncle,
Annibale Bentivoglio, who was living in exile at
Milan. Ippolita herself was barely fifteen, but is
described as tall and beautiful, as well as accomplished

[1] Cod. Vat. Lat., 8211.

and intelligent beyond her years. She inherited a considerable fortune from her mother, and, what especially gratified Madonna Luigia, had been exceedingly well brought up by her relatives at Modena. Up to the time of his arrival at Mantua, Castiglione himself had shown little interest in the matter, and was too much absorbed in the troubles of Urbino to think seriously of the union which his mother was so eager to bring about. But his first meeting with Ippolita seems to have decided the question. Whether he visited Modena on his journey from Bologna, or whether he stopped there on his way back to Urbino, he certainly made her acquaintance that Christmas. The simple charm and beauty of the young girl won his heart, and, in spite of the fact that this suitor was her senior by twenty-three years, the Count seems to have captured Ippolita's affections on the spot. The favour with which the Marquis and all his family regarded the marriage no doubt contributed greatly to its conclusion. Unfortunately, before Castiglione could receive his friends' congratulations, or give himself up to the peaceful enjoyment of these new dreams, the threatening aspect of public affairs summoned him back to Urbino.

He left Mantua before the end of January, and his mother had the pleasant task of announcing the marriage and receiving the congratulations of her friends. One of the first and warmest letters which she received came from Costanza Rangone, who wrote from Modena on February 10, rejoicing with her honoured kinswoman over ' this our common bride.'

' Since she has been educated in this town,' adds the writer, ' I know her better than you do, and am sure that you will have much joy in her, since, not to speak of her beauty, you have gained in her a daughter who has been brought up in Paradise, and is, God knows, as charming and attractive as possible. I pray that God may grant them grace to live happily together for many years. V. S. will kindly wish your daughters La Magnifica Madonna Polissena, and Madonna Francesca joy of this good and gentle sister whom they are gaining for their own. Indeed, for my part, I could not feel greater delight if both the one and the other were my own children, and it is very long since anything of the kind has given me so much pleasure.'[1]

Three days later another of Ippolita's kinswomen, who happened to be an old friend of Madonna Luigia, and had herself many years before proposed a marriage for Baldassare, wrote in the same cordial terms. This was Alda Boiarda, the Marchesana Isabella's favourite maid of honour, who had been lately banished from court by the Marquis, and compelled to retire to Ferrara, where her sister Laura was a nun in the convent of Corpus Christi.

' I learn from your letter of the marriage which you have concluded for your only son, Messer Baldassare, which news gives me the greatest joy ; and Suor Laura, to whom I have shown V. S.'s letter, also feels the utmost satisfaction at this good news. From being friends we have become relatives, and accordingly we rejoice with you as well as with M. Baldassare, and are very glad to hear that he is to wed Madonna Ippolita, who is, I am told, a lovely girl, rich in dowry, and also sweet and gentle, as I learn from a friend of mine in Modena who knows her. And Suor Laura and I pray God and Christ and His Mother, the glorious Virgin Mary, to keep you and

---

[1] Cod. Vat. Lat., 8212.

your son and daughter-in-law eternally happy and joyous together with us, your most faithful relatives.

'ALDA BOIARDA COMITISSA.'

But the most touching of all the congratulatory letters addressed to the happy pair on this occasion, and still preserved in the Vatican archives, was one from the bride's cousin Angelica, the beautiful daughter of Giovanni Gonzaga, who had taken the veil in the convent of Corpus Christi at Mantua, together with the Marchesana's daughter Paola and Castiglione's own sister Laura. The news of Ippolita's marriage had reached the gentle nun, thanks to the thoughtfulness of Baldassare's mother, and Suor Angelica hastened to assure the little bride of her best wishes and fondest prayers for her welfare.

'MAGNIFICENT MADONNA AND MOST HONOURED SISTER,—The peace of Him who rules the whole universe has deigned to lay His protecting hand on your footsteps, and as He has given your life so good a beginning, He will, I doubt not, conduct it to a happy ending. This I conclude from your espousals with the house of Castiglione, and since I have not had any opportunity of intimacy with you, owing to our living so far apart, from our tenderest years, my dear and honoured Madonna Luigia has kindly informed me of this happy union, with what joy, dearest sister, I can hardly tell you, feeling that you are to belong to this her only son. If you are what I believe you to be, you will, I am sure, be her heart's delight. And I rejoice with you, my sister, to think you should wed so noble a cavalier as M. Baldassare, a man who is spoken of to-day as one above all others for his talents and charms, as well as for his beauty. And I do not think anyone can be his equal. So I rejoice with you, and cannot think that this marriage has been arranged by any but the hand of God. And I must write to you, seeing that you are so nearly related to me by blood.

'Your dear sister,

'SUOR ANGELICA DA GONZAGA.'[1]

The fame of the brilliant Count had, it appears, already penetrated these convent shades, and the news of his marriage to a maiden so closely related to herself, stirred the gentle soul of the young nun. Although Suor Angelica had herself been early taken from the world to become the bride of Christ, she had, it is plain, kept a lively remembrance of this peerless knight in her heart, and rejoiced the more in his union to her kinswoman. The lives of the two cousins who exchanged these affectionate greetings offered a strange contrast. Ippolita married at fifteen, and died four years later, before she was quite twenty. Suor Angelica took the veil while still a child, and spent her whole life within the walls of the same convent. She was chosen Abbess of her community five times, and outlived most of the men and women of her generation, dying in 1570, full of years and sanctity.[2]

[1] Cod. Vat. Lat., 8213; Cian, 'Candidature Nuziali,' 40. Appendix XXXII.–XXXIV.

[2] Donesmondi, 'Storia Eccl. di Mantova,' ii. 230.

CHAPTER XXVII

1516

The Pope begins proceedings against the Duke of Urbino—Death of Giuliano de' Medici—Castiglione in Rome—The Duchess Elisabetta at the Vatican—Excommunication and deprivation of Francesco Maria—Invasion of Urbino—Flight of the Duke and Duchesses to Mantua—Lorenzo de' Medici proclaimed Duke of Urbino.

THE doom of Urbino was sealed at Bologna. Francis I. had finally sacrificed his old ally to the ambitious schemes of the Medici, and Leo X. and his nephew returned to Florence resolved to put their deep-laid plot into immediate execution. On January 27 Marin Zorzi, the Venetian ambassador who had accompanied the Pope to Florence, wrote home:

'The Pope has begun important proceedings against the Duke of Urbino, and means to deprive him of his State. He brings two charges against him. One that he murdered the Cardinal of Pavia; the other, that he refused to fight after he had taken the Church's money.'[1]

In vain the Duke appealed for help to friendly powers. The only monarch who made any attempt to save him was the Emperor Maximilian, who wrote from Trent desiring the Pope to abstain from attacking this loyal vassal of his grandson Charles,

[1] Sanuto, xxi. 496.

who in January had succeeded to the crown of Spain and Naples.[1]

But although Maximilian himself led an army across the Alps to oppose the French and Venetians, the ill-success which attended his arms left him powerless to help the Duke, and the good offices of the Constable of Bourbon, who as Viceroy of Milan generously interceded with the Pope on behalf of his cousin's husband, were politely but resolutely declined.[2] In vain Leo X.'s own brother, the being whom he probably loved best in the world, begged him with his dying breath to remember the kindness which he and all his family had received from the princes of Urbino. The Pope turned a deaf ear to Giuliano's repeated entreaties, and told him not to vex his soul with politics, but to try and get well.

On February 6, the first day of Lent, Leo X. attended mass in the Duomo, and after distributing the holy ashes to an immense multitude of people, he went to amuse himself at Poggio. At carnival time Giuliano was dangerously ill, and the doctors who attended him despaired of his recovery ; but with the first days of Lent he rallied a little, and for a moment the hopes of the Duke's friends revived. On the 9th the Venetian envoy reported that the Pope was going to drop the enterprise against Urbino, which his nephew Lorenzo had persuaded him to undertake, to please Giuliano, 'who will not have it on any account.' But Lorenzo and his relatives were too strong for him, and the next day the Pope told Cardinal Riario that it was waste of time to argue the case any longer, and that he was

[1] B. Morsolin, ' Vita di Trissino,' 406.
[2] Pastor, iv. 102.

determined to have done with the traitor once and
for all.[1]

Ten days later the Pope returned to Rome, and
sent the Golden Rose to King Francis I. On March 1
he cited Francesco Maria to appear before the tribunal
appointed to try him, on pain of excommunication
and forfeiture of all his honours and estates.   On
the 14th Cardinal Bibbiena, who had remained in
Florence with Giuliano, wrote from the Badia of
Fiesole, where the sick man had been taken for
change of air, that he was much worse.   Three days
afterwards all was over.   'It has pleased God,' wrote
Bibbiena to his old friend Canossa, 'to call back that
blessed soul to a better and quieter place than this.'
And he told the Marchesana Isabella, to whom Giuliano had been deeply attached :

'The Lord God has called this pure soul to Himself, leaving us all in tears and sorrow, although as
yet we can hardly believe that he is gone.   To-day
the funeral rites have been celebrated with due
honour.   All yesterday his body lay in the church
of S. Marco, where you would have thought, from
the crowds assembled there, that this was the most
memorable thing that had ever happened.   I suppose
that for the last hundred years no one has died in
this city who was more universally beloved and whose
death has been more deeply lamented.'[2]

The Cardinal's grief was shared by all the late
Duke's friends in Rome, and most of all by Bembo,
to whom Giuliano had confided his four-year-old child
Ippolito.

'I could not read your touching and affectionate
letter on the death of our good Duke without tears,'

---

[1] Sanuto, xxi. 510 ; Luzio in 'Arch. st. Lomb.,' 1907, 37.
[2] Baschet-Reumont, 249.

wrote the Papal Secretary. 'And how much greater and more reasonable is your grief when we think how infinitely you loved that blessed soul, and how long and close your friendship had been. Oh, how deeply every detail in your letter affected me—most of all the part in which you told me how the sight of his dog Leo moved you to tears. I had Signor Ippolitino for some time in my room yesterday, and in my arms. He is well, but seemed a little melancholy, as if he realized his great loss. I took him to His Holiness, who caressed him fondly. I will see him often, and have him to meals as often as possible.'

In a postscript he adds:

'I have just paid Signor Ippolitino a visit, and thought him looking handsomer and fatter than ever. He begs you to bring him one of those dancing dolls, and clasped me tightly with his little arms when I told him that I kissed him for you.'[1]

The Pope, on his part, was sincerely grieved, but, as Marin Zorzi remarked, 'It is not in his nature to trouble himself long about anything.' A few weeks later he threatened to excommunicate Giuliano's widow if she did not restore the costly jewels given her by his brother.[2]

Castiglione at the time of Giuliano's death was in Rome, vainly employing all the arts of diplomacy to avert the blow that now seemed inevitable. As a last resource, Francesco Maria sent his aunt, the widowed Duchess, to intercede with the Pope on his behalf. This step had been originally suggested by Bibbiena, and was strongly supported by Elisabetta's relatives at Mantua, who felt that, if anything could move the Pope's heart, it would be the influence of

---

[1] 'Lettere,' i. 33.   [2] Sanuto, xx. 79, 231.

this beloved and venerated lady, who had been so good a friend to the exiled Medici.

Accordingly, on the last day of February Elisabetta Gonzaga arrived in Rome, accompanied by Emilia Pia and a train of ladies and courtiers. The Cardinals and chief officials at the Vatican hastened to pay their respects to the Duchess and assure her of their good-will. Bembo and Sadoleto visited their honoured friends, and l' Unico Aretino delivered his most eloquent improvisations in Elisabetta's presence, and once more professed himself her devoted slave.

On March 1 the Duchess was admitted into the Pope's presence and received with great affability. His Holiness went to meet her, embraced her affectionately, and expressed his pleasure at seeing her in Rome, but said that he was too much engaged to discuss political affairs. At the second audience which she obtained, the Duchess implored His Holiness to forgive her nephew, but the Pope only replied that Francesco was a traitor, and must be punished. On March 10 she made a third, but equally ineffectual attempt to soften Leo's heart.

To-day,' wrote the Mantuan envoy, Carlo Agnello, 'the Lady Duchess has been with the Pope for the third time. This time His Holiness was more severe and implacable than ever, changing the subject repeatedly, and only remaining firm on one point—namely, his determination to punish the Duke, in which he is as firm and immovable as a rock.'[1]

Yet three days later the brave lady returned to the charge, and, gathering courage, reminded the Pope of the hospitality which he and the Magnifico had received at her late husband's court. She recalled

[1] Baschet-Reumont, 248.

the days when she nursed his nephew Lorenzino in her arms, and when they prayed together that the Medici might be restored to their own. 'Surely you, who know what this means, Holy Father,' she said with touching earnestness, 'will not drive us out of house and home, and force us to wander in exile and beggary through the world?' But the Pope did not utter a word in reply. He only looked at the Duchess through his eyeglass and shrugged his shoulders. And, in obedience to his orders, neither the secretaries nor Cardinals in attendance addressed a word to her as she left his presence.[1]

Luigi Gonzaga of Castelgoffredo, whom Isabella sent to Rome to intercede with the Pope on her behalf, met with no better success. The Pope held long and confidential interviews with him, laughed and joked on every kind of subject, and assured him of his affection for the Marchesana and reluctance to injure any of her kindred. But all that either he or the Duchess were able to obtain was the prorogation of the sentence of excommunication, with which the Duke was threatened, until after the Easter festival.[2] Then came the news of Giuliano's death, and the Pope left Rome for his villa of La Magliana, and went to hunt in the forests of Palò, on the Mediterranean shore.

Elisabetta decided to spend Easter in Rome, in the hope that affairs might take a more favourable turn, and Castiglione, who had left no stone unturned on his master's behalf, enjoyed a brief interval of repose.

The letters addressed by Bembo to Cardinal Bibbiena this Easter give us pleasant glimpses of the

---

[1] Cesareo in 'N. Antologia,' 1898, p. 194.
[2] Luzio in 'Arch. st. Lomb.,' 1907, p. 51.

way in which the Count enjoyed his brief hours of leisure during these anxious days.

'To-morrow,' wrote the Papal Secretary on April 3, ' I go with Navagero and Beazzano, and with M. Baldassare Castiglione and Raphael, to visit Tivoli, where I have only been once—twenty-seven years ago ! We shall see both the old and the new, and all that is beautiful in the country round. I go to please M. Andrea [the Venetian scholar and diplomat, Navagero], who leaves for Venice the day after Pasquino [the Feast of St. Mark, April 25].'

And he adds in a postscript :

' Yesterday His Holiness prorogued the interdict against the Duke of Urbino for another week.'

Again, on the 19th, after saying he has been to visit the Duchess of Urbino, and found l' Unico Aretino as devoted to her as ever, Bembo mentions both Raphael and Castiglione :

' Raphael, who commends himself reverently to you, has painted our Tebaldeo so naturally that in this picture he is more exactly himself than he is in reality. I, for my part, never saw so excellent a likeness. V. S. may imagine what M. Antonio says and thinks of this ; and, indeed, he has every reason to be a proud man. The portrait of M. Baldassare Castiglione or that of our good and never-to-be-forgotten Duke, whom may God receive, might have been painted by the hand of one of Raphael's scholars, so inferior are they in point of likeness, compared with this of Tebaldeo. I feel very envious, and really think I must be painted myself some day.

' I had written thus far, when Raphael came in, as if he had guessed that I was writing about him, and begged me to give you this message, which is that he hopes you will send him the other subjects that are to be painted in your little cabinet, or, rather, the inscriptions for the pictures, because those which you sent him before will be finished this week. *Per Dio!* this is no joke, for now M. Baldassare has arrived, and says I am to tell you that he intends to spend this summer in Rome, not to spoil a good habit, and more especially because M. Antonio Tebaldeo wishes it.'[1]

But the joyous freedom of these days was soon ended. M. Baldassare was required to attend to sterner duties. Only the day before he had been to La Magliana for a last interview with the Pope, as he told his lord in the following letter:

' In order that V. E. may understand the situation fully, I must tell you that to-day I once more begged His Beatitude to give us a further respite, explaining that the Duchess desired more time to discuss these matters. Upon which he replied that the delays were nothing but a trick to blind him, and that he would grant no more. I returned that the delays might have been numerous, but that they were certainly short, that there had been no time to send messengers, and that the marriage proposals which I had made could not be entertained without some delay. To this he replied that his honour could not be satisfied unless V. E. came here, as he said before. I endeavoured to show him that V. E. had good reason to be afraid of coming here, as the situation was so serious, and defended your action with all the words and reasons that I could call to mind. At the end he said that V. E. would never trust him until you realized how much His Holiness might have done to injure you, and had refrained from doing, and that he could never trust V. E. unless you gave him this proof of confidence. He was content to promise the Lady Duchess, the Marquis,

[1] ' Lettere,' i. 33-35.

and as many Cardinals as you liked, that you would be safe, by word of mouth, but not in writing, adding that if he wished to deceive you he would do it by bulls and briefs, but that you could believe his words. He further promised that V. E. should be unhurt and safe, and told me that you would be blessed if you came, and that every one who is your friend and servant, ought to advise you to come, saying that anyone who does otherwise is a fool. He said much more in this strain, and I replied much more, by way of excuse and in explanation of the difficulties in your way, and in the end he consented to sanction the delay for which we asked, if the Duchess would promise that V. E. would come. If not, we need not think of it. The matter is so important that it is impossible for a servant to give advice. V. E. must decide as seems best to your own wise and prudent judgment. I kiss your hand, and remain,

'Your devoted servant,

'BALD. CASTIGLIONE.

'ROME, *April* 18, 1516.'[1]

It is clear from this letter that Castiglione realized the gravity of the situation, and did not venture to advise the Duke to trust himself into the hands of the Medici. Elisabetta was still more convinced that it was useless to attempt to propitiate the Pope, as she told her nephew in a letter which Castiglione sent to Urbino with his own, by express, that evening:

'I am certain, from what our best friends say, that the Pope is bent on this undertaking and hopes to find you unprepared. To-morrow I will go to La Magliana and take leave of His Holiness, and then return at once to share your fate and that of the Duchess.'

True to her word, the next morning the good Duchess once more undertook the long journey to La Magliana,

[1] Archivio Gonzaga, Carteggio di Castiglione ; Martinati, 78.

and was received by Leo X. in a farewell audience.
This time he quite refused to listen to her prayers, and
told her curtly she must send the Duke at once to
the Vatican, or it would be the worse for him.   Already the villa was bristling with armed men, and as
Elisabetta left the Pope's presence she saw Lorenzino
and his captains waiting in the hall.   Even the
Duke's enemies, wrote the Mantuan envoy, could not
restrain their pity and admiration at the distress of
this noble lady, whose tears would have melted the
most savage heart.[1]

These letters from Castiglione and the Duchess,
decided Francesco's course of action. He wrote to
his father-in-law, enclosing Elisabetta's account of
her last ineffectual efforts to soften the Pope, and
begging the Marquis for help in the defence of his
dominions.   At the same time he wrote to Castiglione from Pesaro, acknowledging his letter, and
saying that, if it were not a case of risking his life,
he would have hastened to throw himself at the
feet of His Holiness, but that, as it was, he felt it
best to ask his father the Marquis to intercede with
the Pope on his behalf.   He ended by desiring the
Count to assure the Holy Father that he would
always remain his good and faithful servant, and was
ready to sacrifice everything at his bidding, 'saving,'
he added significantly, 'my life and freedom, as I
have said above.'[2]   But the Pope was in no mood to
brook delay, and on August 27 he published the bull
by which Francesco was excommunicated and deprived of all his States and honours. That week the
Duchess left Rome attended by Castiglione. Hardly
had she reached home before the Papal and Florentine
forces, under the command of Lorenzo de' Medici and

[1] Luzio, p. 70.   [2] Martinati, 79.

Renzo da Ceri, invaded Urbino. 'His Holiness,' wrote Carlo Agnello sadly, 'is making such extreme preparations for this campaign that we can only expect to see the utter destruction of this poor young Duke of Urbino.'[1]

Nothing was left Francesco but to make a last gallant stand, and this he prepared to do with the help of Alessio Beccaguto, an able captain whom the Marquis had employed to fortify Mantua, and whom he now sent to his son-in-law's assistance. Unfortunately, the Spanish mercenaries whom he had engaged, quarrelled with the Italians, and one of their leaders was slain by order of Luigi Gonzaga, to whom the defence of Pesaro had been entrusted. The Duke hastened to the spot from Urbino, and broke into so violent a passion that Luigi Gonzaga threw up his command on the spot and took boat for Mantua. Urbino was now attacked on three sides by the enemy, and after a vain attempt at resistance, Alessio Beccaguto, finding his ammunition exhausted, threw his guns into the Metauro and retired to Pesaro. On Saturday, May 31, Lorenzo de' Medici entered Urbino without opposition, and most of the other cities in the duchy opened their gates to the victors. That same day the two Duchesses left the palace at Pesaro by a garden door, with only a few attendants. 'The young Madonna,' remarks a citizen of Pesaro who was an eyewitness of their secret flight, 'could hardly walk, and had to be supported by two of her servants.' So the poor ladies climbed the hill on which the church of the Annunziata stands, and descended to the harbour, where ships were in readiness and their most valuable possessions had already been sent on board. A few hours later the

---

[1] Baschet-Reumont, 248.

Duke, seeing further resistance to be useless, joined
them, and the small fleet of seven or eight ships set
sail. But a terrible hurricane sprang up which
scattered the boats and drove them on the Dalmatian
shores, and several days elapsed before a favourable
wind enabled them to reach Ferrara.[1] On June 8
they arrived at Pietole, the birthplace of Virgil, five
miles from Mantua, where the Marchesana had sent
one of her ladies to prepare rooms for the fugitives and
make them as comfortable as she could. Leonora's
little son Guidobaldo had been sent to Mantua the week
before, and was lodged in the Corte Vecchia, in the
apartments of his uncle Federico, who had followed
the King of France over the Alps. But the Marquis
did not venture to receive the exiles at Mantua without permission from the Pope. All he did was to
send a friendly note from Marmirolo to Castiglione,
who had accompanied the ducal family in their flight,
thanking him for the messages which he had brought
from the Duke and Duchesses. In this he expressed
an earnest hope that he might soon be able to satisfy
their wishes and his own love for them, and receive
them either in his country-house or else at Mantua.[2]
So the friends of the exiled Princes crowded out to
the little village on the banks of the Mincio to hear
the tales of the travellers' adventures, and wept while
the gentle Elisabetta told them how unkindly the
Pope had treated her, or listened with delight to the
spirited language in which her little grandson chal-
lenged his father's foes.[3]

Meanwhile Lorenzo de' Medici had made an easy
conquest of the Duke's State. With the exception

[1] Sanuto, xxi. 310.
[2] Archivio Gonzaga, Carteggio di Castiglione.
[3] Luzio e Renier, ' Mantova,' 228, 229.

of the Rocca of Pesaro, which did not surrender till July, and the strong fortress of S. Leo, where the Duke's nephew, young Sigismondo Varano, gallantly held the enemy at bay for more than four months, the whole duchy of Urbino was conquered in a few days. By June 6, the news reached Rome, and both here and in Florence the Pope and his family celebrated their triumph with fireworks and illuminations. On August 18, a bull was issued by which Lorenzo was proclaimed Duke of Urbino, Prefect of Sinigaglia, and Gonfaloniere of the Church. This document was signed by all the members of the Sacred College, excepting the best and most learned among them, Cardinal Grimani, the Venetian Bishop of Urbino, who had alone dared oppose the Pope in this matter, and who, rather than commit so great a wrong, left Rome, never to return until after Leo's death.[1]

The only concession which the Marquis of Mantua could obtain from the Pope was permission for the exiled Princes to live in his dominions. Accordingly, at the end of August, the two Duchesses took up their abode in the Corte Vecchia, where they spent the next five years, often reduced to great straits, and compelled to pawn their jewels and melt down their finest plate, while the Duke exhausted his resources in vain attempts to recover his patrimony.

The greatest sympathy was felt on all sides for the widowed Duchess, who was driven into exile for the second time in her life, and there were many who, not without reason, compared the Medici to the Borgias. 'The Pope's nephew Lorenzo,' remarked Marin Zorzi, whose reports reflected current opinion in Rome at this time, 'is astute and capable of great things. He is not equal to Valentino, but is little

---

[1] Sanuto, xxi. 323, etc. ; Pastor, iv. 107 ; Alberi, iii. 56.

Photo, Brogi.

LORENZO DE' MEDICI, DUKE OF URBINO.

BY ALLORI (UFFIZI).

To face p. 430, Vol. I.

inferior to him. . . .   He has made himself lord of
Florence, and what he wills is law.'[1]   The new
Duke's haughty airs made him everywhere un-
popular.   He walked through the streets clad in
rich clothes and attended by hundreds of followers,
and openly declared that he meant to wed a bride
of royal birth and take his place among the crowned
heads of Europe.   At the French court the young
Queen Claude listened with tears in her eyes
to Federico Gonzaga's touching account of the
sufferings endured by the two Duchesses, and both
she and her mother-in-law, Louise of Savoy, wrote
pressing letters to the Pope, begging him to allow
the exiles to live in peace at Mantua.   Even
Francis I., who had reluctantly sacrificed Francesco
Maria for reasons of political expediency, made no
secret of his dislike for the Pope's nephew.   When
the Papal bull was issued, he sent Lorenzo a civil
letter of congratulation, but a few weeks afterwards
he remarked to the Ferrarese envoy : ' This is all
Lorenzo's doing, and he is as proud of himself as he
can be ; but he is only a simpleton who plays at being
a captain and a great man, and boasts of these
conquests which have not cost him a single man or a
drop of blood, and wishes to make himself lord of all
Italy.   But if he has any sense he will be content
with this one State of Urbino—I doubt myself if he
will ever manage to keep it !—for remember, after all,
he is only a merchant !'[2]

[1] Alberi, iii. 51.   [2] Nitti, 81 ; Verdi, 27.

APPENDIX

A SELECTION OF UNPUBLISHED DOCUMENTS

I.

Giovanni Stefano Castiglione to Cristoforo Castiglione.

MAGNIFICE ac prestantissime eques et affinis honorandissime: Questo povero homo Bartholomeo da Castiliono vene da la V. M. sperando che quella gli habia a fare una elymosina di quella obligatione che l' ha da lui la quale invero sera una elymosina fiorita per essere lui constituito in extrema necessita et bisogno, e ha a fare cun quello suo cognato el quale per essere stato sua securita di epsa obligatione gli tiene occupato tuto quello che l' ha in questo mondo, si che ben che sapia di quanta bonta sia la V. M. nondimeno m' è parso di scrivergle (*sic*) queste poche parole e ricomandargli epso Bartholomeo, pregando la V. M. sia contenta di liberarlo da quello suo cognato che in vero sera una opera tanto pietosa quanto alcuna altra che potesse fare la V. M.

Ceterum facio intendere a la V. M. como Messer Baldessaro suo figliolo sta bene et è molto ben visto dal nostro Illmo S^{re} e uniuersalmente da tuti e meritamente per che in vero non poria essere ne piu gentile ne piu virtuoso quante è, la V. M. ha a fare pensiero di acompagnarlo qui a Milano e fare qualche parentado honorevole e sera a consolatione de la V. M. e de tuti li suoi parenti. A la V. M. di continuo mi racomando. Mediolani 2 februarij 1499.

M^{tie}. V. affinis JO STEPHANUS DE CASTILIONO.

Mag^{co} ac prestanti equiti affini et tan-
quam patri honoran. Dño Cristho-
foro de Castiliono ec. Mantue. *Cito.*

[Cod. Vat. Lat., 8210, f. 7, partly printed in Cian, Candidature nuziali,' p. 15.]

II.

Baldassare Castiglione to Luigia Castiglione.

Magnifica ac generosa domina et Mater honoranda : Pe-
haver io poco fa scritto a la M. V. non mi extendero molto in
questa · per non haver cosa alcuna nova : Nui stiamo bene
tutti per la Dio gratia : prego la M. V. che dia bon recapito a
le alligate : e me scriva de le cose di la : e come si sta : che si fa
da le bande di la : e come stanno gli amici nostri : Nove qua
sonno impertinente a nui : gran cosa è Roma. Prego la M. V.
che stia sana edi bona voglia : e me racomandi a tutti li nostri :
a quella continue mi racomando : Da Antonius haverete per
otto da ascoltare. Romæ 16 Martii 1503.

Obediens Filius
BALDESAR.

Mag^{ce} ac generose Dm̄e Aloisie de Castiglione Matri honor. Mantue.

[Cod. Vat. Lat., 8210, f. 7.]

III.

Baldassare Castiglione to Luigia Castiglione.

Magnifica ac generosa Domina et Mater honoranda : Credo
che la M. V. a questi di habia hauta una mia littera : cun
la quale era alligata una a Messer Nicolò Phrisia la quale man-
dai per la via di Ferrara : pero non replicaro altramente le cose
ditte in quella. Hora mando el mulatero cun un mulo, e quatro
mazze di fichi : se qui fosse qualche altra cosa meglio, piu
voluntier la mandaria : la M. V. se dignara farne parte a
Mª Polissena e Mª Francescha et a sor Laura. E perche
adesso è la quadragesima io voglio confessare el mio peccato :
che questi fichi io li do ad usura : perche aspetto che la M. V.
mi rimandi qualche salami over caso, cioe formazo, Mª Polissena el medemo : Mª Francescha anchor lei o qualche gelatina
de cotogni : over altri frutti confetti di zucharo : Da la Matre
sor Laura non voglio altro che orationi : maxime adesso che
pur l' andata mia de Inghilterra serà, non interuenendo altro,
come ho speranza in Dio. Se la M. V. harà hauti quelli forceri
da Milano : harò molto caro che la me li mandi.

Oltra questo : se quelli maestri de legnami del borgo haves-sino fatta una mia cassetta ch' io gli ordinai già millanni fa, harei caro haverla per el presente latore.

Anchor perche vorei far qualche coperta de tela per li cavalli, serei contento, che la M. V. mi mandasse quella tela che li resta de quella trabacha vechia, che la mi satisfaria.

Quando ero a Ferrara scrissi a la M. V. che volesse mandarmi panno negro per un paro di calce : a questo la non mi rispose. Vorei hora che la me lo mandasse, ma non bruno : che piu mi piaceria biancho. Vorei ben ch' el fosse bello : e tanto che le calce se potessino fare : e piu presto ne avanzasse un poco che ne manchasse :

La M. V. non harà altro fastidio del Rosso. Io de le cose mie di la non ne scrivo ne dimando a la M. V. perche la vedo tanto timida che la non osa parlare : pur harei caro sapere come le succedano, e se mai se aquietato niente, ne vsato meglior o mancho triste parole di me.

Subito fatto pasqua lo Illmo S^r prefetto credo venirà a Mantua : Questi servitori del Sr Ducca per la piu parte li faranno com-pagnia. Io non, ne alhor ne poi fin che non sapia e non veda esser meglio visto e piu raconosciuto che hora non sono. Qui per la Dio gratia tutti stiamo bene e in pace. La S^{ra} Duchessa ogni modo prima che passi quaresima andrà a Roma. Altro nui non havimo qui de novo ; qualche cosa anchor potrà dire el Rosso a boccha. Aspetto ogni modo che la M. V. mi mandi qualche bon salame : perche qui sono molto in precio e piaceno molto a la Excellentia del Sig^r nostro : et io harei molto caro potergene far gustare. E quando vegniranno in qua, per non paghar dacio se potrà vsar questo modo che usato io de haver una patente che para vengano de lo Illmo Sr Marchese ouer Madamma al S^r duca qui : se pur questa gratia se po impe-trare. Racordo a la M. V. quelli dinari de Messer Timotheo. Credo anchor mandar a la M. V. quelle sopraveste vechie, pur non so certo.

Io facio pensier quando monsignor mio R^{mo} de Mantua serà qui cun noi, ringratiare sua S^{ria} R^{ma} del bon animo suo verso nui : e del accettar mio fratello quando non fosse altro rispetto : e pregarla che sia contenta ch' io gli trovi vn altro patrone : cun mille belle parole. Poi andando a Roma, come ogni modo mi serà necessario per la andata de Inghilterra, so certo che li

troverò patrone : pigliarò anchor bon partito de veder la M. V.
ogni modo : a la quale continue mi racomando. Di questa mia
andata la M.V. non ne parli. Urbini 5 Martii M.DVI.

La S^ra Duchessa mia Sig^ra se racomanda a la M. V. a M^a
Polissena, et a sua comatre, le alligate io le racomando :

De V. M. obed. fil.

Bald. Cast.

[Cod. Vat. Lat., 8210, f. 61.]

IV.

Baldassare Castiglione to Luigia Castiglione.

Magnifica ac generosa Domina et Mater honoranda : La
lettera de la M. V. portata per el Rosso, io la ho hauta qui in
Roma, dove hor sono per alcune mie cosette, e sonovi stato
diece di e starolli fin a quatro di anchora : poi venirò ad
Urbino : poi presto venirò verso a Lombardia per andar al mio
viaggio. Le robe che ha portato el Rosso non le ho viste, ma
intendo ogni cosa essere agionta. Io non responderò a tutte le
parte : perche pochi di fa io scrissi per un messo del Sr Giohanni
assai diffusamente : non so se la lettera sia capitata : pur dove
la M. V. dice che qualche volta bisognaria tenere la briglia in
mano, e non voler estimarsi d' haver piu che non s' ha : e veramente a me non pare meritar questa imputatione : che se la
M. V. considera cun quante bocche e cun quanti cavalli io son
visso hormai dui anni e dove sono visso : la vederà ch' io non
ho cussi alargato la mano comegli pare : e se la considera
quello che la spende lei a Mantua : doue non li bisogna com-
prare ne pane ne vino, ne legne, ne biave da cavalli e stando
in casa sua : et io son privo de tutte queste condicioni : la
vederà che io poco posso haver fatto. Et io el so che qualche
volta et spesso mi sono ritrovato non sapere la matina quello
che havesse a cenare la sera : e pur ogni cosa se suporta cun
sforzo de non perder quel poco de reputatione che s' è aqui-
stata : non già facendo el signore ne 'l gran maestro : ch' io non
lo so fare ne lo facio. Vero che non nego che qualche cosa de
le mie non potessino andar piu ordinate : niente di meno non
è desordine notabile : hor di questo non dirò piu. Venendo io
li provedero oportunamente a Bastiano. Credo che la mia

venuta serà presta : ma per essermi stato fatto cussi bel saluto a l' altra volta io non vorei venire nel paese de lo Illmo Sr Marchese di Mantua, per non mostrare de estimar poco la volunta sua, ma el parer mio seria de venir a Gazolo dove la M. V. volendo potesse trasferirse : et io li la vederia molto voluntiera. Circa questo la prego la se degni avisarmi cio che li pare : perch' io di quel modo mi governarò :

Non scrivo a Mad. Francescha ne a Messer Thomaso per non haver tempo : la M. V. se degni racomandarmi a loro e ringratiarli del suo presente che mi è stato carissimo : a quella sempre mi racomando.   Rome 28 Aprilis M.DVI.

Obed. F. Bal. Castilione.

[Cod. Vat. Lat., 8210, f. 63.]

V.

Baldassare Castiglione to Luigia Castiglione.

Magnifica ac generosa Domina et Mater honoranda : Per la lettera ch' io scrivo el Mag^{co} Messer Zo. Pedro V. M. intenderà cio che qui se è fatto circa lo andar mio : si che havendo risposta o no, o bona, o trista, spero vedere la M. V. a Casatico o vero a Gazolo.   Trovar quella scusa del non andare a Mantua per la peste credo sia superfluo : maxime qui, perche tutto questo stato fa che lo Illmo Sr Marchese non volse ch' io andasse a Mantua, senza altre circumloqutioni : e credo ch' el medemo si sapia a Mantua.   Io metto a ordine per venire e presto : si che non serò piu longo : solo mi racomando a la M. V. et a tutti li nostri : Urbini xxij Maij M.DVI.

De V. M. obe. figliolo
Bal. Castilione.

[Cod. Vat. Lat., 8210, f. 64.]

VI.

Baldassare Castiglione to Luigia Castiglione.

Magnifica ac generosa Domina et Mater honoranda : Non so se la M. V. harà questa prima over quella che è portata per Messer Nicolò nostro, che viene col cavallo.   El quale è stato et è causa de mio fastidio assai : pur per haverne tollerato de

molto magiori tollerarò anchor questo. Prego anchor la M. V.
a non ne haver despiacere alcuno : che forsi è per el meglio
che la vadi cussi : et io me lo persuado. Quella sella che è sopra
detto cavallo e li guarnimenti tutti e la testera : e quella
coperta de panno : prego la M. V. che li voglia far governare
cun diligentia e maxime la sella : che li ferri non arruginis-
chano : el cavallo se rimanderà secundo che nui lo havessimo :
excetto che forsi de la sanità. La M. V. intendera da Scaramella
el progresso de queste cose : io mi partiro ogni modo dimane
piacendo a Dio cun speranza d' haver bon viaggio. Lasso
Francescho qui : el quale aspettarà quello famiglio che ha
menato in la lo cavallo : poi tutti dui mi agiongeranno : e spero
per loro haver littere da la M. V. et anchor da Vrbino che le
desidero assai. Altre lettere per el tempo che ha a venire se
seranno indrizate in casa de li Vismari, ouer de Monsig^r de la
Torre, me veranno drieto. Mando a Mad. Francescha un
ventaglio : e non ge lo ho mandato prima perche mi creda
ch' el racordo fosse fatto per lei : tanto erio balordo : pur la
S^{ra} Mª Margaritta lo mandava a lei : a la quale quando vn altra
volta Mª Francescha scriverà, me piaceria piu ch' el soprascritto
dicesse : Sig^{ra} mia honoranda : che maiore mia honor. avegna
ch' el sia picolo errore, pur a me piaceria cussi. Questo
ventaglio a me par molto bello : lei si tenga quale la vole,
avegna che hormai le mosche siano per dar poco fastidio secundo
me. Non serò piu longo. Solo mi racomando senza fine a la
M. V. et a tutti li nostri senza nominar ad uno ad uno.
Mediolani 3 Septembris M.D.VI.

De V. M. obe. fi.
B. K. (sic).

Le alligate ad Urbino harei a caro che andassino bene e
fidatamente ma non per messo a posta : pur fidatamente per
amor de Dio : alcuno del Cardinale seria bono s' el non è partito.

Post scripta : Io ho preso un poco de securtà cun la S^{ra} M.
Margaritta de aprire la lettera che li scrive Mª Francescha : e
parmi che la non habia ben inteso ciò ch' io scrissi : che è che
Mª Margaritta mandava lei a donarli quello ventaglio e veli :
ch' io non ne paghai niente : pur questo ventaglio adesso lo
mando io.

[Cod. Vat. Lat., 8210, f. 68.]

VII.

Baldassare Castiglione to Luigia Castiglione.

Magnifica ac generosa Domina et Mater honoranda : Ho recevuto una lettera de la M. V. de 27 de agosto : per la quale ho inteso—benche prima lo hauesse presentito—la morte de quel povero figlioletto de Messer Jacomo : e benche el mi para che Dio ne visiti molto spesso in tante e varie cose, pur lo ringratio : et assai mi dole de Messer Jacomo e Mᵃ Polisenna : li quali credo che siano molto afflitti : non piu di questo. Io mando per Messer Nicolò nostro li veli che in ultimo la M. V. me richiede, quelli altri cun el ventaglio, la Illustre Mᵃ Margaritta Sanseverina li mandò lei a donare a Mᵃ Francescha, intendendo ch' io ge li volea mandare : seria suo debito respondergli vna lettera e ringratiar sua S. Me rincresce del male de Messer Thomaso nostro : La M. V. intenderà da Messer Nicolò nostro de questo cavallo benedetto che Dio volesse ch' io non l' hauesse mai visto per mia ventura : e del tutto la ge darà indubitata fede. Questo familio che lo conduce a mano : vorei ch' el tornasse subito subito : e che la M. V. acio ch' el potesse tornare piu presto li facesse havere un roncino : el quale io farò che serà remandato per la via di Crema : ne mi curo che costui stia aspettare ch' el cavallo sia apresentato a lo Illᵐᵒ Sⁱ Marchese : ma come l' è a Casatico harei caro che la M. V. lo spazzasse in qua : poi mandare el cavallo a Mantua in compagnia de Messer Nicolò per Carletto, ouer altro che paresse in proposito : e la M. V. me avisi se la harà inteso cosa alcuna de questo cavallo che habia detto el Sʳ Marchese. Altro non mi occorre per hora : se non infinitamente racomandarmi a quella e pregarla che la se sforci de star sana e di bon animo : perch' io non potrei haver cosa al mundo che piu desiderasse de questa. Messer Nicolò suplirà a bocha : ov' io mancho nel scrivere. Mediolani 3 Septembris M.D.VI.

De V. M. obediente Figliolo
Baldasar Castilione.

[Cod. Vat. Lat., 8210, f. 69.]

VIII.

Baldassare Castiglione to Luigia Castiglione.

Magnifica ac generosa Domina et Mater honoranda. Avegna ch' io non sapia come presto o tardi sia per venir questa lettera a la M. V. pur scrivo : facendoli intendere come io ho hauta la sua portata per Franchesco el qual me ha agionto qui a Lione dove hor sono sano per la Dio gratia e sono stato fermo quatro giorni per lassar reposare li cavalli : che haveano pur un poco temuto el passar de monti. Domatina piacendo a Dio me partiro per el camino nostro. Credo che la M. V. habia hauto una mia lettera portata per Scaramella : et insieme un ventaglio per M* Franchescha : per questa non replicarò le cose sevitte in quella. Me piace assai che Messer Thomaso nostro stia bene : e dolmi de Messer Jacomo assai e de M* Polisenna : bisogna che anchor loro portino in pace li despiaceri inevitabili. Io non so che cosa de qui per scriuere a la M. V. de le cose che di la accaddino : la non se ne pigli affanno alcuno : che se la fortuna e cussi mutabile come se dice a nui sta aspettar hormai qualche prosperità : io mi racomando infinitamente a la M. V. el medemo fanno tutti questi nostri : e la supplico che la voglia sforzarsi star sana : e racomandarmi a tutti li nostri : maxime a sor Laura. In Lione 20 Septembris M.D.VI.

De V. M. Obed^{mo}
Fi. Ba. Casti.

[Cod. Vat. Lat., 8210, f. 70, partly printed by Serassi, ' Lettere,' i. 27.]

IX.

Baldassare Castiglione to Luigia Castiglione.

Magnifica ac generosa Domina et Mater honoranda. Per contento de la M. V. li aviso come io son gionto qui a Lione per Dio gratia galiardo e sano : e presto spero esser li : riser-uandomi di dire el resto a bocha. A la M. V. mi racomando di core : Da Lione xxvj de genaro MDVII.

De V. Mag^{cia} Obed. Figliolo
Bal. Castilione.

[Cod. Vat. Lat., 8210, f. 72.]

X.

Tolomeo Spagnoli to Baldassare Castiglione.

Magnifico messer Baldesar: Mi alegro dil felice et honorato ritorno di V. M^{tia} quanto forsi pochi amici l' habbia. La risposta havuta dal N. Illmo S. circa il caso suo è ch' el si contenta che per qualchi di la possi venir a Casatico a reveder la M^{ca} M^a sua matre come receva la M^{tia} V. la quale prego non resti de commandarmi, ogni volta che la possi seruire : che mi reputarò recever magior beneficio servendola, che se fossi io servito da altri in cosa desyderatissima.   Et a lei sempre mi raccomando : Mantuae xiij Februarii M.D.vii.

M. V. deditus Ptolemeus.

Magnifico Equiti maiori hon. D$\bar{n}$o
    Baldesari Castiglioneo.

[Cod. Vat. Lat., 8211, f. 495.]

XI.

Baldassare Castiglione to Luigia Castiglione.

Magnifica ac generosa Domina et Mater honoranda : La M. V. intenderà come io per Dio son gionto sano e salvo qui a Bologna dove ho trovato la S^{tà} del nostro S^{re} el Sr Duca e tutti dui hozi son partiti de qui.   Io li seguirò dimane, ne credo poter ritornare in quelle bande fin questa pasqua : perche 'l Sr Duca non se ne cura : Fratanto io harei caro che la M. V. procurasse s' el fosse possibile trovar per qualche via qualche denari per questo mio debito ch' io ho fatto col Vismara che sono 25 ducati d' oro prestati : e poi le robe tolte da lui : poi questo debito cun Monsig^r di Ferrara : so bene che la M. V. non pensa mai ad altro.

Bisognaria che la M. V. facesse che Francescho andasse fin a Milano per far fare una cassetta : e mettervi dentro quelle barde che restorno li : e farle mettere in cassa de li Vismara che le mandassino a Mantua, e certe altre robe, come sa Francescho : e perche 'l Sr Duca ha donato a Monsig^r Sanseverino quello cane che se chiama Mordano e quell' altro che se chiama Bombò, vorei che Francescho ge li conducesse e me racoman-

dasse a sua S^{ria} R^{ma} apresentandoli questa alligata : e a quel
Bombò metta quello collaro d' oro : el suo cordone de seta.

Poi subito ch' el sia tornato, subito vorei ch' el venisse in
qua : e facesse condure quelli muli e se quello che amalato non
serà guarito lassarlo li ; e la soma insieme che mancho è
necessaria : e cussi li tre mei caualli cun bona diligentia e
quello turchetto, del quale harei caro che la M. V. se con-
sigliasse cun Sebastiano, s' el fosse bon cavarli un poco de
sangue, fargelo cavare, a me piaceria, per el longo camino
che nui havimo fatto : non vorei anchor ch' el mangiasse niente
di feno se non biava e palia.

Prego anchor la M. V. che volia sollicitare Maestro Francescho da la Scuola : over Hieronimo suo figliolo de un qualche
puto che habia bona mano da scrivere : che volesse venir a star
meco, come ho ditto a la M. V. altre volte, che ne ho grandissimo bisogno : Altro non scrivo a la M. V. se non che a quella
sempre mi racomando : Bononie xxij Februarii M.DVII.

Di V. M. Obediente Filiolo

BALDASSAR CASTILIONE.

[Cod. Vat. Lat., 8210, f. 74.]

XII.

Baldassare Castiglione to Luigia Castiglione.

Magnifica ac Generosa Domina : et Mr. honor : Da Pedrone
e dal Gobbo ho recevuto quelle robbe tutte che mi scrive la
M. V. che mi sono state gratissime, cosi la ringratio assai : el
nostro Gobbo io ge l' ho perdonata : perche la M. V. lo ha
in protectione : altramente io li insegnava bene : sel e cosi
giovenetto che 'l non sappia andar dal Poggio a Mantua sel
non ha la baila. Evangelista è venuto et emi bisognato darli
quaranta scuti : e cosi ho fatto a quelli che haveano de andar a
Fiorenza : si che quando la M. V. potra mandarmene de li altri :
la mi farà gratia assai, per satisfar a questi bisogni : di questo
non dico altro perche so che la non mancherà de sollicitare : e
quelli del conte Boccherino anchor aspetto : overo sua risposta :
li denari ch' io debbo hauer del Carpegnolo sono molto pochi
per satisfar a questi debiti et anchor mi bisogna manzare : che
li va poco men che un ducato e mezzo al di in spesa per me e per

li cavalli: si che io non mi scordo de chi mi die dar denari.
Aspetto che la M. V. mandi Xtoforo e Smiraldo con quelli
cavalli: avegna ch' io per un altra mia ge lo habbia scritto:
vorei anchor che venisse quello Villanetto allevo di Xtoforo:
potria esser che fino a qualche di le strate se rompissino: e forsi
presto. Conforto anchor assai la M. V. a torre altrotanti homini
come la ha in su l' ara: e far expedire prestissimo de batter e
condur quelle biave: perche dubito che non siano travagli a
Mantua: Dio ci metta la mano: Altro non scrivero alla M. V.
se non che a quella sempre mi raccomando. In Bologna a di
xvᵒ de Julio M.D.X̄.

De V. M. ob. fi.

BAL, CASTILIONE.

[Cod. Vat. Lat., 8210, f. 101.]

XIII.

Francesco, Duke of Urbino, to Baldassare Castiglione.

Magnifice dilectissime noster. In questo punto habbiamo
recevuta questa del locotenente della Marcha la qual vi mandamo acciò potiate mostrarla a chi vi parerà. Quelle del altri
Sʳⁱ Cardinali vi manderemo dietro a questa avisatene delle
scomesse che se sonno poste et a quanto per Cento: et chi
indura l' oppinione delli piu circa il papato. Urbini primo
Martii M̄.D.Xiij.

FRANCISCUS MARIA Dux Urbini

S. R. E. Capitaneus Generalis.

Magᶜᵒ dilᵐᵒ nostro Domino Baldasari
  Castigliono. Romæ, cito, cito.

[Cod. Vat. Lat., 8211, f. 479.]

XIV.

Francesco, Duke of Urbino, to Baldassare Castiglione.

Magnifice dilectissime noster. Avenga questa santa creatione
del pontifice si differisca assai: et che cosa molto importante
non habbiate che scriverne. Non dimeno ce sarà caro intendere
qualchi andamenti di costà: et quanto il potete fare per via de
Bolgetta senza spedire Cavallaro aposta.

La qui annexa a messer Ludovico[1] subito farete dare, et la resposta pigliarete cura di mandarne: perche in essa gli domandamo in presto un suo cavallo molto da noi desiderato. Urbini x Martii M.DXiij.

FRANCISCUS M^A Dux Urbini
S. R. E. Capitaneus Generalis.

[Cod. Vat. Lat., 8211, f. 503.]

XV.

Francesco, Duke of Urbino, to Baldassare Castiglione.

Magnifice dilectissime noster. Havemo recevuta la nostra longa piena de gli progressi del papato, li quali desideravamo assai d' intendere: Non vi potressemo dire la contenteza dil animo nostro recevuta per questa nova: Sperando che la servitu nostra sia da questo bono et S^{mo} S^r ricognosciuta: cosi ne raccomandarete in bona gratia di Sua S^{tà} facendogli intendere che non siamo punto meno desiderosi di servire quella che havessemo la santa memoria di nostro zio, et supplicarla ne voglia comandare come a devotissimo servo che gli semo.

Quanto sia di venire a basciare il piede a sua S^{tà} laudamo come bonissimo il parere vostro e siamo del medesmo: ma perche voi sappete ritrovarne mal il modo dove che venendo alla incoronatione vorressimo fare honore et a Sua S^{tà} et a noi: perche essendoui ancora si poco spatio di tempo si semo resoluti di venire il secondo di de Pasqua: salvo se sua S^{tà} non fosse d' altro parere · che havendo bisogno di noi subito exequiremo il suo comandamento; però ne avisarete sopra ciò il volere di quella: standovi a memoria che ne saria dannosa assai il venire prima della incoronatione.

Appresso havevamo commesso ad Horatio che del servitio nostro con la Camera appostolica dovesse farne non so che in nostro servitio, hora intendemo il R^{mo} di Mantua havere levato il mandamento di xx^m ducati pensando retenerli per conti di messer Gal. da Pesaro. Il che ne piace assai: ma voressemo pur intendere come è passata questa cosa. Però ne darete

[1] Lodovico di Canossa.

aviso: accio non siamo ignoranti delle cose proposte. Urbini
xiiij Marzo M.D.Xiij.

Franciscus M Dux Urbini

S. R. E. Capitaneus Generalis.

[Cod. Vat. Lat., 8211, f. 504.]

XVI.

Francesco, Duke of Urbino, to Baldassare Castiglione.

Messer Baltassare amantissimo. N' è stato gratissimo intendere per la vostra che li sia qualche speranza de cavare bon
constructo, sì delli conti vecchi como etiam del Quartarone.
Il che etiam ne replica ser Gabriello. Laudamo l' opera
vostra et summa diligentia, exhortandove quel tempo che
serete li a non desistere de tale impresa, che sapete quanto
sia nostro utile et interesse. Preterea perche Horatio ne
dimanda licentia de venire da noi per qualche di, ve piacera
interim supplire in tenerne de continuo advisato delle nove de
quella Corte et sopra tucto mantenerne in bona gratia del
summo Pontifice et racomandarne alli soi S^{mi} Piedi et bene
valete. Pisauri x Maii M.D.xiij.

Fr. Mª Dux Urbini

ac S. R. E. Cap^s generalis.

[Cod. Vat. Lat., 8211, f. 505.]

XVII.

Francesco, Duke of Urbino, to Baldassare Castiglione.

Messer Baldassare: Havemo recevuto la lettera vostra et
veduto quanto voi ne scrivite circa li crediti nostri quali
habbiamo designati al R^{mo} Mons^{re} de Mantua. Vi respondemo
havere preso, et pigliare tanto dispiacere quanto sia possibile a
dire che Mon^{re} el thesauriero ce manchi de la fede sua: quale
non solum ha dato a noi: et ce l' ha mandata a dare fin qua:
et etiam ha data tante volte al predetto Mon^{re} R^{mo} il che
è contra ogni expectatione nostra: perche si da tucti li altri
homeni del mondo ce trovassimo mancati de la parola loro: da
Mon^{re} Messer Bernardo da Bibiena amico nostro precipuo non

crediamo mai ci devesse mancare in parte alcuna: Tuctavia quando non poterimo fare altro ci dolerimo infra noi medesimi de la disgratia nostra: ma ben volemo che siati cun el predetto Mon^re thesauriero, et ve ne resentiati in nome nostro quanto sia possibile a dire: de questo mancamento de fede facendo molto bene capace S. S. che ultra el danno che recevemo che per non essere satisfacto el predetto Mon^re R^mo noi pagamo ogni mese cento ducati de interessi, ne preme più l' honore che essendosi dato phama (*sic*) che noi ne sia satisfacto, et el sia tucto el contrario che altra cosa del mondo: Volendo che ve ne dogliati fino al vivo core de tale cosa: pregando S. S. che non vogli mancarci de la promessa fede: perche noi in tucte le occorrentie sue serimo per fare tanto, come ne le cose nostre proprie.

Preterea perche Horatio ha da retrovarsi qui per uno bisogno nostro non mancarite de supplicare voi li in advisarne continuamente de tucte le nove de là: perche magiore apiacere non ne poteriste far et maxime retrovandosi el predetto Horatio absente.

Apresso io scrivo vna lettera al Marchese Phoebus[1] et al Marchese Ghirardino[2] la quale serà qui alligata: Et perche ne preme grandemente haverne resposta, volemo che usiati ogni diligentia de darla in mano de Messer Sebastiano Sauli, et pregarlo vogli s' il dovesse mandare uno messo aposta per apiacere nostro mandarla, et farla consignare in mano propria de li decti Marchesi, et fare ogni instantia che prestissimo ne habbiano la resposta perche come è dicto desideramo grandemente tale resposta: Et voi se desiderati farne cosa grata vedete presentialmente che la vadi omnino et per messo fidato: Et benevalete.   Urbini xxviij Iunii 1513.

Franciscus Maria Dux Urbini Urbis
Prefect. ac S. R. E. Capit^s Generalis.

[Cod. Vat. Lat., 8211, f. 509.]

XVIII.

Francesco, Duke of Urbino, to Baldassare Castiglione.

Messer Baldassare: In questo di ultimo de Giugno havemo receuto uno Breve de N^ro S. per el quale Sua B^ne ne manda che

---

[1] Phœbus Gonzaga.   [2] Ghirardo Rangone.

stiamo in ordine insieme cum le nostre Gentedarme (*sic*) al potere cavalchare uerso Verona ogni volta che Sua B^ne celo comandara: Noi che ultra cognoscemo essere obligati etiam desideramo grandemente satisfare Sua B^ne in tucto quello potiamo: Et perho volemo che li facciati intendere che noi et le gente nostre semo sempre prompti et aparechiate a tucti li comandamenti de S. Sta ne altro desideramo che seruire, et satisfare S. B^ne in tucte le cose che ce siano possibile, et spendere non solum el stato ma la vita propria in ogni sua satisfactione et beneficio. L' è ben vero che havendo andare nel luoco dove disegna la Sta Sua noi desideramo che Sua B^ne ne mandi come capitaneo et non come privato conductiero, cio è, cum una guardia de fanti, in modo, che noi potiamo havere la obedientia, et ancho havendo qualche suspecto de li Spagnoli, come sapete, non vorressimo andare ad metterci ne le mano loro: per modo che volendoci loro usare termine nisciuno sinistro, noi non ce potessemo defendere. Voi sete prudente, regete questo caso nostro in quello modo che vi pare sia al proposito nostro: ma ben sopratucto advertirete che nostro S^re resti ben satisfacto de noi, et ch' el cognoschi che dandoci S. Sta una conveniente guardia, come è rasoneuole, non solum che siamo per andare a Verona ma s' el bisognasse nel fuoco proprio per suo servitio: et cusi lo farete cum quelle piu accomodate parole che sia possibile ala Sua Sta de cui ali sanctissimi piedi humilmente ne recomandarite. Urbini vltima Iunii 1513.

Fr. Ma. Dux Urbini etc.

S. R. E. Capit^s Generalis.

Mag^co dil^mo nostro Domino Baldasari
    de Castigliono, etc.
In casa de Mons^re de Tricaricho in
    Borgo.

[Cod. Vat. Lat. 8211, f. 511.]

XIX.

Francesco, Duke of Urbino, to Baldassare Castiglione.

Messer Baldassare: Havemo receuto lettere nostre de ultimo de giugno, et de ij del presente et veduto quanto ne scrivite delo assignamento de Solarolo, che vole fare N^ro S^re a Mon^re nostro R^mo de Mantua: et li dificulta che fa el predetto Mons^re

de pigliarlo cum dire ch' el non vogli de intrata mille ducati :
vi respondemo che noi volemo che havendo voi facte tante
bone opere in questa practica, vogliati anchora vedere conten-
tare el predetto Mon^{re} R^{mo} per via de N^{ro} S^{re} et fare ogni cosa
ch' el non se parta de li che tale affecto non sia facto : perche
altro modo ne via havemo de contentarlo se non questa de
Solarolo o, de altro assignamento che li facesse N^{ro} S^{ve} Et perhò
come è dicto non lassate partendoli al predetto Mon^{re} che
prima l' habbia tale assignamento : perche noi non sapressimo
in che modo contentarlo mancando questo, et tanto più havendo
el credito che havemo cum li Sauli obligato ad altri in una cosa
nostra de grande importantia : tenendoci chiari el predetto
Mons^{re} R^{mo} devere essere satisfacto da N^{ro} S^{re}. Confortarete
S. S. R^{ma} per parte nostra ad acceptare questo Solarolo : perche
per la relatione che havemo da persone digne de fede, semo
certificati decto castello valere mille ducati de intrata. Circa
quanto ne scrivite, che vorresti sapere che havendo noi ad
cavalchare, che numero de fanti vorressimo da N^{ro} S^{ve}, vi
dicemo che questo non ce pare che lo specifichiati a Sua
B^{ne} ma bene ricercarla che havendo noi ad andare, la ce vogli
mandare cum quelli modi, et conditione che se ricerca al officio
nostro, et ala fidelissima servitu nostra verso S. S^{tà} et perciò in
questo vi regularete cum la prudentia vostra, et come a voi
parera per fare capace bene S. B^{ne} essere necessario havendo noi
a cavalchare farci provisione de fanti come parera a lei. In
questo usaretice ogni diligentia et ne tenerete advisati quello
sia el parere vostro circa el nostro cavalchare : Et benevalete
Urbini iiij Iulii 1513.

FRANCISCUSMARIA Duc Urbini

S. R. E. Cap^s Generalis.

[Cod. Vat. Lat., 8211, f. 513.]

XX.

Elisabetta Gonzaga to Baldassare Castiglione.

Magnifico Messer Baldaserra. Semo in Pesaro doue insino
che il caldo estivo non cie caccia credo starimmo sforzandoce de
stare sane : Vi desideramo et expectamovi cum desiderio : de
quanto ne havete scripto per il facto de Messer Augustino

Gonzaga non ui mandamo altra resolutione, essendo il messo in procincto de partire : Altra volta quando haremmo commodo de tempo vi responderimmo : il che non vorrimmo exspectasti ma piu tosto tornasti ad noi subito : Pisauri xj^a Maij M.D.Xiij°.

ELISABET FELTRIA DE GONZAGA

Urbini Ducissa.

Mag^co affini nobis amantissimo domini
  Baldasari Castiliono, etc.

[Cod. Vat. Lat., 8211, f. 307.]

XXI.

Elisabetta Gonzaga to Baldassare Castiglione.

Messer Baldasserra : La Ill. et reveren : M^a sora Clara nostra cognata et sorella honoranda, per uno credito ha cun il s. Pandolpho da Arimino come prima et potiore creditrice, volendo dimandare contra li beni quali lui havea ad Arimino, ha facto domandare a V. S. la commissione di la causa sua : da la quale intendemo haver hauto bona intentione : Hora dubitandosi che sua [S]^tà non la commetti o ali clerici o ali auditori di Camera : et li poi non si facci [im]mortale si per la lungheza solita di la Corte, come ancho per el pocho modo di essa predetta M^a, desiderosa di omne beneficio et commodo suo per el singulare amore che li portamo come sapete : havemo scripto al S. M^co Iuliano vogli operare cun N. S. che si degni commetterla a mons. R^mo de Santo Vitale : vederite ancho voi parlarne a sua S. et cun essa parlarne ancho in nome nostro ala sua Sta et di gratia dimandarli questa commissione in el predetto R^mo Cardinale in el quale effecto non vogliate manchare di opera : ne possibile solertia et studio che veramente non ne potriste fare cosa piu grata. Pisauri xx maii 1513.

ELISABET DE GONZAGA

Feltria de mano propria.

M^co dilettissimo nostro Domino Bal-
  thaseri Castilliono, etc.

[Cod. Vat. Lat., 8211, f. 309.]

XXII.

Chiara di Montefeltro to Baldassare Castiglione.

Magnifico Messer Balthasserra (*sic*) mio : La M. V. sa quanto la Illma Mª Duchessa nostra et io li ho scripto circa le cose mie di Arimino : Et il desiderio ch' io ho obtenere da N. S. che la causa sia commessa in el R^{mo} Cardinale S^{to} Vitale : Et la risposta hauta dal S. M^{co} nostro : di la quale io pur desidero lo effecto : quale più spero per mezo et opera di la predetta V. M. che per altri : Però cun tutto el core la prego sia contenta solicitare talmente : che si ne habbia resolutione cun effecto : Et advisarmi particularmente come et in che termini la cosa sia : che lo ricevero in piacere supramodum grato da la predetta M. V. ala quale mi ricommando.   Urbini viij Iunii 1513.

FELTRIA SOROR CLARA.

Prego con tutto el core la M. V. voglia con la prudentia sua operarse per modo io optenga la gratia quella intendera desidero. So che portiate amore a la felice memoria del S. mio fradello ; per amor suo aiutateme, so ancora sete devoto del glorioso San Franzescho e de Sancta Chiara, perho habiate Idio nante ali ochi e questi doi gloriossimi Sancti, vostra sorella sora e tutte l' altre monache che militano sotto el trionfante vexillo de questa gloriosa Vergine.   El corpo de la quale se farete (*sic*) sia in mano de quelle vivano secondo la sua volonta non dubito ve rendera copiosi meriti in questa vita e in l' altra e ue obligarete tutta la religione nostra perpetualmente pregare Idio per voi.   Per la lettera de la mia S. D. Elisa, intenderete diffusamente el tutto perho iterum atque iterum recomando questa cosa e per l' amor de Idio passi secreta per questa causa scrivo a lo Illmo Iuliano l' aligata.   Non dimentichi etiam quella mia causa d' Arimino.

Al mio M^{co} Messer Balthasserra Cas-
      tiglione.   Romæ.

[Cod. Vat. Lat., 8211, f. 302.]

XXIII.

Chiara di Montefeltro to Baldassare Castiglione.

Magnifico Baldassera.   Essendo io molto desiderosa ch' el locho di Sta Clara di Assisio dove è il glorioso Corpo di quella Sancta si reducesse al Observantia : acio fusse recto et gubernato

come meritamente si dovea : Et fusse levato da le Conventuale :
quale in esso come da molti citadini fui informata : et è notis-
simo viviamo mancho che religiose et honeste : Al tempo di
Papa Iulio fe. mæ. tentai mi fusse dato per tale effecto il dicto
loco : cun animo di andarli pigliarlo et redurlo a la dicta
religione nostra Observantina : Come ancho da molti citadini
mi ne era facto instantia : Sua Sta condescendeva : et era contento : cun ordine ch' io mi elligesse uno confessore : et che
da lui et non altri si facesse la visita : Et non voleva altramente si presto levarlo da la cura di li Conventuali.   Io la
quale non voleva per modo alchuno levarmi da la cura et
totale obedientia di li mei superiori et da la regula in la
quale ho facta la mia professione, non volsi acceptare : Et cosi
rimase la cosa inresoluta : Et havendo pur el medesimo desiderio :
aciò quello locho si reduchi a quello governo et vita che
meritamente si conviene : Sperando che N. S. per la bonta sua
et sanctimonio vivare che lui vole si faccia condescendera a
questo intento et mio ardentissimo desiderio : Prego la M. V.
che cun questa mia credentiale in lei al M^{co} gli ne voglia parlare :
et fare intendere el tutto cun extendarsi in questo come la sapra
fare : et operare insieme cun esso apresso N. S. si efficacemente :
ch' el mi sia concesso a tale effecto el dicto locho : et che si
reduchi a la regula : et governo di la Observantia nostra : che
ultra si fara opera sancta et laudabile et a Dio acceptissima :
et di merito per la M. V. io lo ricevero in piacere tanto grato :
et accepto quanto piu dire non potria da quella : a la quale mi
ricommando : Et la prego adverti governare talmente secreta
questa cosa : che altri ch' el M^{co} et N. S. non intendano questa
praticha : perche sapendosi emuli assai et ancho Conventuali
fariano opera in contrario : Urbini x Iunii 1513.

FELTRIA SOROR CLARA.

[Cod. Vat. Lat., 8211, f. 303.]

XXIV.

Elisabetta Gonzaga to Baldassare Castiglione.

Messer Balthasserra : Voi viderite quanto vi scrive la Ill. et
reveren. M^{a} sora Clara nostra Cognata et sorella honoranda :
Vedate cum omne efficacia di parlarne cun il S. M^{co} et cun N. S.
in nome nostro : et fate omne conato acio la sia compiaciuta di

questo suo et nostro desiderio : che ne farite piacere gratissimo
et singulare.   Urbini x Iunii 1513.

ELISABET FELTRIA DE GONZAGA

Urbini Ducissa etc.

[Cod. Vat. Lat., 8211, f. 311.]

XXV.

Elisabetta Gonzaga to Baldassare Castiglione.

Magnifice Dilectissime noster: Ali giorni passati ve fu per
via de la Bolzecta dirizato un mazo de lettere infra le quale li
erano quelle de la Reverenda M^{na} Sora Chiara nostra cognata
de manu propria, et nostre : Et tamen benche l' habiamo
expectato cum summo desiderio, mai ne havemo habuto risposta :
Ve piaccia adunque satisfare al nostro honesto voto, havendole
recipute.   Et quando fusse altramente (ad cio potiate operare
el bisogno) el tenore de epse è questo : che havesteno ad parlare
prima cum la S. del M^{co} per esser Catholico et inclinato ad
favorire le cose pie, et demum a la Sta de N. S. usando omne
opportuna diligentia in vider de impetrare da sua Beatitudine,
che el Convento de Sta Chiara de Asisi, dove è el sanctissimo
Corpo di quella se havesse ad redure a la Observantia, ad cio in
quel sacro loco se viuesse piu religiosamente che non se fa al
presente, et cum piu timore de Dio.   Et tal peso prehenderia
(*sic*) la predetta Reverenda nostra cognata per tor via tanta
licentia de li, dove se intende esserli spesso tre, o, quattro sore
gravide, et usarlise molti inhonesti et intollerabili termini : in
modo che saria opera sanctissima ad providerli, et condecente
ala predetta Sta et etiam conforme ala natura de lo Illmo M^{co} che
in queste cose sole sempre intervenire volentieri.   Cum favore
adunque de sua Excellentia, sollicitarite la votiva expeditione di
questo, et ce darite celere adviso, che dal canto di qua se fara
anche le debite provisione : Et perche siate piu animoso ad
operare, sappiate che la Roborea natura de Papa Iulio, era gia
mollificata et condescendeva ad tale petitione, che merita essere
exaudita : Bisognando etiam la Comunita de Asisio che non puo
tollerare piu, mandara ambassiatori et breviter se fara omne
expeditione che el caso ricerca.   Et bene valete : Urbini viij Iulii
M.D.Xiij.

HELISABET FELTRIA DE GONZAGA

Urbini Ducissa etc.

[Cod. Vat. Lat., 8211, f. 313.]

XXVI.

Cesare Minutolo to Baldassare Castiglione.

Magnifico et mio observandissimo etc.   La S. V. vedera quanto li serive il nostro Illmo commune S^{re} però non insisto in respondere alla sua, parendome che la lettera di sua Ex^{tia} testificara la mente de quello et il bono animo et fede ha in voi.

Monstrai la partita della vostra lettera a Mª Raphaella, et benche quella me negasse il baso della candida mano, non manchai della mia solita presumptione, sed frustra laboravi. Dice ve debbia fare intendere da parte sua che la mangia bene et beve meglio, dasse piacere et bon tempo et vive allegramente, et per dirve la pura verita non me pare se attristi molto della absentia vostra, non so se proceda da pocho amore, o vero dalla sua mala natura et instabile cervello, che tanto se ricorda del suo amante quanto il vede e a mala pene, et non la intenderia bis Christo.   Sapete quanto l' amo et observo, el premio ne reporto sono rabuffi, villanie et tortuosi resguardi, et quod deterius, me spaccia per Messer Marco Antonio Cosmogerite, o ingrata donna!

De novo qui non è altro se attende al ordine della giostra, et ogni di se prova qualche vno.   Heri sera il S^{or} ruppe tre lancie valorosamente.   Me racomando sempre alla S. V. et al R^{do} Monsignore de Tricaricho et ve prego anchora che siate gran Maestro, ve degnate de gratia allegrarvi da parte mia, con il novo Arcivescovo de Bari, et racomandarmi a sua S. perche me è anticho padrone, et che lo pozza vedere Cardinale.   Io. Batista Bonaventura se racomanda molto alla S. V. et tutta questa corte, et principalmente Mª Raphaella che de sopra m' è scordato dirlo.   Bene Valete.   Pisauri x Maii 1513.

Vostro servitore
CESARE MINUTOLO.

Al Mag^{co} et mio observan. Messer
Baldassare da Castiglione.

[Cod. Vat. Lat., 8211, f. 479.]

XXVII.

Luigia Castiglione to Baldassare Castiglione.

Carissimo mio figliolo: Per messer Aluiso nostro io hebbi una tua lettera, pocho parlassimo a bocha per esser io a la venuta sua in punto d' andare a Casaticho dove gli son stata otto di e iudici e procuratori e nodari per quella differencia d' Antonio da Mantua: Non staro a dir adesso como havemo fatto: spero la sententia sera data che la fossa sia tuta nostra: Heri che fu l' ultimo de aprile per messo a posta de mio fratello hebbi una lettera a Casaticho dove tu mi scrivi haverne mandato un' altra per Paulo Bena° la quale non ho hauta ne luy e venuto secondo quando dicono li suoy: per questa intendo il desiderio hay de haver quello libro dove son notati tuti quelli rason de Casaticho: e cussi subito oze chi è el primo de mazo son venuta dentro: e domandato chi fusse per venir a Roma ho ritrovato don Bernardin Capra lator presente el quale fazeva ben un pocho de dificulta: pur credo questo me servira: e per luy ti mando diece ducati d' oro zioe roverini 9 e un ducato largho: piu non ho potuto ritrovar cussi presto: Prima ch' io partisse per Casaticho intesi el Sr Aluiso da Gonzaga dovesse in breve partir per Roma e cun sua S[ria] messer Francesco Benato parente nostro: e dubitando non esser venuta a tempo: manday al dicto messer Francesco ducati 20 zioè rouerini: ch' io pensai ben che quelli potevano esser spesi: quando son venuta loro non son anche partiti: et ho mandati per haver li dinari e non ho poduto per non essere messer Francesco in la terra: si che alla venuta sua a Roma che diseno sera presto tu haverai anche quelli: Va mo dreto cussi cun deztreza spendendo, perche siamo pur stati mal quest' ano e purche non havessemo bisognato sustenir cussi li nostri cuntadini se gli poteva star: ma seriano a quest' ora morti de fame: Dicemo pur un pocho de la praticha nostra: in quel altra mia io te scrivea como messer Aluiso me havea ditto dovesse un pocho intratenir la cosa e cussi parlay cun m[a] Polissena Rangona dolendomi in nome tuo e mio de molte subtilita che usava el Conte Gi. non specificando pero di quella licentia parendo cusi a mio fratello: Al fine conclusi ch' io volena saper che termini e seguenze haueano ad essere queste e poy te avisaria: Siche questo sera un tenir un pocho

in tempo tanto che possi veder como se puo far di questo ch' io
te scrissi : Per freza non scrivo piu di questa expedicion de
Casaticho so ch' el non bisogna ch' io te ne rischalda altramente : Siamo sani Dio gratia el piu de nuy e molti se ti
racomandano ch' io non staro a dir : El Sr Dio te campa da mal
e periculi : Mantuæ p.^o maij 1513.

ALUISA CASTI : tua Madre.

Al mio Mag^{co} e carissimo figluolo
Baldesaro da Castiglione. In Roma.
In borgo in casa del R^{do} Messer L^{co}
da Canossa, Vescovo de Tricharicho.

[Cod. Vat. Lat., 8211, f. 199.]

XXVIII.

Luigia Castiglione to Baldassare Castiglione.

Carissimo mio figliolo : Dapoy ch' io venne fora al Casaticho
del mese presente ho hauto quatro lettere tue a me tute gratissime : delle quale una ne porto Bochalino qui apresso vene in
persona a visitarme per tua parte : il che me fue de grandissimo
contento a poter parlar cun persona che te hauesse veduto e
certificarme del ben star tuo : Ben mi credeva ch' el mi dovesse
saper dir qualche particularita di queste tue cose de Casaticho
che poco me ne sepe dir sonno cussi gienerale : el mi disse de
quelle zovene de Nuvolara laudando mo le cose ; Dio ce inspira
atacharse al melio : esso Bochalino mi ritrovo in leto amalata
d' una terzana asay fastidiosa, pure Dio gratia, la mi ha lassata
pur trista : tutatvia spero in n. Sr Dio de restaurareme presto :
La lettera tua ne la quale tu me scrivi ch' io veda de metere
insieme ducento ducati : il che faro el possibile, anchora che
adesso sia molto mal ritrovare dinari per essere qualche piu grano
del solito non se atrova chi ne voglia per pocho ne per assay : niente
di meno faro ogni sforzo tanto ch' io spero a mezo agosto o pocho
piu serano aparechiati : li 50 ducati ch' io scrissi son a mano
e non mi son curata fin qui circhare messo che te li porta per
haverme ti scrito ch' io non li mandasse senza tuo aviso : hora
procurarò de mandarli a chaschuno messo che vadi a Pesaro
o a Urbino : Me pare in questa lettera ultima che tu ti resenti
forse per el mio solicitarte de expedir queste tue cose : mi non
vorey za che ti desperasse ne che tu volesse quello che non puo,
che seria pazia : anche ti priego a star di bona voglia e con-
servarti sano ch' io non potrey haver la mazor gratia al mondo :

L' è ben vero che apresso a quanto io desidero grandemente che le cose tue siano ben expedite per honor e utile tuo : ch' io so molto ben che non poy star longamente in Roma che non spendi assay e ch' el star absente tanto tempo da la famiglia genera disordini asay non gli havendo alcuno governo di quello gie sia : e diro pur anche questo pocho : quanto utile pare che seria stato quando vedesse che questa expedicion da Roma andava tanto in longo a far tuore il possesso dil tuo castello per altra persona cun carta de procura : et metergie un homo in nome tuo : et occorendo qualche intradella pigliarli in nome tuo che ti haveria pur dato utile e honore : niente di meno io non posso saper queste cose se non che mi vanno cussi per mente e non scio che far altro se non scrivere : Siche figliolo mio abiate per excusa e pigliale cun quello amore ch' io te le scrivo : e molto piu voluntiera te le direy a bocha quando da Dio mi fusse concessa et alora tu poresse anche ci dir la rason tua : siche se tu venirai in Lombardia a locho ch' io ti possa vedere perche l' havero de suma gratia : fra questo mezo ti conforto ben a vedere de atrovarte un homo da ben, anche duy s' el si puo : un che stesse sempre apresso di te : e di questo ho hauto queste di qualche pensiere a Bochalino che qui l' ha pocho credito : un altro che stia sempre governo de la famiglia tua e sia homo da farse temere e sapia pigliar un partito quando el bisogna : e non guardi a spesa ch' el se la potra molto ben guadagnar : Venendo in Lonbardia e parendoti veder quella cosa da Modena non dispiazera : et anchora quelle de Nuvolara che sera fazil cosa : azio che possiamo una volta dar a terra : Le nostre biave anchora non son fornite de battere, pur a quello si vede starimo molto melio del anno passato ma son venute a ville precio. Non scrivo piu per esser stancha anchora ch' io l' abia scrita in duy di : Circha de star sano aricomandame al veschovo nostro et a messer Agustino se tu te trovi in Roma : como sey a Urbino avisame precise el debito de maestro Abraam ch' el mi insta d' essere pagato : El Sr Dio te guarda da ogni periculo : In Casaticho a di 28 de luio 1513.

Tua madre

Aluisa Casti.

Al carissimo figliolo Bald. de Castiglione.   In Roma o dove si ritrova.

[Cod. Vat. Lat., 8211, f. 202.]

XXIX.

Luigia Castiglione to Baldassare Castiglione.

Carissimo mio figliolo : Da Bindo ho hauto una tua lettera et a bocha da luy ho inteso il ben star tuo dil che ho hauto grandissimo contento : Nui qui a Mantua siamo asay ben sani : ma fora in villa messer Thomaso nostro con tuti duy li figlioli son amalati como da Bindo intenderay che li ha visti : messer L^{co} nostro di Uberti mori merchore proximo passato : non e stato tropo da pianzere per esser ormay decrepito : Hora ti diro di quello che occorre Bindo non era tropo informato di tuto quello volea saper da luy, maxime dicendomi luy che tu volevi venir in queste bande como anche ti me scrivi : gie domanday cussi in secreto che ordine gie havevi zioe cun che licentia : luy disse non lo sapere : sopra quanto io li ho ditto che tu vengi quanto te piaze a Casaticho, e starge diece o quindeci di e piu s' el ti pare : io te diro poi el modo che ho tenuto, ben l' ho ditto anche a luy se te lo sapera dir : ora venendo mi parera ben fato per non parer de far beffe del amico da Modena che passi di li e veder la merchantia se voranno : poy se ritrovara qualche scusa bona de quella da Nuvolara : pur heri parlandone cun Francesco Gonzaga mi disse che certe al iudicio suo la seconda non seria may chiamata bruta et che a luy pareria che venendo qui, tu la vedesse, che seria facillimo ch' el padre la tien sempre a manzar cun luy : e senza dir altro passando di li far uno lozamento ti e vederla : De quella del Conte Nicolò, la mazore fu data a un messer Pietro Fregoso, le altre son chi in qua, chi in la : el padre e in Franza non mi par cosa da pensar. Quel altra del Conte x° me pare una materia che l' è in cussi pocho conto qui quanto si possa dir : M$_a$ Madalena compagna del Illmo Sr Fedrico nostro mi ha pregata ch' io te scriva che tu vedi de saper quello sia venuto d' una zovene che fu nora de messer Bartolomeo de la Rover, moglie di quello suo figlioli chi era cussi un pocho in discordia cun il padre el quale morite in queste bande nostre, hora fu l' anno : dice che l' era da Perosa o vicina, che l' era assay bella e per quanto la intese, havea ducati desdotto milia de dota, poy se asperava anchora una hereditate che seria una bona cosa : la non mi sa dire de chi la fusse figliola, ma dice che l' era d' un signor : fa quello ti pare siando cussi

bona l' è dubio che la sia spazata : L' altro di ti manday cento
ducati per un merchadante nostro mantuano chi drizay a Pesaro
a messer Amato e gli scrissi : a ti scrisse poi per un figliolo de
m^a Iulia el quale sta li a Urbino : horo ne mando per Bindo
ottanta e vinti ne dago al podesta che serano cento : Voleva
ben mandarte li cento ma non he possibile sparger biava se non
a stente, como l' ha visto Bindo anchora che la se buta uia : Te
mando poi molte cose : che serano notate che a una parte gli è
pur bisognato dinari : vederemo questi duy di ch' io staro a
Mantua satisfar a maestro Abraam e dubito bisognaro impegnar
per una parte piu presto che star qui in tempo che l' è molto
bisogno ch' io vadi fora : Quello giovane chi è venuto cun
Bindo ha hauto berete per ducati trentacinque circha io li ho
promesso : vedi per ogni modo non me li pagar che adesso
havero da far assay : A mezo questo mese m^a L^ra e Carlo mi
serano dreto : Venendo in queste bande ti suplico de gratia che
tu reschodi la tua catena e portarla cun tego e cussi se l' hai
qualche veste de seta o brochato che non sia per ti che me la
porta ch' io ne faro qualche fornimenti per casa : e non far
como facesse quand' io era a Urbino che non volessi may ch' io
vedesse ne li tuoy forzeri : Poy venne zente a che non credevi
lassarli e restasse nel danno : l' era pur ben ch' io li havesse
hauti e forne qualche cosa honorevole per casa che lassarli haver
a li tristi. Altro non scrivo per hora. N. Sr Dio ti conserva
in sanità : In Mantua a di 4 septembris 1513. Aricordate de
dar risposta a questi nostri di Uberti che ti scriveno de la
morte del padre.

Aluisa da Castiglione tua Matre.

P^a una fodra de lupi.
7^ecci de panno biancho fino.
Fazioleti 12 ⎫
Scufioti   ⎬ de renso.
              ⎭
Para 6 de calzeti.
Lenzoli 3 grossi.
Peze de mane da cortelli 7.
Peze 2 de formazo pesi 4.
3 fasoli.
3 cisi.
3 milio.

Beretti 2 negri belli.

Pezi 8 de cervelati.

Sachi 6 novi.

Coltre 2 da letto.

[Cod. Vat. Lat., 8211, f. 205.]

XXX.

Luigia Castiglione to Baldassare Castiglione.

Carissimo mio figliolo : Quello di che Bindo parti da Mantua
ro hebbi una tua lettera portata da un ragazo del Sr Duca
patron tuo : ala quale non accade altra risposta : Da poy ch' io
son a Casaticho ne ho hauto un altra del ultimo d' agosto : e
messer Hieronymo, Podesta a Urbino mi è venuto a visitar e
dirme como tu partisse el di de S^{to} Bartolomeo da Urbino per
Santa Mª de Loreto el qual di vien a di 24 d' agosto e pur
questa tua lettera è data a Urbino, siche non intendo como vada
questa cosa : Sia come si voglia pur che tu sii sano como tu me
scrivi bastame : Bindo fu expedito da mi a di 4 del presente e
porto dinari cun molte altre cose le quale ti misi in scripto
excepto due coperte da leto che mi dimentichay : El cavallo che
lui conduceva da luy haveray inteso como è passato, el ne compro
uno de dinari d' altri per sey ducati et io gie lo pagay perche
el potesse portar tela el lino e berete a chi li havena dato
dinari : e porto all' Alda b̄^{ci} 15 de tela de piu da 15 marzelli che
poray far andar in cunto de dinari ch' el dice la debe havere
dati : El podesta è satisfato de li 20 ducati : de la cavalla che
volevi ch' io ti mandasse : venendo ti como spero la vederay
e piazendoti la pigliaray : Di quello amico tuo orefice che voria
condur le robe sue ne ho comisso al fator nostro da Mantua per
mie lettere ch' el fazia quanto tu scrivi : Di quelli veli che
scrivi non essendo io a Mantua ne sapendo como siano fatti
quelli : o di seta o di filo o bambaso che non lo scrivi haveria
faticha a intendere : siche differiremo pur sino a la venuta tua
in qua : la quale aspetto cun gran desiderio e pregoti non la
tardi piu, che ognidi ua pezorando el tempo e le strade, siando
vicini al inverno como siamo : e ti racordo che fazi la via de
Modena e da Nuvolara azio me sapie dir qualche cosa : E
quando veniray racordate lassar bon ordine in casa e quelle robe

che lasseray siano in bone mane che non si achascha qualche disordine, e non ti dimentichar portar la tua cathena ch' io te la voglio salvare : Siamo sani Dio gratia tuti excepto messer Thomaso nostro che ha hauto una longa e fastidiosa terzana come Bindo ti puo haver dito che l' ha visto : Non scrivo piu al presente : Nostro S[r] Dio te guarda da male : Scriveme qualche cosa quando credi de ritrovarte qui a Casaticho perche son molte persone che desiderano venire a vederte : Casatici 21 Septembris 1513.

Tua madre
ALUISA CASTIGLIONA.

Al Mag[co] e Carissimo figliolo B. Castiglione.   In Urbino o dove sia.

[Cod. Vat. Lat., 8211, f. 207.]

XXXI.

Francesco Strozzi to Baldassare Castiglione.

Magnifico fratello mio honorando : A questi di per una lettera vostra e poi a bocha per Bindo ho inteso del ben star vostro, cosa che a me è stata de summo apiacere e voria poterne intendere ogni di et ogni hora che non posso havere el magior contento commo è a sapere che stati bene.   Intendo che sete grasso, che non havete temuto el caldo da questa estate commo habiamo fato nuy, che siamo tuti amalati e venissimo fora qui per paura del caldo da Mantua.   Son stata la prima amalarme e cusi per gratia de Dio la prima a guarire, per potere atendere ali altri.   Messer Thomaso mio è in leto vinti di fa cun una febra terzana non molto grande ma fastidiosa, ha perso in tuto l' apetito che non trova cosa che li piacia e se non vi fussimo da lonze se non una zornata, che credo seria forza a mandar a tore de quello vostro vino che intendiamo ch' è cusi bono che li faria forsi tornar el gusto.   Li mei puti sonno tuti amalati commo siano guariti tuti andaremo a Mantua piacendo a Dio : Ho dimandato a Bindo se sete anchora andato al vostro Castello e me dice de no, e voria che li andasti perche habiamo fato pensiere non venendo vuy in queste bande de venire nuy in quelle e quasi ho fato voto in questo mio male se havesse saputo el nome del santo de quella chiesia lo haveria fato in tuto : E ve ricordo

a tore mogliera prestamente, acioche potiamo venire a noze e a
solazo che faremo de uno viazo duy servicij, che horamai me
comincia a rincrescere aspetare tanto, che dubito che parero poi
vecchia che mi sera vergogna a balare ale vostre noze : Non
scrivero piu in longo per hora se non che a vostra Mag^cia Messer
Thomaso et io se racomandamo per infinite volte, desyderosi
vederlo e goderlo. In Revere adi 5 de setembre 1513.

La vostra amorevole sorella

Francischa Stroza.

Al Mag^co Cavaliero e mio venerando
   Fratello Messer Baldesaro da Castiglione ec. In Urbino.

[Cod. Vat. Lat., 8211, f. 240.]

XXXII.

Costanza Rangone to Luigia Castiglione.

Magnifica quanto sorella honoranda : Per lo amor che io
porto a V. S. sono sforzata ad alegrarmi cum quella dela nostra
comune sposa qualla sono certa che V. S. la conosca, ma per
essersi alevata in queste parte ne ho pur io piu cognitione di
quella, la quale puo havere gaudio che oltra le beleze sue de
haverse aquistato uno figliola alevata in Paradiso, che per Dio
è tanto gentil et acostumata quanto dir se possa ; cusi prego
Idio li concedi gratia de godersi l' una parte et l' altra longo
tempo in alegreza. Anchora V. S. sera contenta in nomo mio
alegrarsine cum le Magnifice m^a Polisena et m^a Francesca soie
figliole, dela bona et gentil sorella se hano aquistato, che a fede io
dal canto mio non ne ho mancho alegreza quanto l' una parte et
l' altra mi fussino figlioli, ne mi par che molti giorni fano fusse
facto cosa piu laudabile di questa : cusi Idio la persevera in bene.
Altro per hora non mi occore se non che a V. S. de continuo mi
racomando. In Modena ali 10 de febraro 1516.

Di. V. S.

Quanto sorella

Costanza Rangona Contessa.

Alla Mag^ca Mª Aloysa da Castione,
   quanto sorella honoranda. In Mantua

[Cod. Vat. Lat., 8212, f. 236.]

XXXIII.

Alda Boiarda to Luigia Castiglione.

Magnifica quanto sorella honoranda : Ho visto per una di
V. M. quanto quella mi ha scripto del sponsalitio che ha facto
V. M. de lo unico figliolo Messer Baldessare.   Io ne ho hauto
sumo contento et gaudio et ho mostrato la lettera di V. M.
a sor' Laura et anchora lei se ne ha hauto grande alegreza.
Havendo inteso la nora, et de amici siamo doventati parenti,
et V. M. se ne relegra, como Messer Baldasar per parte nostra
et mi piace assai che habia hauto Mᵃ Hypolita ch' io intendo ch'
è vna bellissa (*sic*) giovene et anchora richa de dotta et
e gientille cossa ad quello mi ha dito un modeneso amico
mio che la conosso : et sor' Laura et me pregamo Dio Sigʳ Yᵘ
Xto. con la madre sua gloriosissima Vergine Maria, che
mantenga V. M. et il figlio e la nora felici et lieti in perpetuo
con nui altre fidelissime parente.   Et a la M. V. cun bon cuore
et fido animo io mi racomando et suor' Laura si ricomanda a la
bona gratia di quella.   Ferrarie 13 februarij 1516.

ALDA BOIARDA Comitissa.

A Magᶜᵃ quanto sorella Mᵃ Aluysa
  Castiglione honᵐ.   In Mantua.

[Cod. Vat. Lat., 8212, f. 56.]

XXXIV.

Angelica Gonzaga to Ippolita Torelli.

Magnifica et singularissima madonna e come sorella honoran-
dissima.   La pace de quello che gode tutto lo universo se degni
poner mane ad ogni vostro passo como vede per sua gratia si è
dignato dar tal principio, son certa che in vui finira in gran
contenteza, dil che havendo presentito de la amicitia facta
mediante la uostra disponsatione cun la casa da Castione, (*sic*) e
avegna che cun vostra Magnificencia non habia tropo domesti-
cheza per essere state lontanate l' una dal altra insina da li
nostri teneri anni, ma in che in modo habia questo presentito la
mia cara e, honor. mⁿᵃ Aluisa me ne ha dato avviso, e cun
quanto jubilo de core scriver non ve poteria pensate, carissima
sorella, essa à di quello unico figliolo.   Se serite quella che io penso

sarite tutto il suo core, dil che sorella me alegro cun vui che siate apozata a cosi digno cavaliero quanto el Mag^{co} messer Baldesar, homo fra tutti li altri al di de ozi nominato de virtu e zentileza cun beltade, non credo sia el paro a lui. Iterum me alegro e de questo non posso pensare essere proceduto da altro che da la mane de Dio e dal nome de vostra dignissima venustade. Ve ho voluta cun questa mia visitarve per essere mia propinqua de sangue. Non altro me vostra humanissima Magnificencia me aricomando. Ex monasterio nostro Corporis x^i Mantue die xxj Februarii M.D.Xvj.

La Vostra Cara sorella sor

ANGELICA DA GONZAGA.

Alla Mag^{ca} et honor. Madonna Ippolita
   da Castiglione sorella sua colendis-
   sima et amatissima. In Modena.

[Cod. Vat. Lat., 8213, f. 29.]

The last three letters were partly printed in Prof. Cian's 'Candidature nuziali di B. Castiglione,' 40-42.

END OF VOL. I.